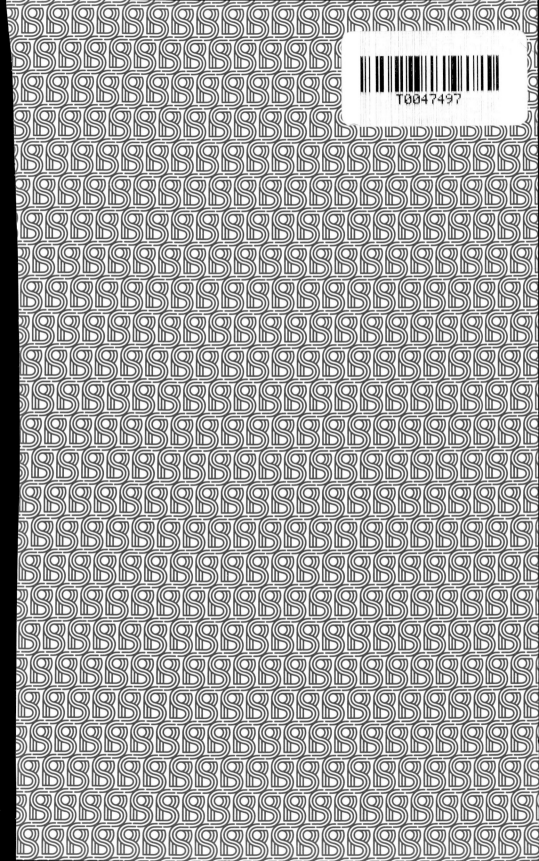

**Stripe
Press**

Ideas for progress
San Francisco, California
press.stripe.com

THE
REVOLT
OF
THE
PUBLIC

THE
REVOLT
OF
THE
PUBLIC

AND THE CRISIS OF AUTHORITY
IN THE NEW MILLENNIUM

BY
MARTIN
GURRI

ABOUT
THE
AUTHOR

Martin Gurri is a geopolitical analyst and student of new media and information effects. He spent many years working in the corner of the CIA dedicated to the analysis of open media. After leaving government, Gurri focused his research on the motive forces powering the transformation of the media environment, and has churned out countless articles, studies, and blog posts on the topic, including co-authoring *Our Visual Persuasion Gap* (Parameters, Spring 2010). His blog, *The Fifth Wave*, pursues the themes first elaborated in *The Revolt of the Public*.

Published in the United States of America
by Stripe Press / Stripe Matter Inc.

Stripe Press
Ideas for progress
San Francisco, California
press.stripe.com

Printed by Hemlock in Canada
ISBN: 978-1-7322651-4-1

Second Edition

TABLE
OF
CONTENTS

MARTIN GURRI SAW IT COMING

I read the first edition of *The Revolt of the Public* in early January of 2016, after Virginia Postrel cited it in her column.† Since then, it has been the book that I recommend whenever I am in a conversation that turns to the Trump phenomenon or the disturbing state of politics in general.

Because Martin Gurri saw it coming. When, without fanfare, he self-published the first edition as an e-book in June of 2014, he did not *specifically* name Donald Trump, or Brexit, or the oddball political figures and new fringe parties that have surged all over Europe. But he saw how the internet in general and social media in particular were transforming the political landscape.

THE RATHER-GATE EXAMPLE

The first edition told a story of elites losing their ability to control the narrative and protect their reputations. I like to illustrate by using an example that he did *not* include—an incident known as Rather-gate.

In 2004, venerable newsman Dan Rather delivered a story on CBS's *60 Minutes* that purported to show that George W. Bush had used political connections to evade real military service in the 1960s. But a participant in the far-right internet discussion group Free Republic, writing under the pseudonym "Buckhead," claimed that one of the documents used by CBS was fraudulent. He pointed out that the document used a proportionally spaced font that was typically not available when the memorandum was supposedly written. Instead, it was likely typed on a computer using word processing software from Microsoft that only became available decades afterward. His analysis quickly spread, serving to discredit the CBS story and Dan Rather as a reporter.

Before the internet, ordinary individuals would not have had access to sufficient information to second-guess an investigation conducted by a major news organization. Nor would someone lacking any sort of formal

† "Democracy's Destabilizer: TMI," *Bloomberg View*, December 28, 2015.

credentials have been able to disseminate his findings as widely and rapidly as they were disseminated in the Rather-gate scandal. The World Wide Web gave a single anonymous individual the ability to humiliate a powerful media conglomerate and one of its most famous reporters.

In the 1960s, the U.S. government was able to hide important information about its involvement in the failed attempt to depose Fidel Castro (the Bay of Pigs invasion of 1961) and about the difficulties it was facing in Vietnam. Today, a similar embarrassment likely would be exposed via YouTube or WikiLeaks. The public has access to information that it did not have 50 years ago, about matters ranging from police shootings to hurricane relief efforts to lurid details of celebrities' sexual misconduct.

With his eyes on this altered media space, Martin Gurri saw what was coming. He saw that the elites would be increasingly despised, as more of their mistakes and imperfections became exposed. He saw that the elites would respond to the public with defensiveness and contempt, but that this would only make the public more hostile and defiant toward authority. He saw that the public's newfound power does not come with any worked-out program or plan, and as a result it poses the threat of nihilism. If the existing order is only torn down, not replaced, the outcome could be chaos and strife.

AN IMPORTANT NEW CHAPTER

This edition of *The Revolt of the Public* contains a major new chapter, called "Reconsiderations," which covers events that have unfolded since the first edition was issued. I recommend reading this chapter twice, once before you begin the rest of the book and once afterward. Writing with greater assurance, passion, eloquence, and urgency, Martin Gurri in "Reconsiderations" spells out the lessons of these events and delivers an important warning about the future.

These days, even though hardly anyone anticipated the way that Donald Trump would turn American politics upside-down, many pundits claim to have the explanation. But Martin Gurri's analysis is the most credible, because he locates it within a trend affecting much more than just one election in the United States. He is able to link the Trump phenomenon to the collapse of the establishment in many other countries. Merely within the last few years, we have seen the revolt of the public play out in Greece, Spain, France, Germany, Italy, Great Britain, Hungary, the Philippines . . . you name it.

And let me repeat the other factor that makes this book's analysis of the Trump phenomenon particularly credible: Martin Gurri saw it coming.

DEMOCRATIZED INFORMATION

Reading this book made me realize that democratized information poses a dilemma for modern society. If the public loses patience and respect for government, the result will be disintegration. If elites choose to dig in, they are likely to resort to repression.

To avoid these extreme outcomes, both elites and the public have to change. Elites will have to cede authority and permit more local variation and experimentation. The public will have to be more tolerant. Imperfections and bad outcomes should not be taken as proof of conspiracy or evil intent. We should pay less heed to those who can only pour out condemnation and blame. We should show greater appreciation for those who make constructive attempts to experiment and fix.

PRELUDE
TO
A
TURBULENT
AGE

Can there be a connection between online universities and the serial insurgencies that, in media noise and human blood, have rocked the Arab Middle East? I contend that there is. And the list of unlikely connections can easily be expanded. It includes the ever faster churning of companies in and out of the S&P 500, the death of news and the newspaper, the failure of established political parties, the imperial advance across the globe by Facebook and Google, and the near-universal spread of the mobile phone.

Should anyone care about this tangle of bizarre connections? Only if you care how you are governed: the story I am about to tell concerns above all a crisis of that monstrous messianic machine, the modern government. And only if you care about democracy: because a crisis of government in liberal democracies like the United States can't help but implicate the system.

Already you hear voices prophesying doomsday with a certain joy.

I am no prophet, myself. Among the claims I make in this book is that the future is, and *must* be, opaque, even to the cleverest observer. Consider the CIA and the collapse of the Soviet Union in 1991, or the Fed and the implosion of Lehman Brothers in 2008. The moment *tomorrow* no longer resembles *yesterday*, we are startled and confused. The compass by which we navigate existence cracks. We are lost at sea.

But we can speak of the present. And I think it demonstrable that an old, entrenched social order is passing away even as I write these words—one rooted in the hierarchies and conventions of industrial life. Since no substitute has appeared on the horizon, we should, as tourists flying into the unknown, fasten our seatbelts and expect turbulence ahead.

INFORMATION IS COOL, SO WHY DID IT EXPLODE?

I came to the subject in a roundabout way. I was interested in information. The word, admittedly, is vague, the concept elusive. Information theory finds "information" in anomaly, deviation, difference—anything that separates signal from noise. But that's not what I cared about.

Media provided my point of reference. As an analyst of global events, I sourced my material by parsing the world's newspapers and television reports. That was what I considered information. I also held the belief that information of the sort found in newspapers and television reports was identical to knowledge—so the more information, the better. This was naïve of me, but, if I say so, understandable. Back when the world and I were young, information was scarce, hence valuable. Anyone who could cast a beam of light on, say, Russia-Cuba relations was worth his weight in gold. In this context, it made sense to crave more.

A curious thing happens to sources of information under conditions of scarcity. They become *authoritative*. A century ago, a scholar wishing to study the topics under public discussion in the U.S. would find most of them in the pages of the *New York Times*. It wasn't quite "All the news that's fit to print," but it delivered a large enough proportion of published topics that, as a practical proposition, little incentive existed to look further. Because it held a near monopoly on current information, the *New York Times* seemed authoritative.

Four decades ago, Walter Cronkite concluded his broadcasts of the *CBS Nightly News* with the words, "And that's the way it was." Few of his viewers found it extraordinary that the clash and turmoil of billions of human lives, dwelling in thousands of cities and organized into dozens of nations, could be captured in three or four mostly visual reports lasting a total of less than 30 minutes. They had no access to what was missing—the other two networks reported the same news, only less majestically. Cronkite was voted the most trusted man in America, I suspect because he looked and sounded like the wealthy uncle to whom children in the family are forced to listen for profitable life lessons. When he wavered on the Vietnam War, shock waves rattled the marble palaces of Washington. Cronkite emanated authority.

It took time to break out of my education and training, but eventually the thought dawned on me that information wasn't just raw material to exploit for analysis, but had a life and power of its own. Information had *effects*. And the first significant effect I perceived related to the sources: as the amount of information available to the public increased, the authoritativeness of any one source decreased.

The idea of an information explosion or overload goes back to the 1960s, which seems poignant in retrospect. These concerns expressed a new anxiety about the advance of progress, and placed in doubt the naïve faith, which I originally shared, that data and knowledge were identical. Even then, the problem was framed by uneasy elites: as ever more published reports escaped the control of authoritative sources, how could we tell truth from error? Or, in a more sinister vein, honest research from manipulation?

Information truly began exploding in the 1990s, initially because of television rather than the internet. Landline TV, restricted for years to one or two channels in a few developed countries, became a symbol of civilization and was dutifully propagated by governments and corporations around the world. Then came cable and the far more invasive satellite TV: CNN (founded 1980) and Al Jazeera (1996) broadcast news 24 hours a day. A resident of Cairo, who in the 1980s could only stare dully at one of two state-owned channels showing all Mubarak all the time, by the 2000s had access to more than 400 national and international stations. American movies, portraying the Hollywood approach to sex, poured into the homes of puritanical countries like Saudi Arabia.

Commercial applications for email were developed in the late 1980s. The first server on the World Wide Web was switched on during Christmas of 1990. The MP3—destroyer of the music industry—arrived in 1993. Blogs appeared in 1997, and Blogger, the first free blogging software, became available in 1999. Wikipedia began its remarkable evolution in 2001. The social network Friendster was launched in 2002, with MySpace and LinkedIn following in 2003, and that thumping *T.rex* of social nets, Facebook, coming along in 2004. By 2003, when Apple introduced iTunes, there were more than three billion pages on the web.

Early in the new millennium it became apparent to anyone with eyes to see that we had entered an informational order unprecedented in the experience of the human race.

I can quantify that last statement. Several of us—analysts of events—were transfixed by the magnitude of the new information landscape, and wondered whether anyone had thought to measure it. My friend and colleague Tony Olcott came upon (on the web, of course) a study conducted by some very clever researchers at the University of California, Berkeley. In brief, these clever people sought to measure, in data bits, the amount of information produced in 2001 and 2002, and compare the result with the information accumulated from earlier times.

Their findings were astonishing. More information was generated in 2001 than in all the previous existence of our species on earth. In fact, 2001 *doubled* the previous total. And 2002 doubled the amount present in 2001, adding around 23 "exabytes" of new information—roughly the equivalent of 140,000 Library of Congress collections.[1] Growth in information had been historically slow and additive. It was now exponential.

Poetic minds have tried to conjure a fitting metaphor for this strange transformation. *Explosion* conveys the violent suddenness of the change. *Overload* speaks to our dazed mental reaction. Then there are the trivially obvious *flood* and the most unattractive *fire hose*. But a glimpse at the chart opposite should suggest to us an apt metaphor. It's a stupendous wave: a *tsunami*.

HOW WALTER CRONKITE BECAME KATIE COURIC AND THE AUDIENCE BECAME THE PUBLIC

What was the character of the change imposed by this cataclysmic force, this tsunami, as it swept over our culture and our lives? That was the question posed to those of us with an interest in media, research, and analysis. A number of *partial* answers presented themselves, before I could truly grasp the big picture.

From a professional perspective, I realized that I couldn't restrict my search for evidence to the familiar authoritative sources without ignoring a near-infinite number of new sources, any one of which might provide material decisive to my conclusions. Yet, despite the arrival of Google and algorithmic search, I found it humanly impossible to explore that near-infinite set of new sources in any but the most superficial way. However I conducted my research, whatever sources I chose, I was left in a state of *uncertainty*—a permanent condition for analysis under the new dispensation.

Uncertainty is an acid, corrosive to authority. Once the monopoly on information is lost, so too is our trust. Every presidential statement, every CIA assessment, every investigative report by a great newspaper, suddenly acquired an arbitrary aspect, and seemed grounded in moral predilection rather than intellectual rigor. When proof *for* and *against* approaches infinity, a cloud of suspicion about cherry-picking data will hang over every authoritative judgment.

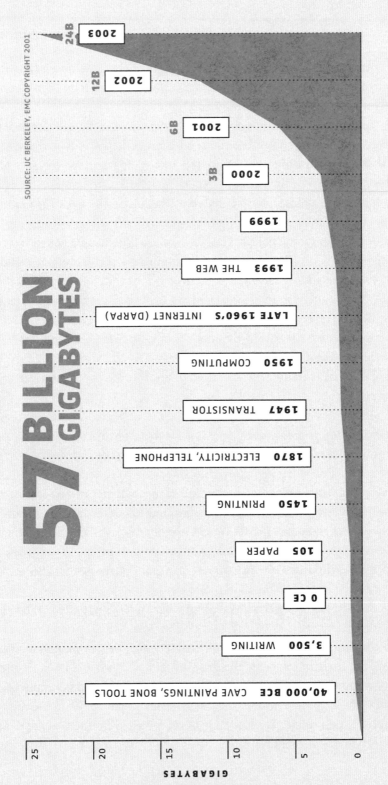

Figure 1: Volume of information is doubling every year.[2]

And suspicion cut both ways. Defenders of mass media accused their vanishing audience of cherry-picking sources in order to hide in a congenial information bubble, a "daily me."

Pretty early in the game, the wave of fresh information exposed the poverty and artificiality of established arrangements. Public discussion, for example, was limited to a very few topics of interest to the articulate elites. Politics ruled despotically over the public sphere—and not just politics but *federal* politics, with a peculiar fixation on the executive branch. Science, technology, religion, philosophy, the visual arts—except when they touched on some political question, these life-shaping concerns tended to be met with silence. In a similar manner, a mediocre play watched by a few thousands received reviews from critics with literary pretensions, while a computer game of breathtaking technical sophistication, played by millions, fell beneath notice.

Importance measured by public attention reflected elite tastes. As newcomers from the digital frontiers began to crowd out the elites, our sense of what is important fractured along the edges of countless niche interests.

The shock of competition from such unexpected and unauthoritative quarters left the news business in a state of terminal disorientation. I mentioned the charge of civic irresponsibility lodged against defecting customers. We will encounter this rhetorical somersault again: being driven to extinction is not just a bad thing but morally wrong, sometimes—as with the music industry's prosecution of its customers—criminally so. Yet the news media wasn't averse to sleeping with the enemy. The most popular blogs today are associated with newspaper websites, for example, while the *New York Times's* paywall discreetly displays orifices that can be penetrated through social media.

Such liaisons beg the question of what "news" actually is. The obvious answer: news is anything sold by the news business. In the current panic to cling to some remnant of the audience, this can mean anything at all. On the front page of the gray old *Times*, I'm liable to encounter a chatty article about frying with propane gas. CNN lavished hours of airtime on a runaway bride. The magisterial tones of Walter Cronkite, America's rich uncle, are lost to history, replaced by the ex-cheerleader mom style of Katie Couric.

One reason the notion of "citizen journalism" never got off the ground was the fundamental confusion about what the *professional* journalist is expected to do, other than squeeze out content like a milk cow.

No part of the news business endured a more humiliating thrashing from the tsunami than the daily newspaper, which a century before had been the original format to make a profit by selling news to the public. True confession: I grew up reading newspapers. For half my life, this seemed like a natural way to acquire information. But that was an illusion based on monopoly conditions. Newspapers were old-fashioned industrial enterprises. Publishing plants were organized like factories. "All the news that's fit to print" really meant "All the content that fits a predetermined chunk of pages."

In substance, the daily newspaper was an odd bundle of stuff—from government pronouncements and political reports to advice for unhappy wives, box scores, comic strips, lots of advertisements, and tomorrow's horoscope. Newspapers made tacit claims that collapsed under the pressure of the information tsunami. They pretended to authority and certainty, for example. But the fatal flaw was the bundling, because it became clear that we had entered on a great unraveling, that the tide of the digital revolution boiled and churned against such artificial bundles of information and "disaggregated": that is, tore them apart.

(My 93-year-old mother has kept her subscription to the *Washington Post* strictly because she loves the crossword puzzles. I have shown her websites teeming with crossword puzzles, but she remains unmoved. My mother wants her bundle, and belongs to the last generation to do so.)

Information sought a less grandiose, less industrial level of circulation. The question was *who* or *what* determined that level. Every possible answer spelled misery for the daily newspaper, but the pathologies involved, I thought, reached far deeper than one particular mode of peddling information, and implicated the relationship between elites and non-elites, between authority and obedience. That passive mass audience on which so many political and economic institutions depended had itself unbundled, disaggregated, fragmented into what I call *vital communities*: groups of wildly disparate size gathered organically around a shared interest or theme.

These communities relied on digital platforms for self-expression. They were vital *and* mostly virtual. The topics they obsessed over included jihad and cute kittens, technology and economics, but the total number was limited only by the scope of the human imagination. The voice of the vital communities was a new voice: that of the amateur, of the educated non-elites, of a disaffected and unruly public. It was at this level that the vast majority of new information was now produced and circulated. The intellectual earthquake that propelled the tsunami was born here.

Communities of interest reflected the true and abiding tastes of the public. The docile mass audience, so easily persuaded by advertisers and politicians, had been a monopolist's fantasy that disintegrated at first contact with alternatives. When digital magic transformed information consumers into producers, an established order—grand hierarchies of power and money and learning—went into crisis.

I have touched on the manner of the reaction: not worry or regret over lost influence, but moral outrage and condemnation, sometimes accompanied by calls for repression. The newly articulate public meanwhile tramped with muddy boots into the sacred precincts of the elites, overturning this or that precious heirloom. The ensuing conflict has toppled dictators and destroyed great corporations, yet it has scarcely begun.

I'd been enthralled by the astronomical growth in the volume of information, but the truly epochal change, it turned out, was the revolution in the relationship between the *public* and *authority* in almost every domain of human activity.

I CHRISTEN THE NEW AGE AND OTHER DEFINITIONAL ILLUSIONS

This book is not a history of the revolution, since it's much too early for that. Thoughtful interpretations of the genesis and nature of the change have been written by Yochai Benkler, Clay Shirky, and Glenn Reynolds, among many others.[3] If you wish to understand the world being formed outside your windowpane, let me introduce you to this growing body of work, then step aside.

Nor am I propounding some world-historical argument for or against the new order. Using terms for analytic style coined by Isaiah Berlin and borrowed by Philip E. Tetlock in his famous study of expert political judgment, I'm afraid that I am a "fox" rather than a "hedgehog." No matter what I believe to be true, there always seems to be another side to the question. If you were to put me to the torture, I'd probably confess that this is my analytic ideal: to consider the question from as many relevant perspectives as the mind can hold.

Understanding 9/11 from the point of view of Al Qaeda incurs, for the analyst, the risk of "going native" and losing his moral equilibrium. That sort of thing happens with distressing regularity in academia, and even in government. But pretending that there is only one point of view aborts even the possibility of analysis. For that, all you need is an original prejudice and a sufficiently narrow mind.

The story I want to tell is simple but has many conflicting points of view. It concerns the slow-motion collision of two modes of organizing life: one hierarchical, industrial, and top-down, the other networked, egalitarian, bottom-up. I called it a collision because there has been wreckage, and not just in a figurative sense. Nations that a little time ago responded to a single despotic will now tremble on the edge of disintegration. I described it as slow motion because the two modes of being, old and new, have seemed unable to achieve a resolution, a victory of any sort. Both engage in *negation*—it is as a sterile back-and-forth of negation that the struggle has been conducted.

So I am writing this book because I fear that many structures I value from the old way, including liberal democracy, and many possibilities glimmering in the new way, such as enlarging the circle of personal freedom, may be ground to dust in that sterile back-and-forth.

The book's temper is reflective. It was written out of a desire to understand. The structure should be intuitive, or so I fervently hope. The chapters are self-standing but thematically connected. Each represents a mystery to be penetrated in this most mysterious of conflicts. Heroes and villains will appear, and because life is meant to be lived rather than analyzed, I have no qualms about saying who I think is which. There will be a scarcity of saints but an abundance of martyrs. That is the way of our moment in time.

To tell my story I must use my own words, but if I am to communicate successfully with you, the reader, you must understand what I mean by them. Terms like *the public* and *authority* are not simple, and require much thinking about. A goal of this book is to flesh out the reality that these terms represent—yet, for obvious reasons, I can't just spring their meaning at the end, like the punch line of a joke. Let me, instead, offer quick-and-dirty characterizations to get the story started, and we can see how these hold up as we go along.

First, the public. It's a singular noun for a plural object. I usually refer to the public as "it," but sometimes, in a certain context, as "them." Whether one or the other is correct, I leave for grammarians to decide. Both fit.

We'll explore later what the public is *not*. My understanding of what the public *is* I have borrowed entirely from Walter Lippmann. Lippmann was a brilliant political analyst, editor, and commentator. He wrote during the apogee of the top-down, industrial era of information, and he despaired of the ability of ordinary people to connect with the realities of the world beyond their immediate circle of perception. Such people made decisions based on "pictures in their heads"—crude stereotypes absorbed from politicians, advertisers, and the media—yet in a democracy were expected to participate in the great decisions of government. There was, Lippmann brooded, no "intrinsic moral and intellectual virtue to majority rule."

Lippmann's disenchantment with democracy anticipated the mood of today's elites. From the top, the public, and the swings of public opinion, appeared irrational and uninformed. The human material out of which the public was formed, the "private citizen," was a political amateur, a sheep in need of a shepherd, yet because he was sovereign he was open to manipulation by political and corporate wolves. By the time he came to publish *The Phantom Public* in 1927, Lippmann's subject appeared to him to be a fractured, single-issue-driven thing.

> *The public, as I see it, is not a fixed body of individuals. It is merely the persons who are interested in an affair and can affect it only by supporting or opposing the actors.*[4]

Today, the public itself has become an actor, but otherwise Lippmann described its current structure with uncanny accuracy. It is not a fixed body of individuals. It is composed of amateurs, and it has fractured into vital communities, each clustered around an "affair of interest" to the group.

This is what I mean when I use the word "public."

Now, authority, which is a bit more like beauty: we know it when we see it. Authority pertains to the source. We believe a report, obey a command, or accept a judgment because of the standing of the originator. At the individual level, this standing is achieved by professionalization. The person in authority is a trained professional. He's an expert with access to hidden knowledge. He perches near the top of some specialized hierarchy, managing a bureaucracy, say, or conducting research. And, almost invariably, he got there by a torturous process of accreditation, usually entailing many years of higher education.

Persons in authority have had to jump through hoops of fire to achieve their lofty posts—and feel disinclined to pay attention to anyone who has not done the same.

Lasting authority, however, resides in *institutions* rather than in the persons who act and speak on their behalf. Persons come and go—even Walter Cronkite in time retired to utter trivialities—while institutions like CBS News transcend generations. They are able to hoard money and proprietary data, and to evolve an oracular language designed to awe and perplex the ordinary citizen. A crucial connection, as I said earlier, exists between institutional authority and monopoly conditions: to the degree that an institution can command its field of play, its word will tend to go unchallenged. This, rather than the obvious asymmetry in voice modulation, explains the difference between Cronkite and Katie Couric.

With this rough sketch in hand, I'm ready to name names. When I say "authority," I mean government—officeholders, regulators, the bureaucracy, the military, the police. But I also mean corporations, financial institutions, universities, mass media, politicians, the scientific research industry, think tanks and "nongovernmental organizations," endowed foundations and other nonprofit organizations, the visual and performing arts business. Each of these institutions speaks as an authority in some domain. Each clings to a shrinking monopoly over its field of play.

* * *

I have one more characterization to propose.

The new age we have entered needs a name. While the newness of the age has often been remarked upon by many writers, and by now is almost a cliché, very little effort, strangely enough, has been invested in christening it. Tony Olcott writes of a "networked age," but I think he means the phrase to be descriptive rather than titular—and it's inadequate in any case. "Digital age" is lame, "digital revolution" better and I will use it in some contexts, but it implies change by means of a single decisive episode, and fails to communicate the grinding struggle of nega-tion which I believe is the central feature of our time. An earlier candidate of mine, "age of the public," I discarded for the same reason. The old hi-erarchies and systems are still very much with us.

So let me return to my original point of departure: information. Information has not grown incrementally over history, but has expanded in great pulses or waves, which sweep over the human landscape and leave little untouched. The invention of writing, for example, was one such wave. It led to a form of government dependent on a mandarin or priestly caste. The development of the alphabet was another: the republics of the classical world would have been unable to function without literate citizens. A third wave, the arrival of the printing press and movable type, was probably the most disruptive of all. The Reformation, modern sci-ence, and the American and French Revolutions would scarcely have been possible without printed books and pamphlets. I was born in the waning years of the next wave, that of mass media—the industrial, I-talk-you-listen mode of information I've already had the pleasure to describe.

It's early days. The transformation has barely begun, and resistance by the old order will make the consequences nonlinear, uncertain. But I think I have already established that we stand, everywhere, at the first moment of what promises to be a cataclysmic expansion of information and communication technology.

Welcome, friend, to the Fifth Wave.

HODER
AND
WAEL
GHONIM

I met Hossein Derakhshan, better known by his blogname "Hoder," at a bloggers' convention in Nashville, Tennessee. We sat around a lunch table with other attendees and ate enormous barbecue sandwiches. Hoder was 30 but looked even more youthful than that, an amiable young man with sparkling dark eyes and a ready smile.

The media always referred to him as the Iranian "blogfather," so it's natural that we talked about the internet, and blogging, and Iran. I asked whether the blog he wrote in both Farsi and English, *Editor: Myself,* was blocked by the Iranian government. He assured me with a grin that he had ways to get his message into the mother country.

Hoder was technically savvy: that was his claim to fame. But, for an Iranian and a supposed dissident, I found him surprisingly naïve in political matters. He felt great anger toward the United States and the Bush administration. Part of that was personal: he had become a Canadian citizen, and getting across the border when your name was "Hossein Derakhshan" and you fit the wrong profile for age and sex was, at the time, a humiliating process. But he was full of strange ideas about neocons conspiring with other Iranian exiles whom he didn't like.

Hoder had just begun his curious and confused trajectory, from anti-regime dissident to frenetic supporter of Iranian president Mahmoud Ahmadinejad's nuclear posture. My brutally honest assessment of the man: a very likable person, possessed of a very ordinary intellect.

That was in 2005, a year and a half before his visit to Israel and three years before he entered into his private Calvary, for reasons that are worth considering.

A TWENTYSOMETHING IN TORONTO OPENS A NEW CONTINENT OF EXPRESSION FOR IRANIANS

Hoder really was an ordinary person, an insignificant man in relation to the great events that, during his lifetime, have troubled his country and the world. He was not a politician, not a revolutionary, not a genius, not a scholar—not an authority of any sort. He represents a type we'll encounter often in this story of the struggle between grand hierarchies and the public: the gifted amateur, propelled to unexpected places by the new information technology.

He was four years old when Ayatollah Khomeini and the Islamic Revolution swept to power in Tehran. That was the only government he knew before he departed into exile, and it came to define his life, for and against. Since that government played the role of villain in this specific story, it would be useful to linger over its characteristics for a moment.

In theory, the Iranian regime is a Platonic republic, with wise guardians protecting the moral and material welfare of all. In practice, it resembles a sterile hybrid begot on the mafia by the Communist Party of the Soviet Union. The men in charge monopolize all the power and much of the wealth of the country. They claim to be revolutionary, and once really were, in the worst way. Decades ago, however, most of them settled into big mansions, bought expensive cars, and became an entrenched ruling class at home, while pursuing ancient Persian ambitions in the region and the world.

They control the resources of a nation that is large, populous—80 million according to the *CIA Factbook*—and rich in oil. Iran is the big boy of the greater Middle East, though for ethnic and religious reasons its influence has never been proportional to its size and strength: a wall of mutual hostility and disdain divides Persian from Arab. The rulers of the Islamic Republic consider the global status quo to be a naked injustice to Iran. They crave a place in the sun.

Recent history has seen cycles of superficial reforms to open up the system, followed by hardened repression. The inner core of the regime, that is, the people and institutions who really hold the levers of power in Iran—the clerics, the militia, the revolutionary courts—remained unreformed and unreformable. But it was during one of the moments of relative calm that the young Hoder began his career as an observer of the digital universe, writing for a reformist newspaper that was soon after closed by the courts.

By 2000, he was in Canada. Because he wished to start a blog, he tinkered with code, and in September 2001 succeeded in adapting blogging software to the requirements of Farsi script. This minor innovation by an ordinary twentysomething was to have long repercussions, not just for Hoder's life but for public expression in Iran. Iranians took to blogging

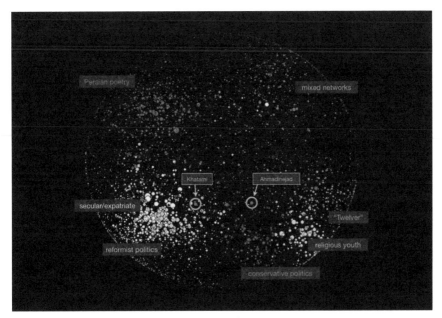

Figure 2: Map of "Blogistan," Iran's blogging universe.[5]
Image courtesy of Morningside Analytics.

with abandon. At a time when Arab countries had only a handful of blogs, almost all of them in English, Iran's "Blogistan" quickly reached tens of thousands of active sites, and continues to grow to this day. Most Iranian blogs were trivial personal diaries. That happened to be the case in every country on earth. Many blogs, however, commented on political news, advocated feminism, or criticized the obvious corruption of regime officials.

The phenomenal expansion of Iran's blogosphere was a nonlinear event, possible only under the conditions of the Fifth Wave. A space abruptly opened for expression that was *not* under the absolute control of the censor. Vital communities formed online, splintered along the usual divergence of interests but sharing a common wish to defend and expand that virtual public space against the predations of the regime.

In consequence, the ruling class confronted what has come to be called "the dictator's dilemma"—a frequent affliction of authority in the new environment. The dilemma works this way: For security reasons, dictators must control and restrict communications to a minimum. To make their rule legitimate, however, they need prosperity, which can only be attained by the open exchange of information. Choose.

Along a spectrum of possible choices, North Korea, for example, stands at the restrictive extreme. Three generations of North Korean dictators have bet big on famine and poverty in exchange for silence and control. As we'll see, the Egyptian dictator Hosni Mubarak lost power in part because of his vacillations on this question. He wanted to toggle between communication and control, but instead betrayed his own panic and an old man's ignorance of the information sphere.

Iran's rulers chose differently. Formally at least, they embraced blogging and the internet. They promoted connectivity (though keeping bandwidth artificially low), and encouraged regime supporters to get online—an attempt to nullify the anti-regime unity of the online communities. Whole swaths of Blogistan are thus dedicated to "conservative" political and religious views. High government figures are expected to communicate online. The most famous blogger in the country is ex-president Ahmadinejad.

Of course, the regime also blocked many websites, and currently holds the world record for bloggers thrown in jail. At least one of them died from the admonishments of his wise Platonic guardians.

In a very nonlinear but, I believe, real way, all of these contortions had been forced on the brutal authoritarians of Iran by an insignificant young man tinkering with code in Toronto, Canada.

AN INSIGNIFICANT MAN THREATENS THE SANCTITIES OF A VERY LARGE NATION

It was the surprised discovery by the West of the Iranian blogosphere that raised Hoder to the status of a minor celebrity. He was invited to an endless round of conferences to speak about that shadowy realm, the internet, which he did with some zest and skill. By the time I ran across him in Nashville, he seemed less a blogfather than an orphaned techno-gypsy, drifting from conference to conference. In January 2007, he attended a conference in Tel Aviv, Israel. He knew perfectly well this barred his return to Iran, but gave idealistic reasons for the visit. Then, in the fall of 2008, Hoder travelled to Tehran. And so it happened that, on the first day of November, the Iranian authorities at last caught up with the insignificant man: they arrested Hoder at his father's home and ushered him into Evin Prison, an unfriendly place within the Islamic Republic's merciless penal system.

Two years passed before his trial. An additional eight months lapsed before the Alice-in-Wonderland sentence was announced: 19½ years of incarceration for the crime of blogging.

Idle to speculate why Hoder returned to Iran: he was, as I noted, of a naïve and unrealistic temperament. Far more useful—far more honest and to the point, if we wish to understand the character of the age in which we now live—is to aim our questions about this wanton injustice at the men who perpetrated it. Why did they arrest Hoder? Why the inordinate punishment? What did they, in full possession of great power and authority, fear from this ordinary person? What did they hope to gain by burying him alive in Evin Prison?

On the surface, these questions may appear no less naïve than Hoder himself. By Western standards, the Islamic Republic was a lawless and despotic government. Despots punish those who express politically unorthodox views or engage in offensive behavior. Hoder fit that profile on both counts.

Moreover, repression aimed at internet dissidents has become so commonplace that it hardly excites attention. Throwing bloggers in prison seems to be the way of the world: it isn't news. In February 2007, for example, an Egyptian court condemned blogger Abdel Kareem Nabil Suleiman, who was all of 22 at the time, to four years in prison for "insulting the president" and "vilifying Islam." That was under the old Mubarak regime. In June 2013, another court in Egypt condemned blogger Ahmed Douma to six months' imprisonment, also for insulting the president. That was under the new elected government formed by the Muslim Brotherhood. I cite these two men as random bookends: other Egyptian bloggers were persecuted and jailed in between.[6]

China employs a veritable army of internet censors and is the only nation in serious competition with Iran over the all-time record for bloggers jailed. In Cuba, dissident blogger Yoani Sánchez was thrown in the back of a car and beaten by agents of the regime. In Vietnam, blogger Nguyen Hoang Vi was knocked off a motorcycle, had the windows of her car smashed, and was stripped and subjected to a body search by the police, before being arrested. And in Iran, Hoder was only one of many bloggers abused and jailed during a hardening of the regime in recent years.[7]

Life is bad if you're a blogger in many parts of the world. That can be the simple story of Hoder's private Calvary. He angered the wrong people in the wrong country, then, inexplicably, he put himself in their hands.

This account is accurate enough but superficial. It asks us to accept as given many things we could well question: for example, that powerful authoritarians are angered by, or fearful of, information. Yet the relationship between power politics and information is, and always has been, opaque. The cause for anger or fear in a person of great material authority confronted with information generally—with information *as* information—is thus *never* a given, I maintain, but rather is a mystery in need of analysis and interpretation. This is very much the case when "information" is represented by an insignificant man posting his thoughts on a blog.

Along with countless trivial subjects, Hoder posted his opinions of the Iranian regime, for and against. But he had no standing in Iranian politics, no political standing anywhere. He wasn't really much of a dissident, in any sense of that word. His one claim to influence was technological: almost accidentally, he had opened a space for public discussion and made it available to ordinary Iranians. And, being an idealist, he had become a sort of traveling salesman on behalf of blogging and self-expression.

A way forward into the mystery, then, would be to hypothesize that for Iran's rulers, Hoder—blogfather, blogger—stood for something larger and more threatening than himself. In fact, he stood for the loss of monopoly over information, the loss of an absolute control over public communications.

My preferred method of analysis—I have said this before—is to examine a story from every possible perspective. Understandably, Hoder's story is always presented by news media and human rights activists from the perspective of the youthful victim. But to penetrate to the heart of this particular mystery, to make sense of the terms of the asymmetric struggle between great power and mere information, we must shift our point of view to that of the unattractive mongrels—half gangsters, half ideologues—enthroned at the top of the political pyramid in Iran.

A good place to start is with the formal charges lodged against Hoder. These formed a confused hodgepodge of accusations, including making propaganda against the Islamic Republic and "cooperating with enemy states," a reference to the visit to Israel. The most revealing charge, however, was "insulting the sanctities" of the Iranian nation. No doubt religion was meant, but the words expressed a more profound and generalized concern by the authorities, and show us the way into their perspective.

Bloggers, and in general all dabblers in digital communication, are often accused of insulting sacred things: presidents, religion, property rights, even the prerogatives of a democratic majority. They speak when there should be silence, and utter what should never be said. They trample on the sanctities, in the judgment of the great hierarchical institutions that for a century and a half have controlled, from the top down, authoritatively, the content of every public conversation. The idea is not that some forbidden opinion or other has been spoken. It is the *speaking* that is taboo. It's the alien voice of the amateur, of the ordinary person, of the public, that is an abomination to the ears of established authority.

So to arrive at the destination mapped out by our hypothesis, we must set aside the salient characteristics of the men in charge in Tehran. What matters is *not* that they are thugs, or that they oppress their own countrymen. That simply speaks to the range of actions open to them. The meaningful bit is that they belong to a larger class or category of people, found in every country and in most walks of life, who long ago persuaded themselves that they alone have the authority and legitimacy to speak and act within their own domains. This—not from selfish motives, no, not in the least—for the good of humanity. Their authority rests on the moral order of the world. Any challenge, however insignificant, isn't just a potential threat to *them* but a violation of that order, a perversion that must be crushed utterly in the name of all that is good and true.

With regard to Hoder and his 19½-year sentence, what counted was less any political dissidence on his part than the perception by the men in authority in Iran that the young blogger was a moral monstrosity.

Democratically elected governments have reacted in the same way. Turkish president Recep Tayyip Erdogan is his country's most popular politician in generations, having comfortably won several national elections. His influence and that of his party has spread to a soft, but effective, control of mass media. Erdogan speaks and acts within an echo chamber of great authority—legitimately so, by democratic standards.

When protests broke out in Istanbul over government plans to build a shopping mall on the site of a park, then spread throughout Turkey and acquired a definite anti-Erdogan edge, the Turkish news media ignored the events. CNN Turkey, partly owned by Turkish interests, famously showed a documentary about penguins. (The visual joke of protesting penguins spread through the web with astounding rapidity.) The authorities had decreed silence. Anti-government forces—the protesting public— turned to Twitter to exchange information, with a preference for vivid photos showing the size of demonstrations and, more importantly, the violence of the police in repressing them. These images were persuasive. The West's perception of Turkey as a benign Muslim democracy suffered a sharp jolt.

Erdogan headed a democratically elected government. His presence on Twitter had attracted 2.5 million followers. But when he spoke about the June 2013 protests, it was not as a democrat or a participant in social media. His was the voice of authority, in the grip of moral outrage no different from that experienced by the despots in Tehran: "There is a curse called Twitter, all sorts of lies are there. This thing called social media is a curse on societies." Turkish tweeters had insulted the sanctities. Dozens were arrested. A few days later, Erdogan's minister of the interior announced that "provocations on social media" were to be targets of criminal investigation. [8]

This visceral repugnance, amounting almost to nausea, toward the intrusion of the public into the domain of authority is by no means restricted to government. I noted that people in the news business have converted the economic failure of the daily newspaper into a danger not just to their own livelihoods but to the fabric of democratic life. When, for example, Nicholas Kristof brooded on the "decline of traditional news media," which pays his salary, he evoked a dismal future of "polarization and intolerance." [9]

The classic case of insulting *corporate* sanctities involved the file-sharing program Napster. The story of Napster is that of Shawn Fanning, prototype of the many young men, like Hoder, who stumbled on a formula to leverage information technology in ways that threatened the established order. Fanning released the first version of Napster in June 1999. He was 18, an unknown teenager without money or business connections, yet the shock of that beta release would send the profits of a mighty industry on a downward spiral, from which it would never recover.

Napster invited Fanning's fellow teenagers to exchange song files without first stopping at the cash register to pay the recording companies.

The noise of condemnation by defenders of the music and allied industries was Erdogan-worthy. In a friend of the court statement for the 2001 lawsuit against Napster, Jack Valenti, head of the Motion Picture Association of America, portrayed the corporate interests he represented as "the backbone of America's creative community" and the Napster business model as "theft." "If the courts allow Napster and services like it to continue to facilitate massive copyright infringement," he added pointedly, "there is a grave risk that the public will begin to perceive and believe that they have a right to obtain copyrighted materials for free."

The best summation was delivered by Hilary Rosen, head of the Recording Industry Association of America: "What Napster is doing ... is legally and morally wrong." The immoral act in question, let's recall, consisted of teenagers exchanging music files.[10]

Few incidents better illustrate the pervasiveness of authority as a belief system that anoints the chosen few, or the implacable fury of the anointed against a trespassing public. If Jack Valenti had had the power to sentence Shawn Fanning to 19½ years in a federal penitentiary, I'm fairly certain he would have done so.

A BURNING MAN ON FACEBOOK LIGHTS THE WAY FOR POLITICAL CHANGE IN TUNISIA

You could object that this has been a tragic tale, signifying nothing. Even if Hoder threatened the Iranian authorities on the plane of morality, little was changed down here on planet Earth. The Islamic Republic rolled on, dictatorial as always, still ruled by unpleasant men. Hoder agonized in Evin Prison for four years, until he was pardoned in November 2014 by Ali Khamenei, Supreme Leader of Iran. His 19½-year sentence remains the longest ever pronounced against a blogger in Iran.

The gap between online freedom and political change was never crossed—possibly, never *can* be crossed, because of the fundamental mismatch between virtuality and reality.

These objections loop back to the mysterious relationship between political power and information. The word used for power is "hard," while information is supposed to be "soft"—so it all seems like a game of rock–paper–scissors, with scissors eternally cutting paper and no other structural outcome possible. Brute force beats smart talk, forever. Such a *null effect* interpretation of the Fifth Wave has been proposed by certain

Figure 3: Man on fire: Mohamed Bouazizi, December 16, 2010.[11]
Photo © 2011 ievolve.org/ZUMA Press

scholars, and those of us who observed digital activists being abused and imprisoned over the years could only wonder whether the contrarians were right.

I'll return to the power–information equation in a little more depth soon enough, when I relate the story of *Homo informaticus*. Here and now, I want to bring up, for your consideration, real events, *hard* events, which were variously—and, yes, mysteriously—entangled in webs of information.

The first is the least persuasive, but it concerns Hoder's country, Iran, and so deserves mention. The huge protests that erupted in Tehran and elsewhere in that country following the contested presidential elections of June 2009 soon bloomed into the anti-regime Green Movement, and received instant media acclaim as a "Twitter Revolution." In a rare moment of techno-euphoria, the starched-collar worthies of the State Department intervened with Twitter to postpone a planned shutdown, ostensibly so the revolutionary tweets could continue.

The best information available, however, suggested that relatively few Twitter users could be found inside Iran—the immense spike in traffic during the protests was generated by émigrés and others outside the country. The Green Movement was almost certainly *not* a Twitter revolution or reliant on social media, although it was certainly a digitally assisted revolt: protesters used cell phone texts and videos to powerful effect.

But the main lesson here was the violent repression of the Green Movement by regime militia. Scissors cut paper. While it was really impossible to say, as I did with Hoder's incarceration, that nothing had changed, the political facts on the ground in Iran remained fundamentally the same: for the next four years, Ahmadinejad and his faction ruled.

Matters turned out differently in Tunisia with the uprising of December 2010–January 2011. Less than three weeks after the first anti-regime protests, the country's president of very long standing, Zine El Abidine Ben Ali, fled to Saudi Arabia. The question, for us, is the degree to which the Fifth Wave of information was implicated in this outcome.

The catalyst for the Tunisian uprising came in the form of a truly insignificant man: Mohamed Bouazizi, a street vendor in the provincial town of Sidi Bouzid, who set himself on fire in despair over humiliations he had endured at the hands of regime officials, and later died of his burns. You will note that I wrote "catalyst" rather than "cause": even the simplest human events constitute complex systems ruled by nonlinearities. Within such systems, teasing out a single episode and proclaiming it the prime mover makes as much sense as picking a grain of sand and calling it "the beach."

This tangle of causation is why analysts who get paid big bucks to play the part of prophet invariably get the future wrong—or, at least, whenever tomorrow fails to resemble yesterday.

The trajectory by which Bouazizi became a *cause*—in both senses of that word—deserves a bit of reflection. Nine months before his fatal moment, another street vendor called Abdesslem Trimech, from the provincial town of Monastir, set himself on fire over his mistreatment by the government, and later died. No protests ensued. In fact, nothing at all happened. Trimech, I imagine, was mourned by family and friends, but otherwise remained obscure and inconsequential.

Trimech was a different man acting in a different time and place from Bouazizi. True enough. But another significant difference leaps out, if we wish to understand why these two similar deaths had such dissimilar effects. Bouazizi burned to death in front of a camera. For as long as digital images hold true, we will watch him explode into flames, still walking, at a nondescript public square. This image was impossible to absorb without feeling pain and horror. Without words, seemingly untainted by special pleading, it told the story of a man driven by his rulers beyond the last measure of despair. The photos of Bouazizi's self-immolation were posted on Facebook, and aroused strong emotions in and out of Tunisia. In contrast, the unphotographed Trimech died a faceless shadow.

Tunisia's revolution demonstrated one decisive change between the old and new information dispensations. The industrial age depended on chunky blocks of text to influence government and opinion. The new digital world has preferred the power of the visual. What is usually referred to as new media really means the triumph of the image over the printed word.

But another observation to take away from events in Tunisia is that the divide between old and new media is largely fictitious. It may be useful to speak of the internet or social media and contrast these with mass media, but what exists in reality is a single, deeply matrixed *information sphere*.

Al Jazeera, for example, is a digital satellite TV channel aimed at a mass audience. It's new and it's old. Both sides of the Tunisian conflict believed, with good reason, that Al Jazeera influenced the outcome by favoring the insurgency in its coverage. That could be considered a case of Big Media "setting the agenda." But most of Al Jazeera's Tunisia footage came from cell phone videos, taken by the public on the spot and communicated via Facebook. They were then reposted online—on Al Jazeera's website, on YouTube, and on thousands of niche sites. So this was also a case of new media driving news coverage.

The point I want to drive home is that there is now massive redundancy in the transmission of information. That's another change from the old ways. You can jam Al Jazeera's signal, but you can't jam YouTube. You can shut down the internet—as Egyptian authorities did when they faced their own uprising—but you can't shut down the information sphere.

A GOOGLE EMPLOYEE IN DUBAI SCHEDULES AN EGYPTIAN REVOLUTION AS A FACEBOOK EVENT

The success of the Tunisian uprising reversed the polarities of power as we have so far observed them. A mostly disorganized public toppled a regime which had ruled with unquestioned authority for 23 years. Paper beat scissors, somehow. Many factors played into this outcome, but I will venture to say, without straying into controversy, that one important factor was the effect of the information sphere—on the global public, on the Tunisian public, and on the Tunisian authorities themselves. Much of the information coming out of Tunisia during the protests reflected the work and the will of the public.

Still, there's no doubt that the turmoil in that country began spontaneously, on the streets. That was not the case with the last event I want to consider. It originated online, as a virtual invitation to revolution scheduled on Facebook Events.

If you were to ask me to name the most significant geopolitical transformations since the fall of the Soviet Union, the 2011 uprising in Egypt, which followed close on the heels of Tunisia's and repeated the same pattern, would rank very near the top. Egypt is the most powerful and influential country in the Arabic-speaking world. The fall of the old regime there sent shocks and aftershocks into the region, the effects of which are still in play today. Many good accounts, from both Western and Egyptian perspectives, have been written about this sudden turning of the hinge of fate—I have no wish to add another.

Here's what I intend to do: to touch on three brief moments of that uprising, which reflect how supposedly "hard" political events were shaped by soft information.

The first and last moments, the alpha and omega, share the same protagonist: Wael Ghonim, a young Egyptian whose talents lacked even a name a generation ago. Ghonim was Google's head of marketing for the Middle East, and had moved to Dubai, a sort of Disney World of emirates, for his work. He was 29 when he created his Facebook page, 30 when he was kidnapped off the streets of Cairo by anonymous agents of the regime. I hesitate to call him ordinary or insignificant, as I have done with Hoder and others. Even before he provided the spark for the revolt, his life had not been a typical one for an Egyptian.

Ghonim himself, however, had decided opinions on the matter. He posted on his site that he had no wish to "start a revolution or a coup," and did not view himself as "a political leader of any sort." He then went on:

> I'm an ordinary Egyptian who cheers the Ahly team, sits at the local café, and eats pumpkin seeds . . . and who becomes miserable when our national team loses a game . . . the bottom line is that I just want to be proud that I'm Egyptian . . . [12]

And it is true that, in the decisive TV interview given after his release, he was perceived by many ordinary Egyptians as one of them: a decent young man, humble in demeanor, markedly different from the pompous officials, angry revolutionaries, and otherwise peculiar personalities prevalent in Egypt's politics.

Let us agree, then, that Wael Ghonim was an *extraordinary* ordinary person. He forged, on Facebook, a vital community that helped lead the charge during the early phase of the events of January–February 2011. His own telling of those events, the autobiographical *Revolution 2.0*, I recommend to anyone who wants to understand, from a very human perspective, the destructive effects of new information on a fossilized political system. Ghonim may have been the closest digital equivalent to Walter Cronkite: mediator to a disparate virtual public, whose authority was earned daily from below rather than accredited for all time from above.

He called his Facebook page "We Are All Khaled Said." The name signified a person, an event, and an image. Khaled Said was a young Alexandrian who, for reasons that remain obscure, was savagely beaten to death by thugs in the employ of the Mubarak regime. Such abuses took place with impunity and in public silence. Khaled Said was different, however. He had been a nice-looking, middle-class young Egyptian, first of all. More importantly, his family, using a cell phone camera, had secretly photographed Said's mangled face as he lay in the morgue. The difference from earlier photos of the handsome, smiling young man was appalling. In Egypt as in Tunisia, a powerful and disturbing image stood at the starting-place of revolution.

Ghonim used the images, and the story of Khaled Said, to fuel what was essentially a marketing campaign against regime injustice on his website.

At that point, Hosni Mubarak had been in power over 30 years—longer than Ben Ali in Tunisia, much longer than Ahmadinejad in Iran. His rule had acquired a monumental inevitability, and there was talk that the pharaoh's crown would pass to his son Gamal. The political system in Egypt rested on pure gangsterism, lacking any ideological justification other than the *authority* of the men in charge: they alone, it was claimed, possessed the expertise to maintain security, grow the economy, and manage the complexities of a modern government.

In fact, the Egyptian government was less incompetent than it has since been portrayed, but that carried little weight with Egyptians, most of whom detested the regime for the everyday indignities and occasional brutality it visited on them. The problem was inertia. Political change seemed impossible, because it had never happened: and with such a dearth of hope, fear easily won the day.

I will pass over the marketing techniques applied by Ghonim to help members of his community overcome the fear barrier. The fascinating details can be found in *Revolution 2.0*. Instead, I want to move directly to a specific moment: January 14, 2011, when Ghonim, inspired by events in Tunisia, posted on the "Khaled Said" page a call for protests for January 25, the "Police Day" holiday in Egypt. Ghonim gave the event its name: "Revolution Against Torture, Poverty, Corruption, and Unemployment." And he created a Facebook Event for it.

Ghonim linked his call to revolution to other anti-regime websites and activists. His aim was remarkably ambitious: nothing less than to bridge the gap between virtual and real, and to do so in the domain of hard politics. From a Facebook page, he sought to mobilize the Egyptian public against their government. Consider the implications. If this leap was possible, the modes of organizing a mass movement prevalent since the French Revolution would be superseded—and attacking power and authority could become the work of amateurs, ordinary people, the untutored public.

Not long ago, a revolutionary was a dedicated professional. To achieve his goal, he needed an *organization* to command and control, a published *program* to explain the need for radical change, resting on an ideology that persuaded and attracted large numbers of the public—who would then be formed into a mass movement by means of *command* and *control*. Organization, program, printing presses, ideology, mass command and control: this costly, slow-moving machinery, with its need for hierarchy and obedience, could be transcended by a single click of the mouse if Wael Ghonim won his bet.

Though he had scheduled a revolution, Ghonim specifically denied being a revolutionary. He claimed to be an ordinary Egyptian.

* * *

Besides the obvious danger of regime repression, two technical obstacles might have barred the way to his goal. Since these have been cited by writers who even now doubt that web politics can be transferred to the real world, I want to deal with them briefly. One obstacle pertained to the number of Egyptians Ghonim could actually reach with Facebook. The other raised the question whether the psychological distance between virtual and real was, under any circumstances, simply too great to be crossed.

The problem of numbers was a significant one. Egypt lagged in internet penetration, falling behind not just the West but also Iran and the wealthier Arab countries of the Gulf. A previous online call for an "anti-terrorism" demonstration, to be held on July 24, 2005, attracted a handful of well-to-do, university-educated young Egyptians who were quickly and peaceably dispersed by the authorities. It was more comic opera than protest. Internet penetration at that time probably hovered between 7 and 10 percent.

By January 2011, internet penetration in Egypt exceeded 20 percent. You may well ask whether, at that level, Ghonim's message could have reached a large enough segment of the public—and, more generally, whether we have any idea what the minimal level of diffusion must be, for a message to enter the consciousness of the public. The answer to both questions is: yes.

Roland Schatz, a brilliant commercial practitioner of agenda-setting theory, has identified a level of media diffusion below which a message sinks without notice, but above which it quickly rises to public attention. Schatz calls this boundary the *awareness threshold*, and has estimated the tipping point at 15 percent of diffusion. Scholars have charted a similar trajectory for the adoption of every kind of innovation, including new political beliefs. "Critical mass" occurs at between 10 and 20 percent of adoption—the level at which enough diffusion networks become "infected" by the virus of change to make the latter self-sustaining.[13]

The levels of internet and social media penetration in Egypt were consistent with a potential to break through the awareness threshold. During the 2011 revolt, this potential was realized. I believe Wael Ghonim won his bet. According to his own numbers, by January 25, the day of the protest, over a million persons had viewed his Facebook Event invitation, and around 100,000 had announced their intention to participate. It has been argued that most January 25 demonstrators weren't there because of

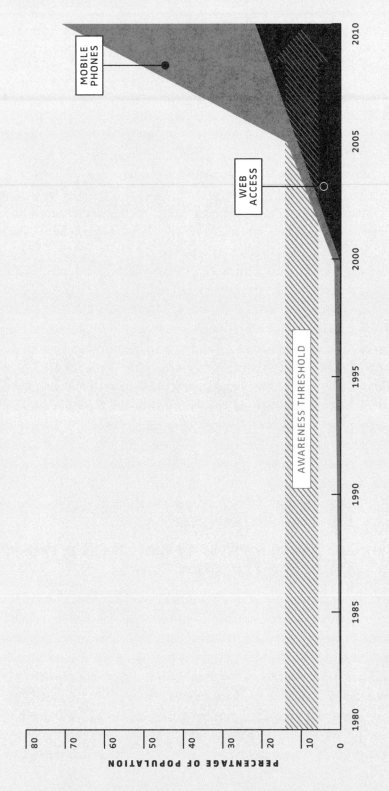

EGYPT: PHONE AND WEB ACCESS (MILLIONS)

MOBILE PHONES

WEB ACCESS

AWARENESS THRESHOLD

PERCENTAGE OF POPULATION

80
70
60
50
40
30
20
10
0

1980   1985   1990   1995   2000   2005   2010

Firgure 4: Egypt's new media break through the awareness threshold. [14]

Facebook. That's certainly true in terms of ultimate motives, possibly true in a more proximate sense. But many—maybe most—demonstrators were there because they had learned about the protests online. They had toggled from soft information to the hard pavement of the streets of Cairo, from virtual to real, from clever talk to pitched battles with the riot police. Almost incidentally, on the way to political change, they had carried out a revolution in Egypt's information balance of power.

I should add that the regime clearly believed that "We Are All Khaled Said" played an important part in the revolt. So did the protesters, who accorded Ghonim a place of honor in Tahrir Square. So did Ghonim himself, with good reason. When he asked protesters in Tahrir how they had found out about the event, many answered, "From 'We Are All Khaled Said,'" or mentioned other anti-regime Facebook groups.

If that was the case, the issue of psychological distance was answered empirically. It's simply false to say that the public can't make the leap between virtual and real politics. The problem has been posed in terms of online "weak bonds" as against real-life "strong bonds"—a proposition I will explore later in greater depth. All we need to know about the "strong bonds" objection, in connection with the Egyptian uprising, is that it applies *only* to the old mode of forming a mass movement. If the protesters had sought to replace the regime with a specific set of people, programs, and principles, the weak bonds of the digital world would have been insufficient.

But that's not what brought out the variegated Egyptian public to the streets. They just wanted to get rid of Hosni Mubarak.

A VERY OLD MAN SHUTS DOWN THE WEB, THEN FALLS THROUGH THE TRAPDOOR OF THE INFORMATION SPHERE

I want to make very clear what it is that I'm claiming—and what I'm not. I'm not saying that Ghonim and the internet caused Egypt's revolution. Because human beings aren't billiard balls, the application of Newtonian mechanics to political events invariably ends in confusion, and often in error. Ghonim and the internet were *one* cause out of many. If you have eyes to see, that should be remarkable enough.

I'm also not asserting the primacy of the internet, even under the conditions created by the tsunami of new information. Primacy goes to that massively redundant information sphere, which has absorbed new and old

Figure 5: Wael Ghonim on Dream TV.[15]

media alike. Within the information sphere, in the age of the image, I'd imagine that the most popular and persuasive medium is still television.

My second moment—chronologically the last—concerns the interview given on February 7, 2011, by Wael Ghonim to Mona El-Shazly of Dream TV. Let's unpack these elements.

Ghonim had just been released by the authorities after 11 days of detention in a secret state security prison. He looked gaunt and pale. Dream TV was a privately owned Egyptian channel, essentially the product of the dictator's dilemma. Hosni Mubarak wished to modernize Egypt. Modern countries boasted an abundance of TV channels and content. Mubarak gambled that his regime could control the information pouring out of new channels. The owners were beholden to the regime, the content was heavily censored. However, compared to state-owned television, this was indirect control. It was more tenuous. During the recent political turbulence, private channels could pivot away from the regime's interpretation of events. El-Shazly, the interviewer, made clear her sympathy with the protesters.

Here was a confluence possible only in the information sphere: old media mainstreaming a new media voice belonging to a central figure in a revolution. Dream TV was no Al Jazeera: its audience consisted of entertainment-minded, nonpolitical Egyptians.

At the time the program aired, the uprising had reached a crisis point. Six days before, Mubarak had delivered a televised speech in which he cited his service to the country and promised to step down at the end of his presidential term, in six months' time. Many protesters felt the old man should be allowed a dignified exit. Others were wavering. Crowds at Tahrir Square grew smaller.

Ghonim's raw, emotional performance on Dream TV has been credited with turning the tide decisively in favor of the protesters. It was a testament to the power of TV to capture and communicate sincerity: his sorrow when confronted with photos of dead demonstrators was both compelling and painful to watch. Before a mass audience, Wael Ghonim, that extraordinary ordinary person, gave the revolutionaries a face that ordinary Egyptians could identify with. He *embodied* information, which changed the direction of political life in his country. His interview went viral on YouTube, new media compounding the effect of the old. The crowds in Tahrir swelled in size. Four days later, Hosni Mubarak resigned from office.

* * *

The reality of the new environment is that the global information sphere, rather than any one medium or platform, erupts into nearly every political conflict, and not infrequently helps determine the outcome. Unlike, say, TV or Facebook, the information sphere can't be blocked by government. It's too redundant. Information leaks into the conflict anyhow.

This was demonstrated under almost laboratory conditions in Egypt on Friday, January 28, 2011: the moment the government shut the door on its population's access to the internet. Mobile phone service was disrupted as well. Mubarak, on the brink of the precipice, wanted to change sides on the dictator's dilemma, withdraw his gamble on modernity. He imagined he could push Egypt back into the past, to the comfortable days before the Fifth Wave.

The reason *why* Mubarak's minions shut down the web was no mystery. They were afraid of it. The causes of this fear—which they never explained or even admitted—hinted at a revolution much deeper and more disruptive of existing human relations than any purely political upheaval. Starting with the octogenarian Mubarak, the people who ran the regime had come to power during the industrial age of information. They had

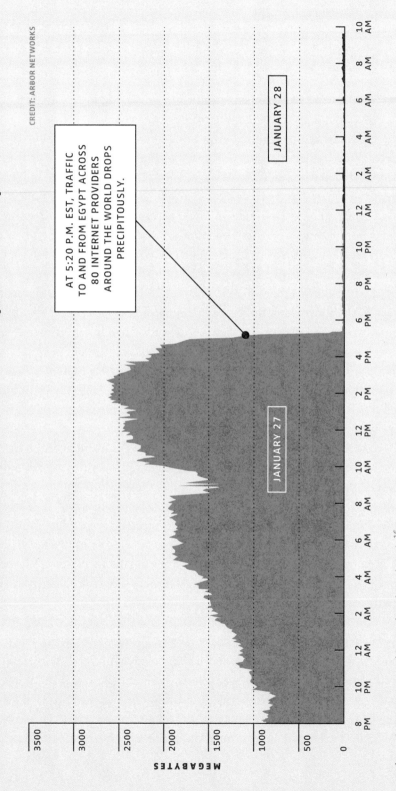

Figure 6: Reverse tsunami: Egypt shuts down the web.[16]

been lords and masters of what *could* and *could not* be said in newsprint, what *could* and *could not* be shown on television. And they dimly comprehended the irreparable erosion of this monopoly, the loss of control over the story Egyptians told about their rulers.

Demonstrations planned after Friday prayers in many Egyptian cities were the immediate cause of the shutdown. But let's inhabit the skins of the old men who ruled Egypt on January 28. What were they thinking? Very likely, that they were snatching away the means of communication and organization from the unruly public: that they had flipped a switch and cut off the public's voice. The internet represented the enemy.

Yet streams of information still surrounded and invaded Egypt, beyond the ability of political power to control.

Shutting down the web made history in the worst way. In Egypt and abroad, the move communicated a feeling of crisis and panic in the regime. In exchange for a political placebo, the government incurred real economic costs and alienated powerful business interests. But the most important effect of the shutdown was to create a silence—filled at once by Al Jazeera, which among its many agendas had pursued a long-running campaign to delegitimize Egypt's ruling clique. Here was redundancy with a vengeance.

The dominance and influence of Al Jazeera's coverage of the Egyptian uprising has probably been exaggerated, but there's no question that the channel exemplified to many observers the power of the information sphere. The regime certainly felt this way. Its agents dropped Al Jazeera's signal from the Nilesat satellite, and orchestrated the physical intimidation of Al Jazeera staff in Egypt. These efforts collided with the redundancy factor and came to nothing. Other Arab channels offered Al Jazeera space on their satellites, and much of Al Jazeera's footage came from amateurs who could not be shut down or intimidated.

The channel kept the story of the uprising alive by streaming it to every corner of the globe. From snowy Davos, Switzerland, where I was attending a conference, I witnessed street violence in Cairo on my laptop, via Al Jazeera in English. Many others there did the same. My guess is that Al Jazeera was instrumental in framing the event to the world as a struggle between idealistic youth and a vicious thugocracy. It led Western public opinion—including, it may be, in the White House—to a tipping point favoring the end of Mubarak's reign, despite real fears about the consequences of instability in the cradle of the Muslim Brotherhood.

YouTube amplified this sentiment, re-hosting video from Al Jazeera and other broadcasters, as well as raw footage from cell phone cameras that somehow found a path to the web. Unlike TV or live streaming, YouTube could select the most visually dramatic moments, and make them searchable. It archived spontaneity: a defiant young man suddenly gunned down by security forces, a bizarre horse and camel charge by Mubarak supporters into the crowd at Tahrir Square.

Virtually all YouTube videos favored the protesters. In the aggregate, the result was a brilliant exercise in geopolitical persuasion, wholly unco-ordinated, but the more authentic and effective because of that.

The men who pulled the plug on the web must have known that they couldn't keep ordinary Egyptians from learning about events. Hundreds of TV channels flooded the country's airwaves. Possibly, they imagined they could reconquer some control over the framing of images. If so, that was a generational mistake. The images swirling around the uprising showed protesters as pro-democracy underdogs, the heroes of the struggle. The public never lost its mighty voice. It was in this context that Ghonim's appearance on Dream TV delivered a decisive blow to Mubarak's hopes of clinging to power.

I began this chapter with the story of an insignificant man—the Iranian blogfather, Hoder. In hindsight, with Egypt's revolution and the "We Are All Khaled Said" page in mind, we can see that, in their persecution of Hoder, the Iranian authorities were motivated by self-preservation no less than moral outrage. They worried about the practical political consequences of giving ordinary people the means of public expression. Like all despots, they understood the fine points of control.

I end the chapter by observing, yet again, the strange embrace between information and power, now personified by the opposing figures of the drama in Egypt: Wael Ghonim, the Google marketing man turned Facebook agitator, and Hosni Mubarak, the Air Force pilot turned hard authoritarian. Together, they blew away our rock-paper-scissors theory, with its naïve faith in the supremacy of hard politics, and reaffirmed how information interacts with power in ways that are open, unpredictable, mysterious.

Every step of Ghonim's progress through the labyrinth of the Egyptian uprising would have been impossible when his antithesis, Mubarak, first assumed the presidency 30 years before. From the perspective of information, the two men grew up in different countries. Neither, therefore, understood the other, but Ghonim was a carrier of the Fifth Wave, an aggregator and connector, a drop of rain in a global storm, while Mubarak in his moment of crisis could only grope for a switch to turn out the light.

You don't need to accept the idea that Facebook pages can defeat tanks and bullets to perceive—faintly, like a pale shadow over the events in Egypt—a cataclysmic transformation in human power relations.

MY
THESIS

Consider this book a canvas. My job will be to depict the strange chaotic world that was born with the new millenium and, I feel certain, will remain with us for a little while longer. I'm not a visionary prophesying doom, however, or a scientific wizard forecasting the shape of things to come. I don't know the future, and I'm pretty sure they don't either. If I describe the present accurately, I will have achieved my goal.

Very little of what I have to say will be original: maybe only the composition.

If, after all these admissions, you were to ask me why you should read on, I would respond: because the world I'll describe is probably very different from the one you think you're living in. The problem is that there are so many superficially dazzling aspects of the information tsunami. When I sit in my study in Vienna, Virginia, and Skype with someone in Beirut, Lebanon—that's dazzling. It feels remarkable even as I'm doing it. So, naturally enough, attention has focused on the capabilities of digital platforms like Skype, Facebook, and Google, on the proliferation of communication and collaboration around the globe, or on the unprecedented growth in the volume of information. I understand the fascination—my own journey started with these concerns.

But it turns out that fascination with surface glitter has obscured our view to what is transpiring in the depths. There, human beings interact with platforms and information, and are changed by the interaction, and the accumulated changes have shaken and battered established institutions from companies and universities to governments and religions. The view from the depths is of a colossal many-sided conflict, the outcome of which, for good or evil, remains uncertain. In fact, the outcome will largely depend on us. And because we still think in categories forged during the industrial age—liberal and conservative, for example, or professional and amateur—our minds are blind to many of the clashes and casualties of this underground struggle.

This is the story I want to tell—the reality I aim to describe as accurately as I can.

A WAR OF THE WORLDS, DEDUCED FROM THE DEVIL'S EXCREMENT

My thesis is a simple one. We are caught between an old world that is decreasingly able to sustain us intellectually and spiritually, maybe even materially, and a new world that has not yet been born. Given the character of the forces of change, we may be stuck for decades in this ungainly posture. You who are young today may not live to see its resolution.

Famous landmarks of the old regime, like the daily newspaper and the political party, have begun to disintegrate under the pressure of this slow-motion collision. Many features we prized about the old world are also threatened: for example, liberal democracy and economic stability. Some of them will emerge permanently distorted by the stress. Others will just disappear. Many attributes of the new dispensation, like a vastly larger sphere for public discussion, may also warp or break from the immovable resistance of the established order.

In this war of the worlds, my concern is that we not end up with the worst of all possible worlds.

Each side in the struggle has a standard-bearer: *authority* for the old industrial scheme that has dominated globally for a century and a half, the *public* for the uncertain dispensation striving to become manifest. The two protagonists share little in common, other than humanity—and each probably doubts the humanity of the other. They have arrayed themselves in contrary modes of organization that require mutually hostile ideals of right behavior. The conflict is so asymmetrical that it seems impossible for the two sides actually to engage. But they do engage, and the battlefield is everywhere.

The perturbing agent between authority and the public is *information*. For my description of the present to make sense, I will have to show how such a vague, abstract concept can be wielded as a weapon in the war of the worlds.

Irreconcilable differences between old and new can be found in something as seemingly trivial as naming conventions. The industrial age insisted on portentous-sounding names of great seriousness and formality, to validate the organizations that spoke with the voice of authority: "Bank of America," "National Broadcasting Corporation," "*New York Times*." Each of these three names stood for a professional hierarchy that claimed a monopoly of specialized knowledge. They symbolized a starched-collar kind of mastery, and they meant to impress. Even the lowest-ranking person in these organizations, the names implied, had risen far above the masses.

The digital age loves self-mocking names, which are a way to puncture the formal stiffness of the established order: "Yahoo!," "Google," "Twitter," "Reddit," "Flickr," "Photobucket," "Bitcoin." Without having asked the people in question, I feel reasonably sure that the founders of Google never contemplated naming their company "National Search Engine Corporation" and Mark Zuckerberg of Facebook never felt tempted by "Social Connections Center of America." It wasn't the style.

The names of two popular political blogs from the early days of blogging, Glenn Reynolds's *Instapundit* and Andrew Sullivan's *Daily Dish*, poked fun at the pretentiousness of the news business. Bridge-bloggers who posted in English from foreign countries leaned toward even more attention-getting names: *Rantings of a Sandmonkey* and *The Big Pharaoh* in Egypt, for example, and my favorite, the Venezuelan *The Devil's Excrement*. Names of blogs have tended to become less outrageous with time—but the pull of digital culture is still toward goofiness and informality. The names asserted non-authoritativeness. They created a conscious divide between the old order and the new.

Try to imagine the response of a CIA briefer telling the president of a crisis in Venezuela, who is asked for his source of information: "It's *The Devil's Excrement*, Mr. President." Regardless of the cost in information missed, the briefer will avoid using any sources with such awkward names. His professional dignity—not to say, his professional success—demands the imposition of taboo.

I don't want to make too much of the conflict over naming styles. It's a skirmish, a surface manifestation of our struggle in the depths. I touched on the subject because it clarified, in an almost comical way, the nonnegotiable claims of identity implicit in the two contending structures: how each side has come to be organized.

The incumbent structure is *hierarchy*, and it represents established and accredited authority—government first and foremost, but also corporations, universities, the whole roster of institutions from the industrial age. Hierarchy has ruled the world since the human race attained meaningful numbers. The industrial mind just made it bigger, steeper, and more efficient. From the era of Rameses to that of Hosni Mubarak, it has exhibited predictable patterns of behavior: top-down, centralizing, pain-fully deliberate in action, process-obsessed, mesmerized by grand strate-gies and five-year plans, respectful of rank and order but contemptuous of the outsider, the amateur.

Against this citadel of the status quo, the Fifth Wave has raised the *network*: that is, the public in revolt, those despised amateurs now con-nected to one another by means of digital devices. Nothing within the bounds of human nature could be less like a hierarchy. Where the latter is slow and plodding, networked action is lightning quick but unsteady in purpose. Where hierarchy has evolved a hard exoskeleton to keep every part in place, the network is loose and pliable—it can swell into millions or dissipate in an instant.

Digital networks are egalitarian to the brink of dysfunction. Most would rather fail in an enterprise than acknowledge rank or leaders of any sort. Wael Ghonim's passionate insistence on being an ordinary Egyptian rather than a political leader was an expression of digital culture. Networks succeed when held together by a single powerful point of refer-ence—an issue, person, or event—which acts as center of gravity and orga-nizing principle for action.

Typically, this has meant being *against*. If hierarchy worships the es-tablished order, the network nurtures a streak of nihilism.

THE CENTER CANNOT HOLD AND THE BORDER HAS NO CLUE WHAT TO DO ABOUT IT

Another way to characterize the collision of the two worlds is as an epi-sode in the primordial contest between the *Center* and the *Border*. The terms were employed by Mary Douglas and Aaron Wildavsky in another context, long before the advent of the information tsunami, but they are singularly apt for our present condition.[17]

"Center" and "Border" can be applied to organizations embracing specific structures, ideals, and beliefs about the future. The two arche-types are relative to each other, and perform a kind of dance, which deter-mines the direction of social action.

The Center, Douglas and Wildavsky write, is dominated by large, hi-erarchical organizations.

It frankly believes in sacrificing the few for the good of the whole. It is smug about its rigid procedures. It is too slow, too blind to new information. It will not believe in new dangers and will often be taken by surprise.[18]

The Center envisions the future to be a continuation of the status quo, and churns out program after program to protect this vision.

The Border, in contrast, is composed of "sects"—we would say "networks"—which are voluntary associations of equals. Sects exist to oppose the Center: they stand firmly against. They have, however, "no intention of governing," and develop "no capacity for exercising power." To the Border, rank means inequality, hierarchy means conspiracy. Rather than articulate programs as alternatives to those of the Center, sects aim to *model* the behaviors demanded from the "godly or good society."

Making a program is a center strategy; attacking center programs on behalf of nature, God, or the world is border strategy.[19]

To maintain unity, the sectarian requires "an image of threatening evil on a cosmic scale": the future is always doomsday. The Border somehow reconciles a faith in human perfectibility with the calm certainty that annihilation is just around the corner.

Sects resolve internal disputes by splintering. Their numbers must remain small. This may be the one strategic difference between the face-to-face sect, as described by Douglas and Wildavsky, and the digital network: the latter can inflate into millions literally at the speed of light.

Viewed from within this scheme, the stories of the last chapter appear in a new light. Hoder, Wael Ghonim, and Shawn Fanning emerged as sectarian heroes of the digital Border, striking at the forces of monopoly and centralization. Ahmadinejad, Mubarak, and Jack Valenti each represented a mighty hierarchy of the traditional Center, slow-turning yet implacable, perfectly willing to smash the individual to preserve the system. Two of the young sectarians, Hoder and Fanning, received disproportionate punishment. The third, Ghonim, spent 11 nights in the dungeons of the Center. But at the end of the day two great hierarchies—the Mubarak regime and the recording industry—had been toppled.

The confrontation has followed a predictable pattern. Whenever a Center organization thought it owned a document or file or domain of information, the networks of the Border swarmed in and took over, leaving the landscape littered with casualties from such guerrilla raids. Thus the music business collapsed, newspapers shed subscribers and advertisers, political parties shrank in numbers. The U.S. government lost control of its own classified documents. Book publishers and the TV and movie industries, still very profitable today, depend on technical and copyright regimes, which could be breached at any moment.

Since power wasn't a file that could be copied or shared, the political battleground has tilted more in favor of hierarchy. Iran, we saw, imprisoned Hoder and brutally repressed the 2009 protests. The Chinese trained their famous "internet police." Cuba and Vietnam abused and imprisoned dissident bloggers. Even the U.S. government during this period has been allowed to operate on the assumption that the public are the enemy—for example, in airports and federal buildings.

The Center held the advantage in the political domain, but not absolutely—not as scissors forever cutting paper. Networks exploited their speed, near-invisibility, and command of the information sphere to inflict pain and confusion on the Center. On 9/11, a minuscule network of violent men slaughtered thousands of Americans, while the government stood by, blind and helpless. In 2008, Barack Obama, propelled by online networks that generated funds, volunteers, and an effective anti-Center message, crushed the Democratic and Republican establishments. And we have seen how Wael Ghonim's Facebook invitation to revolution led—through a complex and nonlinear labyrinth—to the overthrow of Mubarak.

Yet in the next stage sectarian advances have been reversed. My suspicion is that they *must* be reversed, if sects—the public in revolt—truly have no interest in governing and possess no capacity for exercising power. Consider Al Qaeda: it failed to achieve the objective for 9/11, which was to terrorize the U.S. into leaving the Middle East. President Obama's fortunes have been more equivocal, and I want to postpone for a bit consideration of his unique place in the struggle between Center and Border. Suffice to say, for now, that the president lost his governing coalition after the 2010 elections. In Egypt, the secular protesters who overthrew Mubarak were almost immediately swept aside by the hierarchical forces of the Muslim Brotherhood and the Egyptian military.

And this is the deeper pattern of the conflict. The programs of the Center have failed, and have been *seen* to fail, beyond the possibility of invoking secrecy or propaganda. Let the disastrous performance of the rating and oversight agencies before the 2008 financial crisis, and of the intelligence community in Iraq, stand for many more examples of Center failure. At the same time, the fracturing of the public along niche interests has unleashed swarms of networks against every sacred precinct of authority. Failure has been criticized, mocked, magnified.

The result is paralysis by distrust. The Border, it is already clear, can neutralize but not replace the Center. Networks can protest and overthrow, but never govern. Bureaucratic inertia confronts digital nihilism. The sum is zero.

The world I want to depict isn't stalemated. The contending forces are too unlike, too asymmetrical to achieve any kind of balance. My thesis describes a world trapped in a sociopolitical combat zone, in which every principle of living, every institution, I want to say every *event*—the choice of what is meaningful in time—has been fought over and scorched in the crossfire. It would be natural to expect one side to prevail in the end, but I have my doubts. I can't picture what Wordsworth's blissful dawn of 1789 would look like under present conditions, or a forced march to the status quo ante as in 1848. The Center can't bring back the industrial age. The networks can't engender an alternative.

The closest historical parallel to our time may have been the wars of religion of the 17th century. I say this not *necessarily* because of the chaos and bloodshed of the period, but because every principle was contested. If an educated person of that era were transported to the present, his first question would be, "Who won—Catholics or Protestants?" For us the question has no meaning. Both sides endured. Neither won. Something different evolved. Much the same, I suspect, will occur with the dispute of hierarchy and network.

* * *

In this conflict, my concern as an analyst is to pay attention to the right subject at the right level of description. I was trained, as even the youngest of us were, to think in terms of the old categories: to think, for example, that the direction of American politics depended on the balance between Democrats and Republicans. Yet both parties are, in form and spirit, organizations of the Center. Both are heavily invested in the established order, offering the public minor differences in perspective on the same small set of questions. Surprises in America's political trajectory are unlikely to come from the alternation of Democrat and Republican.

The analyst searching for *discontinuities*—for the possibility of radical change—must wrench his mind free of the old categories and turn to the subterranean strife of hierarchy and network: in the political parties, between "netroots" activists and a variety of Tea Party networks on one side, and the Democratic and Republican organizations on the other. There, different languages are spoken, and potent contradictions can be found.

My great concern as a citizen is for the future of liberal democracy.

Democracy as an *ideal* can be abstracted from every attempt to implement it—in fact, democracy has often been used to condemn democratic systems that fall short of perfection. Representative democracy as it has evolved *historically* in the U.S. and elsewhere, however, is a procedural business, necessarily integrated with the ruling structures of the time. In the 18th and early 19th centuries, the procedures of representative democracy reflected a distrust of centralized power and the faith that wealth and land ownership conferred personal independence. In the industrial age, procedures became tightly centralized, top-down, rule-bound, and oriented toward the masses rather than the individual.

That democracy became hierarchical, organizational, an institution of the Center, is less a paradox or a conspiracy theory than a historical accident. The consequences are beyond dispute. Many aspects of representative democracy have become less democratic, and are so perceived by the public. The defection of citizens from the voting booth and party membership gives evidence to a souring mood with the established structures. Many have been moved to a sectarian condemnation of the entire system as ungodly and unjust. The more assertive political networks today proclaim our current procedures to be the tyranny of Big Government or a farce manipulated by Big Business.

In the collision of the old world with the new, democracy has not been absolved from harm. It too is a battleground, like the daily newspaper. It may survive, but that is not a given, and it almost certainly will be changed. *How* it changes may depend on the aggregated decisions of individual citizens—in other words, on us—no less than on procedural reforms. This is part of my thesis—and the one place where I will deviate from a pure description of the world, to contemplate what *ought* to be done.

CYBER-UTOPIANS, CYBER-SKEPTICS, CYBER-PESSIMISTS, AND HOW ALL THEIR SOUND AND FURY SIGNIFIES VERY LITTLE

Before the start of recorded history, we find hierarchies managed by elites in authority. For all that time there was a bottom of the social pyramid, more or less inert. How this inchoate lump became the public is a story for a later chapter. Two preconditions had to be met, however. For a public to exist it had to achieve *self-consciousness*—some irritation or dissatisfaction was needed to pry it apart from the elites. For the public to voice its thoughts and opinions, and thus transform itself, potentially, into a political actor, required a *means of communication*. This became a possibility only after the spread of the printing press.

My thesis holds that a revolution in the nature and content of communication—the Fifth Wave of information—has ended the top-down control elites exerted on the public during the industrial age. For this to be the case, I need to show how the perturbing agent, information, can influence power arrangements. Information must be seen to have real-life *effects*, and those effects must be meaningful enough to account for a crisis of authority.

A century of research on media and information effects has delivered confusing if not contradictory findings. The problem for the analyst is again one of complexity and nonlinearity. Intuitively, it should be a simple matter to establish the effects of information. I see a truck bearing down on me, for example: that's information. I move out of the way: that's behavior caused by information. Or I watch television news of the U.S. invasion of Iraq: that's information. I form an opinion for or against, and agitate politically accordingly: that's behavior caused by media information.

Politics in modern countries, however, takes place beyond the immediate perception of the public. Political information is thus mediated rather than direct—almost always resembling the Iraq war example rather than the truck I can see with my own eyes. This sets up a large number of variables in the interaction between an individual, the mediator, and the information.

Do I, in my condition as a member of the public, accept *all* the mediators' information, and act accordingly? This has been proposed, originally by thinkers like Walter Lippmann, who were intellectually imprinted by their experience in World War I. Through the use of persuasive stereotypes and other techniques, Lippmann argued, those who controlled information—the people in authority, the elites—also controlled "the pictures in our heads." Propaganda, on this account, injected new opinions and actions directly into the gullible brains of the public.[20]

Or do I accept *none* of the mediators' information, because my moral and political beliefs were formed by "strong" social bonds, like church and family, rather than "weak" links like reading a newspaper? That also has been proposed, most recently by Malcolm Gladwell to disparage the possibility of social media "revolutions." Alternatively, I may be invulnerable to mediated information because I'm encased in an armor of prejudice, and dwell comfortably in an information bubble, or daily me.

Or do I engage in a "two-step" process, in which I first absorb the opinions of a strong personal connection, like a trusted friend or minister, and only then accept certain mediated information? That was proposed way back in the 1940s, and has been found applicable to the manner in which Twitter users "follow" information.[21]

Or is it the case that mediators have no power to control how I think or act, but can command my attention to those public issues and events I think *about*? That is the premise of agenda-setting research, which has been applied with some success in the marketplace. Roland Schatz, for example, has correlated the public's disaster donations with the amount of media attention received by an event.[22]

All the findings and theories on information effects are suggestive. None, in my view, are even remotely conclusive. In the story of *Homo informaticus*, which completes this chapter, I will aim for some of the immediate clarity in effects of that truck bearing down on me. Here I propose to skip a level, and pause for a peek at the desultory quarrel about the effects of new media: whether its impact on us has been good, bad, or indifferent.

* * *

The global proliferation of the internet in the 1990s and of social media in the early 2000s inspired equal measures of applause and alarm, with a residue of doubt. Some writers saw in digital media a boost to human collaboration and democracy. Critics dubbed this tribe cyber-utopians. Others found in the internet all manner of ills—the corruption of our culture, for example, or an invitation for governments to spy on their citizens. These were the cyber-pessimists. A third, much smaller group wondered whether anything important had really changed: call them *cyber-skeptics*.

There is less to this dispute than meets the eye.

Let the last come first. Malcolm Gladwell, fittingly in the pages of the *New Yorker*, compared the strong personal ties of the civil rights activists in the 1960s with the weak ties between participants in online causes like the Save Darfur Coalition. Only strong ties, argued Gladwell, made possible the informal coordination of sit-in protesters in the Jim Crow South. Only the mutual support induced by strong ties could embolden a group to face "high risk" situations and achieve political change. As for "Facebook warriors," Gladwell allowed that they might accomplish minor feats of collaboration—finding a donor for a bone marrow transplant, for example. But real politics happened among comrades and in the flesh.[23]

Clay Shirky has noted that a committed activist with strong personal ties to others *also* can expand his reach by becoming a Facebook warrior. There's no contradiction involved. But I want to push beyond this argument. Gladwell's contentions have simply been proven wrong by events. The initial protests in Egypt were the work of ordinary people, most of them connected digitally, if at all. Wael Ghonim, the Google marketing man, administered his Facebook page from Dubai, under a pseudonym. The strong tie that held together the protesters he summoned to action was loathing of the Mubarak regime.

Gladwell is a thinker of the Center, a mind of the industrial age. This doesn't prove or disprove his ideas—but it places them in a certain context. He explicitly identified strong ties with hierarchy, weak ties with network, and he could not imagine how one might be toppled by the other: "If you're taking on a powerful and organized establishment you have to be a hierarchy." Political change, for Gladwell, was a job for trained professionals, requiring the imposition of a new system, with a new program and ideology, to replace the old. But we have seen how this formula has been contradicted by the sectarian logic of the Fifth Wave. To stand for change now means to be anti-system, anti-program, anti-ideology.

Gladwell at least grounded his skepticism on a traditional conception of power: hard trumped soft, scissors *always* cut paper. I find it harder to make sense of the warnings of the cyber-pessimists. They shout from the rooftops that dictatorships have used digital tools to spy on dissidents and manipulate public opinion. This, of course, is true. We saw an example in

Iran, where the regime threw disagreeable bloggers in prison while flooding the blogosphere with its own stooges. The Chinese are supposed to be even cleverer at cyber-spying and manipulation.

As analysis, the exhortations of the pessimists hover somewhere between pointless and trivially true. Of course dictatorships wish to spy on dissidents, just as dissidents seek to avoid detection—a game made vastly more difficult for those in power by the proliferation of digital hiding places. Of course dictatorships wish to manipulate media of all kinds to influence opinion. In the industrial age, however, they did so boldly and officially, from authority, while under the new dispensation that despots must try to *impersonate* the public to have any hope of influencing it. Instead of injecting slogans into the brains of the masses by means of banner headlines on *People's Daily* or a televised speech of the *lider maximo*, they are now forced to ride the tiger of real opinion, and face the consequences should it turn against them.

Pessimism tends to be the province of the disillusioned idealist and the false sophisticate. That seems to be very much the case when it comes to the loudest voices of cyber-pessimism. I have noted their cautions. Let's move on.

The favorite goat of cyber-skeptics and cyber-pessimists has been Clay Shirky, whose 2008 book, *Here Comes Everybody*, was described by Gladwell as "the bible of the social media movement"—that is, of the cyber-utopian crowd. Shirky walks on the sunny side of the street, but he's no utopian. He prefers optimistic anecdotes, which infuriates the curmudgeons, but in the offending book he gave social media credit for *sharing*—photos on Flickr, for instance—and *collaboration* on the Wikipedia model, while admitting that examples of collective action inspired by digital tools were "still relatively rare." That was true in 2008.[24]

His message was that the new digital platforms made it easy for groups to "self-assemble," and that the rise of such spontaneous groups was bound to lead, sooner or later, to social and political change. Very much unlike Gladwell, Shirky foresaw the possibility of the events of 2011, and the part a networked public, connected to the information sphere, could play in revolution. In an article published just before the outbreak of revolt in Tunisia, he addressed the arguments of the skeptics and the pessimists:

Indeed, the best practical reason to think that social media can help
bring political change is that both dissidents and governments think
they can. All over the world, activists believe in the utility of these
tools and take steps to use them accordingly. And the governments
they contend with think social media tools are powerful, too, and
are willing to harass, arrest, exile, or kill users in response.[25]

Today we know both partners in this political minuet were correct. Digital media can be exploited by self-assembled networks to muster their forces and propagandize for their causes, against the resistance of those who command the levers of power.

But this understates the distance between the old and the new. A churning, highly redundant information sphere has taken shape near at hand to ordinary persons yet beyond the reach of modern government. In the tectonic depths of social and political life, the balance of power has fundamentally shifted between authority and obedience, ruler and ruled, elite and public, so that each can inflict damage on the other but neither can attain a decisive advantage. That is the non-utopian thesis of this book. And it was arrived at, in part, by pursuing threads of analysis about the nature and consequences of new media that were first spun by Clay Shirky.

HOMO INFORMATICUS, OR HOW CHOICE CAN BRING DOWN GOVERNMENTS

There remains the question, central to my thesis, of how information can influence political power. The answer isn't intuitive. Information is soft and abstract. Power is as hard and real as a policeman's bullet. Yet, as Shirky observed with regard to new media, the wielders of power have always assumed a close and vigilant relationship to information. Governments have worked hard to control the stories told about the status quo— that is, about them.

This anxiety to control information in those who already controlled the guns should alert us that political power may be less "hard," and more intangible, than supposed.

Power, from our perspective, is a particular alignment between the will of the elites and the actions and opinions of the public: a matter of trust, faith, and fear, apportioned variously but involving both sides.

Brute force plays a part, but as the fall of the brutal Muammar Qaddafi demonstrated, no government can survive for long solely on the basis of killing its opponents. A significant fraction of the public must find the status quo acceptable, and the larger the number of true believers, the more solid the foundation underneath a regime. Thus the potential influence of information over political power flows more from its fit into *stories of legitimacy* than from, say, investigative reporting or the dispensing of practical knowledge.

My analysis of this question centers on the rise of a restless, disruptive organism, which I have taken the bold step to name *Homo informaticus*, Information Man. You and I, and possibly a majority of the human race today, are him: end products of an evolutionary process involving the spread of education, expanded levels of wealth and security, and improved means of communication. Our traits can be explained only in reference to an ancestral environment—in this case, a parched information landscape. That's the logic of evolution. So before I present *Homo informaticus*, we must first encounter his less fortunate predecessor, whom I will call, in plain English, Unmediated Man.

As his name implies, Unmediated Man lacked access to any media. He was likely to be illiterate, and had neither the means nor the interest to travel very far. His only channels of information were the people around him. While he may sound like an implausible fiction, Unmediated Man described the typical Egyptian of 1980, and represented most people's relationship with information from the dawn of our species until very recently.

In the nature of things, Unmediated Man lived and died within a political system: let's make it an authoritarian regime with great, but not absolute, power to control information. The problem confronting this regime was one of communication rather than control. To impose its will on Unmediated Man, it had to find a way to convey the particulars to him, in the context of a persuasive justifying story.

In reality, of course, *all* information is mediated. The question is whether mediation is conducted directly, face to face, or indirectly by print and electronic sources. Unmediated Man depended on his community for information: extended family, friends, neighbors, local religious and political authorities, bosses, underlings, co-workers, his butcher, his barber, "the street." The single most important aspect of this information

POLITICAL REGIME: "OUR JUSTIFYING STORY"

UNMEDIATED MAN:
"MY STORY OF THE WORLD"

Figure 7: The problem: A regime confronts an Unmediated Man.[26]

environment was that so very little was new. The range of interests was narrow, the set of sources small. Unmediated Man woke up every morning expecting a world quite unchanged from the day before.

So for the regime to communicate and interact with Unmediated Man in terms advantageous to its story of legitimacy, it needed only to control the community—which, of course, it did in many ways. The regime appointed the local authorities, including the political headmen, police, military, tax and land assessors, business-license granters, health inspectors, census takers, teachers, etc. Everyone coming in contact with Unmediated Man knew his version of the regime's story of legitimacy—and those who failed to do so egregiously enough were removed and silenced.

All things being equal, Unmediated Man lacked the means to conceive of an alternative story to the one that justified his present way of life. He may have protested, even violently, against local conditions, but he could never seek to overthrow the political system.

Feedback from below was extremely limited under such constraints. Probably nothing of Unmediated Man's private fears and frustrations reached the ear of the government. This meant the government could (and in fact must) behave as if the public didn't exist. For political purposes, the public became whatever the government told it to be.

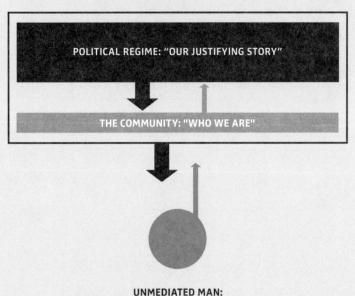

Figure 8: Control the community and you control the Unmediated Man's information horizon.

It is at this point that our newly evolved hero makes his entrance on the stage. *Homo informaticus* is a differently endowed member of the public: he's literate, and has access to newspapers, radio, movies, TV. He has been exposed to a larger world beyond the immediate community.

His arrival confronts the regime with a new threat: the public with a longer reach may gain access to information that subverts its story of legitimacy. In the regime's worst nightmare, the public actually conceives of an alternative form of government and acts to attain it.

To cover the threat, the regime must deploy a costly and elaborate state media apparatus. It acts vigorously to own, or at a minimum to control, the means of mass communication: newspapers, radio, TV, books, cinema, etc. The content of state media plays, in harmony, theme and variations of the regime's justifying story.

The ideal for the regime would be to reconstruct, in the controlled media, voices similar to those of the local community through which it dealt with Unmediated Man. In many ways, the structure of mass media fits smoothly into regime schemes of control: it is top-down, one-to-many, monopolistic, and it demands an undifferentiated, passive mass audience.

However, sheer volume makes the reconstruction of the small world impossible. Even in the most controlled media, the amount of information

HOMO INFORMATICUS:
"MY STORY OF THE WORLD"

Figure 9: New problem: regime confronts *Homo informaticus.*

is far greater than what was available in Unmediated Man's village. Too much of the content is new and unsettling, too much covers distant and alien conditions. As messages and images proliferate, it becomes progressively harder to determine exactly what their relationship is to the regime's justifying story. As more intermediaries are used, it becomes progressively more likely that dissonance will be introduced into the information stream.

The simplicity and perfect fit between the public's perception of the world and the regime's story of legitimacy are gone forever. Under these conditions, the best outcome for the regime is acceptance by the public that the world is too complex to be understood yet too dangerous to be left alone, and must be placed in the care of those whose job it is to manage the nation's affairs. Examples of mediated acceptance of the status quo are the Soviet Union under Stalin and North Korea today.

By its structure and composition, state mass media allows an even narrower feedback path than did the local community of Unmediated Man. The presence of mediators increases the distance between those at the top of the power pyramid and everyone else.

The decisive transformation of *H. informaticus*'s mental universe arrives with the introduction of independent channels of information.

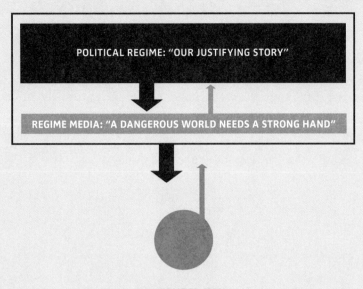

Figure 10: State media is an expensive way to achieve limited control.

A single such channel—a privately owned newspaper, say, or a satellite TV station like Al Jazeera—can work a prodigious change in the public's perception of the world.

To understand why, we must return to the thorny subject of information effects. Recall that information must be either directly perceived or mediated by others. Recall, too, that complexity makes the positive effects of mediated information impossible to determine. I can't say that the "We Are All Khaled Said" Facebook page caused the revolution in Egypt. I wouldn't know how to go about proving such a proposition.

But with *negative* effects we stand on solid analytic ground. If all the information available to the public reveals the political system to be fixed, like nature itself, for all time, then revolution becomes an absurdity. If everything I know persuades me that no alternative exists to the status quo, then I may despair even unto violence, but I cannot seek what I do not know—political change. The public in these cases is like a blind person standing in the street with a truck bearing down. Negative effects funnel human beliefs, and in this way shape human behavior. They are intuitive and powerful.

That single independent channel of information thus holds the potential for radical change. It broadens *Homo informaticus's* field of vision to encompass alternative values and systems. Most importantly, it shatters the illusion that his way of life is inevitable and preordained, a first, necessary step toward revolution. Whether revolution will ultimately happen will of course depend on a multitude of factors, many of which have little to do with information. The transition from negative to positive effects must end in nonlinearity, but we can say with confidence that it won't be triggered unless the public is shown a differently ordered world: a choice.

Information can influence actions by revealing something hitherto not known or believed possible. Scholars have called this *demonstration effects*. A trivial example would be a TV commercial for a new, improved dishwasher detergent. A political example was the jolt of hope experienced by the Egyptian opposition after the fall of Ben Ali in Tunisia. Arab dictators had always died in power and in bed. Their rule had seemed immutable, until the first one collapsed. We can feel the excitement of new possibilities in Wael Ghonim's words, written on his website shortly after Ben Ali's flight:

> *After all that's happened in Tunisia, my position has changed. Hopes for real political change in Egypt are much higher now. And all we need is a large number of people who are ready to fight for it. Our voices must be not only loud but deafening.*[27]

In reality, nothing had changed for Egypt. The transformation had taken place in Ghonim's mind.

Sheer volume of information is subversive of any narrative: alternatives are demonstrated. State-controlled media had generated too much information, too much that was new, but when effective it had convinced *Homo informaticus* that no safe alternatives existed to the present state of affairs.

By necessity, an independent channel will deliver demonstration effects contradicting the regime's justifying story with equally plausible explanations.

When judging his government, *H. informaticus* can then do so in light of alternative possibilities—different views of the same policy or event, different values invoked for an action or inaction, different performance by other governments, real or imagined. The first step toward skepticism

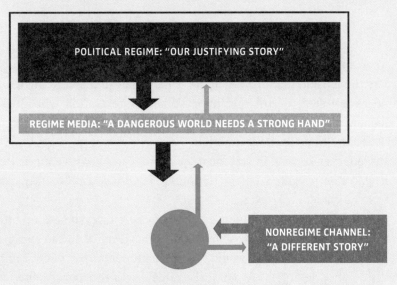

Figure 11: Independent channel: The psychological revolution.

is *doubt*, and *H. informaticus*, exposed to an independent channel, must confront choices and doubts when constructing his story of the world.

As this evolutionary fable approaches the present moment, content proliferates. A vast global information sphere, churning with controversies, points of view, and rival claims on every subject becomes accessible to our hero. Its volume and variety exceed that of the controlled media by many levels of magnitude.

If *H. informaticus* were to try to absorb this mass, his head would explode. This is not what transpires. He will pick and choose. So will other members of the public. By that very selectivity, that freedom to choose its channels of information, the public breaks the power of the mediator class created by mass media, and, under authoritarian rule, controlled by the regime.

The fall of the mediators, all things being equal, means the end of the regime's ability to rule by persuasion.

Governments of every stripe have had trouble grasping the sudden reversal in the information balance of power. Proud in hierarchy and accreditation but deprived of feedback channels, the regime is literally blind to much global content. It behaves as if nothing has changed except for attempts by alien ideals—pornography, irreligion, Americanization—to

GLOBAL INFORMATION SPHERE: "MANY DIFFERENT STORIES"

HOMO INFORMATICUS:
"MY STORY OF THE WORLD CAN BE CRITICAL OF THE REGIME"

Figure 12: Overwhelmed: The incredible shrinking state media.

seduce the public. Most significantly, the regime in its blindness fails to adjust its story of legitimacy to make it plausible in a crowded, fiercely competitive environment.

An accurate representation based on volume would show state media to be microscopic, invisible, when compared to the global information sphere. This is how *H. informaticus* experiences the changed environment: as an Amazonian flood of irreverent, controversy-ridden, anti-authority content, including direct criticism of the regime.

The consequences are predictable and irreversible. The regime accumulates pain points: police brutality, economic mismanagement, foreign policy failures, botched responses to disasters. These problems can no longer be concealed or explained away. Instead, they are seized on by the newly empowered public, and placed front-and-center in open discussions. In essence, government failure now sets the agenda.

As the regime's story of legitimacy becomes less and less persuasive, *Homo informaticus* adjusts his story of the world in opposition to that of the regime. He joins the ranks of similarly disaffected members of the public, who are hostile to the status quo, eager to pick fights with authority, and seek the means to broadcast their opinions and turn the tables on their rulers.

Figure 13: Fall of the mediators: when the public talks back.

The means of communication are of course provided by the information sphere. The unit of broadcasting can be a single individual—a Hoder, a Wael Ghonim, any member of the public, including *Homo informaticus*. The level of reach is billions, distributed across the face of the world.

At this stage, the public, clustered around networked communities of interest, has effectively taken control of the means of communication. Vital communities revolve around favorite themes and channels, which in the aggregate reveal the true tastes of the public, as opposed to what mass media, corporations, or governments wish the public to be interested in.

Under authoritarian governments, vital communities will tend to coalesce in political opposition as they bump into regime surveillance and control.

The regime still controls the apparatus of repression. It can deny service, physically attack, imprison, or even kill *H. informaticus*—but it can't silence his message, because this message is constantly amplified and propagated by the opposition community. Since the opposition commands the means of communication and is embedded in the global information sphere, its voice carries beyond the reach of any national government.

This was the situation in Egypt before the uprising of January 25, 2011. This is the situation in China today. The wealth and brute strength of the modern state are counterbalanced by the vast communicative powers of the public. Filters are placed on web access, police agents monitor suspect websites, foreign newscasters are blocked, domestic bloggers are harassed and thrown in jail—but every incident that tears away at the legitimacy of the regime is seized on by a rebellious public, and is then broadcast and magnified until criticism goes viral.

The tug of war pits hierarchy against network, power against persuasion, government against the governed: under such conditions of alienation, every inch of political space is contested, and turbulence becomes a permanent feature of political life.

Objective conditions and the nature of the political system must be accounted for, when it comes to the evolutionary process I have just described. The viciousness of the regime matters. It was safer to protest against Ben Ali in Tunisia and Mubarak in Egypt than against Qaddafi in Libya or Assad in Syria—or, for that matter, the Kim dynasty in North Korea.

But the rise of *Homo informaticus* places governments on a razor's edge, where any mistake, any untoward event, can draw a networked public into the streets, calling for blood. This is the situation today for authoritarian governments and liberal democracies alike. The crisis in the world that I seek to depict concerns loss of trust in government, writ large. The mass extinction of stories of legitimacy leaves no margin for error, no residual store of public good will. Any spark can blow up any political system at any time, anywhere.

I began by posing a question about how something as abstract as information can influence something as real as political power. Let me end the chapter by proposing an answer, in the form of three claims or hypotheses.

1. *Information influences politics because it is indigestible by a government's justifying story.*

2. *The greater the diffusion of information to the public, the more illegitimate any political status quo will appear.*

3. *Homo informaticus, networked builder and wielder of the information sphere, poses an existential challenge to the legitimacy of every government he encounters.*

I will explore the implications in the remainder of the book.

WHAT THE PUBLIC IS NOT

I borrowed Walter Lippmann's definition of the public because I found it honest and unpretentious: "The public, as I see it, is not a fixed body of individuals. It is merely the persons who are interested in an affair and can affect it only by supporting or opposing the actors." The philosophical assumptions underlying these words were typical for Lippmann, who possessed an almost mystical faith in experts and elites—the "actors" he mentioned. But taken baldly and innocently, the definition happened to fit the facts of the subterranean conflict that is the theme of this book.

There is no single body of the public. There are many publics, each of them embedded in a particular culture and circumstance. Nor is the public organized to endure as a permanent fixture of social life. If the interest in an affair that has brought a public into being somehow dissipates, the public itself, like the Marxist hope for the state, will wither away.

The difficulty for the analyst is that he must characterize this heterogeneous beast. The public is a protagonist in my story. In its multiple manifestations, it has exhibited *common habits of behavior* made possible by the conditions prevalent today: the Fifth Wave of information. To cite just one example, I noted the remarkable affinity with Border-sectarian loathing of authority described, in a different context, by Douglas and Wildavsky. Only those blinded by archaic categories will fail to see that that public, once synonymous with "the audience," is no longer silent, no longer passive—that it has leaped onstage and become a leading actor in the world-historical drama.

Yet any feature I might depict in my portrait of the public can be falsified by some example, and any attempt I might make to simplify or personalize the subject will result in caricature and error.

The most promising way forward, it seems to me, is to follow N.N. Taleb's "subtractive knowledge" method of analyzing complex questions. Rather than assert what the public is, I explain what the public is *not*. This resembles the sculptor's approach of chipping away at the stone until a likeness emerges, or the bond trader's formula of identifying safe investments by subtracting risk.[28] Since the public is an unstable and undetermined entity—a complex system—this negative mode of characterizing its behavior is least likely to fall into the fallacy of personification, of inventing some new Marxian-style "class" with a single consciousness and will.

Taleb's method is also helpful because the term in question, "the public," has been made to stand for so many things that it has become obscured under layers of confusion and special pleading. So one last metaphor: my task resembles that of the archaeologist, who brushes away foreign matter until the object is restored to its original identity.

THE PUBLIC IS NOT THE PEOPLE, BUT LIKES TO PRETEND THAT IT IS

On June 29, 2013, a year and four months after the fall of Hosni Mubarak and exactly a year after free elections had installed Mohamed Morsi as the new president of Egypt, the Egyptian public took to the streets in enormous numbers demanding the overthrow of the government. Morsi, a member of the Muslim Brotherhood, had alienated many with his narrowly partisan approach to government. The protesters were led by secular groups, which had found themselves marginalized soon after the collapse of the Mubarak regime.

But what matters here is what each side was made to represent in a desperate moment, when grand ideals collided with political necessity and interested parties needed to justify their actions.

On July 3, the Egyptian military ousted Morsi, installed an interim government, and began a purge of the Muslim Brotherhood. The military had always feared and detested the Brotherhood, but that was not the reason given for their intervention. They claimed to be abiding by the will of the people. "The Armed Forces . . . have been called by the Egyptian people to help," affirmed the defense minister, Abdul Fatah Khalil al-Sisi, in the initial statement following the rebellion. Although Morsi had been the elected president, al-Sisi maintained that he had failed to "meet the demands of the people."[29]

A similar argument was put forward by Mohamed ElBaradei, the new prime minister in the interim government:

In a democracy, when you get 20 million people in the street, you resign. Unfortunately, we don't have a process of recall or impeachment like you have. It was a popular uprising rejecting Mr. Morsi's continuing in power . . . . People went to the street on the 30th of June and were not psychologically ready to go home until Morsi left office.[30]

For the military to push Morsi from power, ElBaradei insisted, "was no different than what happened under Mubarak."

These accounts appealed directly to the central doctrine of liberal democracy: the people were sovereign. Only they possessed the authorizing magic of legitimacy. Political power at every level must be derived from the people as a whole, above the claims of any institution, faction, or person. Thus the people were entitled to organize or reorganize the government as they saw fit.

In a rhetorical device at least as old as the French Revolution, al-Sisi and ElBaradei identified the protesting public with the Egyptian people. The public was sovereign. It was the legitimate ruler of Egypt, and Morsi, by failing to meet the public's demands, had lapsed into tyranny.

A problem with this argument was the fractured condition of the Egyptian public. Many were "interested in the affair" of getting rid of Morsi, but many others sided with the president and his Islamist allies. Which was the true public? By Lippmann's definition, both were. Which could be identified with the Egyptian people? I will answer momentarily, but first let's remind ourselves that Morsi, unlike Mubarak, had been voted into office by 51 percent of the electorate, a clear majority. Over 13 million Egyptians had cast a ballot for Morsi: hadn't *they* spoken for the people? Opposition voices were concerned enough on this score to engage in fantastic claims—20 million protesters on the streets, 22 million signatures petitioning Morsi to step down, much larger figures, always, than the president's vote.

But democratic legitimacy doesn't reside in numbers, and the political authority of the public can be determined independently from the question of whether the July events in Egypt were a revolution or a coup.

The public is not, and never can be, identical to the people: this is true in all circumstances, everywhere. Since, on any given question, the public is composed of those self-selected persons interested in the affair, it possesses no legitimate authority whatever, and lacks the structure to enforce any authority that might fall its way. The public has no executive, no law, no jails. It can only express an opinion, in words and in actions—in its own flesh and blood. That was what transpired in Egypt. The roar of public opinion precipitated political change, but it was the Egyptian military, not the public, that compelled Mubarak and Morsi to step down.

The public can never be the people because the people are an abstraction of political philosophy. The people, strictly speaking, don't exist. Thinkers like Locke and Jefferson, who affirmed the sovereignty of the people, were preoccupied with protecting the freedom of action of the individual citizen against the crushing embrace of the state. The famous "We, the people" of the preamble to the Constitution was a rejection by the framers of the ultimate authority of state governments. The people themselves were eternally absent.

The public, in Egypt and elsewhere, was thus *not* sovereign. Its authority has always been based on persuasion rather than law. Representative democracies have instituted procedures such as elections and jury trials, in which the public, conventionally speaking, may be said to embody the people. But it is precisely the overflow of the public's activity beyond the channels of democratic procedures—sometimes, as in Egypt, in revolt against them—that represents the great imponderable of our time.

In an older generation, the lack of fit between public and people engendered deep pessimism about the future of democracy. Lippmann came to his definition in despair. The work in which it is found was titled *The Phantom Public*—phantom because it was "an abstraction" and "not a fixed body of individuals." In brief, it was not the people. In 1927, two years after *The Phantom Public* appeared, John Dewey published *The Public and Its Problems*—problems because, in the "machine age," the public had become "lost," "bewildered," and "cannot find itself." Like a troubled wraith, the public haunted the mansions of democracy.[31]

Lippmann's pessimism rested on two shrewd observations and a questionable assumption. He observed, presciently, that even in the industrial age public opinion influenced matters of policy and government. Always the elitist, he believed that the public "will not possess an insider's knowledge of events," and "can watch only for coarse signs indicating where their sympathies ought to turn." Because the public was clueless, the political weight of its opinion was likely to be misguided or manipulated by cunning insiders. This led Lippmann to a conclusion that remains largely accurate today:

> *We cannot, then, think of public opinion as a conserving or creating force directing society to clearly conceived ends, making deliberately toward socialism or away from it, toward nationalism or empire, a league of nations or any other doctrinal goal.*[32]

Programmatic goals, we have seen, are the business of the Center, and will be rejected by a public which has clung to Border ideals from Lippmann's day to our own.

What broke Lippmann's heart was the assumption that the people of political philosophy must exist in political reality. He knew that the public was the only candidate available for the job, and, as an astute observer of events, he felt keenly the disproportion between his hopes and the truth. The ideal of the "sovereign and omnicompetent citizen" was unattainable. The public was born of expediency among private citizens who shared an interest—civic or selfish—in an affair, and would be aligned differently, or simply vanish, phantomlike, on other issues. In principle no less than in fact, this mutable entity could not be identified with the people.

Yet the claim has proved irresistible to those who wish to challenge an established government or political system. This has been true not just for manipulative institutions like the Egyptian military, but for the public itself. The "Occupy" groups in the U.S., with tiny numbers on the street compared to Egypt's protesters, still claimed to represent the "99 percent" against the predations of the elite.

To assume the robe and crown of the sovereign is an intoxicating experience, I imagine, but the effect has been to devalue the democratic process, and the end result, given the mutable nature of the public, can only be chaos. As I write these words, large crowds of Morsi and Muslim Brotherhood supporters are rallying in the streets of Egypt. They believe that *they* embody the will of the Egyptian people. The military, exasperated, has called for giant counter-demonstrations to combat "terrorism." The last act of this drama is nowhere in sight: when everyone is king, power *must* be divorced from legitimacy.

THE PUBLIC IS NOT THE MASSES, BUT WAS ONCE BURIED ALIVE UNDER THEM

The Spanish philosopher José Ortega y Gasset, whose title I cribbed for this book, once noted that in pre-industrial society ordinary people lived "dispersed." The rules that defined them were local and particular to class, religion, sex, age, and profession.[33] In Spain, as late as the 1930s, country women wore shawls and only city women were allowed hats. Punishment of transgressors was swift and harsh, but the reality was that few thought to transgress. It never occurred to the Gascon peasant that he shared many attributes in common with a professor of law in the Sorbonne. It never occurred to the professor, either. Each looked on the other as on a different species of humanity.

These narrow enclaves for the mind were swept away in the 19th and 20th centuries. Education raised the intellectual, and technology the material reach of the ordinary person. The triumphant ideology of the time, liberal democracy, preached the universal equality of man and citizen. No differences in worth or conduct existed, it turned out, between Christian and Jew, man and woman, peasant and professor. The crooked timber of humanity was planed into a generalized, universal form.

Whether this transfiguration took place because it suited the economic pressures of the age, I am not qualified to say. But industry needed mass labor for production and a mass market for consumption. By "mass labor" I mean a generalized pool of workers equally trainable to the highest pitch of efficiency. Forging and deploying such a mass became the goal of "scientific management" and its great apostle, Frederick Winslow Taylor. With time and motion studies in hand, the scientific manager could program his workers' every move as if they were a single instrument—a human machine.

> *The work of every workman is fully planned out by the management at least one day in advance, and each man receives in most cases complete written instructions, describing in detail the task which he is to accomplish, as well as the means to be used in doing the work.*[34]

The system was top-down, intrusive, and impersonal, but it became orthodoxy in the industrialized world, and it caught the attention of influential persons. Henry Ford and Lenin were Taylorists, each in his way. Both believed in an infallible vanguard commanding a mass of undifferentiated humanity.

The industrial age was Taylorist to the core. The ordinary person, so hopelessly parochial through all of history, got flattened into the masses: better educated, more affluent and mobile, and organized into gigantic hierarchies for every domain of activity. The masses functioned as the anti-public. More precisely: the masses *impersonated* the public for the benefit of the hierarchy, while stripping it of all spontaneity and repudiating its authentic interests. In the marketplace, for example, the mass consumer was created by stripping away all particularities and recognizing only certain universal needs and tastes: those satisfied by mass production.

In politics, the Taylorist organizing principle reached an extreme with the mass movements whose prestige crested just before World War II—laborists, anarchists, syndicalists, fascists, socialists, National Socialists, communists. Here in the U.S., political machines—wonderful phrase—controlled much of the electorate. National parties were only slightly less skewed. The selection of presidential candidates by party elders invited as much democratic participation as a papal conclave. The Democratic and Republican masses could only say yes or no on election day, or abstain from voting. Often they were bullied or bribed into going along with leadership decisions.

Intoxicated by the successes of industrial organization, the founders of mass movements, and their admirers and imitators, sought to reduce political action to pure mechanics. This was true right and left, and regardless of the actual content of the movement's ideology. The latter was usually a hash of pseudoscience, in any case: racial Darwinism for the Nazis, for example, or "scientific materialism" for Marxist-Leninists. What mattered was control of the masses. Movement members were disciplined with military rigor. The leadership, in turn, maneuvered the political machine toward a new conception of power, in which the whole of society was absorbed into the movement and the masses displaced the sovereign people.

There was no question of pursuing a personal interest in an affair under such a scheme: no space for a freestanding public. When we come across despairing words about a "phantom public" that "cannot find itself," we should recall that this was the political landscape confronting Lippmann and Dewey. The two men knew that in an earlier time the public had shown a muscular independence. The public of the 18th century had been composed of networks of persons with knowledge of science and the arts, connected virtually, by correspondence. They called themselves, informally, the Republic of Letters, and their labors proved almost indecently fruitful: they helped popularize the scientific revolution, articulated the principles of liberal democracy, and inspired political revolutions in America and France.

In Dewey's "age of the machine," that assertive public appeared as extinct as the fashion for powdered wigs. The masses had buried alive the public, so it seemed, and with it the prospects for a democratic future.

Here I want to break the historical narrative, and fast-forward to the present. Anyone paying attention will have noticed surprising similarities between the periwigged citizens of the Republic of Letters and our own networked public. Both are largely virtual, informal, spontaneous, and networked rather than hierarchical, open to quality rather than accreditation. And it's true: they resemble each other more than they do the intervening masses of the industrial age. Whether this resemblance is an optical illusion or reflects some underlying causal link is a worthy subject for study and reflection—but it isn't part of my story.

I'm more interested in considering the one significant difference between the two: the Republic of Letters, in the end, was an elite club, an intellectual Olympus far removed from the sight of Ortega's particularized humanity. In contrast, the networked public today is composed of ordinary persons. It spends more time on images of cute cats and pornography than on revolution or political philosophy. The new public, in fact, closely corresponds to the old masses, now escaped from Taylorist control and returning, in vital communities, to its particular interests and tastes.

So questions immediately arise: how did this strange escape occur? By what historical acrobatics did the machinelike masses, so totally in the grip of elites with scientific pretensions, emerge as the anti-authority public of today? Why were Lippmann and Dewey—brilliant men—so wrong about the future?

I don't know how such questions can be answered with any confidence. Like the present and the future, the past is a tangle of complex interactions, each pregnant with possibilities. Causes are everywhere, and can be cherry-picked at will. The fall of European communism in

1989–1991, for example, has been ascribed by different analysts to causes internal or external to the system, political or economic or even military in nature. Each explanation is true to some extent. The problem is that we can't run different versions of history, controlling for each factor. We have only the single instance on which to build our theories. Fascination with one cause at the expense of another often reveals more about the analyst than the event.

The best way to proceed is by sticking close to the facts. And fortunately the facts are not controversial. In the 85 years following the publication of Lippmann's *The Phantom Public*, mass movements were defeated in war and outcompeted economically and at the ballot box. They lost their hold on ordinary persons. By the time the Soviet Union went out of business in 1991, the mass movement, in the eyes of its potential followers, had become a dead relic from a forgotten time. Desiccated specimens, which clung to places like Cuba and North Korea, served as illustrations of its utter failure.

On a somewhat different time scale, the great hierarchies around which liberal democracy had been organized during the industrial age also began a process of disintegration. Political machines were torn apart by reformers. The parties lost much of their authority, including the ability to dictate presidential candidates. Not surprisingly, their membership began to defect to more rewarding arrangements, such as participation in advocacy groups. A similar loss of authority, as we will see, undermined government, business, and the scientific establishment. The decline, so far, has been less disastrous than that of the mass movement, but in both cases authority drained away from once-powerful hierarchies toward informal, spontaneous groups.

My hypothesis with regard to the public and its miraculous resurrection from burial by the masses is this. Every public must behave in both an active and reactive manner, but the proportion of each at any period of history depends entirely on the structural options available. The 18th-century public was minute but highly active. The public in the industrial age was immense but bullied into a reactive posture. The masses absorbed the hundreds of millions of ordinary persons who entered history in the 19th century, and placed them under the command of structures that allowed few authentic decisions, few real choices of opinion and action.

But the public never disappeared under the weight of the masses. That is a crucial claim of my hypothesis. The public never became an inert prop on the social and political stage. Public opinion retreated to a reactive mode, but it remained a factor, it always mattered—even to Nazi Germany, which invested heavily in a persuasion and propaganda apparatus. The same was true for all mass movements and the regimes that sprang from them. They were obsessively concerned with shaping public opinion—more so, by far, than the liberal democracies.

Propaganda was the totalitarian's admission that his power wasn't total. Unlike democratic politicians, leaders of mass movements lacked feedback mechanisms: they had no idea what the masses were thinking, and could only hope to inject the desired opinions directly into the brains of their followers. Call it Taylorism for the soul.

But the masses could fail to oblige. The public, with its peculiar interests and opinions, still lived in them. It was not inert. And the power to react made it dangerous to autocrats. East Germany in 1953, Hungary in 1956, Czechoslovakia in 1968, and Poland in 1980 saw the public cash in the ultimate choice: life-and-death revolutions against communist regimes. By 1989, all the propaganda in the world couldn't save those regimes from being swept away. By 1991, the mother ship—the Soviet Union and its communist party—had foundered.

The old public had been reactive because, structurally, it could be nothing else. TV viewers in the 1950s, for example, could only *react* as consumers to three channels, by either watching or tuning them out. For obvious structural reasons, members of that public were unable to develop their own TV programs. They couldn't act. The same held true in politics, even in democracies—where, I have already noted, political machines and powerful parties reduced the structural options open to the public to a very few. The same was true of the industrial economy: mass producers invented a mass public with tastes that matched what was actually produced. And the same was true in information and communication, which saw a caste of mediators, under the motto "All the news that's fit to print," arbitrarily control the content available to ordinary persons.

Our age is characterized by a radical shift along this spectrum: from a public that was almost entirely reactive to one that is hyperactive and ultra-intrusive. This was made possible by a proliferation of choices. The process resembled the radical strategic reversal described in my fable of

Homo informaticus. As more structural options became available to ordinary people, the latter began a migration back to their original interests, and the institutions that had once hemmed their behavior lost the power to do so.

TV viewers became YouTube posters. Movement and party members morphed into advocates for personally meaningful causes, often grouped around virtual meeting places such as the "We Are All Khaled Said" Facebook page. In business, design took priority over production, and personalization emerged as the grand ideal for design. In information, technological innovation released an astronomical number of capabilities for use and abuse by ordinary persons, reconstituting the new public and enabling its assault on the temples of authority.

This last development can help explain why Lippmann and Dewey got the future wrong: like every other person on planet Earth, they failed to foresee the advent of a *personalized* information technology.

That industrial organizations espoused Taylorist ideals and worked to convert the public into masses is, I think, beyond dispute. My hypothesis about the reemergence of the public can be summarized briefly. *First*, the public never disappeared behind the embrace of the masses or the control of hierarchical organizations. The public endured, though forced into a reactive mode by the stripping away of its structural options. Second, a combination of geopolitical developments and technological innovation opened an immense frontier of choices and capabilities to the public, which awakened from its reactive slumber and began to *act*. The public as actor immediately collided with the old institutions, and these, accustomed to control, reacted with anger and incomprehension, sometimes tottered, and not infrequently fell to pieces.

I mean to say that the new public has been the turbulent edge of the Fifth Wave. To the extent that it has intruded on events, established institutions have gone into crisis and faced the threat of dissolution.

THE PUBLIC IS NOT THE CROWD, BUT THE TWO ARE IN A RELATIONSHIP (IT'S COMPLICATED)

In this book, I have described the uprisings in Tunisia and Egypt as the triumph of the public over authoritarian regimes. If you possess a literal cast of mind, however, you might arrive at a different interpretation. You would note that it was the crowds that brought down the Ben Ali and Mubarak governments—crowds never more than a small fraction of the population of the two countries. Since the public has not been shown to be identical to the crowd, you, in your literalness, could reasonably wonder why the former has been given so much credit for what the latter achieved.

The relationship between the public and the crowd is not transparent. Though closely associated with one another, the two are never identical. The public, we know, is composed of private persons welded together by a shared point of reference: what Lippmann called an interest in an affair, which can mean a love of computer games or a political disposition. Members of the public tend to be dispersed, and typically influence events from a distance only, by means of "soft" persuasion: by voicing and communicating an opinion.

A crowd, on the contrary, is always *manifest*, and capable of great physical destructiveness and ferocity. It is a form of action that submerges the desires of many individuals under a single rough-hewn will. In direct democracies like ancient Athens, it could be said to represent the will of the sovereign people. Everywhere else, the crowd can represent nothing but itself. Yet the persons who integrate a crowd invariably make larger claims of identity: with political crowds, such claims often reflect the more emotive aspects of the public's agenda. A crowd can thus perceive itself, and be perceived by others, as the public in the flesh, "the people" or "the proletariat" or "the community" in action.

On occasion—think of the civil rights march on Washington or the storming of the Bastille—the crowd has attained a powerful symbolic importance, with an influence far beyond its numbers or even its moment in history. It is then turned into a form of communication.

The public mediates the transformation of the crowd into a symbolic force. It can seize on a event, like demonstrations in Istanbul against the demolition of a park, then mobilize its organs of opinion on behalf of the demonstrators, in the process adding sentiment and meaning that may not have been present in the actual event. Used in this manner, the crowd becomes an instrument to communicate public opinion. But the crowd itself can also crystallize into a new focus of interest, toward which the public gravitates in ever larger numbers—that is in fact what transpired in Turkey, where the protests quickly spread beyond Istanbul and turned into a political uprising.

If the public can be said to re-create the crowd into a form of communication, it is equally true that such a crowd, once convincingly expressed, will create its own public.

A fateful example of this type of two-way influence took place in June 1979, when Pope John Paul II travelled to communist Poland, his native land. At every step of the pope's nine-day journey, immense crowds gathered—and the crowd by its sheer size communicated a transcendent truth to the scattered members of the anti-communist opposition.

> *I was there, along with friends from the resistance, at the Tenth Anniversary Stadium. We, and a million others. For the first time, I saw a sea of people, with my own eyes. We understood then, we and our kind—the "outcasts" and "instigators" of the nation—that we were not alone, that we had a purpose, that it was not over, and that no one had broken us, the Polish people, down.*[35]

Here we encounter the demonstration effect at its most vivid and powerful. Individuals may have joined the crowd attending the pope from political, religious, or patriotic feelings, or for many other private motives. It didn't matter. To the opposition, the crowd was literally a revelation—a flash of self-awareness that merged the identity of a small community of interest into a far larger public than it had imagined possible. With perfect sincerity, a handful of dissidents assumed the mantle of "us, the Polish people," and turned the pope's crowd into a persuasive argument against the communist regime. Many, inside Poland and out, accepted this interpretation. After 30 years of rule, the communist grip on Eastern Europe appeared to be suprisingly precarious.

The history of the public's love affair with the crowd, with its impassioned rendevouz and heartbreaking abandonments, is a tale that has not yet been told. Here, however, my concern is only to note that, like the freestanding public, the spontaneous crowd almost disappeared in the age of the masses. It was reduced to an appendage of hierarchical organizations—mostly political parties and labor unions, but on occasion less established groups agitating for prohibition or civil rights.

The organization scripted the crowd with Taylorist care. This was done in the first instance by providing it with slogans, placards, and appropriate settings, but also symbolically, by proclaiming an event's meaning

Figure 14: Injecting a blond worldview: Nazi poster. *Courtesy of Library of Congress.*

before it occurred. Such events were mere tests of strength for the organizations involved: industrial-era facsimiles of true public opinion.

The alienation of the public climaxed with the advent of the mass movement, whose primary function was to put a well-disciplined crowd on the street, often in military uniform and to violent ends. In Weimar Germany, for example, the police force was pushed aside while communist and Nazi "masses" murdered one another in street battles. On conquering power, these groups deployed the masses in splendid rituals to communicate their superiority over rival doctrines. Thus Hitler's rallies at Nuremberg and Stalin's May Day parades. Fossilized remnants of this system can be observed today: Cuba's Castro regime on festive occasions still herds the masses to bask in their approval, and organizes "rejection-ist" crowds to harass the opposition.

The mass movement buried alive the public and deprived the crowd of all spontaneous life and independence of purpose. Everything was scripted, and the scripts appeared insincere almost by design—a tendency that attained a pathological intensity in North Korea, where the masses were made to perform acrobatic tricks usually reserved for the circus. The shock caused by the joyous papal crowds in Poland owed much to the contrast with the official ones.

In the new millenium, the public returned with a vengeance, and its command of the information sphere permitted much greater intimacy with the crowd than had been structurally possible before. The public could invite itself to a protest on Facebook, comment from the streets on Twitter, and reflect on the larger meaning of the event on blogs, Tumblr, Reddit, and other open platforms. For the first time in history, public opinion could fuse, moment by moment, with the actions of the crowd. Such intimacy with the public enabled the crowd to escape predictable scripts and communicate itself directly to the world by posting cell phone videos on the web, endowing the contagion of revolt with the speed of light. This, in turn, transformed the street into a domain of political uncertainty frightening to all forms of authority.

The unpredictability of the crowd mirrored the public's networked structure and sectarian temper. We discern in both the invertebrate profile of Shirky's "self-assembled" groups: no leader, no hierarchy, no program, only a shared interest in an affair to bring the public to life and push out the crowd to the street. To authoritarian rulers like Hosni Mubarak and Syria's Bashar Assad, the millennial crowd represented a terrifying new thing under the sun. Repression in the past aimed to cripple rival mass movements, like the Muslim Brotherhood in both Egypt and Syria. If it succeeded at this task, the regime owned the street.

Now the crowd spontaneously self-assembled. This could take whimsical form, as with the "flash mobs" that have engaged in bizarre behavior to show a disrespect of established authority. But it could reflect serious political planning, conducted virtually and adjusted moment by moment on the streets: "spontaneity" in such cases meant regime surprise caused by technological blindness. No wonder the first instinct of authoritarians has been to turn back the clock to simpler times—shutting down the web in Egypt, switching off the electric grid in Syrian cities, like Daraa, which were strongholds of the opposition.

Access to the global information sphere amplified the reach and impact of the demonstration effects resulting from crowd action. Members of the public could still experience the crowd as a personal revelation, an impossibility made real—particularly in Arab countries that had not seen protests of any size for two generations. Wael Ghonim's reaction after reaching Tahrir Square on January 25 echoed the wonder and exaltation of the Polish activists watching the throngs around John Paul II.

> *The scene at Tahrir was one of the most enthralling I had ever seen. Enormous numbers of protesters—thousands, if not tens of thousands—covered most of the ground space in the square. This was when I realized Jan25 had succeeded. It would be marked as a historic day for Egypt's opposition movement.*[36]

But the January 25 protests had been inspired in large part by the success of the Tunisian crowds in chasing Ben Ali from power. Images of Mohamed Bouazizi's self-immolation had reached Egypt. His death was mourned by the public in both countries. Members of the Tunisian crowd had documented their existence with the use of cell phone videos. In Tunisia, these videos could not be posted directly to the web, but Al Jazeera obtained and broadcast them into Egypt and the rest of the world—and by this path they entered the web, where they could be searched and viewed at will. Here was the information sphere at work.

The Tahrir crowd, in turn, assumed a heroic dimension for the Arab revolts that began in 2011. Caught in a crossfire between irreconcilable political antagonisms, Egyptians today speak with longing of the "Tahrir spirit." The crowd, for a moment, transcended the fractiousness of the public. Incidents like the failed camel charge by Mubarak supporters achieved a kind of viral fame. Al Jazeera streamed live from Tahrir Square around the clock. The broadcaster made no effort to conceal its sympathy for the crowd. Other international newscasters, while less blatant, also portrayed the Tahrir crowd as the hero of the story.

The whole world followed the fortunes of the Tahrir crowd as if it were an epic adventure. Demonstration effects, as always, are tough to show conclusively, but the chronology of the Arab uprisings is suggestive. Ben Ali fled Tunisia on January 14, 2011. The Tahrir crowd first gathered on January 25, and persuaded Mubarak to resign on February 11. Large-scale protests followed in other countries: Yemen (February 3), Bahrain (February 14), Libya (February 15), and Syria (March 16).

No sane analyst would insist on a straight line of causation between the crowd in Tahrir and protests in other Arab countries. Human affairs aren't like billiard balls or the orbits of the planets. I have said this before. But demonstration effects, while indirect, can be very powerful. News-casters and web videos glamorized the Tahrir crowd to people whose background and political circumstances were not too different from those of the Egyptian protesters. The watching public in Yemen and Syria strongly identified with the crowd in Egypt: the love affair could now be conducted at long distance and across borders. The revolts that erupted within weeks of each other could hardly have been unaffected by these feelings, or by a knowledge of each other.

In the worldwide political collision between the new public and es-tablished authority, the image of the crowd has assumed a decisive impor-tance. A willingness to face down power, even to die, in front of cell phone cameras, has equalized the asymmetry of this conflict to a surprising ex-tent. A government can respond with old-fashioned brute force, as it did in Syria, but at the cost of tearing to shreds the social contract and becom-ing a global pariah. Every beating and every shooting will be recorded on video and displayed to the world. Every young man killed will rise again in the information sphere, transformed, in the manner of Mohamed Bouazizi and Khaled Said, into a potent argument for revolt.

If the demonstration effects of Tunisia and Tahrir helped inspire the Arab uprisings, the heroic image of the Arab crowd stirred those in the West interested in the affair of political change. They sought to repeat the drama of Tahrir in a democratic setting. The vector of contagion was the information sphere, the weapon of choice was the crowd. The resulting convulsion deserved a catchy name, but given the failure of the global imagination on this point, I will call it, simply, the year 2011.

PHASE
CHANGE
2011

My story—I repeat—concerns the tectonic collision between a public that will not rule and institutions of authority progressively less able to do so. My misgiving is that democracy will be ground to pieces under the stress. An immense psychological distance separates the two sides, even as they come together in conflict. This gulf is filled with dark matter: distrust.

The elites who control the institutions have never really trusted the public, which they considered animalistic and prone to bouts of destructiveness. In effect, they sought to neuter the public by herding it into a mass and attaching it to established hierarchies. A glimpse at any American airport today will confirm that this horror of the top for the bottom has, if anything, grown more intense.

What has changed, then, is the public's distrust for authority—and its increased power, in the age of the Fifth Wave, to translate that distrust into action.

Pierre Rosanvallon, one of the few interesting political analysts today, has written of the "rise of the *society of distrust*."[37] The public, in a complex society, must depend on specialists, experts, and intermediaries such as political representatives, organized institutionally and hierarchically. When the experts fail, the public can only appeal to other experts, often from the same failed institution. The process has resembled a mutual protection pact among the elites. Failure typically gets blamed on insufficient support: the CIA, for example, demanded and received a bigger budget after 9/11.

An exasperated public has countered by notching up the vehemence of criticism and the frequency of its interventions. At times, in some places, the public has abandoned all hope in modern society and lapsed into a permanent state of negation and protest.

This chapter is about the year 2011, when distrust reached a tipping point and the public in many countries took to the streets to demand change. First came the Arab uprisings, with a familiar script. Protesters clamoring for freedom confronted dictatorships endeavoring to repress them. The fatal rupture of trust in the Middle East could be explained without stretching the analytic imagination: authoritarians cheat and lie.

By spring, however, the tide of revolt had swamped the liberal democracies—Spain, Israel, the U.S., Britain, many others. These were relatively open societies, bastions of personal and political freedom, but the public there deeply identified with the Arab protesters and envied their revolutions.

So here is my theme for the chapter. At some moment of 2011, the script went awry. Toxic levels of distrust sickened democratic politics. People began to mobilize for "real democracy," and denied that their elected representatives represented *them*. They were citizens of liberal democracies, but they demanded something different. They wanted radical change, and the great mystery, casting a shadow beyond 2011, was what this change *away* from current democratic practices might look like.

A word on method. Many historians have scoffed at the idea that any year, or any cluster of years, could comprise a meaningful causal unit. I was taught at school that everything flows: the Italian Renaissance, with its love of the classical form, represented a moment in a series of classical rebirths going back to Charlemagne and forward to Washington's Lincoln Memorial. History, I was assured, advances in a stately procession, not in leaps and bounds.

When it comes to the behavior of complex systems, I now believe this is flat wrong. Let me explain why.

Social and political arrangements tend to accumulate noise. The internal and external forces holding them together inevitably shift in ways that drive the system ever farther out from equilibrium. Such pressures work silently and invisibly, beneath the surface. They are cumulative, slow to take effect. But when change comes, it is sudden and dramatic. Pushed beyond disequilibrium to turbulence, the system disintegrates and must be reconstituted on a different basis.

Thus water is just water interacting with falling temperatures, until abruptly it becomes ice. The Soviet Union was an evil empire and a superpower until suddenly it was neither. Hosni Mubarak was an immovable pharaonic figure, then in two weeks he was gone.

Whether the events of 2011 represented such a dramatic phase change remains uncertain. Not enough time has passed for the consequences to be manifested, much less analyzed. But that is my working hypothesis. I believe 2011 marked the moment when the public first equalized the asymmetry in power with government. It did so by deploying digital tools to mobilize opinion and organize massive street protests. I also believe 2011 first exposed the gulf of distrust between the public and elected governments in many democratic countries. Liberal democracy itself came under attack. Since no alternatives were proposed, the events of 2011 may be said to have launched a fundamental predicament of life under the Fifth Wave: the question of nihilism.

As for the consequences, they bear watching. A complex system can be transformed by a phase change, or it can be annihilated. The view on the far side of the change can look like an embrace of new organizing principles, or like increased disorganization—perpetual turbulence. The state of affairs in Syria and Egypt as I write this suggests that this isn't a purely theoretical concern.

THE LIMITS OF OUTRAGE, OR THE SOUND OF A SILENT SCREAM

On May 15, 2011, tens of thousands of mostly young demonstrators took to the streets in more than 50 Spanish cities. Their motto: "We are not merchandise in the hands of politicians and bankers."[38] The demonstrations were boisterous but peaceful, and very well organized. Yet they were not associated with the political parties or the labor unions, and they had received little notice from the news media. For this reason alone, they caused an earthquake in Spanish politics. The authorities had been caught by surprise. Spain was a top-down country, and those at the top had no idea what to make of the young demonstrators. They seemed to have come from nowhere.

An inconclusive debate began among the elites about the meaning of it all: whether the crowds in the street were a symptom of political health or sickness.

In the next few days, an "assembly" of Madrid protesters voted to "take" the large plaza called Puerta del Sol—it became their version of Tahrir Square. The move would inspire a rash of "Occupy" movements in the U.S., Britain, and elsewhere. The Spanish protesters called themselves the "15-M movement," from the date of the first demonstration, but they were better known as the *indignados*: the outraged. The label had been borrowed from a pamphlet by a 93-year-old French writer, Stéphane Hessel, whose message to young people was "It's time to get angry!"

The protesters sounded more earnest than angry—and they were clever, popularizing a string of witty slogans. The Spanish news media compensated for having initially missed the story by falling in love with the well-spoken *indignados*.

By June, protests were attracting millions of ordinary citizens. Opinion surveys showed strong levels of support for the movement. This was extraordinary, since the only clear position taken by the *indignados* was their rejection of Spain's existing political and economic systems. The youngsters who had come from nowhere wanted social life to start again from nothing.

In reality, of course, they had come very much from somewhere: the internet, a place of mystery to the authorities in Spain, as it had been in Egypt. The demonstrations were not spontaneous, but had been planned for months on Facebook. A Facebook group calling itself "Real Democracy Now" had appeared in January, and had been embraced by an odd assortment of bloggers, activists, and online sects with suggestive names like "Youth Without a Future." Most participants were young professionals or university students. Egypt's uprising—which they had followed, like the rest of the world, in the global information sphere—served as an inspiration and, in many ways, as a model. The organizers kept a tight focus on the unifying point of reference, the affair they, and so many other Spaniards, were interested in: what they stood against.

Objective conditions in Spain supplied a conspicuous target. After decades of prosperity, the country had been battered by the financial crisis of 2008 and a collapse of the national real estate market. Unemployment was highest in Europe: among the young, it touched 45 percent. Housing was scarce despite the drop in prices. The socialist government, elected for its opposition to the Iraq war and concerned mainly with social issues, seemed out of its depth. Politicians, bankers, experts—all appeared detached from reality. Their solutions entailed more pain for the population. In the distance, Germany and the European Union demanded austerity.

The first demonstrations had been scheduled a week ahead of Spain's local elections, presumably to influence the vote. The manifesto drafted for that original protest was a marvel of nonpartisan, nonideological inclusiveness:

We are normal ordinary people. We are like you: people who get up in the morning to study, to work or to look for work, people with family and friends. People who work hard every day to make a living and win a future for those around us.

Some of us consider ourselves more progressive, others more conservative. Some are believers, others not. Some have well-defined ideologies, others consider ourselves apolitical ... But all of us are worried and outraged by the political, economic, and social landscape we see around us. By the corruption of the politicians, businessmen, bankers ...[39]

The organizers went on to condemn the "political class" for "paying attention only to the dictates of the great economic powers" and forming a "partycratic dictatorship." The "obsolete and anti-natural current economic model" was blamed for enriching the few while reducing the rest to poverty. In the Manichean scheme of the *indignados*, democracy and capitalism, as these existed in Spain, were the forces of destruction.

This being the case, you would expect a call for drastic action—if not the guillotine, then prison time for corrupt members of the political and business class. The language of the movement virtually trembled with desire for radical change. But none was proposed. The single positive proposal in the manifesto seemed strangely unequal to the magnitude of the crisis it described. It was brief and stated in the passive voice: "An Ethical Revolution," it read, "is needed."

The revolt of the *indignados* brought together, uneasily, two distinct tendencies animating the events of 2011. All of the protest's leading spirits belonged to the same demographic as Wael Ghonim and Hoder: young, university educated, and brilliant at navigating the pathways of the information sphere. Lenin would have labeled them the vanguard. We would call them early adopters. Some espoused the culture of the web as well, reconciling a meticulous egalitarianism with the sense that they had become more highly evolved than their opponents. An instinctive rejection of authority, of existing structures, of the past, allowed this group to believe that they had transcended political parties, even ideology: that their revolt rested on a universally accepted standard of justice.

Some of the organizers, however, subscribed to the dizzying array of causes of the contemporary left: in their own words, "anarchists, . . .

alter-worldists, feminists, ecologists," and more.[40] The *indignados* struck an inclusive pose, but it didn't require much depth of analysis to discern the leftist flavor of the anti-capitalist, anti-"system" demonstrations. In the revolutionary jargon emanating from Puerta del Sol, the class struggle and the anti-globalization crusade loomed almost as large as the Arab uprisings. These people possessed "well-defined ideologies," a universalist vision, and a variety of programs for change. They had found an opportunity, in the protests, to smash a despised political order and hatch a revolution.

People of the web mobilized in awkward tandem with people of the left. The one provided a persuasive message, the other experience with street protests. They were united in their loathing of the established order—united also, and with no contradiction, by the sectarian outlook that pervaded their culture and generation to the core.

If, in the laboratory of rebellion, a political movement were stitched up to match perfectly Douglas and Wildavsky's description of the Border sect, the *indignados* would lumber forth from the operating table. According to these authors, the sect rejected every form of leadership in favor of a fierce egalitarianism, and condemned, in principle, bureaucracies and programs as the root of all evil. Decisions demanded long debates, and failure to decide, for the sectarian, was less problematic than abdicating responsibility to a leader or politburo.

So it went with the Spanish protesters. They refused to acknowledge leaders, even spokespersons. Instead, each individual was encouraged to speak on his or her own behalf. They met in general assemblies, which resembled nothing so much as an internet chat room: there were no moderators, and everyone who wished to speak, on whatever subject, was allowed to do so. Majority votes were considered an abomination of representative democracy. Ideologies and programs were tolerated as personal beliefs, but repudiated as drivers of group action. In this regard, at least, the culture of the web overwhelmed the people of the left.[41]

Damning ideology and party politics attracted many to the protest. Sheer negation, hostility toward the status quo, became the shared point of reference for networks and individuals advocating mutually inconsistent ideals. But after the crowds and the occupations, the point had been made. The logical next step was political change—and for change something more substantial than outrage or witty slogans seemed in order.

Enter the riddle: What now?

Some form of this riddle confronted the public during every collision with authority in the turbulent year 2011. What next? What structures will replace the old, despised institutions? How should society be reorganized? In every case no satisfactory answer was given. Given the public's sectarian temper, none might have been possible.

A favorite gimmick of the Spanish demonstrators was the "silent scream": to every man his own internal revolution. The misty "priorities" of the Real Democracy Now organizers also verged on political mutism: "Equality, progress, solidarity, free access to culture, ecological sustainability...."[42] The question of how to stack and pay for these priorities was never broached, and the omission was willful. Every step toward an ideology or program meant the embrace of something old, something hierarchical, something unequal and corrupt. Since the *indignados* lacked the imagination to articulate a society both universal and sectarian, they vented their thoughts in silence.

With elections came a moment of fatal clarity. The May protests had been timed to coincide with local elections in Spain, but the movement's approach to the vote was, to put it generously, confused. Fabio Gándara, one of the more articulate Real Democracy Now organizers, stated that he only asked the public to "vote their conscience." Gándara was a political activist. He must have held strong opinions. He acknowledged he was going to vote, but he refused to say for whom, calling it a "private" decision.[43]

Others were less timid. They labeled themselves "neither-nor" to denote a repudiation of the electoral process and the "dictatorship" of the political parties. A "Don't Vote Them In" campaign flourished online, and word spread that a blank ballot was the way to endorse the demonstrators.

In the event, election results appeared wholly disconnected from the protests. The conservative Popular Party won big in May, primarily because of an implosion by the ruling socialists. This trend was exacerbated in the November general elections. The socialists were swept out of office with their lowest vote ever, and the conservatives gained absolute control of parliament. Regional and radical parties increased their vote, but were powerless in the face of an overwhelming conservative dominance. The informal spoiled-ballot campaign lacked any discernible impact.

Spain's 2011 electoral season thus ended with the annihilation of the established left and the decisive triumph of the right. In the dazzling

Figure 15: A silent scream in Madrid.[44] *Photo by Juan Santiso*

clarity of a great national reorientation, the *indignados*, disdainful of leaders, spoke with many minds. Some felt the elections confirmed the hopeless corruption of the system, but they remained silent about what could or should be done. Others concluded that true change could only be achieved by going to the people and creating more democratic social structures—a sectarian dream amounting to political abdication.

The people of the left knew better. They understood the dimensions of the defeat. Their hopes had been blasted by the electorate, and the destruction of the socialists ensured conservative rule, essentially without opposition, for many years.

Contemplating the wreckage, some of them reconsidered the wisdom of neither-nor. To write off the socialists as "the same old shit" had been wrong, wrote one regretful *indignado*: "They may be a shit, we'd have to discuss it, but it isn't the same shit . . . ."[45] This was as incisive as the movement's political analysis got.

On December 19, 2011, less than a month after the parliamentary elections, the last occupiers of Puerta del Sol declared a period of "indefinite active reflection." They could sense the tide of public opinion flowing away from their cause.

The 15-M is losing participation, we see it in the demonstrations, in assemblies, in the neighborhoods, in activities, in the internet. . . . This is the time to stop and ask ourselves some deep questions . . . Have we stopped listening to each other? Are we reproducing the forms of old activism that have been shown to be useless because they exclude so many people?[46]

The sectarian impulse had generated vast crowds, excitement, self-righteous condemnation of Spain's ruling institutions. Digital networks had become a political force. The legitimacy of representative democracy and capitalism had been damaged. The socialist party, comfortably in office when the demonstrations began, had been gutted. Everything was different, but nothing had changed. Not a single project or policy or idea representing the worldview of the *indignados* had been put in place. It was time for the occupiers to go home.

THE SOURCES OF OUTRAGE VIEWED FROM BELOW, VIEWED FROM ABOVE

I want to measure the distance between the rhetoric of the *indignados* and the conditions that were the source of their outrage. To do this, I will peel back a few layers of Spanish political and economic life, and examine these from two perspectives. One is from below, from ground level, the way the young people of the movement experienced their situation. From this place, the revolts of 2011 can be explained by the colossal failure of Spain's ruling institutions. The second perspective will be the bird's-eye view of history—and it will show that the revolt of the *indignados* was propelled by a self-destructive contempt for the world that had created the young rebels.

The two perspectives, I fear, are not mutually exclusive, and may well be complementary. It is perfectly possible for the elites to lapse into paralysis while the public staggers into nihilism. Indeed, this could be our future.

The view from below immediately presents us with a fundamental question: What should be the public's expectations of government? We know the *indignados*, along with millions of Spaniards, felt cheated of their expectations to the point of outrage and revolt. Were they justified? The answer depends, in part, on what is possible for a modern government to achieve, the kinds of activities it can perform competently. This secondary question, though encrusted with ideological concerns, is to some extent an empirical puzzle: I promise to give it full attention in Chapter 7.

But our answer also depends on the government's claims of competence over whole domains of activity—whether such claims are sincere and true, wishful thinking but false, or purely fraudulent. Once the public accepts the claims, an expectation will have been formed, and failure to perform will appear like a breach of the social contract.

If we had examined the Spanish government on the eve of the economic crisis, we would have found it to be, in many ways, typical of the modern Leviathan. It wielded power and requisitioned treasure—just under 30 percent of the country's wealth in 2007, a moderate figure by global standards. It gathered vast amounts of information. A large bureaucracy, after presumably consulting this information, reallocated both power and treasure though a tangle of obscure, often contradictory programs. As has been true of all national governments, transparency mattered less than the care and feeding of favored constituencies. And as has been generally the case, the government seemed incapable of balancing the books—accumulated debt also stood at 30 percent of GDP in 2007. It was rapidly declining, however.[47]

Certain circumstances were unique to Spain. Central authority was squeezed from below by a bevy of "autonomous" regional governments—19 in all, with some, like the Basque country and Catalonia, harboring pretensions to independence. The Spanish government was thus forced to share power and treasure with political entities that were, at best, indifferent to its success, and at worst actively opposed to its rule.

It was also squeezed from above by the monetary and regulatory machinations of the European Union. The E.U., in 2008, consisted of 27 countries that had yielded to an administrative superstructure some aspects of their sovereignty. The administration was pure Center hierarchy—bureaucratic, unelected, and largely unaccountable. The powers ceded by the member states were vague and controversial.

The surrender of traditional control over the currency was clear enough, however. In 1999, Spain became part of a "euro zone" with 16 other E.U. countries. The reasons behind this monetary union need not concern us here. What was important was the government's loss of authority over fiscal issues that previously had been settled by political means, and the increased distance between the Spanish public and those who determined monetary policy. Money in Spain was controlled by shadowy experts in Frankfurt. This destroyed the sense of trust needed in case the economy went bad—which it did, in a big way, after 2008. Predictably, the E.U. and the German chancellor, Angela Merkel, ranked high in the *indignados'* gallery of villains.

Leviathan is a massive but invertebrate monster. Add the separation of authorities normal to a parliamentary democracy, and you have, in the Spanish government, a babble of voices, a muddle of cross purposes, and a multitude of decision centers. The system could work only if the elites at all levels broadly agreed on the direction of governance, and a large enough segment of the public could be persuaded that the system worked to its benefit.

That's precisely what transpired. The protesters were correct to charge the two major parties with espousing identical principles and similar policies. Socialists and conservatives differed on marginal questions—Middle East policy, social affairs—but were of one mind on democracy, capitalism, the welfare state, the euro, and the E.U. In a hindsight clouded with failure and distrust, this looked like collusion, even corruption. At the time, however, it would have been self-evident that, absent such a consensus on policies, the lumbering machinery of the Spanish state would have ground to a halt.

And for many people over many years, the system seemed to work wonderfully well. A 25-year-old in 2011 would be able to remember only peace, relative social tranquility, and endless prosperity before the crisis. The last year of negative growth had been 1993. A majority of Spanish workers enjoyed ironclad security in their jobs. For obvious reasons, this segment of the public embraced with some passion the "two-party, one-system" formula. The substantial minority of workers with little or no job security included young people disproportionately—but like most young people in ordinary times, they were politically unimportant.

Both major parties behaved as if they had solved the riddle of the Sphinx, asserting far-reaching claims of competence over many domains of social life. They were democratic politicians. It was in their nature to take credit for the apparent success of the system. Questions of luck or complexity never entered the political discourse. The Spanish public certainly didn't raise such questions, or the possibility that the economy might have prospered despite, rather than because of, the politicians. It was a democratic public. It wished to believe the exaggerated claims of the government. There were no serious street protests in the fat years.

Between 1996 and 2004, the conservative government invested much of its energies in an ambitious but fruitless foreign policy. Between 2004 and 2008, the socialist government focused primarily on social issues such as gay marriage. A visitor to Spain in 2007 could have watched on TV a government-sponsored commercial showing people literally hugging a tree, and another that featured two women kissing. In May 2006 the socialist party had proposed in parliament that certain "rights" be granted to four species of great apes.[48] The tacit assumption of the elites was that they had left far behind the basic questions of war and peace, wealth and poverty, and now confronted the task of lifting the country to a higher ethical plane.

When the economy began to wobble, the government denied the seriousness of the problem. The public agreed. In the elections of March 2008, on the verge of economic catastrophe, the socialist party won a record number of votes and was returned to office with a larger plurality than in 2004.

Recall Douglas and Wildavsky's observation about the Center hierarchy: it is often surprised. Modern governments can keep an eye on a thousand moving parts, but they can't predict discontinuity. They can't comprehend phase change. When the crisis arrives, they are slow to grasp its dimensions. When the effects become palpable, they reflexively reach for the crude tools they have at their disposal, whether or not these will improve the situation. In essence, governments can throw money at unwanted change, or they can hurl bombs and policemen.

Despite later complaints about austerity, the Spanish government threw large amounts of money at the economic crisis. President José Luis Rodríguez Zapatero promised to "pour out the investment capacity" of the state, and he was true to his word. Money was given to promote public works, to the autonomous regions, to the banks. Remarkably, as the economy continued to deteriorate, the government hardened its claims of competence. Zapatero insisted that the crisis had vindicated the importance of government relative to the markets. "Our policy is the correct one," he said in November 2008. "Citizens and businesses can maintain a degree of tranquility."[49]

To a young person, that must have sounded like fiddling while the future burned. In the 12 months before Zapatero's statement, unemployment had ballooned by 37 percent. By 2011, total unemployment surpassed 21 percent, with youth unemployment nearing 50 percent. The unprotected class of workers naturally suffered most, but even public employees experienced cuts in pay and benefits. Prospects looked dismal as far as the eye could see.

The question, at ground level, was whether this disaster reflected only incompetence by the elites, or also corruption and criminal negligence. The answer, in large part, depended on the bonds of trust previously established between the public and their rulers—and there was no trust. There were only continued assertions of competence on one side, and increased economic pain and hopelessness on the other. Distrust poisoned the public's perception of politics and politicians. The digital platforms favored by the young lent themselves to conspiracy theories. It was natural to believe the worst.

The Spanish elites and the institutions they inhabited had never made much of a case for themselves beyond prosperity. They failed on their own terms. In their experience as in that of so many others, authority turned out to be not terribly authoritative. Under the conditions of the Fifth Wave, the human consequences of their failure couldn't be swept discreetly under the rug. The *indignados* were born on Facebook, and Twitter globalized their grievances. The economic crisis thus resembled a plane crash, a cataclysm out in the open, more than a problem in economics. The government had nowhere to hide.

The view from below, in Spain, in the troubled year 2011, fixated on the people at the top, on the ruling elites, on their empty claims, on what seemed like the decisive failure of established institutions to deliver on the social contract. Expectations of the good life had crashed and burned. The breach of trust, for many, extended well beyond any one party or policy to a "partycratic dictatorship" stuck in fossilized immobility. The socialists, after all, had been swept away to oblivion, yet the conservatives retained many of the same old policies.

Out of hopelessness, digitally expressed, a public had crystallized that was interested in the affair of abolishing the whole system. The "key message" of the protesters, wrote Manuel Castells, a student of the move-ment and a participant in it, "was a rejection of the entire political and economic institutions that determine people's lives."[50] This meant noth-ing less than the elimination of representative democracy and capitalism. If these idols of the modern world could be overturned, society would be purged of exploitation and distrust, and the individual would once again be free to determine his own existence. So the *indignados* believed.

A central question for the view from above—by which I mean from the Olympus of history—is whether these beliefs were grounded in reality. Analytically, this is probably impossible to discover. Almost immediately you smack into the problem presented by alternative or experimental his-tories: there aren't any. The *indignados* imagined that, without the "entire political and economic institutions," they as a group, and the Spanish public as a whole, would be better off. But the question remained: com-pared to what?

Compared to recent Spanish history, the demands of the *indignados* sounded strangely out of tune. Take the dismissal of representative de-mocracy. For 40 years, until 1975, Spain was ruled by a military dictator-ship. This regime tolerated no dissent, much less public protests. A move-ment based on street protests and occupations of public places became possible only because of the rights of expression guaranteed by liberal de-mocracy, which the movement wished to do away with. I presume the *in-dignados* had no wish to raise Francisco Franco from the grave. But given the alliance between a protesting public and the military in Egypt, forged in opposition to democratic results, this possibility shouldn't be treated as just a witticism, either.

A similar dissonance applied to economic matters. Spain had been a very poor country within living memory. If "capitalism" meant the eco-nomic practices and institutions dominant since the end of the dictator-ship, its accomplishments had been remarkable. In 2011, three years into the crisis, per capita GDP was five times what it had been in 1980: around $32,000 compared to just over $6,000. Even adjusted for inflation, this is a significant increase. By the standard definition of such things, Spain was now a middle-class country, no longer a poor one. Percentage of imports to GDP, always a good measure of wealth, had nearly doubled, from 17 percent in 1980 to 31 percent in 2011. The value of the Spanish stock mar-ket had jumped from $91 billion to over $1 trillion in the same time frame.

In 2012, four years into the crisis, there were more cell phones *and* cars per person in Spain than in the U.S.

The accumulation of wealth had predictably beneficial social effects. Life expectancy increased by seven years between 1980 and 2011, for example. This was due in part to a reduction of the mortality rate for children under five, from 18 per 1,000 in 1980 to only 4 per 1,000 in 2011. Educational enrollment at all levels improved significantly. Internet penetration reached nearly 70 percent in 2011. That year Spain ranked ninth in the world for Facebook penetration, with nearly nine million users.[51]

I don't believe it would be an exercise in phrase-making to say that liberal democracy and capitalism created the class out of which the *indignados* and their protest emerged. For all their deeply felt sense of grievance, the protesters were well read, highly educated, mobile, affluent enough to have access to laptops and cell phones, and extremely adept at mobilizing the online social networks where the movement in fact began. They took democratic protections and freedoms for granted, as they did the air they breathed.

In the view from above, the *indignados* appeared in revolt against two distinct foes: the political and economic elites in Spain and the historic forces that had brought them, the protesters, into being. Failure against the elites was probably inevitable, given the sectarian character of the movement. Results on the second front were less clear. Tides of opinion can take time to swell into a crisis of legitimacy: Spanish democracy, or capitalism, or both, may have been fatally shaken by the events of 2011, and now wait only for some political tremor to collapse. There is no way to know until it happens.

But such a victory would be self-defeating. If the *indignados* somehow managed to destroy the system they so deeply despised, they would have extinguished themselves and their movement by eliminating the conditions that made both possible. This is not a riddle or a paradox, but a political pathology frequently encountered in the wake of the Fifth Wave.

The Spanish protesters' unwillingness to offer an alternative program to the status quo left them mired in negation. They could only mock, condemn, reject. That was perfectly in harmony with their mode of thinking. The documents they produced showed little historical awareness. Their few positive suggestions were vague and contradictory. It was only with a negation that implicated the awful present but also the dynamic past that the *indignados* found their true voice.

Pure negation is nothing and leads nowhere. Neither-nor resembles a curse in a fairy tale because it's open-ended. Under its spell, a revolutionary can never declare victory, nor even glimpse the promised land from a high place. He can only batter away at the established order, until every trace of history has been erased from social life. Then he too, as a child of history, will disappear.

So I pose here, for the first time, in the context of the Spanish street revolts, the question of nihilism. By this word I mean the will to destruction, including self-destruction, for its own sake. I mean, specifically, the negation of democracy and capitalism, with a frivolous disregard for the consequences. The view from above portrayed the *indignados* and their movement, in certain moods at least, as a preternatural hybrid of revolutionary aspirations and a societal suicide pact. They were a privileged generation, which, when confronted with an existential challenge, chose to cut and tear at their own roots. And they were not powerless or marginal. They commanded the great persuasive power of the global information sphere, and, according to the polls, they enjoyed considerable support from the general public. Even if they failed to overthrow the system, they could and did undermine its legitimacy—possibly, as I said, to a fatal extent.

The question of nihilism, now posed, will hover like a doleful spirit over the political landscape in 2011.

HOW A TENT CITY IN TEL AVIV BECAME A CIRCUS OF MIDDLE-CLASS DISCONTENT

The tent-city protests that convulsed Israel in the summer of 2011 bore a strong family resemblance to events in Spain, and, earlier, in Egypt and Tunisia. By now this should not surprise us. Information generated turbulence. Demonstration effects were at work. On their televisions and laptops, a restless Israeli public had witnessed the power of the multitudes to humble even ruthless dictators. They knew what had been done, and how it had been done.

These eruptions of public discontent resembled one another because all were part of the great underground collision that is my story—and all exemplified the turning of the hinge that is the theme of this chapter.

The Israeli protests began, ostensibly, in Tel Aviv, but really in the same place where the trouble had started in Egypt and Spain: on Facebook. And among the same demographic group: the young, university educated, digitally connected. Daphni Leef, a 25-year-old video editor and film-school graduate, played the part of Wael Ghonim—although, I think, with a difference. She was, by most measures, an ordinary person. She led no political party or social organization, had stirred not a ripple as a public figure in her country. She represented herself.

Early in July, Leef had learned that the lease for her Tel Aviv apartment would not be renewed. When it became clear that she could not afford another apartment within the confines of the city, Leef posted an invitation to a Facebook event: pitching tents on fashionable Rothschild Boulevard to protest the cost of housing.

The gesture succeeded beyond anyone's expectations. On July 14, Leef and a few friends spent the night at Rothschild Boulevard. In the following days, student and labor organizations jointed the protest. By July 23, a tent city sprawled between the boulevard's shops and cafes, and 30,000 persons, chanting the slogan "The people demand social justice," marched to the Museum of Art. On the next day, tent cities and demonstrations sprang up in Jerusalem and over a dozen Israeli cities, including the working-class towns of Negev and Holon. As in Egypt and Spain, the dimensions of the protests expanded much faster than the ability of the authorities to make sense of what was transpiring. Two weeks after the first demonstration, more than 300,000 took to the streets—it was said to be the largest protest in the short history of Israel. Marchers in Tel Aviv unfurled a giant banner that read "Egypt is here!"[52]

The protesters' message was savagely critical of the market-friendly government of Benjamin Netanyahu, and blandly admiring of themselves: words like "awakening," "renewal," and "rebirth" were thrown around by them, in an effort to describe the transcendental change they imagined they had brought about. They were not alone in applauding their actions. Opinion surveys showed remarkable levels of public support for the protests—up to 88 percent in one poll.[53]

The tent-city dwellers, though born on the web, quickly became the darlings of the Israeli news media. Sometimes it seemed as if all who could articulate a cause or an idea, in that articulate nation, had projected their hopes on the rebels, as on a blank screen. To read the early coverage and analysis of the "Israeli summer" of 2011 is to wander through a maze of wishful thinking.[54]

The Israeli protesters attracted contradictory political fantasies because of the fuzziness of their definition. This repeated a pattern established in Egypt and Spain. The lack of leaders, programs, and organizational structure was, if anything, more pronounced. Those who spoke to the media on a regular basis, like Leef, were attractive and clever, but they lacked the power to command or decide, and they quarreled constantly among themselves. The question of whether to negotiate with the government divided the protesters. The goal of social justice—supposedly the North Star of the uprising—appeared to be as foggy a notion to them as to their media admirers.

Nevertheless, they unleashed a prodigious amount of kinetic energy, and for two months turned the very settled Israeli political landscape upside down. To explain this blind surge of pressure—to grasp the relation between events in Israel and my hypothesis of a 2011 phase change—I need to clarify who, exactly, the tent-city protesters were, and what, in the end, they really wanted.

The who was plain enough. The protesters received support from the general public, and benefited from the active participation of some working-class elements—but this wasn't them. They did not represent the Israeli population or its proletariat. Nearly all the organizers and most of the demonstrators came from Tel Aviv's affluent, secular Ashkenazi families. This was a revolt of middle-class hipsters, not of the downtrodden. Daphni Leef, for one, had been born into a well-to-do family, and partook of the generic leftist attitudes favored by the artistic community to which she belonged. She had refused to serve in the military, apparently out of sympathy with the Palestinians. In this, Leef differed from her prototype, the more conventional, politically ambivalent Wael Ghonim.

To judge by the groups that joined the tent protests, the people of the left played a more active part in Israel than they had in Spain. In fact, some on the right have dismissed the entire episode as an exercise in manipulation, perpetrated by the leftist parties. This strikes me as unlikely for many reasons—not least that, if Israel's moribund political left knew how to conjure up enormous crowds, it would have done so long before the summer of 2011. The left failed to insert any organizational strength or programmatic clarity into the protests. If leftists were abundant, the

sectarian spirit of the people of the web was a far more powerful influence over the young rebels.

Hence the carefree incoherence of their demands. To give just one
example: proposals were floated to eliminate university tuition and increase benefits for the faculty.[55]

Even more than their Spanish counterparts, the young Israelis, as a
class, had benefited from the success of their country's political and economic system. Israel had managed to avoid the worst of the 2008 crisis.
Per capita GDP had climbed to over $31,000 in 2011 from $27,600 in
2008. Even accounting for inflation, this was a noteworthy improvement.
At 5.6 percent, unemployment was not an issue. The majority of the demonstrators either held down jobs or fully expected to do so when they
graduated. They were not a youth without a future. By some measures, inequality in Israel had increased, but the protesters' demographic had been
among the beneficiaries of this trend. Educated urbanites stood at the top
of the pyramid. Arab Israelis and the ultra-Orthodox, with the highest
poverty rates, languished at the bottom, and neither group participated in
the protests of 2011.[56]

The people taking to the streets were the golden youth of Israel. That
was the view from above and the view at ground level. Yet, like the *indignados*, they wished to cut away at their own roots. They wanted to be other than they were. They felt deeply, as one of them put it, that "something
in Israeli society is lacking; something is wrong with our collective priorities." That refrain was repeated over and again. Something was missing
from their lives. Something was wrong with their country. "This is not
about housing," a young journalist explained. "It is a welcomed attempt at
patricide."[57] In the negation of their world and of themselves lay the beating heart of the revolt.

The feeling infused life and urgency into the vague calls for social
justice. By this phrase, the protesters meant many things. At the level of
the system, it meant a repudiation of the Netanyahu government's "swinish capitalism" and a reversal of market-oriented policies endorsed, over a
decade, by the voters. Since 2001, the Israeli left had been decimated. The
venerable Labor Party, which had midwifed the country during the epic
years after its foundation, lay fractured and in ruins. The youngsters in
Rothschild Boulevard often expressed a longing for the idealism of the
old times. Although they liked to play at revolution—a mock guillotine

went up in the tent compound—they imagined the future in terms of the past, and asked for nothing more radical than a return of the welfare state.

Social justice also meant fixing the high cost of life in Tel Aviv. Daphni Leef's grievance had been personal before it became political, but it resonated with large numbers of people of her age and class. The young demanded affordable housing. Students wanted lower tuition. Parents conducted a "stroller protest" against the cost of child care. Doctors went on strike for higher salaries. It's hard to avoid the suspicion that the zeal for "patricide" among this group was directly proportional to its loss of earning power.

From the tent city in Rothschild Boulevard came few calls for the elimination of the system, or democracy, or even capitalism of the non-swinish kind. But there were fantastic, almost messianic, expectations placed on the shoulders of modern government.

What Israel's mutinous youth really wanted was this: They wanted the government to make things right. They wanted it to legislate a meaningful life for them in an egalitarian, fraternal, and, of course, affordable society. They had no plans to achieve this, or even a definition of what it meant, but it didn't matter. That, too, was the government's job—to listen to the politicized crowd, "the people" who demanded social justice, then somehow make it so. Israeli citizens, Leef asserted, "understand that we all deserve more; understand that they are allowed to demand more from the government." [58]

The contradiction between the free-market predilections of Netanyahu's government and their own haphazard calls for state intervention didn't trouble them overmuch. They weren't revolutionaries, but neither did they make a fetish of representative democracy—and, at the height of their popularity, they believed Rothschild Boulevard could dictate terms to Jerusalem. "From now on, the young people will shape the government's vision," declared Itzik Shmuli, 31-year-old head of the National Union of Israeli Students and one of Leef's rivals as media face of the protests. [59]

During the protests, the government, though shaken by the magnitude of the revolt, reacted more nimbly than the Spanish government had done under similar circumstances. Three weeks after the tent city was first pitched, Netanyahu appointed a committee chaired by economics professor Manuel Trajtenberg, and tasked it with proposing, within a month, specific policy changes to address the grievances behind the protests. In an admission that the mechanisms of representative democracy had failed in this instance, the committee was asked to act as intermediary between the government and "different groups and sectors within the public."[60] That was code for the tent-city people.

The recommendations of the Trajtenberg committee included housing subsidies, tax breaks for low-income earners, and tax increases for the wealthy and businesses. These measures went against the grain of the Netanyahu government, but they were approved in October 2011—a small, tentative step toward the welfare state desired by many of the young protesters. The size and volume of the demonstrations had represented a kind of political force majeure, to which the government responded because it felt it had no choice. Whether they were a fig leaf, as the protesters claimed, or sincere compromises, the Trajtenberg-inspired laws would never have received consideration if it hadn't been for the tent-city revolt. In this sense, they represented a triumph for the rebels.

That was not the way they saw it. To people with boundless faith in the powers of government, small bounded steps appeared like craven obstructionism. To those who hoped for personal transformation by means of radical politics, an offer of economic support looked like a bribe—and an insultingly tiny one at that. To a public animated by blanket negations, anything positive, anything specific, was experienced as a threat.

The demonstrators weren't prepared to declare victory on any terms. That was true of the *indignados* in Spain, and true also, with some local differences, of the crowd in Tahrir Square. It has proved impossible for the multiple revolts of 2011 to move beyond negation and reach an accommodation with reality. In Israel, the group around Daphni Leef refused outright to talk to government negotiators. They remained inflexible in their sectarian virtue. But even those who reached out to the government, like Schmuli and his students' union, repudiated the outcome.

By then, the protests had passed their high-water mark. The last large demonstration was September 3. On October 3, police dismantled the Rothschild Boulevard tent city. Sporadic demonstrations continued into 2012, but with smaller crowds and diminished media attention. Political energy focused on the general elections called by Netanyahu for January 2013. Two prominent protesters—one of them Schmuli—ran on the Labor Party list and won seats in the Knesset. Their transformation from street revolutionaries to conventional politicians was a sign that the Israeli summer of 2011 had yielded up its soul to the Center.

The election results of 2013 lacked any clear connection to the events of 2011. Netanyahu's party, Likud, lost seven seats but remained the most popular. Netanyahu himself kept the prime minister's office. He may have been somewhat weakened by the protests, but, unlike Mubarak and Zapatero, he was not overthrown. The Labor Party gained a few seats, but remained stuck in third place.

Daphni Leef continued to thunder against swinish capitalists and the government that supported them. No longer an ordinary person, she had become a celebrity of sorts. The protests she started had worked out well for her, even if they failed to achieve their goal of social justice and left few marks on the Israeli electorate.

The protests also demonstrated that the powerful current of negation beneath the inscrutable surface of the public required little provocation to break into large-scale political action. The Egyptian public had endured 30 years of Hosni Mubarak. The *indignados* at Puerta del Sol had suffered a loss of future prospects because of the severity of the economic crisis. In Israel, the public's existential challenge to the established order came because Leef had found it unendurable to lengthen her commute.

OCCUPY WALL STREET AND THE BAFFLING POLITICS OF NEGATION

The events of 2011 in Tunisia, Egypt, Spain, and Israel were true mobilizations of the networked public, which fused fractious communities of interest into a single political movement. In each case, the numbers were enormous, the organizers were political amateurs, and the protests they began almost immediately acquired a life of their own. Large segments of the general public gave their blessing to the protesters.

Many of these benchmarks were not met by the various "Occupy" groups that sprang up across the United States in September 2011. The numbers were minuscule—they never remotely approached the 300,000-plus who took to the streets in Israel, a country with one-thirty-ninth of the U.S. population. With such limited participation came the possibility that the episode reflected the will of semi-professional activists and grievance-mongers, rather than a tide of opinion sweeping along a substantial portion of the public. And in many Occupy factions, including the original in New York, this possibility came close to the reality on the ground. As for the American public, it wavered in its opinion of the episode: pluralities tended to support the cause but disapproved of the method.

Despite these differences, I have not hesitated to include the Occupiers as part of the 2011 phase change. Let me offer up three reasons why.

One: I found strong demographic and behavioral affinities between Occupy Wall Street participants and the public that took to the streets in Egypt, Spain, and Israel. They were the same people, in different countries: young, middle class, university educated—and, in the case of OWS, predominantly white. Sectarian ideals propelled them to politics. All repudiated, in principle, the need for leaders, programs, and top-down organizations.

The organizers in New York and many other Occupy sites were, disproportionately, anarchists. To a somewhat lesser extent, that had been the case in Spain as well. Anarchists introduced the mechanisms and principles of decision followed by the Occupiers—the "general assemblies" and the demand for consensus or "direct democracy," for example. These were not ordinary people. They were experienced, if not hardened, veterans of street battles, who rejected capitalism and all its works and despised liberal democracy.[61]

But, again, if anarchist groups had the knack to organize hundreds of protests across the United States, they would have done so before 2011. Most of the participants shared that lack of positive political definition that characterized the protests of 2011—by one count, 60 percent of the OWS people had voted for Barack Obama in 2008 and felt disappointed with the results.[62] Like the tent dwellers of Tel Aviv, they wanted more. It's worth noting that anarchism is by far the most sectarian movement on the left, with an ideological predilection for individualism and self-expression. The difference between a young anarchist and a young disillusioned liberal was not likely to be noticed by either.

Two: To a remarkable extent, the Occupiers lived virtually. They organized on the web so they could occupy a physical space, and they occupied a physical space so they could talk about it online. More completely than the other protesters of 2011, they were creatures of the Fifth Wave, able to extend their reach digitally beyond their small numbers. The "We Are the 99 Percent" campaign on Tumblr, in which ordinary people told their stories of victimization on a single sheet of paper, had a tremendous impact on liberal commentators and the news media in general. Every

Occupy site had an elaborate Facebook page. Every violent act by a cop trying to dislodge a young Occupier was caught on mobile phone video and posted online. City governments, embodying the slow-moving Center, were driven into awkward rituals of attack and retreat, as public opinion swung between irritation over the disruption caused by the protests and anger over the level of force necessary to disband them.

All this bore a striking similarity to the other encounters I have covered in this chapter.

Three: Like their brethren in Spain and Israel, the OWS protesters were energized primarily by the force of their repudiations. They made no demands, but they felt free to accuse. The objects of their loathing—a predatory economic system, a corrupted government, a society ruled by money—united them in a way that common goals did not. They spread the notion that the top 1 percent of Americans tyrannized the bottom 99—and that they, a handful of white, middle-class youngsters, represented the vast American public, the people, in revolt. OWS injected these once-marginal attitudes into the mainstream, where they became fodder for liberal politicians. The romance of condemnation, in my judgment, has become the most conspicuous feature of President Obama's mode of governance. The demonization of millionaires was a rhetorical pillar of the president's successful 2012 campaign.

Among my concerns in writing this book has been the fate of democracy in the indecisive conflict between the public and authority. From this perspective, OWS's numbers may have been small, but the message was consequential. It helped tip American politics at the highest level toward pure negation and distrust, eroding the legitimacy of democratic institutions. For this reason alone the Occupy protests belong with the bigger revolts in my investigation of phase change.

* * *

That said, the number of odd occurrences surrounding OWS seemed to defy the laws of probability—although, when all was said and done, that's what I would guess was at work. From early 2011, a number of attempts had been made to disrupt Wall Street for the obvious symbolic reasons. These attracted sparse attendance and zero media attention. The first notable protest against the headquarters of American capitalism was launched by an online Canadian anti-consumerist magazine, *Adbusters*, which in June registered the #occupywallstreet hashtag, and, on its blog, posted the following proposal: "Are you ready for a Tahrir moment? On September 17, we want to see 20,000 people flood into lower Manhattan, set up tents, kitchens, peaceful barricades and occupy Wall Street for a few months." [63]

The few hundred demonstrators who showed up on that date were chased out of public spaces by the police, until they found refuge in Zuccotti Park, where, in a strange muddle of ideals, they were protected by the sanctity of private property. When the media ignored the initial occupation, the organizers forgot their anti-consumerism and turned to a commercial public relations firm, Workhorse Publicity, for help with spreading the word of their revolution. The company did so well that it actually won a professional award for its efforts. [64]

Beyond such quirks, the story of the OWS movement can be told in few words. From September 17 until November 15, the Zuccotti Park encampment waxed and waned with the flow of events. Larger crowds came invariably after attempts by police to arrest or disperse protesters. Mobile phone video of a New York cop pepper-spraying a group of young women, for example, went viral and aroused much indignation. Following the arrest of 400 Occupiers for disrupting traffic on the Brooklyn Bridge, some 15,000 protesters marched on October 5 from Foley Square to the park. Shortly after, occupations began to spread across the U.S.—to over 600 sites, according to one source. Numbers for each site remained small, but media attention of the movement grew large, and, particularly in New York, was not unsympathetic. Labor unions, including the AFL-CIO, offered their support, though union members mostly stayed away. As in Tel Aviv, this was not a working-class revolt. Nor did OWS manage to attract African American or Hispanic activists in any numbers.

Every Occupy site embraced nonviolence, but some were more nonviolent than others. In Oakland, protesters fought pitched battles against police, with each side accusing the other of brutality. Occupy Oakland's "General Strike and Anti-Capitalist March" on November 2 managed to close the Port of Oakland—probably the only significant economic impact of the protests.

Sanitation was always a problem, and was frequently cited by the authorities as a pretext for clearing out the encampments. Crime became a concern with the passage of time, as the homeless and other distinctly non-middle-class elements drifted into the sites. On November 15, giving unsanitary conditions as a reason, New York police swept the protesters out of Zuccotti Park. Within days, city governments had done the same in every Occupy site around the country. Sporadic protests and attempts to re-occupy continued for months, but the numbers involved dwindled into insignificance, and public opinion, insofar as it cared about the movement, had turned negative. Mostly, though, the public and the media had stopped paying attention.

The rigidly sectarian mindset of OWS proved more seductive to American political life than the actual protests. In calling for the first occupation, *Adbusters* had presented a single demand: a presidential commission "tasked with ending the influence of money" over politics. This was immediately forgotten. As in Israel, media commentators and intellectuals rushed in with suggested schemes for the protesters to embrace. They were ignored. The Occupiers refused to make demands as a matter of principle. They felt it was beneath them to petition an illegitimate government. Here is a statement from the discussions in the "demands committee" of the Zuccotti Park general assembly:

> *The movement doesn't need to make demands, because the movement is an assertive process. This movement has the power to affect change. It does not need to ask for it. The OWS does not make demands. We will simply assert our own power to achieve what we desire. The more of us gather to the cause, the more power we have. Make no demands for others to solve these problems. Assert yourself.* [65]

We have heard this sentiment before, the hope—the expectation—that hierarchy would be decontaminated by making it subservient to the sect. "From now on, the young people will shape the government's vision," Itzik Shmuli had said. The government was not to be overthrown. The government was to become an instrument of sectarian virtue. Zuccotti Park would command Washington and achieve what it desired. As a general proposition, this was disconnected from the realities of American politics. But on any given issue, not so much: OWS could mobilize public opinion, substantially enough, it may have been, to inflict a fatal wound on the target of its repudiation.

What the Occupiers desired to achieve was what all the rebels and street insurgents of 2011 desired: to negate a host of historical conditions, institutions, and relations whose persistence had driven them to revolt. They wanted history to abolish history, hierarchy to eliminate hierarchy, government to bring down the temple of authority.

The list of things OWS stood against was long and deep. The "Declaration of the Occupation of New York," adopted on September 29 and one of the few formal statements of the movement, consisted of a crazy quilt of complaints against authority, ending with a bland call to "create a process to address the problems we face."

> We come to you at a time when corporations, which place profit over people, self-interest over justice, and oppression over equality, run our governments. We have peaceably assembled here, as is our right, to let these facts be known.
>
> They have taken our houses through an illegal foreclosure process . . .
>
> They have taken bailouts from taxpayers with impunity . . .
>
> They have perpetuated gender inequality and discrimination . . .
>
> They have poisoned the food supply . . .
>
> They have continuously sought to end the rights of workers . . .
>
> They have held students hostage with tens of thousands of dollars of debt on education . . .
>
> They have consistently outsourced labor . . .
>
> [. . .] They have sold our privacy as a commodity.
>
> They have used the military and police force to prevent freedom of the press.
>
> [. . .] They have perpetuated colonialism . . .
>
> They have participated in the torture and murder of innocent civilians overseas.[66]

The disproportion between such systematic injustices and the proposed actions—the "process" I cited above, a cursory exhortation to "assert your power"—reflects a form of logic that should be familiar to us by now.

Revolution, in 2011, meant denunciation. Actual change was left for someone else.

Manuel Castells, a sympathetic observer, perused the online records of the Occupy sites' general assemblies, and compiled a roster of changes the participants expected to work on the world. It made exhausting reading.

> *...controlling financial speculation, particularly high frequency trading; auditing the Federal Reserve; addressing the housing crisis; regulating overdraft fees; controlling currency manipulation; opposing the outsourcing of jobs; defending collective bargaining and union rights; reducing income inequality; reforming tax law; reforming political campaign finance; reversing the Supreme Court's decision allowing unlimited campaign contributions from corporations; banning bailouts of companies; controlling the military-industrial complex; improving the care of veterans; limiting terms for elected politicians; defending freedom on the [I]nternet; assuring privacy on the [I]nternet and in the media; combating economic exploitation; reforming the prison system; reforming health care; combating racism, sexism, and xenophobia; improving student loans; opposing the Keystone pipeline and other environmentally predatory projects; enacting policies against global warming; fining and controlling BP and similar oil spillers; enforcing animal rights; supporting alternative energy sources; critiquing personal leadership and vertical authority, beginning with a new democratic culture in the camps; and watching out for cooptation in the political system...*[67]

The action words used for these improvements of the status quo connoted negation and elimination: "reform," "control," "reverse," "limit," "combat," "fine," "critique." Added up, they conveyed a feeling of revulsion with the established order of American politics. The Occupiers didn't deal in alternatives, but they wished to sweep away most of the standing political and social arrangements propping up their world.

It is instructive to consider the protesters from the perspective of the elites whose legitimacy they denied. A vast psychological distance distorted that perspective. Politicians at the top of steep hierarchies heard the shouts and slogans from the street as a confused babble. Because they were guardians of order, they felt compelled to offer some response to the disorder outside their doors. Their dilemma was that any response placed the government eyeball to eyeball with the insurgents, immensely raising the stature of the latter.

Those who wielded power peered at the rebellions of 2011 through the thick lenses of their institutional assumptions. If the rebels wanted to abolish history, the political elites were imprisoned by it, and behaved, in each case, according to the logic of their time and place. Government actions thus appeared strangely tactical, local, disconnected from ideology.

Mubarak had believed that if he denied the existence of the demonstrations, they would cease to exist. While pitched battles bloodied the streets of Cairo, state-owned Egyptian TV kept showing cheerful crowds in shopping malls. Unperceived by the aging dictator, however, the day of *Homo informaticus* had arrived: his regime no longer had the power to dictate reality. By the time Mubarak realized he had to respond directly to the protests, it was too late.

Zapatero, a socialist, felt the allure of revolt and repudiation but found himself the target of both. Ideologically, he came from an egalitarian tradition. In reality, he was president of Spain, with all the pomp and distance—and hostility from a rebellious public—his position entailed. Zapatero and his party never resolved this fundamental dilemma.

Netanyahu, the free marketeer, responded by swallowing his principles and addressing the more concrete complaints coming out of Rothschild Boulevard. His government moved with unusual tactical speed, and may well have survived for this reason.

In the U.S., the Occupy movement never remotely threatened the federal government. City governments, almost all of them run by liberal Democratic politicians, struggled to assume the proper posture toward local occupations. Even New York Mayor Michael Bloomberg, a billionaire and "one percenter" if ever there was one, relied on technicalities first to tolerate then to shut down Zuccotti Park. Bloomberg kept reporters away from the site while it was being cleared—again offering vague technical reasons for doing so.

On occasion, President Obama was asked by the media for his opinion of the Occupy groups. He invariably responded with sympathy for the protesters, whose grievances he identified with the economic problems that had won him the presidency in 2008. Here is a fairly typical statement from the president: "I think it [the Occupy movement] expresses the frustrations the American people feel, that we had the biggest financial crisis since the Great Depression, huge collateral damage all throughout the country...and yet you're still seeing some of the same folks who acted irresponsibly trying to fight efforts to crack down on the abusive practices that got us into this in the first place."[68] To underline the message, the White House, on October 16, proclaimed that President Obama was "working for the interests of the 99 percent."[69]

It may seem puzzling for a sitting president to embrace a movement that repudiated the legitimacy of government because it was run by corporations. The president's motives may have included some element of political calculation. Many of the young protesters had been Obama campaign activists in 2008.

But I would venture that President Obama was as sincere in his sympathy for OWS as anyone in politics is allowed to be. I also think that the movement's negations were precisely what appealed to the president. They were in harmony with his intuitive assessment of the world, his ideas about how to navigate events without surrendering his virtue. OWS didn't influence the president. The arrow of causation moved the other way. President Obama anticipated many of the movement's rhetorical features during his 2008 electoral campaign, which was one reason so many of the 2011 Occupiers participated in it.

President Obama's place in the shadowy war of the worlds has been unique and significant, but it belongs to a larger topic—the fate of democratic government—which I will consider in a later chapter. Here I note only that OWS offered the president the opportunity to break out of an institutional perspective he had never found congenial. Like Zapatero, Obama likely viewed himself as both rebel and president, but unlike Zapatero he did not feel attached, in either capacity, to any particular structures.

President Obama represented the sectarian temper in power. The protests allowed him to frame a critique of the country's ruling institutions, and to voice, without equivocation, his own doubts about their legitimacy.

LONDON IN AUGUST, OR THE RECURRING QUESTION OF NIHILISM

At 6:15 p.m. on Thursday, August 4, 2011, Mark Duggan was shot dead in a confrontation with police in the London neighborhood of Tottenham. Because of the impenetrable bureaucracy surrounding police shootings in

Britain, the details of this episode remain uncertain to this day. Duggan, 29, was apparently armed, and was said to be involved in criminal activity.

In the afternoon of Saturday, August 6, a crowd of around 120 protesters gathered in front of the Tottenham police station. A government-commissioned report on the London riots said the group was composed of Duggan's "family and supporters," but I wonder whether the dead man's personal connections really stretched that far. Some may have been drawn by the joys of accusation. Most shared an honest loathing of the police. The protest was initially peaceful, but by 8:30 p.m. serious disorders had broken out, with police cars being attacked and set on fire.

So began four days of riots and looting, which blighted dozens of neighborhoods in London and spread to other British cities. In the bloodshed and destruction, the Duggan shooting was soon forgotten. It had been the spark, but it was not a cause in any sense of the word. Before the end, five people had died, dozens had been hospitalized and left homeless, and half a billion pounds' worth of damage had been inflicted.

There were no Facebook invitations to the London riots, as there had been to Tahrir Square and Puerta del Sol. But there was active use by the participants of BlackBerry Messaging Service, or BMS, a private texting channel favored by the young in the affected communities. *The Economist* christened the disturbances "The BlackBerry Riots."[70] The global information sphere was at work in London in August 2011.

Also unlike the other events of 2011, criminal behavior was the salient feature of the riots. Many of those arrested had experienced previous brushes with the law, and one in four had committed more than 10 past offenses.[71] But the episode was not, as some imagined, a crime wave on fast-forward. It was a breakdown in the authority of the law and its enforcers: not at all the same thing. In a sense, the role of criminals in London paralleled that of the anarchists in Zuccotti Park. They demonstrated by their actions a new set of rules of the game, in which all could play.

Identifying the "causes" of the riots became a growth industry for months after. Two cosmic narratives eventually crystallized and confronted one another. The first told a story of social oppression and deprivation: it blamed the riots on government cutbacks and the ensuing loss of services, and on unemployment, inequality, racism. The second narrative condemned the moral collapse of the British: the rioters, on this account, had been the product of an entitlement culture, which tolerated misbehavior while demanding nothing in the way of responsibility or self-restraint.

The 2011 London riots were, in truth, a massively complex set of human interactions. I have no idea how to go about proving that a single reason or a few were responsible for the event. The search for such cosmic causes, I suspect, has been driven more by political and ideological enthusiasm than by analytic curiosity.

I don't have to explain the riots, so I won't. What I will do is frame the event in the context of the global conflict between the public and authority. I will also show that it adds to the evidence of a phase change in 2011: that is, of a great strategic reversal favoring the public, which now commanded the heights of information and communication.

None of this appears especially challenging.

* * *

A public is a public even when engaged in criminal behavior. Around 15,000 people participated in the riots across Britain. They shared an interest in a particular affair: stealing and smashing things with impunity. To achieve this objective required the effective nullification of established authority—the government, protectors of property, the hated police. The rioters accomplished this early on in the game. Images disseminated by the news media and on the web showed young people breaking into stores and looting while the police stood by, looking bewildered. At the onset of the riots, the authorities in Britain were as helpless and slow to respond as the U.S. government had been on 9/11.

Participants in the riots compounded their advantage in numbers with tactical command of communications. They rampaged in the less affluent areas of London, where, presumably, they lived, but they also used BMS to organize assaults on the cathedrals of consumption in the city's shopping district.

> *Everyone from all sides of London meet up at the heart of London (central) OXFORD CIRCUS!! Bare SHOPS are gonna get smashed up so come get some (free stuff!!!) fuck the feds we will send them back with OUR riot! >:O . . .*[72]

Oxford Circus, in fact, became the location of a disturbance.

The tactical advantage BMS provided to the rioters became a strategic nightmare for the police, which could eavesdrop on the messages but were quickly overwhelmed by the sheer volume of available information. London's Metropolitan Police Service report on the riots makes interesting reading on the subject of social media.

> *The events of August demonstrated how social media is now widely used as a planning and communication medium by people intent on causing disruption.*

> *[…] The MPS could not comprehensively monitor social media in real-time and was therefore not in a position to be moving ahead of events.*

> *Specifically, there was insufficient resilience in both trained staff and technology, to review, capture, and download the vast volume of open source data which needed to be processed.*[73]

The words could have been written by a mandarin in the ruling hierarchies of Tunisia, Egypt, Spain, or Israel. They seethed with repressed outrage. That someone "intent on causing disruption" should out-communicate and outsmart the authorities was a violation of the natural order: a trampling of the sanctities. The information tsunami had swept away the power of the British government and the London police.

The perpetrators belonged to the same age group as the political rebels of 2011. They were not, however, a golden youth, though their mastery of BMS showed they could afford the same type of electronic devices. Hatred of the police was one of the shared points of reference that fused the rabble in the street into a true public. The police stood for a structure of authority they wished would vanish from the earth. Otherwise, they were empty of politics or ideology. When asked why they looted, the most frequent response was: because they could. One participant flipped the question around: "Why are you going to waste the opportunity to get new stuff?"[74]

Violence and criminality were not indiscriminate. They focused on specific objects: the police, stores specializing in digital products. By the magic of YouTube, you can still witness the young looters of 2011 walking out of shattered London shops with plasma screen TVs and armloads of video games. They wanted the prestigious gadgets and entertainment which attended great affluence. But like rebels in other democratic coun-tries, they effected a strange mental separation between the life they wished for and the structures that made that life possible. This indirect method of self-destruction again raises the question of nihilism, about which I'll have more to say momentarily.

The authorities in Britain, as should be clear by now, not only failed in their responsibilities during the 2011 riots but failed out in the open, where all could see. The head of the government, home secretary, mayor of London, and leaders of opposition parties all were vacationing abroad, and had to scramble back to the country. Official statements of reassur-ance and control seemed disconnected from the images pouring out of TV screens and laptops. The police, detested by the rioters, now earned the hostility of property owners. Self-protection civilian groups formed spontaneously, which the media, somewhat pejoratively, labeled "vigilan-tes," but which could be said to represent sensible behavior in a situation bordering on the state of nature. In multiple places, during those four days of August, the legitimate functions of government lost their grip.

In the shocked aftermath of the riots, the British government consid-ered the matter of its disadvantage in information and communication. The explanations it came up with would have made Hosni Mubarak laugh out loud. Control of image and perception—of demonstration effects—was paramount, as had typically been the case with the hierarchies of the Center in 2011. The government-appointed panel took note that

> *The Home Affairs Select Committee has said that the single most*
> *important reason for the spread of the disorder was the perception,*
> *relayed by television as well as social media, that in some areas the*
> *police had lost control of the streets.*[75]

But loss of control wasn't a perception. It was the reality on the ground. So here was the implicit idea: if television portrayed a different re-ality, real reality would cease to exist. The panel recommended that "broadcast media" should "continue to work" to improve its accuracy and clarity, and maintain the "highest journalistic standards." While this fell short of suggesting that happy Britons in shopping malls be televised during public disorders, the spirit of the thing was the same.

The government's take on social media was also predictable. The member of Parliament for Tottenham proposed that the BlackBerry

Messaging Service be shut down. Prime Minister David Cameron agreed that rightful authority needed to impose limits on the public's capacity to express itself digitally. "When people are using social media for violence," he said, "we need to stop them."[76] He didn't say how, and nothing much came from the brave talk. The mindset, however, was revealing. Belief that political power could switch off the information sphere was shown to be more than an aging dictator's hallucination. It was a persistent delusion of the Center.

The British riots differed from the other events of 2011, though not in the obvious way. The difference lay less in the criminality than in the consistency between the public's views and desires and its actions. The young disturbers of the peace in Tottenham and Oxford Circus loathed authority and behaved accordingly. Properly considered, their actions were also in harmony with the worldview of the political protesters—more so, in fact, than the actions of the protesters had been. Disorders turned violent only in Britain because the rioters alone, in their actions, pushed the negations of 2011 to their logical conclusion.

I can illustrate what I mean with a thought experiment. It goes like this:

Assume that the Occupiers' long roster of negations accurately described social and political reality in liberal democracies. Elected government isn't accountable to the people, but is, in effect, a dictatorship of the corporations. While banks and businesses exploit workers and poison nature, the government they control represses freedom of expression, and murders and tortures innocents overseas. The rules of the democratic game are a trick, a ruse to conceal the oppression of women by men, of people of color by whites, of the bottom 99 by the top 1 percent.

If that truly described life under capitalistic representative democracy, what would be a rational response?

The political rebels of 2011 waffled on the question. Most were the children of the comfortable middle class, too interested in the drama of the moment to accept the implications of their own rhetoric. So they occupied a public space and they protested against the status quo, hoping that some external force—presumably, the government they so despised—would bring about change.

The British rioters acted as if the government, the police, and the law lacked legitimacy. I freely grant that they didn't think this through. They didn't write manifestos or shout clever political slogans. But neither was theirs a silent scream: they stole, and burned, and sometimes killed, because they could. They embodied the change the political protesters kept calling for. While the latter rejected the political and economic system under which they lived, the rioters acted out the consequences.

The rioters existed in a world of effects without causes. However dimly, they envisioned a desirable mode of living—one weighed down with mobile phones, video games, plasma TVs—but they vandalized the processes that made that life possible. They behaved as if desirable things were part of the natural order, like the grass under their feet. Detestable systems of authority only stood in the way.

I compared the British government's stumbling response to the riots with that of the Mubarak regime in a parallel circumstance. At a certain point, the mandates of Center and hierarchy appear to matter more than democracy or authoritarianism: that was the complaint of the protesters in democratic countries. But, equally, there is a point at which negation and repudiation by the public must pose the question of nihilism. The criminal public in Britain most closely resembled the political public elsewhere in its blindness to that boundary.

WHAT GUY FAWKES'S MASK CAN TEACH US ABOUT THE TURMOIL IN 2011

The 2011 protesters connected with political violence only in a Hollywood version, through their fantasy lives. At virtually every protest described in this book, you found people wearing the Guy Fawkes mask popularized by the 2006 movie *V for Vendetta*. This was unique for would-be revolutionaries. I can't imagine Lenin or Mao or Castro allowing their comrades to impersonate a fictional character.

Fascination with a revenge melodrama offered a hint about how the young transgressors of 2011 viewed themselves—and what they imagined they were doing.

Guy Fawkes was executed in 1606 for his part in the Gunpowder Plot to blow up Parliament. The mask is traditionally worn on Guy Fawkes Night, which celebrates with bonfires the discovery of the plot. Hollywood turned this story on its head. The film depicted a future Britain ruled by a

Figure 16: "V" at Zuccotti Park.[77] *Tony Savino/Getty Images*

fanatically religious authoritarian government, whose persecutions sounded like a catalogue of victims from Occupy Wall Street: "Immigrants, Muslims, homosexuals, terrorists, disease-ridden degenerates...." "V," a mysterious figure in a Fawkes mask, perpetrates an orgy of violence to bring down the government. The movie ends with an immense crowd in V masks overwhelming the security forces, while the Parliament building and Big Ben explode musically in the background.

In his disgust with his place and time, V sometimes sounded like an *indignado*. "The truth is, there is something terribly wrong with this country," he brooded. But mostly he was an action hero who, in the 132 minutes of the film, personally slaughtered a significant portion of the ruling class. The lust for righteous mayhem, in good movie fashion, was untroubled by doubt.

While this was hardly the political model in 2011, there can be no denying the influence of *V for Vendetta* on the participants. Wael Ghonim turned to the Guy Fawkes mask to underline his anonymity as administrator of the "We Are All Khaled Said" Facebook page:

> *In 2006 I had seen the movie **V for Vendetta** and fallen in love with the idea of the mysterious warrior fighting against evil. I was still influenced by this idea when I created the Facebook page: the*

notion of an anonymous sentinel who tries to wake up the people around him and spur them to revolt against the government's injustice. For my article "Who Are You, Mr. Admin?" I used the distinctive mask worn by the movie's protagonist as the main image.[78]

"I identified with V's desire for change," explained the mild-mannered Ghonim, "although in no way did I approve of his violent means." To anyone who has watched the film, this was an extraordinary statement.

The mask was originally introduced to protest politics by the hacker group "Anonymous," which claimed for itself prodigious powers not unlike those of the protagonist in *V for Vendetta*. Anonymous can only be described as a mutant offspring of the Fifth Wave, spawned from the most nihilistic elements of the web, and it has played an uncertain part in the struggle between the public and authority. Its members sometimes talked like revolutionaries but often behaved like the London rioters, stealing data and vandalizing sites just because they could. None of them, when finally identified, turned out to be engaged in radical politics of any kind. They had meant it when they boasted, "We do it for the lulz."[79]

Anonymous' endorsement of the Occupy Wall Street movement generated a great deal of buzz. In a series of bombastic YouTube videos featuring the mask, the hackers made many threats—for example, to "flood into lower Manhattan" with their supporters, declare "war on the NYPD," and "erase" the New York Stock Exchange using their hacking prowess. This proved to be more drama than reality. One video disseminated the name and personal data of the cop who had pepper-sprayed protesters. Denial-of-service attacks slowed down the NYSE, and pushed it offline for a few minutes. Other than that, the one lasting contribution of the hacker community to the turmoil of 2011 was to reconnect it with the V mask.[80]

I don't want to make too much of this. Like dueling naming conventions, the infatuation with *V for Vendetta* was a symptom, not a cause, of the larger conflict. It revealed an emotional orientation among the protesters: they were self-dramatizers to an extreme degree. The disconnection between their words and their actions, between their understanding of effects and their indifference to causes, can be explained by this trait.

Figure 17: Self-dramatizing with Anonymous. *Meme available widely online.*

As with V, their self-dramatizing was manifested in gestures of negation—of repudiation, accusation, destruction, erasing history and leaving the future blank. The movie ended with the demolition of the old regime. The rest would take care of itself. "With enough people, blowing up a building can change the world," V had proclaimed. But that was true only in fiction.

Wael Ghonim got the chance to play the role of V almost to perfection. As an anonymous political force, he tormented the Mubarak regime, assembled its opponents, and helped engineer its overthrow. At the moment of victory, however, more than negation was needed. The movie had ended, but the drama in Egypt moved on. Ghonim, the real-life V, lacked a script to follow once the oppositional gesture lost its potency.

Because political conditions were much less dangerous in democratic countries, self-dramatization there seemed proportionately more extravagant.

Political rebels in Europe, Israel, and the U.S. felt betrayed by the failure of the structures of authority, particularly the government and the economic elites. The feeling wasn't entirely unreasonable. The masters and regulators of finance had placed large foolish bets, but when the bottom fell out in 2008 it was the public, not them, who paid the losses. There was ample room for criticism, even for cynicism.

In the end, however, a term like "failure" can only be applied relative to some expectation—and we have seen that the rebels' expectations of modern government were at once fantastical in their scope and vaporous in definition. They ascribed magical or, I venture to say, divine qualities to cumbersome, all-too-human bureaucracies. They believed government could work miracles: it could give meaning to their personal lives. This faith was most evident in Israel, a country that quickly overcame the effects of the crisis. Protesters there were affluent and employed, but expected the government to deliver personal fulfillment within a context of social justice. What that meant was never explained. Most of the American Occupiers also held down jobs. Conversely, those nearest to poverty never participated in any of the 2011 street revolts.

Even in the rhetoric of the protests, the connection to the economic crisis was, at best, indirect. Manuel Castells had it right when he wrote that "the movement" was about "everything and nothing at the same time."[81] 2011 never fixated on 2008: the impulse was to abolish history entirely, and open up a future purified of cause and effect.

In their eagerness to play a part in some world-historical drama, the rebels often gave the impression that they were searching for causes. They disdained specifics—ideology, policy—but excelled at lengthy menus of accusations. Stéphane Hessel, French prophet of outrage, understood this process of self-aggravation.

> It is true, the reasons to get angry may seem less clear today, and the world may seem more complex. Who is in charge; who are the decision makers? It's not always easy to discern. We're not dealing with a small elite anymore, whose actions we can clearly identify. We are dealing with a vast, interdependent world that is interconnected in unprecedented ways. But there are unbearable things all around us. You have to look for them; search carefully.[82]

A life spent in search of unbearable things will be necessarily destructive of the legitimacy of most standing institutions and social arrangements, including those which created and sustained the destroyers.

Unlike the fictional character V, the actual protesters of 2011 were unable to wipe clean the slate of power and society. Mubarak fell, the Spanish socialists were voted to near extinction, Netanyahu compromised, Obama borrowed the slogans of OWS—but the consequences,

That was the most profound consequence of 2011: sowing the seeds of distrust in the democratic process. You can condemn *politicians* only for so long before you must reject the legitimacy of the system that produced them. The protests of 2011 openly took that step, and a considerable segment of the electorate applauded. Like money and marriage, legitimacy exists *objectively* because vast numbers of the public agree, *subjectively*, that it does exist. If enough people change their minds, the authorizing magic is lost. The process is slow and invisible to analysts, but, as I have noted, the tipping point comes suddenly—a matter of weeks for the Ben Ali and Mubarak regimes. How far down this road existing liberal democracies have proceeded is a matter of guesswork. We still have time to discover that the street revolts of 2011, in V's words, did "change the world," and not in a good way.

three years down the road, nowhere matched the glittering expectations of participants. The old systems still stood. The hierarchies of the industrial age, with their top-down myopia, stumbled on. The behavior of these structures obeys an inner logic: despite Itzik Shmuli's utopian proclamation, government never became a servant to the forces of revolt.

But the hypothesis I presented in this chapter was not that the public in 2011 had the interest or the capacity to replace current institutions of authority. It had neither. Sectarian to the core, the public would have felt corrupted by the *thought* of assuming the functions of the Center. The phase change concerned, at the most obvious level, a new capacity to mobilize large numbers of the public and so to command the attention of all political players, from government leaders to the media to ordinary voters. This was a new thing under the sun, and it became possible only in the altered landscape of the Fifth Wave. Digital platforms allowed even rioters who wished to loot London stores to organize and act more intelligently, for their purposes, than the authorities.

The consequence wasn't revolution but the threat of perpetual turbulence. The authorities felt, and still feel, their *in*capacity keenly. Governments are aware that the public could swarm into the political arena at any moment, organizing at the speed of light, hurling anathemas of repudiation. Political elites in democratic countries have become thoroughly demoralized. Whether this was deserved or not is a separate question, to be examined in the next two chapters. But the crisis of confidence among established politicians has precluded the possibility of bold action, of democratic reform.

The phase change began in 2011, but the end is not in sight. In the Italian general elections of February 2013, a new party, the Five Star Movement, won 25 percent of the vote for the lower house of parliament and became the second-largest entity there. The party was the creation of a comedian-blogger who called himself Beppe Grillo, after the Jiminy Cricket character in *Pinocchio*. In every feature other than its willingness to stand for elections, Five Star reproduced perfectly the confused ideals and negations of the 2011 protests. Despite receiving more than eight million votes, it lacked a coherent program. The single unifying principle was a deep loathing of the Italian political establishment. The rise of Beppe Grillo had nothing to do with reform or radical change, but meant the humiliation and demoralization of the established order.

A
CRISIS
OF
AUTHORITY

The street protests of 2011, while ostensibly political, were part of a global assault on the guardians of authority across every domain of human activity. The protesters stood in the same relation to government that bloggers and social media did to newspapers, YouTube to television, Napster to the recording industry, massive online courses to universities, Amazon to shopping malls, the open-science movement to the scientific establishment. From the commanding heights of the information sphere, the public sought in each case to break a monopoly held by an accredited elite.

Authority, as I use the term, flows from legitimacy, derived from monopoly. To some indeterminate degree, the public must trust and heed authority, or it is no authority at all. An important social function of authority is to deliver certainty in an uncertain world. It explains reality in the context of the shared story of the group. For this it must rely on persuasion rather than compulsion, since naked force is a destroyer of trust and faith. The need to persuade in turn explains the institutional propensity for visible symbols of authority—the patrician's toga, the doctor's white frock, the financier's Armani suit. Authority being an intangible quality, those who wield it wish to be recognized for what they are.

And they have been, historically, the only actors in the social drama, with the public relegated to the audience, able only to weep or applaud. Authority is an expansion of author, which originally meant something like "initiator"—the active human element in an otherwise inert population.

Current structures of authority are a legacy of the industrial age. The public, when it needs answers, turns to institutions rather than to charismatic individuals. These institutions have been subjected to a Taylorist process of rationalization: they are, without exception, top-down, specialized, professionalized, prone to pseudoscientific rituals and jargon. To enter such a precinct of authority requires a long and costly accreditation process—years of academic education and apprenticeship. Many are called, few are chosen. The elect believe themselves to be unquestioned masters of their special domain—and so they were for many years. From the middle of the 19th to the end of the 20th century, the public lacked the means to question, much less contradict, authoritative judgments derived from monopolies of information.

Most people in authority today came to their positions in that happy time. On moral as well as intellectual grounds, they dismiss the outsider out of hand. Their reflexive loathing of the amateur trespasser inspired Hoder's 19½-year sentence and the mutual annihilation lawsuits against Shawn Fanning and Napster.

Of course, the ferocity of this response can be explained in part by a fear of losing access to power and money. Authority has been closely associated with both—it's a natural connection. Power needs accurate intelligence on which to act. Monopoly has always been a position from which to exploit the market. If I stop thinking in generalities and imagine a concrete person in authority, I'll conjure up a policeman, a politician, a banker.

The links between authority on one side and power and money on the other are dense and often invisible to the public. But each exerts a discrete influence on social relations, and of the three I believe authority to be easily the most consequential.

Even in purely practical terms, persuasion has always trumped compulsion or bribery. The authorizing magic of legitimacy can channel social behavior more deeply and permanently than the policeman's club or the millionaire's check. These propositions should be considered truisms, but they are not. Not by the public, which, as we have seen, assumes that every failure of authority must be explained by a collusion of money with power. And not by many analysts, who embrace some version of the old Marxist concept of "false consciousness"—the idea that the public can be persuaded to heed authority against its own best interests.

False consciousness can be invoked in a world in which the laws of history, and thus the shape of future events, are perfectly understood. Only then, with the tree of causation lucidly in mind, are we allowed to speak of the relation between a sane conscious decision and reality as "true" or "false." But that is not the world we live in. That is not the human condition. Between every decision and its consequences rises an impenetrable veil of uncertainty. The present can only guess at the future—and the track record, as we'll soon see, isn't good. Even among experts, the track record is terrible. The reason isn't false consciousness but the stupendous complexity of human events, which renders prediction impossible.

When asked about the impact of the French Revolution, Zhou Enlai was supposed to have responded: "It is too soon to say." In that one instance, if true, Zhou spoke as an honest political analyst rather than a revolutionary prophet.

The crisis of authority hollowing out existing institutions didn't arise because these institutions prostituted themselves to power or money. That was an explanation after the fact—one that happened to be believed by much of the public and many experts. The fact that needed to be explained, however, was failure: the painfully visible gap between the institutions' claims of competence and their actual performance. The gap, I maintain, was a function of the limits of human knowledge. It had always been there. What changed was the public's awareness of it.

In the industrial age, the pratfalls of authority had been managed discreetly, camouflaged by the mystique of the expert at the top of his game. Today failure happens out in the open, in public, where everyone can see. With the arrival of the global information sphere, each failure is captured, reproduced, multiplied, amplified, and made to stand for authority as a whole. Crisis has followed logically from the destruction of the persuasive power—the legitimacy and credibility—possessed by established institutions.

The focus of this book has been on politics, because I am personally concerned about the future of democracy, but also because I was an analyst of political events for most of my life. That was my own special domain. But I could just as well have made the precarious future of scientific institutions or the universities the overarching theme of my book. The battleground is everywhere. The assault on authority has expanded to virtually every point in the social landscape where an established hierarchy confronts a public in command of the new platforms of communication.

My intent in this chapter is to illustrate some aspects of this broader conflict, and to reflect on the consequences. A few domains of authority— science, the financial establishment, business—have been made to stand for the rest. Many other institutions could have been slotted for the same role in a similar tragicomedy of loss and confusion. Government was secondary here, but never wholly absent from the picture. It has funded science to the tune of billions and regulated banking and businesses to uncertain effect. Power and money can never be wholly dispensed with—a source of satisfaction to conspiracy theorists.

The truly interesting question, on the other hand, is how to explain the crisis of authority and the erratic behavior of the institutions, if there were no conspiracies to account for them.

IF SCIENCE IS THE MODERN DEITY, THEN THE PUBLIC IS ON THE VERGE OF DEICIDE

The epochal moment for the prestige of modern science among the public came on November 6, 1919, when the Royal Society, meeting in Piccadilly, London, announced the findings of Arthur Eddington's expedition to the island of Principe, and the city of Sobral in northern Brazil. At stake was the very shape of the universe.

Eddington, head of the Cambridge Observatory, had measured the gravitational curvature of light during the solar eclipse of May 29. The Newtonian universe, with its notions of absolute space, predicted a curvature of 0.87 arc seconds. Albert Einstein's general theory of relativity, however, had done away with absolute space. It posited a self-folding universe, finite yet limitless, and predicted a gravitational curvature roughly double that of the old model. "Stars ought to appear to be displaced outwards from the sun by 1.7 seconds of arc," Einstein had written in 1916.[83]

The illustrious scientists gathered in Piccadilly knew they were witnesses to history. Eddington's measurements placed the curvature of light at slightly over 1.7 arc seconds. Sir Frank Dyson, Astronomer Royal, underscored the significance of the findings: "There can be little doubt that they confirm Einstein's prediction." With those words, the universe assumed a new form.

A media frenzy followed. "REVOLUTION IN SCIENCE," headlined the *Times* of London. "NEWTONIAN IDEAS OVERTHROWN." Einstein's theory, the paper enthused, will "require a new philosophy of the universe, a philosophy that will sweep away all that has hitherto been accepted." Not to be outdone, the *New York Times* called the confirmation of Einstein's prediction "one of the greatest—perhaps the greatest—of achievements in the history of human thought." Its headline the following day read, "LIGHTS ALL ASKEW IN THE HEAVENS."

This reaction could only be understood in a historical context. Since the 18th century, when intellectuals like Voltaire felt obliged to dabble in chemical experiments, science had been considered the most rigorous

Figure 18: Albert Einstein (1920).[84]

domain of human knowledge. To be scientific meant to speak with great authority. Frederick Winslow Taylor, we have seen, labeled his system "scientific management." A few decades earlier, Marx had called his political ideals "scientific socialism," to differentiate them from utopian schemes.

In general, the prestige of the scientist derived from the belief that he journeyed to realms of mystery and brought back material benefits for the human race. But certain conditions particular to the event helped amplify the resonance of Einstein's achievement.

It was the first major scientific breakthrough in the age of mass media—and it occurred in a field that was impenetrable to all but a handful of brilliant specialists. When told that people believed only three scientists in the world could understand general relativity, Eddington grew quiet. "I'm just wondering who the third might be," he explained. The public was told by the news media that the structure of the universe had been changed in incomprehensible ways by men of superhuman intellect. Scientists were presented in the guise of Platonic guardians: as a class above and apart.

The episode took place in the immediate, and bitter, aftermath of World War I, yet transcended the petty rivalries of nationalism. A British-sponsored expedition had proven a German theorist right, at the expense of an English genius. The old idea that practitioners of science were disinterested pursuers of truth seemed validated.

This was strongly reinforced by Einstein's public image. He became the first scientist media star, and he labored with care to fit into a stereotype once applied to the Christian saint and the philosopher of classical times: a person so devoted to truth and wisdom that he left every worldly desire far behind. With his sad eyes, big mustache, and crazy hair, Einstein embodied science for two generations of the public, projecting to the world a rumpled indifference to the normal human passion for wealth, power, and self-interest.

I find it instructive to compare that moment in November 1919 with our own time. Then, scientists spoke with unquestioned authority. The institutions to which they belonged—Britain's Royal Society, the Prussian Academy of Sciences—served as guarantors for the quality of their work. The news media, in turn, found an eager audience when reporting on this esoteric subject.

The hierarchies of the industrial age stood unchallenged. Nobody doubted Eddington's findings or demanded to see the raw data. Curiously, if anyone had done so, they would have discovered problems. Science work is messy. Eddington didn't simply come up with a single measurement of 1.7 arc seconds for the gravitational curvature of light. There were many measurements, some from Principe, some from Brazil, which needed to be assessed and averaged somehow.

The number announced to the Royal Society was arrived at by more or less arbitrarily throwing out the outlier. Eddington's findings turned out to be valid, but they were based as much on his faith in Einstein's calculations as on the data his expedition had gathered.

In the century or so since Einstein's triumph, the practice of science has been transformed. Vast amounts of money have been poured into science and technology research and development: around $400 billion in the U.S. alone for 2009.[85] The price of affluence has been the centralization and institutionalization of research. An iron triangle of government, the universities, and the corporate world controls the careers of individual scientists. Consequently, the ideal of the lonely and disinterested seeker after truth has been superseded by that of the scientist-bureaucrat. Though the various fields of science differ greatly, scientific success, in general, has been defined less by the quality of the findings than by the ability to bring in "research support"—funding for the institution.

Practitioners have risen to the top of the science establishment by serving, faithfully and with few qualms, their institutional masters. This was true in Hitler's Germany and Stalin's Russia no less than in democratic countries.[86] The power of government over research has inevitably introduced political considerations. President Richard Nixon, for example, declared a "war on cancer." Today research on HIV/AIDS and climate change take political pride of place. The pressure generated by public expectation of specific outcomes has complicated the conduct of honest science.

Much has been claimed for the scientific method, but the only method to which all scientists subscribe is the peer review process. It too has been under strain. Peer review presupposes the existence of independent-minded experts who evaluate manageable data sets. Often, in the age of the Fifth Wave, neither condition applies. Scientists today work in teams, and the subject matter can be so specialized that only a handful of individuals will be able to understand and review the literature. Authors and reviewers can trade places in a chummy circle of mutual admiration and protection. In extreme cases, this constriction of knowledge leads to what one analyst has called "research cartels," which actively stifle minority or unorthodox views.[87]

At the same time, as in every other domain, the volume of data that must be reviewed has proliferated beyond the capacity of the establishment to absorb. Complicated computer programs have become necessary to array and model the data, and high-level statistical skills are routinely required to assess the validity of any finding. Many scientists, including reviewers, have not been up to the job. The peer review process, relic of a simpler time, has thus become progressively less able to guarantee the integrity and legitimacy of research in many fields of science.[88]

Since 1919, in sum, the practice of science migrated from the sectarian Border, where Einstein clearly originated, to a Center dominated by large, bureaucratic institutions. Practicing scientists were absorbed into hierarchies responsive to command from the top. The distance between professional and amateur—Einstein, let us recall, was one of the latter—grew immensely, and the usual barriers were erected to keep out trespassers from the inner temple of authority. The cost of scientific journals, for example, became prohibitive, so that only institutions could afford a subscription. Titles and tenure and awards proliferated. In this regard, the behavior of the scientific establishment paralleled that of government, the news industry, and the other institutions of the industrial age. All claimed monopolies over information to justify an assertion of unquestioned authority.

It might be expected that an unruly public would eventually take on such a pillar of the established order—and that has been the case. Amateurs have swarmed into the precincts of science along many fronts. For the purpose of this chapter, it should be enough for me to touch, however lightly, on two revealing incidents.

The first began with a familiar ritual: the public, in control of the information sphere, maneuvered in a fashion utterly surprising to authority. On November 19, 2009, someone who had hacked thousands of emails from the Climatic Research Unit (CRU) of the University of East Anglia, Britain, released them to the public on an obscure Russian server. The names on the emails belonged to the most eminent climatologists involved in global warming research, and included many of the leading contributors to the United Nations' Intergovernmental Panel on Climate Change (IPCC). The release had a pointedly political purpose. A gathering of world leaders to coordinate policy on climate change was scheduled for December in Copenhagen.

From the emails, an unflattering portrait emerged of the hierarchy of climatology, caught *en famille*. The scientists sounded vain, petty, intolerant, obsessed with media coverage, and abusive to outsiders. They often appeared clueless when it came to their own data sets and computer programs. In this, they faced the same problem as Eddington: the past temperature of the Earth wasn't a single number but an interpretation of very many temperature "proxies," such as tree rings and ice cores. The emails made it clear that the published assertions of the climatologists exceeded their confidence in this data—much of which, in any case, had been lost. And here they confronted a new, more serious problem, one unknown and probably inconceivable to Eddington: a stream of requests under the Freedom of Information Act (FOIA) for the data sets cited in their papers.[89]

The alpha bureaucrats, ensconced at the top of the pyramid, were Michael Mann of Penn State University, for the U.S., and Phil Jones, head of the CRU, for Britain. The two men nominated each other to awards and pressured colleagues to sign petitions supporting the IPCC orthodoxy. Questions of loyalty and disloyalty, of sustaining the information monopoly of the group, absorbed their emails. The threat that enraged these institutional gatekeepers was the intruding outsider, the interested amateur, the "skeptics" and "contrarians" who filed all those FOIA requests.

Mann, Jones, and the circle of scientists around them wrapped themselves in the mantle of the peer review process, which the "skeptics" had avoided. They were accredited science professionals, published in legitimate journals. This was their creed, the source of their authority. But since the group largely controlled peer review for their field, and a consuming subject of the emails was how to keep dissenting voices out of the journals and the media, the claim rested on a circular logic. The supposedly anonymous review process, it was apparent, had become something of a cozy club in climatology. Here is Jones writing to Mann:

> You may think Keith or I have reviewed some of your papers but we haven't. I've reviewed Ray's and Malcolm's—constructively, I hope, where I thought something could have been done better. I also know you've reviewed my paper with Gabi Hegerl very constructively.[90]

When dissident authors at last managed to publish a peer-reviewed paper in *Climate Research*, Mann's reaction was to attack and delegitimize the publication.

> So what do we do about this? I think we have to stop considering Climate Research as a legitimate peer-reviewed journal. Perhaps we should encourage our colleagues in the climate research community to no longer submit to, or cite papers in, this journal.[91]

Disgusted by the "crap science" in *Climate Research*, Tom Wigley, a senior figure at the National Center for Atmospheric Research, proposed going "direct to the publishers and point out the fact that their journal is being perceived as a medium for disseminating disinformation under the guise of refereed work."[92] Wigley had in mind a sort of exorcism of the journal, including a purge of the editor who had allowed the offending paper.

Mike's approach to get the editorial board members to resign will probably not work—must get rid of von Storch too ... I have heard that the publishers are not happy with von Storch, so the above approach might remove that hurdle too.[93]

Mann seemed particularly horrified by the fact that one of the authors of the contrarian paper had been a credentialed astrophysicist from Harvard.

This latest assault uses a compromised peer-review process as a vehicle for launching a scientific disinformation campaign (often vicious and personal) under the guise of apparently legitimately reviewed science, allowing them to make use of the "Harvard" moniker in the process.[94]

The emails showed the world's leading climatologists busily working to organize a research cartel. Peer review was a legitimate source of authority when the process supported their positions. It was compromised, if not malicious, when it offered critics of the orthodoxy a platform. The wish to crush dissenting views, in their minds, had become indistinguishable from the pursuit of truth. In this attempt they ultimately failed, but not, the emails revealed, for lack of trying.

Behind much of the bureaucratic hand-wringing loomed the shadowy figure of Steve McIntyre. We have heard his story before: the amateur who has crashed into the inner sanctum of authority. McIntyre, a Canadian with a talent for mathematics, had developed an interest in climate science around 2002. His blog, *Climate Audit*, became the central point of reference for a noisy vital community of climate-data doubters. Almost all the FOIA requests for data bemoaned in the emails came from McIntyre and his supporters.

McIntyre stood in the same relation to climate science that Wael Ghonim did to the Mubarak regime. He was a man from nowhere, empowered by disruptive new technologies to conduct himself in ways that the bureaucrats from the Center found appalling.

"I must admit to having little regard for the web," wrote Jones in one of the earlier emails. "I would ignore the so-called skeptics until they get to the peer-review arena." "I know the world changes and the way we do things changes," Jones reflected much later, with evident regret, "but these requests and the sorts of simple mistakes [sic], should not have an influence in the way things have been adequately dealt with for over a century."[95] His was the voice of the great industrial institutions, watching their world dissolve into chaos.

Although the climatologists, in their internal emails, occasionally acknowledged that McIntyre's calculations were correct, externally they felt compelled to denigrate and condemn him at every step, without compromise. "Personally, I don't see why you should make any concessions for this moron," Mann admonished a British colleague.[96] In an email to Jones, Mann took an ever harder line: "I would not give them anything. I would not respond or even acknowledge receipt of their emails. There is no reason to give them any data, in my opinion, and I think we do so at our own peril!"[97]

Ben Santer, of Lawrence Livermore National Laboratory, best expressed the shared conviction that McIntyre represented the barbarian inside the gates:

> I believe our community should no longer tolerate the behavior of Mr. McIntyre and his cronies. [...] In my opinion, Steve McIntyre is the self-appointed Joe McCarthy of climate science. I am unwilling to submit to his McCarthy-style investigation of my scientific research. . . I will continue to refuse such data requests in the future. Nor will I provide McIntyre with computer programs, email correspondence, etc. I feel very strongly about these issues. We should not be coerced by the scientific equivalent of a playground bully.[98]

The object of such fear and loathing, we should remind ourselves, wasn't a U.S. senator like Joseph McCarthy, or any kind of political force. McIntyre was an obscure blogger, with no other power than that of persuasion. It was the act of being questioned by a trespasser—a novelty since Einstein's day—that the scientists found intolerable. In their communications, too, the leading practitioners of climatology came across as nothing like Einstein. They sounded self-interested and close-minded, the exact opposite of the public's idea of what a scientist should be—and, after the release of the emails, they were exposed in this unflattering aspect for the world to see.

Coverage of the CRU emails played out in an erratic manner typical of the global information sphere. Mass media, uncertain what to make of the story, at first shied away from it, but the content of the emails exploded across the blogosphere, beginning with the vital community around *Climate Audit.* On November 20, the *Telegraph* published a tendentious column titled "Climategate: The Final Nail in the Coffin of 'Anthropogenic Climate Change?'"[99] With that, the incident received its permanent, if unimaginative, name. The news media now rushed in, with the slant of coverage wholly dependent on the source's editorial line on man-made climate change. CRU scientists, just as unimaginatively, insisted they had been taken out of context, and that the episode unmasked a campaign of "character assassination" conducted by "skeptics."[100]

The consequences were uncertain. Erosion of trust in climate science possibly played a part in the failure of the Copenhagen summit, but this would be difficult to prove—and, in any case, falls outside the scope of this chapter. Several of the climatologists involved in the emails, including Mann and Jones, were investigated by the institutions for which they worked. Though their careers as bureaucratic lords of science were over, all were exonerated. Given that it was the Center investigating the Center, this judgment was predictable. Of much greater interest was how the public judged the matter.

I believe the public judged science more severely than the scientific institutions judged themselves. I grant that this, too, is hard to prove: there are no measurements of public trust in science before and after Climategate that I am aware of. There is no data going back to 1919. Existing surveys show a significant decline in trust,[101] yet I suspect they understate the case: many people, when asked about science, still think of Einstein rather than the Climatic Research Unit of the University of East Anglia. They fondly recall the solitary seeker after truth and fail to see the master bureaucrat. Only when focused on specific issues does the public admit, even to itself, the full measure of its distrust.

People on the left believe that science is a tool of Big Business, that scientists are willing to poison us with genetically modified food and torture laboratory animals to earn a bigger profit for their paymasters. This may be an exaggeration, but, as a general proposition, it's accurate enough. Corporations undeniably pay for and control a substantial percentage of all scientific research.

For people on the right, science has become the handmaiden of Big Government, raising climate and environmental scares to justify the imposition of ever more restrictive political controls over every aspect of life. And this, too, while overstating the case, is generally correct. Government favor is the single most important factor in science research today. It's disingenuous to imagine that such favor would be granted without considerations of power and political advantage.

The revelations in the CRU emails likely drove the public one more step down a path in which its perception of science and the scientist have been radically transformed. The beneficent guardian of truth has become, at best, a self-serving ally of remote elites, and at worst the amoral lackey of money and power. The transformation has been partial and erratic, and at any given time can exclude favored fields of science. This doesn't matter in the larger picture. Legitimacy, like marriage, is a yes-or-no proposition. You can't be partially married, and you can't be partially legitimate.

I could trace the crisis of authority of the scientific establishment indirectly to that moment in 1919, and the expectations formed in the mind of the public regarding the power of science and the nature of the scientist. These expectations were wholly unrealistic, but a lack of realism has characterized the public's relationship to the great institutions. In the past, this inflated the prestige of the institutions. Today, it has left them exposed to accusations of conspiracy and fraud. The failure of the scientist to live up to his exalted image has eroded the legitimacy of his position, I suspect to a fatal extent.

My final incident offered a glimpse into the possible repercussions for individual scientists of this fall from grace.

On April 6, 2009, the ancient Italian city of L'Aquila suffered a devastating earthquake. L'Aquila's buildings, old and new, collapsed like matchsticks, leaving more than 300 dead and over 65,000 homeless. In the aftermath, the Italian public's fury turned against the scientists of the National Commission for the Forecast and Prevention of Major Risks—an institution whose unfortunate name was felt to be the opposite of its performance. Prosecutors indicted seven Commission members for manslaughter, charging that they had provided "inexact, incomplete, and contradictory information" about the risk of a killer earthquake.[102] In October 2012, the seven men were convicted, sentenced to six years in prison, and fined over $10 million.

This may have seemed like a case of outrageous expectations gone bad, Italian-style—and, on the surface, it was. But the episode contained many layers of conflict and confusion.

L'Aquila, like California, sat on a major fault line, and had experienced several smaller earthquakes leading up to the April 6 disaster. Days before tragedy struck, the scientist-bureaucrats of the risk commission had met in the city to assess the situation. Their attention had been divided between two topics, however. One was the possibility of a major earthquake in the region. The other was the intrusion of an amateur into their special domain, in the person of Gioacchino Giuliani.

Giuliani, a local man, claimed to have invented a method to forecast earthquakes by using unorthodox indicators, such as radon levels. He wasn't a seismologist or any kind of a scientist: *The Economist* described him, somewhat derisively, as a "laboratory technician" at a nuclear physics institute.[103] But he had attracted a considerable amount of attention for himself, and spread some alarm among the public, by forecasting that a serious earthquake would hit the nearby town of Sulmona precisely on March 29.[104] This turned out to be a false alarm.

It was Giuliani and his tramping into the precinct of rightful authority, as much as the threat of seismic catastrophe, that concerned the men of the risk commission at their meeting in L'Aquila. In their discussion of the science, behind closed doors, they acknowledged multiple times that the possibility of a major earthquake couldn't be ruled out. When they emerged to face the media, however, they appeared more interested in refuting Giuliani's alarmist statements.

"The scientific community continues to confirm to me that in fact it is a favorable situation, that is to say a continuous discharge of energy," affirmed Bernardo De Bernardinis, a high official in the Italian government's scientific bureaucracy and the only one of the seven who was not actually a scientist. When asked whether the public should relax with a glass of wine, De Bernardinis replied, "Absolutely, absolutely," and recommended a local vintage.[105] Six days later, L'Aquila lay in ruins.

The public needed an assessment of risk. It reasonably concluded that the Risk Commission was doing just that. The public heard an expert forecast: the "continuous discharge of energy" from the smaller earthquakes meant a negligible risk of a dangerous one. But the experts on the Commission didn't think they were making a forecast. The scientist-bureaucrats believed they were countering bad science, and re-asserting their authority against an illegitimate practitioner—a trespasser. The risk commission's statements, as one perceptive analyst observed, "were not specifically about earthquakes at all, but instead were about which individuals the public should view as legitimate and authoritative and which they should not."[106]

Public anger over perceived institutional failure drove the criminal prosecutions, while the convictions evoked public satisfaction. But for the scientists, the entire episode was incomprehensible. "I still don't understand what I was convicted of," one of them, a geophysicist, exclaimed after being sentenced.[107]

It's a fair question. I'd like to end my brief examination of science as an institution of authority with an attempt to answer it.

The risk commission experts were convicted because they had been unwilling to admit, in public, to the degree of uncertainty that science imposed on them.[108] They had been unwilling to say, out in the open, "We don't know whether or not a major earthquake will strike L'Aquila in the short term." In this unwillingness, they behaved in a manner typical of the Center hierarchy. The climatologists at CRU had also felt that announcing the statistical level of uncertainty in their findings would get in the way of their message. "It is not right to ignore uncertainty, but expressing this merely in an arbitrary way . . . allows the uncertainty to swamp the magnitude of the changes through time," Keith Briffa had complained.[109]

Institutions such as the risk commission represented authority, which is another way of saying they dealt in certainty. They claimed competence over truth and falsehood, each in its domain. Any hint of doubt undermined this claim. Public uncertainty created an opportunity for unscrupulous outsiders—people like Gioacchino Giuliani and Steve McIntyre—to pollute the mind of the public with "crap science."

The pose of infallibility, however, required Einstein-like levels of success, and a monopoly of the means of persuasion. In the event, neither condition was remotely met.

The Italian experts were convicted because they had stumbled into the ditch between their aspirations as scientists and their power as authoritative bureaucrats. The expertise they possessed had raised them up to be members of the risk commission, but as members of the Commission they had concentrated their energies on chasing off intruders like Giuliani, rather than on the substance of their expertise.

The seven were convicted, finally, because the exaggerated expectations of science by the Italian public could only lead, sooner or later, to disenchantment and the perception of failure. Science would never be God. Scientists weren't commanders in a war against cancer, or saviors of the Earth against climate change—or, in this case, farseeing prophets of imminent catastrophe. Einstein's predictive power, it turned out, didn't extend beyond his special field of inquiry. In a time of overabundant information and collapsing institutional barriers, within societies of distrust, the result was bound to be a sense of betrayal and a desire to punish.

None of this justified prosecution, much less incarceration. That wasn't the argument I intended to make. My argument was this: the deep conflict between the public and authority is not merely political but total. No established institution has been forgiven, not even science, once the most revered. In the context of Italy, the prosecution of the risk commission scientists must be viewed as part of a larger revolt against the elites, which was to produce, in 2013, electoral victories for a political party from nowhere, the Five Star Movement.

The public, in command of the information sphere, has found corruption everywhere at the Center, and has wielded its new persuasive power to attack the legitimacy of every authoritative institution. The criminalization of scientific error was just one clash in this war of the worlds. The tendency has been to dismiss the episode as somehow peculiarly Italian, but the conflict, I repeat, is structural and global. Italy's government, it may be, was peculiarly weak, and easily stampeded by the public. If this was the case, then Italy in 2009 may have provided a peek at the future of other democratic governments.

THE PANIC OF THE EXPERTS, OR HOW THOSE WHO THOUGHT THEY KNEW DIDN'T

If Pierre Rosanvallon's society of distrust had an official date of birth, it would be Monday, September 15, 2008: the day the Lehman Brothers investment bank, after a protracted agony, finally went bust. In the economic carnage that followed, the experts and political elites betrayed astonishing levels of cluelessness, and did so at center stage, where the whole world could see. Bankers and regulators, politicians and bureaucrats—all turned out to have made drunken-sailor bets on the future, in effect help-ing to push the U.S. economy over a cliff of illiquidity and bad debt. The consequences were immediate and devastating. Across the world, ordi-nary people lost trillions of dollars. Unemployment rose to the highest levels in a generation.

Six years later, in early 2014, the afflicted economies had yet to re-cover from the wreckage of 2008—and trust in economic experts had van-ished, probably forever.

My story, of course, concerns this shipwreck of the expert class rath-er than the crisis itself. A fitting place to start is with the life and times of Alan Greenspan, the man who transformed the economic expert into a glamorous, almost mythical figure.

In 1987, President Ronald Reagan appointed Greenspan chairman of the Board of Governors of the Federal Reserve System—a portentous name for the central bank of the United States, usually called, without af-fection, "the Fed." By law, the mission of the Fed was, and still is, to main-tain the stability of prices while promoting sustainable growth and full employment. The claims behind these goals possessed what I can only de-scribe as a magical quality. They presupposed powers of prophecy and control wholly detached from economic reality. The chairman of the Fed, like the genie in the *Arabian Nights*, was expected to tame the whirlwind.

Greenspan's appointment came in August. Two months later, on Black Monday, October 19, 1987, the stock market dropped over 500 points. A trillion dollars of held wealth disappeared overnight. The 22-percent one-day decline was the largest in history—by comparison, the stock market crash that preceded the Great Depression had amounted to less than 12 percent. On the following day—"Terrible Tuesday"—stocks of many fa-mous companies stopped trading on the New York Stock Exchange. They could not find buyers.

No one, inside the Fed or out, had any idea why the markets had tum-bled. No one knew how to reverse the free fall—or how to prevent a finan-cial catastrophe from swallowing up the economy. The new chairman re-ceived panicked, contradictory advice. Although the Fed's staff had drafted a long, technical statement to reassure the markets, Greenspan opted for a terse proclamation: "The Federal Reserve, consistent with its responsi-bilities as the nation's central bank, affirmed today its readiness to serve as a source of liquidity to support the economic and financial system."[110] This signaled a change in Fed policy toward cheaper money.

By the end of Terrible Tuesday, the markets had rallied to a record gain. In the ensuing weeks, stocks resumed their upward climb. The reasons for the recovery were no less inscrutable than those for the initial collapse, but Greenspan received much of the credit.[111] Relieved elected officials and the news media alike determined that someone must have been in charge during the crisis, and the chairman of the Fed, whose job description hinted at superhuman powers, was the logical choice.

The episode established the pattern for Greenspan's 18-year tenure at the Fed. During that time, the U.S. economy enjoyed an uninterrupted run of growth, coupled with low inflation and unemployment. Because of his position, Greenspan was thought to deserve the lion's share of applause for the continuing prosperity. Greenspan himself avoided making this claim. Like every good analyst, he understood that the future was unknowable, and he felt keenly the limits of his ability to influence the economy.[112]

But he was chairman of the Fed. He stood at the pinnacle of a great hierarchy of authority, and my suspicion is that he believed he had to be perceived as prophetic and in command of the situation. Instead of voicing his doubts openly, he developed a tortured style of communication that allowed different observers to draw diametrically opposed conclusions about what he had said. He called this "constructive ambiguity."[113] Every word Greenspan uttered in public was parsed for meaning, like holy writ. Even his silences were interpreted as conspiratorial.

Greenspan received praise for engineering a "soft landing" for the economy in 1995–1996: to many, he appeared to have repealed the iron necessity of the business cycle. In a rare moment of pride, Greenspan compared the theory of the soft landing with Einstein's theory of relativity, and his own search for meaningful economic data with Eddington's excursion to Principe and Brazil.[114] This was more perceptive than he knew. Greenspan, like Einstein, had risen to become a towering figure in his field, an expert's expert, to be sure, but also a celebrity to ordinary people. Bob Woodward's 2000 biography of the Fed chairman was titled *Maestro,* evoking the image of a genius conductor, leading the economy to a flawless performance with a wave of his baton.

FTSE 100 INDEX (1098–06–19 THROUGH 1988–01–19)

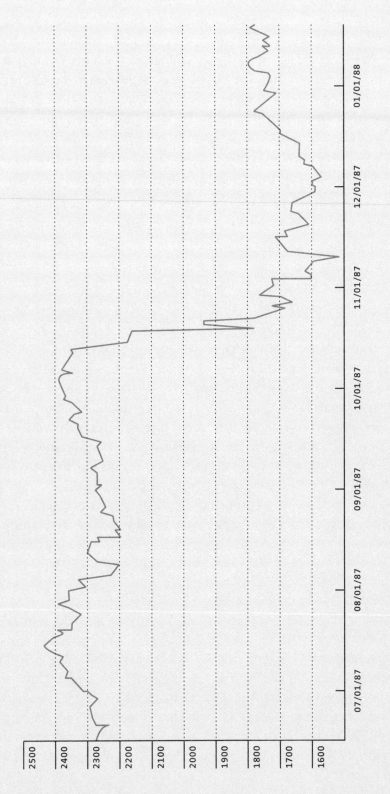

Figure 19: Big dip: Black Monday, 1987.[115]

When, at the age of 79, Greenspan retired from the Fed in January 2006, an article in *The Economist* alluded to his "near god-like status" and observed that he was often called "the second most powerful person in the country." "Alan Greenspan has dominated American economic policy for two decades," the article reflected. "Who can fill his shoes and what will happen to the Federal Reserve once he is gone?"[116] Greenspan's most significant achievement had been to persuade the elites and the public that the pursuit of material happiness required supervision by a brilliant specialist.

Greenspan represented a relatively new type of public person. He was something of an economic authority but very much a master bureaucrat. This hybrid, the expert-bureaucrat, belonged in the same class with the journalist, the corporate CEO, the university administrator, and, indeed, the scientist-bureaucrat. All seemed to be part of the eternal order of things, but were in fact creatures of the industrial age.

As late as 1922, Walter Lippmann had celebrated the arrival of the "specially trained man" who was "oriented toward a wider system of truth than that which arises spontaneously in the amateur's mind." Increasingly, Lippmann noted, "the more enlightened directing minds have called in experts who were trained, or had trained themselves, to make parts of this Great Society intelligible to those who manage it."[117] Put in simpler terms: governments craved control, and the experts, in exchange for a place in the hierarchy, offered to demonstrate how it could be imposed.

The modern economy is a prodigiously complex swirl of human activity. During the 20th century, the "more enlightened directing minds" in government, arm in arm with their experts, erected an intricate structure of authority around this transactional blur. The Fed occupied the heights, and was granted independent authority to avoid pollution from the democratic process. But there were many mansions in the economic bureaucracy. Consider the following very partial roster of the economic institutions maintained by the federal government at the time of the 2008 financial crisis: Office of the Comptroller of the Currency (established in 1863), Federal Reserve System (1913), Securities and Exchange Commission (1934), Federal Deposit Insurance Corporation (1934), National Credit Union Administration (1934), Commodity Futures Trading Commission (1936), Federal National Mortgage Association (1938), Financial Industry Regulatory Authority (1939), Federal Home Loan Mortgage Corporation

(1970), Bureau of Economic Analysis (1972), Bureau of Labor Analysis (1972), Financial Crimes Enforcement Network (1990).[118]

The expert-bureaucrats who staffed these agencies made specific claims of competence. They held that the vast throng of amateurs involved in economic activity regularly succumbed to a disorder John Maynard Keynes had labeled "animal spirits" and Greenspan called "irrational exuberance." Primitive emotions blinded the public to the big picture and the common good. The expert, however, was a disinterested seeker after knowledge. Given a measure of political power, transformed into an expert-bureaucrat, he would predict the economy's trajectory and achieve outcomes beneficial to all—higher employment rates, say, or a more equitable distribution of income. That was the immanent faith manifested in the Fed's mission. Those were the claims seemingly validated by the triumphant career of Alan Greenspan.

And so we circle back to 2008. The blithe unawareness of the expert class as it drove the financial system over the brink, and the obvious confusion, often amounting to panic, with which it confronted the disaster, falsified in pain and loss its claims to competence. Every institution in the system failed catastrophically, beginning with Greenspan's Fed, which encouraged a casino atmosphere by flooding the markets with easy money. Investment firms like Lehman Brothers took that money and "leveraged" it, betting $30 for each dollar they actually held in their hands. The rating agencies like Moody's and Standard and Poor's, designated by the government to assess investment risk, gave the complex, untested subprime securities a AAA rating: when all was said and done, Moody's had missed the mark by 20,000 percent.[119] The White House and Congress pumped the housing bubble by pressuring regulators to accept ever riskier mortgages.

It was a total bankruptcy of the elites—only the public paid the bill.

While the financial system fell to pieces, the people in authority reacted with uncomprehending shock. "How did we get here?" President George W. Bush wondered.[120] He did not receive an answer. "What happened? How the fuck did we get here?" asked investment financier Peter Weinberg during a frenzied meeting in New York.[121] "How could the government have allowed this to happen?" demanded a member of the Lehman board, betraying, in extremis, an unshaken faith in the ideal of the expert-bureaucrat.[122]

Afterward, most players in the economic melodrama insisted that failure to predict the meltdown had been universal. "S&P is not alone in having been taken by surprise by the extreme decline in the housing and mortgage markets," the head of Standard and Poor's testified before Congress. "Virtually no one, be they homeowners, financial institutions, rating agencies, regulators, or investors, anticipated what is coming."[123] This wasn't strictly true. Warnings about a housing bubble abounded before the fall, but the people who voiced them had been ignored or marginalized.[124]

Whether the crisis was or could have been predicted, or whether all the economic prophets, right or wrong, merely rode a thin stream of randomness atop a massively complex system, in the manner described by N.N. Taleb, I am not qualified to say—thankfully, I'm not an economic analyst.[125] But it was an extraordinary defense of the performance of the expert class to say that none of them, at any level, had known what was coming.

Barack Obama's election to the presidency offered this class one last chance at redemption. Candidate Obama had called the crisis "the logical conclusion of a tired and misguided philosophy that has dominated Washington for far too long."[126] Once in office, President Obama reiterated the thesis that "failed economic theories" had brought the crisis about. "I reject those theories," he asserted bluntly.[127] Political considerations, the new president argued, had corrupted expert judgment in the Bush years. A new team, free of such animal spirits and guided by sound economic theories, would restore the country to prosperity.

The economic stimulus legislation, crafted by administration experts and passed by Congress in February 2009, implemented the president's thesis. To help sell the $787 billion package, two White House economists, Christina Romer and Jared Bernstein, provided hard projections of how the measure would bring down unemployment.[128] Their report, I'd like to think, reflected the sincerity of President Obama's intentions, but it was a political miscalculation.

Unemployment stood at 7.3 percent as of December 2008. Romer and Bernstein calculated that, absent a stimulus, it would climb to around 9 percent by early 2010, but with the stimulus in place it would peak lower, at 8 percent, and it would decline faster, by the middle of 2009. Here was a bold attempt at prophecy by the new team of experts; in the event, it was wildly over-optimistic. Unemployment peaked at 10.1 percent after the

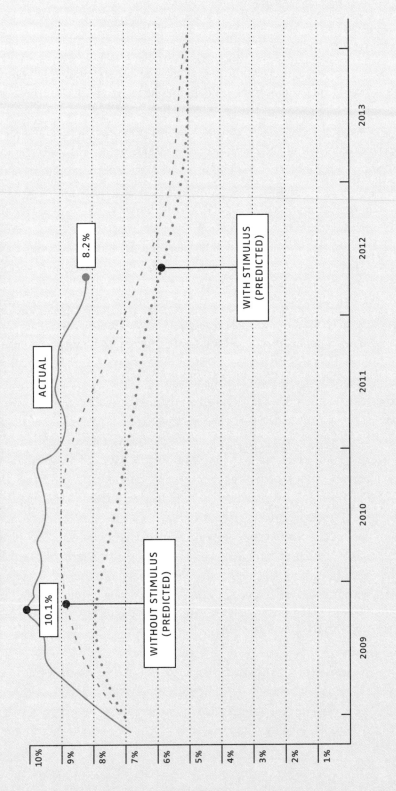

Figure 20: Failure of prediction and control.[129]

stimulus bill passed, and didn't touch 8 percent until late 2012—much worse than the worst-case projections without the stimulus.[130] In human terms, the White House numbers had missed the plight of over three million unemployed Americans.

Statistician Nate Silver offered two reasons for Romer and Bernstein's disconcerting failure at prediction, and neither of them seemed flattering to the expert class. The first was ignorance of actual economic conditions. The economy in 2009 happened to be in far worse shape than the experts, for all their statistical wizardry, had realized. The second reason was overconfidence in tracking the trajectory of unemployment. It had never been possible to predict the movement of major economic indicators, such as unemployment, with anything like the decimal-point accuracy claimed by Romer and Bernstein.[131]

Yet I suspect that it was equally impossible for a personage high in a structure of authority—a sitting president, a White House economist—to acknowledge, in public, the impossibility of prophecy. Within this contradiction, much about the crisis of authority of the institutions can be explained.

The experts in the new administration, it turned out, had performed no better than their discredited predecessors. The new economic theories had been no more successful at achieving desired outcomes than the old, failed ones. The bankruptcy of the expert class was a bipartisan affair. By publishing hard projections, the Obama White House had gambled on the qualitative difference between its expert-bureaucrats and those who had come before. It would have been better served by emulating Alan Greenspan's purposeful obscurities.

Not that Greenspan's reputation survived the shipwreck. The former chairman, once above criticism, was hauled before Congress in October 2008 and badgered by politicians desperately seeking a scapegoat. Greenspan himself, so adept at letting others perceive him as infallible, now admitted to being "in a state of shocked disbelief" and to have made a "mistake"—he had found "a flaw in the model...that defines how the world works."[132]

"A critical pillar to market competition and free markets did break down," Greenspan concluded, adding what might be considered the epitaph for the class he had helped raise to the heights of influence: "I still do not fully understand why it happened."[133]

The failure of the elites in 2008 took place before the bewildered eyes of the public. A feeling of betrayal, of having been lied to, thus compounded the general fearfulness about the future. Of course, the public had bought into the impossible expectations heaped on the expert-bureaucrats. The public assumed that *someone* would be in control, demanded that the institutions of prosperity function smoothly, but left the dirty details to the machinations of the Center. Few complained during the fat years, but when the crack-up came, an unconquerable sectarianism shielded the public from any sense of responsibility, and allowed it to place the blame squarely on the shoulders of the people in authority.

Recriminations followed predictable patterns. People on the left blamed the crisis on the deregulation of the banking industry. To a certain extent, they were correct. People on the right blamed massive political interference in economic activity. They too had a good case to make. But both critiques, as well as others involving "greed" and more elaborate conspiracies, missed the larger point. One side assumed that only legislators and regulators could control the future, the other that only the markets could do so. On the evidence of 2008, however, the gap between the institutions' claims of competence and reality had been vast and deep. *Nobody* knew what was coming.

The search for culprits was less divisive than the search for causes. All who had been in a position of authority when the disaster struck were denounced as frauds and scoundrels. All the justifications that had propped up the political and economic status quo were put in question. Trust in government as a whole reached all-time lows.[134] The Bush administration departed in disgrace, and the Republican Party lost the presidency and both houses of Congress in the 2008 elections. After the failure of the stimulus, the tide of distrust turned against President Obama and the Democrats, who had their ruling coalition shattered in the 2010 midterm elections.

Trust also tumbled in the banks, the stock market, corporations.[135] Many people pressured the government to prosecute bankers responsible for the crisis—a criminalization of failure roughly parallel to the L'Aquila earthquake affair in Italy. One opinion poll showed a large majority of Americans favoring a public audit of the Fed, while another survey of U.S. investors showed minimal trust in Fed chairman Ben Bernanke.[136] The expert-bureaucrat had been discredited and dethroned. The alternative to the expert, however, was always *another* expert: Bernanke for Greenspan,

Janet Yellen for Bernanke. The elites' failure in economic governance confronted a public unwilling to do much more than condemn and punish. The non-economic consequence of the 2008 financial crisis, therefore, was a feast of negation, celebrated with rare unanimity in both mass and social media.

A CORPORATE BUM'S RUSH, OR THE ECONOMIC RAMIFICATIONS OF THE FIFTH WAVE

Enter any large shopping center if you wish to challenge my hypothesis. Enter, for example, Tyson's Galleria, a golden temple of consumption for upscale shoppers, which I sometimes visit on rainy days. Built in 1988, it was expanded in 1997 and made to appear—so the designers believed—"like a European streetscape." In reality, it looks a bit like a hallucination by the artist M.C. Escher.

Here, you will be insulated from the bitter negations of 2008. You will encounter no discernible effects from the great insurgencies of 2011. In this book, I have described traumatic assaults by the public on the centers of authority in every domain: meanwhile, Tyson's Galleria rolls on, imperturbably ostentatious. Stores come and go, but the system endures, untouched. A top-down, brick-and-mortar, hierarchical structure—the shopping center—appears to be surviving, in fact thriving, in a networked age.

If you pursue this line of questioning, you will soon arrive at a fundamental dilemma. The disasters of 2008 were at bottom a failure of capitalism. The people in authority who were discredited and swept away in the aftermath could be described as the capitalist elite. They had claimed authority over the sources of prosperity, but were shown to be clueless and unsteady. The closest thing to a papal figure in capitalism, Alan Greenspan, now acknowledged that the system failed to grasp how the world really worked.

Yet here you are in Tyson's Galleria, a dazzling little chapel in the capitalist church. You might as well have been there in the boom years before 2008: little has changed. Capitalism, it would appear, is still very much with us.

So my dilemma is how to square the revolt of the public and the crisis of the institutions with the apparent survival of capitalism. Note that I am prevented, by my own methods, from claiming that a reckoning will take place in the future. I have rejected prophetic analysis. The story I tell must be bound to the empirical evidence, which means, generally speaking, that I am bound to talking about the present and the past.

Because I find this dilemma to be rolled up into layers, like an onion, I will try to peel them back, one at a time.

If the question is whether capitalism survived the trauma of 2008, the answer must be "Yes, so far." It may have suffered terrible wounds that will be the cause of its demise. We may look back some day and realize 2008 was the end of the capitalist era. That is unknowable. At the moment, six years after the crash, no alternatives exist, no one is calling for revolution, and Tyson's Galleria opens its doors to affluent consumers rather than protesters.

If the question is whether the revolt of the public has constituted a threat to capitalism, the answer must be "Not really." The people of the left denounced capitalism in 2011, but they had always done so. The proclamations of the *indignados* in Spain and the U.S. occupiers were sprinkled with anti-capitalist and anti-"system" rhetoric, and even Israel's tent city protesters, mildest of the lot, felt compelled to attack "swinish capitalism." If my interpretation of 2011 was correct, however, anti-capitalism was only one element in the vast utopian ambitions of the street insurgents, who aimed to abolish history, the determinism of cause and effect, and ultimately themselves, on behalf of a purified future. That such airy ideals were unrealizable fit the sectarian temper of the rebels: they meant to *protest*, not replace. Anti-capitalism was never an alternative to capitalism. It was another path to negation—when pushed hard enough, to nihilism.

The people of the web, on the other hand, pictured the perfect future in terms of powerful personalized technologies, and glorified the venture capitalists, and, above all, the techno-hipsters like Steve Jobs, who made those technologies possible.

The prosperity of Tyson's Galleria, and of similar gilded places all over the globe, indicates that the public in revolt hasn't been notably anti-capitalist, anti-business, or even anti- any particular corporation, no matter how unpopular or powerful. No protests took place against BP during the 2010 Deepwater Horizon oil spill. Google and Microsoft have inspired anxiety in Europe's political class, but the European public has been happy to exploit the platforms provided by these companies to evade and abuse their elites. Similarly, the campaign against Walmart in the U.S.

has been conducted by organized pressure groups and elected officials, and is not the result of a revolt from below.

The public *can* strike at a corporation, ferociously and with the speed of light, when it feels that its peculiar interests have been threatened. An example was the backlash against GoDaddy after that company announced its support of the Stop Online Piracy Act (SOPA), a measure that sought to expand the reach of copyright law over web content. A boycott organized online was so successful that within 24 hours GoDaddy had caved in and proclaimed its opposition to SOPA. The incident was short-lived: once GoDaddy changed its stand, the protests ended. But it demonstrated the public's ability to unleash chaos on the marketplace, if it were interested in doing so.

Moving on to the next layer: if the question is whether a networked public has influenced the conduct of business, the answer must be "Yes, in spades." The public has imposed a single all-important demand on business, the same as it has done on government, politicians, educators, media, and service providers: that every transaction treat the customer as a *person,* with active tastes and interests, rather than as a passive and undifferentiated member of a *mass.*

Remember that ugly word "disaggregation." Meaning: to unbundle, to unpack—to tear apart. As it was in politics, the disaggregation of the masses has been a revolutionary *economic* event. It marked the passing of John Kenneth Galbraith's "new industrial state," in which Big Business and Big Labor divided the spoils of the modern economy at the consumer's expense. Today, Big Business faces a radically shortened life expectancy, Big Labor is in full retreat, and the consumer—the mutinous public—is in command.

Companies that cater to idiosyncratic tastes have flourished. The standard example is Amazon, with its vast inventory and "people like you" algorithm, although a host of online stores fits the bill as well. (The trajectory of the $1.4 trillion commercial web can serve as Exhibit A for the public's lack of interest in anti-capitalist jihad.) For a success story in brick and mortar I would nominate Starbucks, where you can linger as long as you wish, sipping "latte" with cinnamon and caramel but no trace of milk, if that's what you happen to crave.

But these are momentary victors, who may be—many certainly will be—defeated and replaced tomorrow. The revolutionary economic impact

CONSUMPTION SPREADS FASTER TODAY

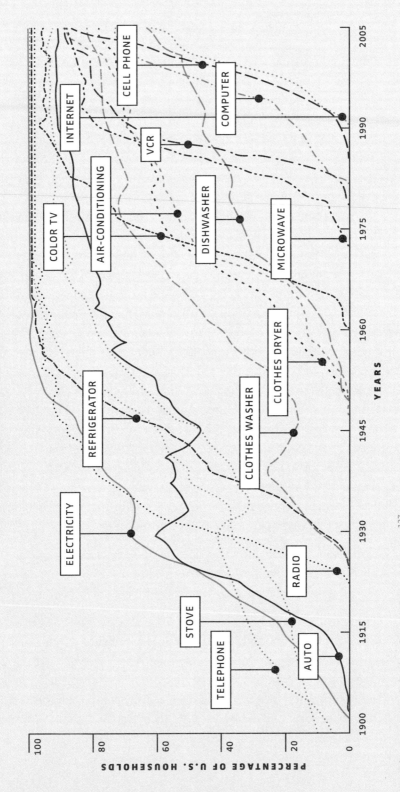

Figure 21: Rate of adoption of new products, 1900–2005.[137]

of the demand for subjectivized treatment is not to be found in "long tail effects" or the growth of the digital bazaar, but rather in the marketplace turbulence such a demand must cause—in the churning of innovation and production, of corporate organization and corporate extinction. Industrial behemoths that imposed on the public the inflexibilities of their production systems are being toppled—the economic equivalent of the Mubarak regime is surely GM. Their successors, however, will lead an impermanent existence in a landscape swept by contradictory impulses.

The mass consumer was an invention of the industrial age: "One size fits all" followed the logic of the assembly line. The conversion of the masses into a networked public, we have seen, only became possible with the arrival of digital technologies and the development of the global information sphere. A very different logic now seems to be at work—innovation has caused an atomization of demand, and atomized demand has driven ever faster rates of innovation in nearly all fields of economic activity. It is not an illusion that life today feels like a sequential wrestling with one new thing after another, in a vertiginous cycle of change.

In *Race Against the Machine*, Erik Brynjolfsson and Andrew McAfee conjectured that this frenzy of innovation was a major reason for the stagnant economic growth since 2008. "The root of our problems is not that we're in a Great Recession or a Great Stagnation, but rather that we are in the early throes of a Great Restructuring," they argued. "Our technologies are racing ahead but many of our skills and organizations are lagging behind." Normally, these authors wrote, a "well-functioning economy" would adjust to the current transition in consumption patterns.

> *However, when the changes happen faster than expectations and/or institutions can adjust, the transition can be cataclysmic. Accelerating technology in the past decade has disrupted not just one sector but virtually all of them.*[138]

I find Brynjolfsson and McAfee's thesis somewhat speculative. But reflect, for a moment, on the chart opposite. It isn't just speculation that this churning of new things must be disastrous for companies that specialized in producing the old things. Half the firms listed on the Fortune 500 in 1999 had dropped out by 2009.[139] According to Richard Foster, the average lifespan of a company on the S&P 500 has declined from 67 years in the 1920s to 15 years today.[140]

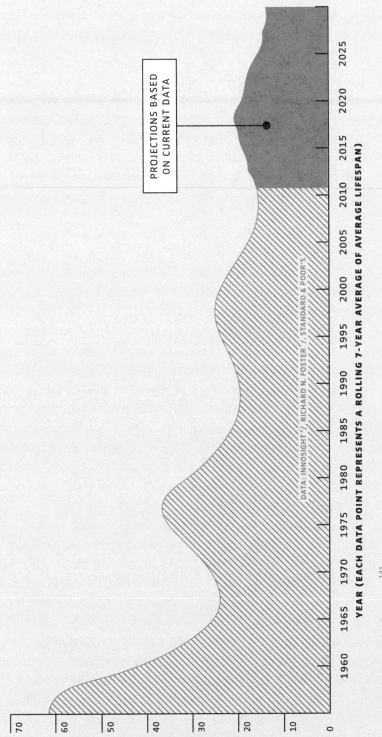

AVERAGE COMPANY LIFESPAN ON S&P 500 INDEX (IN YEARS)

PROJECTIONS BASED ON CURRENT DATA

DATA: INNOSIGHT[1] / RICHARD N. FOSTER[1] / STANDARD & POOR'S

YEAR (EACH DATA POINT REPRESENTS A ROLLING 7-YEAR AVERAGE OF AVERAGE LIFESPAN)

YEARS

Figure 22: A corporate extinction event.[141]

If the information in both charts (Figures 21 and 22) is integrated, the story that jumps out is of a business environment riven by conflict and stress. Whether or not the flood of innovation has disrupted the economy as a whole, as Brynjolfsson and McAfee believed, it has been associated with something resembling an extinction event for individual corporations. The reality of change and hardship behind the story, I note, is consistent with the expected effects of the Fifth Wave on the marketplace.

Individual shops at Tyson's Galleria *do* indeed come and go. Shopping malls rise and fall. It has been Tyson's good fortune (so far) to count among the risers.

The public has been perfectly indifferent to this rolling massacre of the corporations. And so it should be: out of the carnage, it gets what it wants. *Some* companies deliver the goods. That others tried and failed—and died—is of little consequence. The first are now last, and the consumer is in charge.

We come here to a great paradox and tentative explanation about why the networked public, so destructive of the status quo, has tolerated and to some extent embraced the standing economic system. The market is pure trial and error. In business, as in nature, most new trials fail. This is true of every sphere of human activity. Most new government policies fail to meet their intended goals, for example. Most educational reforms fail. Most scientific hypotheses fail. The *trial* part of trial and error entails mostly error, unless the set of trials is large and competitive enough to produce a possible success, and the system is smart and agile enough to recognize success and reward it.

Many of the structures battered by the global struggle between the public and the elites have been captives of single-trial processes, and sought to define success hierarchically, from authority. New initiatives typically have failed—and failure has been typically explained away and doubled down on. The CIA, we saw, demanded and received more money after 9/11. Advocates of the $787 billion stimulus blamed its failure on the insufficient amounts spent. Such arguments persuaded only while the institutions held a monopoly of the means of information and communication—in other words, only so long as they went unquestioned. Today, of course, the public always questions, and will usually find the answer in the information sphere.

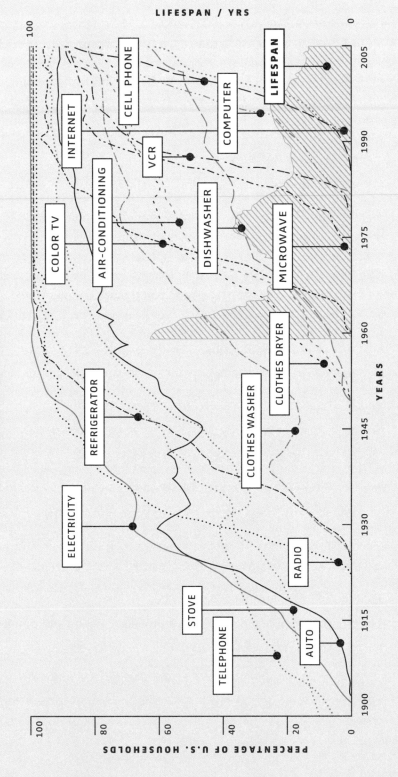

Figure 23: Consumption spreads faster today while S&P average company lifespans decline.[142]

In business, an immense variety of trials gets conducted in parallel for every potentially profitable outcome, and success or failure is determined from below, by the consumer. If a company fails badly enough, it's gone. The void will be filled by a more successful company. The quickening of the rate of extinctions has represented the remarkable adaptation of capitalism, as a system, to the hostile conditions of the Fifth Wave, including the pervasive anti-authority sentiment.

I want to be precise. I am not saying that business has been smarter or more effective than government. Corporations invest heavily in being smart and effective, but economist Paul Ormerod has shown that, allowing for the difference in time scales, the failure rate of businesses recapitulates the mindless, random pattern of species extinction.[143] Nor am I claiming that the corporate CEO has demonstrated greater prophetic powers than, say, the scientist or the bureaucrat. On this point, I will simply cite sociologist Duncan J. Watts: "Corporate performance is generally determined less by the actions of CEOs than by outside factors, like the performance of the overall industry or the economy as a whole, over which individual leaders have no control."[144] It would be strange, anyhow, to glorify the captain of a ship whose expectation of sinking increases by the moment.

In the current environment, as I understand it, businesses have proved no wiser, more farseeing, or successful than other institutional actors. But capitalism, as a whole, has made more productive use of the failure of its parts than most institutions under assault by the public. To borrow Taleb's terminology, capitalism appears to be "antifragile": it "regenerates itself continuously by using, rather than suffering from, random events, unpredictable shocks, stressors, and volatility."[145] This has allowed the system to prosper despite the horrors of 2008, while, not unrelatedly, bestowing on the consumer a multitude of new technologies and products.

For the individual company, however, the speeded-up environment has felt like a bum's rush—an unmitigated disaster. And this brings up the last, strange wrinkle in our economic dilemma.

If the question is whether the individual corporation stands in a similar relation to the mutinous public as do all the hierarchies of the Center, the answer must be "It sure looks that way." At the level of the single company, the new marketplace, dominated by personalized demand,

resembles the larger conflict I have described in this book, only in minia-
ture and on fast-forward. The heart of the matter is structural. Today's
companies were organized for the industrial age. Beyond a minimal size,
each company is a little bureaucracy set up to do one thing, or a few
things, well. A company may do its thing better or worse than competitors, but if asked to do something different, or to keep changing what it
does, it will perform terribly. Bureaucracies are good at conservation, dis-
mally bad at change.

The corporate world is aware of the contradiction, and has been engaged for some time in a frenzied tinkering on the margins of the status
quo in the hope of finding a solution. Calls for "changing the culture," for
implanting a "culture of innovation," for "thinking like a startup," have
become part of the background noise of doing business. Unfortunately,
the trouble isn't cultural or psychological. It's structural, and it threatens
the authority of powerful persons and groups within each corporation.
Few of them can be expected to embrace the threat. Attempts have been
made to replace hierarchy with "councils," and bureaucracy with a more
networked approach. I don't know of any signal successes from these experiments, which run up against the spirit of bureaucracy—and, I suspect,
against the grain of human nature.

Beyond the intrusion of business consultants skimming billions off
their corporate clients, little has changed structurally since Henry Ford's
day. If change does arrive—if the speed and freedom of networking can
somehow be wedded to the mass and stability of hierarchy—it will represent a transformation in human relations as radical as any in history. Until
that apocalyptic moment, I imagine that the savage churning of corporate
births and deaths will continue to accelerate.

UNCERTAINTY, IMPERMANENCE, AND OTHER SYMPTOMS OF LIFE WITHOUT AUTHORITY

The story I presented in this chapter didn't amount to mathematical proof
of a crisis of authority. Human events are rarely susceptible to that kind of
analysis. Deep changes in human relations are also difficult to perceive,
much less quantify, while they are taking place—and my story concerns a
collision of worlds far below the horizon of cultural awareness. Most
Victorians, I imagine, had no idea that they were living through an industrial revolution.

I made specific claims using specific types of evidence. I intended to *describe* what a crisis of institutional authority looked like, and to *illustrate* a handful of instances, rather than to demonstrate the proposition beyond a shadow of a doubt. So: my analysis could be falsified. A cluster of unconnected causes could be responsible for the collapse of the public's trust in institutional actors: scientists, experts, bankers, and the like. I don't believe this to be the case—but I've been wrong before, and not just once.

If I were a doctor attempting to diagnose this particular sickness—the crisis of authority—I would look for definite causal patterns and symptoms. Among the patterns I would include exaggerated expectations by the public, abetted by exaggerated claims of competence by authority. I must believe that seismologists can save me from earthquakes, that the chairman of the Fed has tamed the business cycle—and these authorities must either believe the same thing, or, at a minimum, collude in my delusions.

A second causal pattern would be the elites' loss of control over the story told about their performance, particularly when it has failed to meet expectations. Such control, I noted, is a function of monopoly, so another way to diagnose this pattern is to determine whether the public has broken the institutions' grip on information and communication. Climatologists conspiring to silence dissident views must believe that their data is a professional secret and their private emails are inviolable, while the public must be able to see the emperor in all his nakedness, and to disseminate that unimpressive image globally. The effect will be a growing distrust and loss of legitimacy.

A third pattern would be the rise of alternative centers of authority. This is a corollary of the loss of monopoly. Once the conversation broadens and the public takes command, the dynamic isn't that of Einstein scrutinizing the cosmos from his mountaintop, but of Michael Mann and the Intergovernmental Panel on Climate Change looking over their shoulders at Steve McIntyre and his blog. Each vital community formed by amateurs interested in an affair becomes a threat to the authority of the institutions.

I believe I've dwelled on these patterns extensively enough to show that they are everywhere around us, undermining the established order. But there are manifestations of the crisis—since I'm impersonating a doctor, let's call them *symptoms*—that haven't found their way into this story. And I want to discuss two of them, very briefly, at this point.

The political and expert classes claimed competence over settled truth. That's who they were, what they did: they produced certainty and erased doubt. But if certainty is a function of authority, then a symptom of authority's decline will be a radical and generalized *un*certainty surrounding important questions. Alas, no instrument exists to measure certainty or its lack, but it is instructive to compare our mindset on this question with that of our parents and grandparents.

Sixty years ago, Einstein spoke with the voice of God. Thirty years ago, Walter Cronkite every day told us "the way it is," and the *New York Times* delivered to our doorsteps "all the news that's fit to print." Twenty years ago, Alan Greenspan applied infallible formulas to ensure our prosperity. When I was a boy and factual disputes arose in my family, they were settled by consulting the *Encyclopedia Britannica*. Back then, the world of information was shaped like a pyramid. Those at the top decided signal from noise, knowledge from fraud, certainty from uncertainty. The public and mass media embraced this arrangement. All things being equal, authority was trusted and relied on.

Today we drown in data, yet thirst for meaning. That world-transforming tidal wave of information has disproportionately worsened the noise-to-signal ratio. According to Taleb, "The more data you get, the less you know what's going on."[146] And the more you know, the less you trust, as the gap between reality and the authorities' claims of competence becomes impossible to ignore. If the IPCC climatologists fear a dispute with skeptics, how can they be believed? If the risk commission seismologists can't warn us about catastrophic risk, who will? As I tried to show in this chapter, the public has lost faith in the people on whom it relied to make sense of the world—journalists, scientists, experts of every stripe. By the same process, the elites have lost faith in themselves.

And the magisterial *Encyclopedia Britannica?* Gone the way of the dodo. Its place has been taken by Wikipedia, which, with its "edits" and "reverts" for many entries, leaves the reader uncertain about the agenda of any given version.

Lack of certainty isn't ignorance: it's a splinter of doubt festering in all we know, a radical disillusionment with the institutions of settled truth. One important effect has been a sort of cultural barroom brawl, as every question of significance becomes an irritant and source of strife between interested parties. What, for example, can be said without qualification about Christianity or Jesus? Two of the more ferocious edit battles in Wikipedia happen to rage around these subjects.

This state of affairs invites counterrevolution by the established order. Again and again, in subject after subject, accredited experts have attempted to regain control over the levers of epistemic closure. At every opportunity, institutional actors attacked the public on the grounds of its uncertainty. For example, the public stands accused of cocooning into a daily me, of conducting a "war on science," of indulging in unprecedented partisanship, and more. Such nagging gives the game away. The counterrevolution of the authoritative elites has floundered, because the elites are themselves tormented by that terrible splinter of doubt.

You would expect, in a time of uncertainty, a landscape crowded with frauds and con artists peddling *positive* formulas for happiness, love, sex, good health, and better government. You would expect, too, the most trivial assertions to be attended with much noise and thunder—absent authority, every message must be shouted to have a hope of being heard. Stridency will infect every mode of communication, but will be most disruptive of political rhetoric. Just to keep an audience, politicians and commentators will have to scream louder and take more aggressive positions than the competition.

Whether I just described with any accuracy the outlines of social and political life today, I leave it for the reader to decide.

With that, I turn to a second symptom: impermanence. Authority has always fostered an illusion of inevitability. For obvious reasons: if an expiration date were stamped on the federal government, defection from its mandates would begin today. To the extent that the public doubts the permanence of the institutions, the authority of the latter will be subverted.

I grant that impermanence, like uncertainty, is a perception of reality, impossible to measure precisely. But there's a hard empirical world that confronts perception at any moment in time, and, analytically, I find it safest to stick close to that world.

A good place to start is with our relationship to technology. This used to be a matter of mastering self-contained tools and procedures—learning to drive a car, make a telephone call, operate a lathe or a harvester. Now, it's about the capacity to absorb open-ended change. The chart above showed the accelerated rate at which we adopt technological innovations. That's the hard reality of it. New devices, systems, and media now succeed one another at an impossible pace. Old technical knowledge quickly degrades and becomes useless, like the floppy disks and audiocassettes that clutter the dusty corners of our homes.

There's a belief that digital is forever—that the naked photos of your youth will haunt you to the grave. The opposite is closer to the truth. Digital means ephemeral. Online authority, influence, and attention fluctuate rapidly. Websites go up, have their brief moment on the speaker's platform, then turn mute. Their words and images sometimes persist, fossilized, but just as often disappear. Vast volumes of emails, text messages, same-time chats, have vanished as if they never were. Old links point to nothing. Old platforms like AOL or Friendster are worthless today. Old formats are "incompatible" with new ones—a very good word. Impermanence means nothing more than the incompatibility of the present with even the recent past.

Consider, too, our engagement with work and government. Another chart in this chapter depicted the life expectancy of S&P companies in term of an extinction event: old, illustrious brand names, with their products, crash and burn at a much faster rate than a century ago. The worker has adapted to this churning of the workplace: the average time he will spend with any one company is down to 4.4 years.[147] Those are empirical measurements of the vanity of economic success.

Government, I admit, is more speculative, but in the last decade the world has witnessed wild tumbles of the political wheel of fortune. Barack Obama crushed the Democratic and Republican political establishments in 2008, saw his ruling coalition swept away in the 2010 midterm elections, then was comfortably reelected in 2012. Regimes frozen solid for decades, like those of Tunisia and Egypt, suddenly melt into air.

The world of hard facts confronting our perceptions has become unmoored from the past, and appears to be in the process of devouring itself. How we have responded, subjectively, to this world—that's open for discussion. I'd like to raise just one interesting possibility.

You would expect the loss of a stable existence on earth to drive a search for fixity on a higher sphere. If this is the case, a rise in the appeal of fundamentalism will testify to the *experience* of impermanence. That takes me deep into the realm of subjectivity, but there are empirical hints and signs. In Egypt, we saw, the old regime was initially replaced by the Muslim Brotherhood, which won the country's only fair elections to date. The hard reality in the Middle East is that Islamist groups have prospered wherever secular Arab authoritarians have wobbled. In the U.S., the more demanding faiths—evangelists, Mormons, Hasidim—have grown at the expense of older institutions which too much resemble the earth-bound hierarchies of the Center. The spread of Christianity in China is among today's best-kept secrets.

For the governing classes and articulate elites of the world, this turn to religion is both appalling and incomprehensible—but this is a denial of human nature. If the City of Man becomes a passing shadow, people will turn to the City of God.

At the violent extreme you come to groups like Al Qaeda, whose alienation from the established order both blindly strikes at and embod-ies the spirit of the age: there's no more searing image of impermanence than that of the collapse, in fire and dust, of the World Trade towers. Western intellectuals often dismiss Al Qaeda as a primitivist organiza-tion run by blinkered fanatics, but it is nothing of the kind. The group op-erates at the merciless front lines of the revolt of the public against au-thority, and its disregard not just for human life but for nearly every structure that binds people together poses again, with some urgency, the question of nihilism.

Uncertainty and impermanence are symptoms of social life under the conditions of the Fifth Wave. That, in any case, is my conjecture. It may be that both attributes reflect the reality of the human condition more accurately than the mastery and confidence assumed by the indus-trial age. Alan Greenspan and the Italian seismologists *really* felt uncer-tain about what the data meant, whatever they said in public.

But the conflict at the heart of this book isn't a debate about the na-ture of reality. It's a struggle for supremacy, in which blood has been spilled. Uncertainty, in this struggle, reflects a negation of the standing structures of knowledge. Impermanence signifies the demolition of the current structures of power and money. A large empty space, a conceptu-al hole, a nothingness, is in the process of creation, where once a complex society wrestled institutionally with its own contradictions and fallacies.

Liberal democracy has been the chief mechanism for mediating such internal flaws. The question of nihilism, now inextricably tangled with the crisis of authority, will be answered in terms that either affirm or negate the legitimacy of the democratic process. As I move to consider the effect of the crisis on government, this remains, for me, the most consequential and least noticed imponderable of our moment in time.

THE
FAILURE
OF
GOVERNMENT

The previous chapter extended my hypothesis to virtually every domain of human activity and every exercise of authority once considered legitimate. The conflict, I maintain, is everywhere. Particular skirmishes, like Tahrir Square and Climategate, are what philosophers call "epiphenomena," surface effects rather than causes, the crack and rumble of a dissolving glacier. Underneath these events, and far more consequential, has been the strange reversal in the relationship of the public—ordinary people who are interested in an affair—and the elites.

As I turn my attention back to politics, a number of troublesome questions have yet to be addressed.

Most pressing, in my view, is the evolution of democracy in an atmosphere made toxic with negation and distrust. Even a secure democratic government in prosperous times, like Benjamin Netanyahu's in 2011, can confront a sudden uprising sparked by a loathing of the status quo. Similar insurgencies swept Barack Obama to office in 2008 and brought the anti-Obama Tea Party to prominence in 2010. Democratic governments have failed, and have been perceived to fail. Their replacements, too, have failed, and have been perceived to fail. Individual political figures have been discredited and discarded, but at some point the entire system must become implicated in failure—the cumbersome machinery of representative democracy will then appear, to those impatient for change, as part of the reason for failure.

Having prepared the ground and made the necessary throat-clearing noises, I begin, in this chapter, an analysis of how democracy has fared within societies of distrust like our own.

The question of the *terms* of government failure, which I raised in the context of the events of 2011, must now be made explicit. Government can only be said to fail relative to its own claims or the public's expectations. If democratic governments really have failed with increasing frequency—as I maintain they have—then the balance between claims, expectations, and reality has somehow gotten out of whack. In this, as in so many other matters, I have been struck by the peculiarity of our historical situation.

The utopian ambition of governments from the industrial age, which sought to perfect the social order, hangs ridiculously, like an outsized suit of armor, on their feebler, latter-day heirs. Yet the quixotic pose has been maintained. The fiction of extraordinary ambition and mastery has persisted, without irony, in our political language.

The rhetoric of democratic politics seems to have gotten out of whack with the reality of what democratic governments can achieve—and I propose, in the present chapter, to ponder the reasons why. The destructive effects of the Fifth Wave have played a part, but they are only one side of the equation. Government found itself in a digital fishbowl, for all the world to see, but what the world saw still hinged, to a considerable extent, on the claims and performance and persuasiveness of government.

I am conscious of entering a landscape haunted by ideological disputes. At the back of many questions regarding political failure stands a larger question about the reach and limit of power. Modern governments have been around for a century and a half, largely pounding away at the same projects: increasing national wealth while keeping down unemployment, for example. We know by now that they fall short of omnipotence. An *empirical* boundary must exist, therefore, beyond which the application of power becomes self-defeating. Any claims that cross the boundary will proceed, with the inevitability of a Greek tragedy, to failure.

Work has been done on the boundary conditions of effective government, but anyone with the slightest awareness of contemporary partisan politics will have no difficulty guessing the fate of this research. It has been drowned out by the din of special pleading.

For what it's worth, my purposes in this chapter are analytical rather than ideological. I have treated the limitation of government as a function of the limits of human knowledge, not of ideological preference, and in this approach I have stuck close to Paul Ormerod's brilliantly researched and happily titled book, *Why Most Things Fail*.

The mystery under analysis is the decline of the great democratic institutions, from the heights of ambition to today's poster children for Ozymandias's lament: look on my works, ye mighty, and despair.

HOW JFK WON BY FAILING WHILE OBAMA SUCCEEDED HIS WAY TO DEFEAT

It wasn't always this way. Scroll back 50 years, and you come to an American government still able to tap into a seemingly inexhaustible pool of public sympathy and trust, even in the face of failure. So the first question to examine, let me suggest, is how we got here from there.

On April 17, 1961, around 1,400 armed Cuban exiles landed on the southern coast of Cuba, in a place called the Bay of Pigs. Their objective was to overthrow the regime of Fidel Castro. The exiles had been organized, trained, and supplied by the CIA. The operation had been vetted by the Joint Chiefs of Staff and approved by the new president of the United States, John F. Kennedy. Everyone in the world, friend and foe, understood the attack in Cold War terms: as an attempt by the U.S. government to knock out a budding Soviet ally in a country too close for comfort to Florida. A veil of deniability had been provided, but it was threadbare.

Within three days, the anti-Castro exiles had been utterly routed. All were either killed or captured by Cuban government forces. The fantastic theory that the might of a modern government could be overthrown by 1,400 men was falsified. Responsibility for acting on this peculiar notion fell squarely on the U.S., its government, and, inevitably, its young president.

The Kennedy administration was approaching the 100-day mark by which it had asked to be judged, so the timing of the Bay of Pigs debacle could not have been worse from a political perspective. The president's youth, so far a source of glamor, risked becoming identified with inexperience. After all, his older predecessor, Eisenhower, had been Supreme Commander of Allied Forces in Europe while Kennedy was serving as a PT boat captain in the Pacific.

The news media did not minimize the magnitude of the defeat. The tone of coverage and commentary conveyed a sense that the moment had become decisive for the new administration. "For the first time in his life, John F. Kennedy has taken a public licking," wrote James Reston, top columnist for the *New York Times*. "He has faced illness and even death in his 43 years, but defeat is something new to him, and Cuba was a clumsy and humiliating defeat, which makes it worse. . . . How he reacts to it," Reston concluded, "may very well be more important than how he got into it." [148]

In private, Kennedy despaired that the incident had cost him any chance at reelection. Publicly, he met with Republican worthies in a show of bipartisanship, and he delivered two statements on the Cuban situation: a nationally broadcast speech to the American Society of Newspaper Editors on April 20, and a televised press conference on the following day. More than the bloody facts on the ground in Cuba, those presidential statements shaped U.S. public perception of the Bay of Pigs crisis. It makes for a fascinating analytic exercise to imagine how they would be received today.

In his speech to the newspaper editors, the president denied what everyone knew to be true: that the invasion had been a U.S. show from start to finish. He gave credit to "Cuban patriots" for the attack, and insisted they had secured nothing more substantial than goodwill from the U.S. government. Having established American nonintervention in the affair, the rest of the president's speech was a fairly hard-line assertion of the right of his administration to intervene, if necessary, in the future, to meet its "primary obligations, which are to the security of our Nation."[149]

At the press conference, a journalist asked whether, given the "propaganda lambasting" the country was taking because of the attack on Cuba, it would not be useful "for us to explore with you the real facts behind this, or our motivations." President Kennedy's reply seemed aimed at a different question, but became central to the media story that emerged about the Bay of Pigs misadventure and the president's part in it.

> One of the problems of a free society, not met by a dictatorship, is this problem of information. . . . There's an old saying that victory has 100 fathers and defeat is an orphan. . . . I have said as much as I feel can usefully be said by me in regard to the events of the past few days. Further statements, detailed discussions, are not to conceal responsibility because I'm the responsible officer of the Government—that is quite obvious—but merely because I do not believe that such a discussion would benefit us during the present difficult situation.[150]

It's important to mark the terms under which JFK expected the discussion of his foreign policy failure to be conducted. First, he denied any American responsibility for the affair. This wasn't really a question of misleading the press, which already knew the extent of U.S. involvement, but it was a bald untruth—and it closed a door to accountability. He then apparently accepted responsibility for the defeat as the "responsible officer of the Government," but since officially the U.S. had not participated, it was difficult to say just what the president was taking responsibility for. Finally, when invited to enlarge on the subject of the U.S. government engaging in secret conspiracies, he refused outright, and cited national security reasons for doing so.

From the perspective of the reflexive negations of our own times, it seems surprising how completely the news media bought into the president's terms. No member of the White House press corps mocked the fiction of nonintervention. No secret documents were published in the press exposing the depth of CIA involvement in the Cuba operation. Few if any media voices were raised to object that the secrecy blackout was politically self-serving.

For the speech to the American Society of Newspaper Editors, the White House had solicited input from two of the lions of journalistic opinion, Walter Lippmann and Joseph Alsop. Their words made it into the delivered text. This type of exchange wasn't a new practice, but it obviously made media criticism of the administration's response less likely. In fact, the media as an institution "appeared to rally to Kennedy's support." Failure was transformed into a positive experience. As Thomas W. Benson observed in *Writing JFK*, the young president was typically described in the media as learning from defeat, after having assumed responsibility for it. The implication was that Kennedy, though inexperienced, possessed the intellect to master the demands of the presidency, and the strength of character not to shirk responsibility that was his alone.

Because of his untimely death, President Kennedy never stood for reelection, but neither did he suffer the slightest political damage from the failure of the Bay of Pigs invasion. The public in large numbers continued to trust the president. A Gallup poll taken two weeks after the incident gave him an 82 percent approval rate, a 10 percent improvement over the previous poll. "The worse I do, the more popular I get," Kennedy joked.[151] He was probably the last occupant of the White House to be able to say that. The Bay of Pigs and Kennedy's inexperience in foreign affairs did not materialize as issues in the 1962 midterm elections, which saw the Democratic Party maintain a lopsided majority in the House and increase its majority in the Senate to around two-thirds of the seats in that chamber.[152]

Failure at ground level became for JFK a stepping-stone to political success. How this was achieved lies beyond the scope of this book. Kennedy had mastered a formidable rhetorical arsenal. He was popular with the press, which worked to protect his reputation during a difficult time. But it is just as persuasive, for me, to say that coming out of World War II, and standing deep in the heart of darkness of the Cold War, the media and the public felt they were on the same side as the president—that his successes and failures were theirs as well. Such loyalty to an institution today would be considered corrupt or motivated by false consciousness.

To recognize how far the ground has shifted in the relationship between elites and the public, we need to fast-forward to an incident with somewhat similar attributes, much closer to the present.

Barack Obama won election to the presidency as the financial system of the United States and the world crumbled to pieces, with brutal economic consequences. The new president, like JFK, was young, popular, eloquent, and relatively inexperienced. The crisis Obama faced was more painful and fundamental to the public than a failed attack on a Caribbean island: but, unlike the Bay of Pigs for JFK, it was not of his making. The catastrophe had taken place on his predecessor's watch, and political blame flowed entirely in that direction.

In the last chapter I sketched out President Obama's reading of the crisis and how he expected to surmount it. His was an uncompromising sectarian critique of the Center: corrupt institutions, seduced by false, outmoded theories, had brought calamity down on themselves and the nation. His new administration, Obama believed, was free from the stain of the past. His experts were thus true experts. Their theories were data-driven and up-to-date. We already know where this logic ended: with the stimulus.

In the months after his election, President Obama gave two major speeches on the American Recovery and Reinvestment Act, as the stimulus package was formally known. One was at George Mason University, on January 9, 2009, before he was inaugurated, and the second was before a joint session of Congress on February 24, after the bill had already been enacted into law. What was remarkable about both speeches, beyond the rhetoric developed by the president in his advocacy of the bill, was the dissonance between what was condemned and what was proposed.

The president's analysis of the causes of the recession was strategic, far-reaching, and coherent. The crisis, President Obama argued at George Mason University, "is largely of our own making"—a moral failure more than an economic downturn. "We have arrived at this point due to an era of profound irresponsibility that stretched from corporate boardrooms to the halls of power in Washington, D.C.... It's time to trade old habits for a new spirit of responsibility."[153]

But the practical proposals to demonstrate this new spirit, as explained by the president, were all over the place. The stimulus bill was expected to jump-start the economy and "save or create" 3.5 million jobs, but it was also about promoting sustainable energy, repairing infrastructure, reforming our children's education, improving the competitiveness of the American worker, and delivering better health care to all. At more than 1,000 pages in length, the legislation lacked a guiding thought: its mandates could drift, potentially, toward any corner of social or political life.

Such programmatic fracturing has typified government action under the conditions of the Fifth Wave. The effect on the public has been to engender alarm and suspicion of hidden motives.

Congress enacted the stimulus measure in February 2009, with the vote divided along party lines. It was, on the face of it, a triumph for the president, who had implemented a major piece of his political agenda less than a month after inauguration. White House experts had gone confidently on the record prophesying in detail how the provisions of the bill would reduce unemployment. We know today that they were wrong, and that the stimulus failed on its own terms, but it took time for this fact to become apparent. The Bay of Pigs had been an immediate and undeniable disaster for JFK—by contrast, the stimulus, in February 2009, was a successful if controversial presidential initiative.

Yet the public, which in 1961 rallied to President Kennedy, in 2009 rose in revolt against President Obama and shattered his governing majority in Congress at the 2010 midterm elections.

The emergence of the Tea Party movement in 2009 anticipated many of the patterns followed by the insurgent groups of 2011. It began online. On the day before the stimulus bill was signed into law, Keli Carender, a 29-year-old Seattle blogger, organized a protest that drew over 100 people. Before the event, Carender had posted an ambitious challenge on her blog, *Redistributing Knowledge*:

Make no mistake, the President will be signing that bill tomorrow, I have no illusions that he will actually listen to us. BUT, maybe, just maybe we can start a movement that will snowball across the nation and get people out of their homes, meeting each other and working together to redirect this country toward its truly radical founding principles of individual liberty and freedom.[154]

The group of local activists that coalesced around Carender's call for action called itself Seattle Sons and Daughters of Liberty.

Two days later, on February 19, an obscure TV business reporter called Rick Santelli broadcast an anti-stimulus rant from the trading floor of the CME Group in Chicago. The thrust of Santelli's complaint was that the bill promoted "bad behavior" by bailing out irresponsible mortgage borrowers. He left no doubt about the source of the problem: "President Obama, are you listening?" Santelli concluded with an activist message: "We're thinking of having a Chicago tea party in July. All you capitalists that want to show up to Lake Michigan, I'm going to start organizing!"[155]

Santelli's cable TV channel, CNBC, had a minuscule audience, but the global information sphere provided amplification: conservative and libertarian bloggers chatted up video of the rant, which immediately went viral on YouTube. The popularity of this pedestrian TV performance should have been a warning that something was in the air. Tea Party protests erupted in at least 40 American cities on February 27. On April 15, 2009—Tax Day—around 750 protests took place across the U.S. A "Taxpayer's March on Washington" on September 12 drew between 75,000 and 300,000 persons, depending on who did the counting.[156]

After less than a year in office, President Obama confronted a new movement dedicated to frustrating his objectives.

* * *

The Tea Party was a party in name only. Geographically as well as by temperament, these were Border types, people from nowhere constituted into hundreds of local networks, interacting by means of digital platforms like Meetup and Facebook but firmly rejecting any official organization, hierarchy, leadership, and spokespersons. The handful of national groups that helped with planning and funding, like FreedomWorks and Tea Party Express, were never embraced as representative of the movement, and tended to be viewed with suspicion. Alliances among Tea Party networks were described by one author as "tenuous, often arising for a single lobbying effort or political event, then disintegrating."[157]

The ideals propelling Tea Partiers into action were wholly sectarian, that is to say, against: against Big Government, high taxation, the deficit, the debt, Washington politics and politicians in general, and President Obama's legislation, like the stimulus and the health-care plan, in particular. This was a revolt against the Center, which Tea Partiers viewed as tyrannical and self-seeking. The seductive appeal of the Tea Party movement, like that of the Occupiers who were to follow, was the joy of negation, of bringing down the roof on the temple of political authority. Beyond a fundamentalist respect for the Constitution, any positive proposals inspired either lack of interest or fractious disputes.

The Obama administration, the grandees of the Democratic Party, and even the Republican establishment—all objects of the Tea Party's uninvited attention—reacted to the uprising with surprise and disbelief. That has been true of every collision between the public and authority I have documented in this book. The Center, Douglas and Wildavsky wrote, is easily surprised. It finds it hard to fathom why anyone would question its decisions. In this particular instance, the president and the Democrats were fresh off a decisive victory in the 2008 elections. The most satisfactory explanations, from their perspective, were conspiratorial.

When, in August 2009, Tea Party activists disrupted town hall meetings held by congressmen across the country to discuss the president's health-care legislation, Democratic Party leaders dismissed the participants as "astroturf"—Republican operators faking a grassroots movement. Once it became clear that mainstream Republicans were more likely to be targets than beneficiaries of Tea Party political activity, an alternative conspiracy theory was put forward: the movement had been "co-opted" by corporate interests, notably the brothers David and Charles Koch of Koch Industries.[158]

There is always some truth to such blanket accusations. Republican candidates no doubt wished to ride the tiger of an anti-Obama revolt. The Koch brothers donated money and organizing muscle to libertarian groups, including some associated with the Tea Party. As hypotheses to account for the sudden eruption of people from nowhere into U.S. political life, however, elaborate conspiratorial notions appeared, at best,

Figure 24: Tea Party demonstration, Washington, D.C.: September 12, 2009.
Photo © 2009 Chase Whiteside

insufficient. If the Republican Party or the Koch brothers could really play Pied Piper to the libertarian masses, why on earth had they waited to do so until *after* the presidential elections? If "co-optation" meant altering the direction of the movement, basic analytic questions about *what* the change was, and *when* and *how* it had occurred, needed to be addressed.

A simpler explanation was that the public was on the move. The Tea Party represented a substantial number of persons interested in a particular affair. This had happened before, in the antiestablishment insurrection that was Barack Obama's 2008 bid for the presidency, and it was to happen again, in the phase change of 2011 and after. The public was on the move, on this occasion from the right instead of the left. The tectonic collisions that define our age had been resumed. That the institutions were blind to the situation—that they could not perceive a threat in mere amateurs, and needed to concoct elaborate stories that placed other elites in command of events—did not invalidate the reality of what was taking place.

As in every other recent uprising of the public against authority, the rebels of 2009 didn't belong to the proletariat or the downtrodden, nor were they untutored know-nothings. They came from the affluent middle class. Tea Party shock troops appeared to be somewhat better educated, wealthier, whiter, and older than the average American. If the *indignados* considered themselves a youth without a future, the Tea Partiers could be described as families afraid for theirs. But by any historical or global comparison, their present was prosperous.[159]

A strong tendency within the movement was libertarian, a reflexively anti-authority attitude embraced by many voters who had been politicized by Ron Paul's presidential candidacy in 2008. These people were indifferent or hostile to religion, and tolerant, in principle, of what John Stuart Mill called "experiments in living." Another wing of the movement was occupied by the religious right, which focused on social issues like gay marriage and abortion. The two groups had nothing in common except their negations: for a time, at least, that was enough.

The Tea Party and Occupy Wall Street have often been paired as ideological mirror images of each other.[160] I wouldn't push this parallel beyond its natural limits. The Tea Party was about personal liberty, OWS about social and economic justice. Each, in a sense, was the beast in the other's nightmare, the living horror their country seemed on the verge of becoming. If a similarity existed, it was found in the sectarian temper that identified the two movements as the work of political amateurs from the Border. Both feared the great institutions of power and money yet disdained to organize or appoint their own leaders. Both believed themselves to be the last outpost of civic virtue in a landscape of moral and political desolation. Between libertarian and anarchist, it may be, the distance can be reduced to a quarrel about private property.

Ideological differences have powerful consequences, and I don't intend to downplay them. I only observe that ideology, left and right, must now accommodate itself to the deeper struggle—to the crisis of authority and the sectarian character of the public.

Unlike the Occupiers, Tea Party adherents swarmed head-on into electoral politics. Here was a difference that made a difference. And unlike the Five Star Movement in Italy, the Tea Partiers did not strike out on their own. Instead, they focused their energies into transforming the Republican Party and making it the vehicle for their ideals. Success was partial, but still remarkable: in the 113th Congress, 48 Republican congressmen and five senators belonged to the "Tea Party Caucus." Many governors and state officials were also associated with the movement.

The high-water mark of the insurgency came at the 2010 midterm elections. To an unusual degree, the Tea Party turned congressional races into a national referendum on President Obama and his programs: in one survey of voters, 56 percent stated that they had cast their vote either for or against the president.[161] The approach favored the party with an edge in enthusiasm—in this case, the Republicans, who won big at the federal and state levels. The House flipped from a Democratic to a Republican majority, while in the Senate the Democrats lost five seats and, with that, their filibuster-proof majority.

For Barack Obama, this electoral calamity meant the end of one mode of governing and the beginning of another. His transformation was unique enough to become part of my story: I'll pick up this thread at the end of the chapter. But any hope by the president to assert strong claims of competence from the Center—any idea that he could emulate FDR and LBJ with big programs aimed at big "problems"—had to be abandoned. Partisan legislative battles devolved to the margins of budget and taxation decisions. After 2010, not a single major program pushed by the president became law.

In less turbulent times, the Tea Party might have been expected to build on its surprising victory and challenge for control of the government—for example, in the presidential elections of 2012. Just the opposite occurred. Once President Obama's political agenda had been checkmated, the movement began to lose cohesion and force. It was a revolt of the sectarian Border, motivated by the negation of the Center, and lacked positive proposals around which believers could rally and move forward after that negation had been achieved.

* * *

I have described failures of government under two administrations, spaced some 50 years apart: the Bay of Pigs for President Kennedy and the stimulus legislation for President Obama. The consequences differed in fundamental ways. JFK, whose troubles were clear and self-inflicted, found his popularity on the rise. The public rallied to a floundering president. In the case of President Obama, failure was, at the time, as much a matter of opinion as of reality, yet he faced a revolt of the public that wiped out his governing majorities in Congress.

The answer to what changed between 1961 and 2009 would fill a much fatter book than this one. In a sense, everything changed. I am less concerned with this trajectory than with providing some connective tissue to my theme: the revolt of the public and the crisis of authority, developments very much tangled up in President Obama's difficulties but not at all in President Kennedy's.

For governments to "fail" in the way I have used the word at least two circumstances must be present. Some empirical event must occur that is perceived as a failure. That much is obvious—but not enough. Just as important is a rupture in the relationship between government and the governed. Habits of command and obedience, trust in the competence of higher authority, faith in the stories that justify the elites—all of these relations must be frayed or broken, for failure to bear political consequences.

The presidency from which John F. Kennedy governed was a protected institution. His failure at the Bay of Pigs was blamed by the media on the new president's youth and inexperience: he had not yet grown into the office. Kennedy's ambivalent acceptance of responsibility allowed the media to tell a positive story about a young president learning his job. The Bay of Pigs wasn't a failure. It was an important learning experience. The public embraced the story and supported JFK.

Matters stood quite differently with President Obama. Almost immediately after he began to implement his program, a chasm of distrust opened up between the president and a significant slice of the public. Rather than offer protection, the presidency, as an institution, exposed the incumbent to debilitating levels of suspicion. Obama the candidate had cashed in on this revaluation. As president, he was swiftly punished by it.

Barack Obama ran for the presidency as a righteous voice from the Border, rising up against a failed, unprincipled Center represented by Hillary Clinton within his own party and by President Bush as the retiring Republican incumbent. This made the U.S. presidential elections of 2008 an early instance of the public on the move against the established order. As in all such events I have considered, the public possessed a new strategic advantage: control of the information sphere. The Obama campaign enjoyed unparalleled success telling its story, raising money, and recruiting volunteers online.[162]

But the public in revolt also faced a strategic dilemma: having originated in a political vacuum, it lacked a unifying organization, ideology, program, or plan. The solution, hit upon virtually everywhere that the public has enjoyed political success, was an unrelenting focus on the particular wrong or injustice under assault at the moment. Negation, digitally amplified, has been the glue holding together a multifarious public.

Recall that the protesters in Cairo's Tahrir Square comprised many ideals and opinions, but all were united in hostility to the Mubarak regime. The Occupiers, anarchists and liberals, stood against an economic system that favored the "1 percent." The Tea Partiers, who could be libertarians or religious conservatives, jointly opposed Big Government, exemplified by the stimulus and health-care laws. Advocating a positive program would have shattered these groups: participants felt energized by what they opposed, but were murky and divided about what they stood for. In fact, when circumstances demanded that they spell out an alternative to the status quo, all three movements faltered and splintered.

Much the same happened to President Obama's public support. He had been a sectarian candidate, vehemently *against,* earning his political spurs as an opponent of the Iraq war and running for president on a platform of total repudiation of the Bush legacy. His positive program, however, was vague and unformed. A slogan like "Change we can believe in" appealed to many contradictory political opinions. Once he was elected, any program he espoused was bound to alienate a portion of his base. Strong evidence suggests that the Tea Party was nourished by independents defecting from the president's camp—many of them, I suspect, libertarians who had been disgusted with President Bush but remained suspicious of Big Government programs.[163]

The rupture between President Obama and the Tea Party was prefigured by the decline in the legitimacy of the office of the presidency. Multiple causes drove that decline, not all of them connected to the conflict that is the theme of this book. At some point after the congenial era of JFK, the elites fell out of love with politics and politicians. The news media, preeminently, withdrew its protection from democratic institutions, including the presidency, and began to portray elected officials in the guise of inveterate liars.[164] For my purposes, it should be enough to say that, by the time the public arrived as a force on the political stage, the presumption of a common purpose that hedged Cold War presidents had dissolved in an acid bath of distrust.

One similarity endured, however. The claims of competence made by the government over which Barack Obama presided were as extraordinary and improbable as those asserted in JFK's time. Everything had been diminished except the talk. The radical disconnect between the rhetoric and the reality of government was apparent to anyone with eyes to see, and, amplified by the information sphere, was itself a major vector for the contagion of distrust.

HOW BRASILIA AND CABRINI-GREEN BECAME DODD-FRANK AND THE E.U. CONSTITUTION

The claims made by governments today, and possibly even believed by them, were inherited from their predecessors of the industrial age. The same applies to the public's expectations of government. The public looks past the feeble figures of their actual rulers to the towering ambitions of the industrial age. These ambitions, I note, were almost never realized, but that doesn't matter. They were impressive and persuasive, they were articulated at a time when government controlled the means of communication, and they have become, without much thought or discussion, the default setting of democratic politics today.

So any attempt to examine the claims of government against the reality of what is possible must necessarily begin with a bit of history.

What political scientist James C. Scott has called the 20th century's "high modernist" approach to government routinely gambled on colossal projects designed to bring perfection to the social order.[165] Authoritarian examples of such projects were Stalin's collectivization of Soviet agriculture, Mao Zedong's Great Leap Forward for China, and Julius Nyerere's villagization of Tanzania. Democratic examples included the building of the city of Brasilia, "urban renewal" housing projects like Chicago's Cabrini-Green, and the various "wars" waged by the U.S. government against poverty, crime, drugs, and cancer.

The purpose in each case was to engineer perfection in social relations by the application of political power. High modernist ideology was a utopian faith: it assumed that rational planning and scientific know-how, if imposed on a gigantic enough scale, could eradicate the miseries of the human condition, from tyranny and inequality to hunger and disease. The enemy was history, mother of superstition and disorder. The hero was the expert-bureaucrat, who could wipe the slate clean. We have met this character before: Lippmann's "specially trained man," magically wielding his "wider system of truth."

High modernism suited the hierarchies of the industrial age. In politics, this was true for dictators and elected presidents, left and right. The appeal was structural. Everything cascaded from the top down. Only the elites possessed the technical and scientific training to rationalize society. The public at that time was still considered a formless mass—carrier of the imperfections that it was the ambition of government to eliminate forever. The ruling elites wished to raise this human mass closer to their own higher state of being. Their ambitions were altruistic. Their intentions were pure. If they were ruthless in their means—these included, at different times, forced relocation, intrusive surveillance, even incarceration and death—it was because they believed, with an unwavering conviction, in the justice of their cause.

Under the spell of this ideology, governments defined conditions like economic backwardness as "problems," and focused on some immediate solution with an almost manic intensity. "The clarity of the high-modernist optic is due to its resolute singularity," Scott wrote. "Its simplifying fiction is that, for any activity or process that comes under its scrutiny, there is only one thing going on."[166] The tendency to political gigantism followed naturally from this mindset.

The construction of Brasilia can stand as an example of the stupendous ambition of government in the last century. The project began in 1957 under Juscelino Kubitschek, democratically elected president of Brazil. A new capital would be built out of nothing in the northern wilderness of the country, and by sheer force of rational planning and technology, it would cut, at a single stroke, the knot of poverty and underdevelopment. Vast apartment blocks, laid out in perfect geometric grids, were provided with ideal living spaces, as determined by experts. Fantastically wide highways, devoid of sidewalks, crisscrossed the city. Naturally, the whole design was oriented toward the centers of political power, whose palaces were often isolated by enormous empty spaces. Naturally, only the ruling elites, the politicians and the expert-bureaucrats, were to dwell in this glorious City of Man. But the project meant to transform Brazil into a modern nation and radically improve the lot of ordinary Brazilians. It was utopian in spirit and intent. Building the city, Kubitschek promised, would win Brazilians "fifty years of progress in five."[167]

Brasilia stood for the negation of Brazil: of the real country, with an actual history, with habits and styles evolved from past experience. To achieve perfection, the world had to be made anew. That was the extraordinary claim of high modernist government—handed down, in the form of immoderate rhetoric, to the governments of our own time.

No less extraordinary was the fact that virtually all attempts to enforce this claim met with failure, yet failure never became part of the

Figure 25: Government ministries, Brasilia. *Photo by Ben Tavener*

story. The laborers who built Brasilia, for example, were supposed to leave after their work was done, but instead stayed on, lodged in wholly un-planned, ramshackle housing. Wealthy persons who needed to live near the capital disliked the antiseptic apartment blocks and built irrational mansions around the periphery. By 1980, according to Scott, "75 percent of the population of Brasilia lived in settlements that had never been an-ticipated," and this messy, unofficial Brasilia sustained and underwrote the austere modernist capital.[168] The dream of fast-forwarding Brazil's economy had been forgotten long before.

Under authoritarian governments, the zeal to make the world anew inflicted horrors on the public. Dozens of millions of human beings died in Soviet collectivization and the Great Leap Forward. This story is well known, yet rarely linked to its cause. Nyerere's villagization campaign was a version of Soviet-style collectivization, 30 years after the disastrous failure of the earlier initiative should have been apparent. While the tally of victims in Tanzania was somewhat less appalling, the results were es-sentially the same.

Similarly, Cabrini-Green, like most housing projects, has been razed to the ground. The wars waged by the federal government against social conditions have ended with the enemy standing more or less where he was before hostilities began. The failures of high modernist democracy also are well known, but disconnected from their source. I say here that the connection *must* be made, if you wish to understand the predicament of representative democracy.

All of us, public and elites, live under the historic shadow of governments that sought to re-create the human condition.

Today, few governments imagine this to be possible or desirable. Since the fall of the Soviet Union, the mania to make the world anew has gone out of fashion. But instead of acknowledging that they have awakened from a nightmare of perfectionism, elected governments appear ashamed of their impotence, frustrated by their ineptness. Instead of entering into a new age, political life in democratic countries feels old and late. Politicians shiver under the immense shadow of the past. They sense that the public is divided on the question of high modernism. The *indignados* and the Occupiers, for example, demanded the abolition of history and the release of human relations from the prison of memory.

To return to my concrete examples: President Kennedy belonged to a different age. The Bay of Pigs was a typically ambitious high modernist project, an attempt to spark the overthrow of an established regime with a few hundred armed men. Typically, too, the project failed, yet failure lacked negative political consequences and never became part of the story.

President Obama, however, is very much a man of our own day—what I propose to call, in this context, *late* modernism, to capture the prevalent feeling of the times. The political landscape around him has grown flatter. The circle of possibilities has contracted. I have dealt briefly with the path between then and now: whatever the chain of causation, the change itself has been undeniable.

When Barack Obama entered into office, he stood in the shadow of his predecessors. He looked back with envy and nostalgia to FDR, LBJ, even Ronald Reagan. Like all his contemporaries, President Obama imitated the high modernist habit of defining specific conditions as immense problems, which demanded equally large solutions. In the recession of 2009, he found the need to make "a clean break from a troubled past, and set a new course for our nation."[169] President Bush had done much the same after the atrocities of 9/11. Instead of focusing on the group that perpetrated the attack, he declared a global "war on terror."

Late modernist governments have asserted their claims of competence from the same peak of ambition that launched the high modernist projects. This has placed them in a false and dangerous position. High modernism failed, but it involved governments in actions of monumental proportions, which dazzled elites and public alike by the scope of their objectives. The story told about these projects wasn't one of failure but of epic activity, high drama, reaching for the stars.

It is too late in the day now for such romance: government has lost the will for heroic effort.

The economic situation of 2009 was framed by President Obama as demanding a clean break from the past and a new course for the country. Yet he lacked the manic "singularity" of high modernism, and his proposed solution, the stimulus, was a grab bag of activities needing over 1,000 pages to describe, costing nearly $800 billion, but somehow, after all that, generating very little drama. The president never followed up on the premise of a new start for the nation, never engaged in epic combat against the dead hand of history. His mode of governing was wordy, tactical, splintered among many objectives. He wanted every deserving cause to get a donation. The stimulus never came close to matching the razzle-dazzle of Brasilia or the war on poverty, and it attracted a fierce, determined opposition from the start.

The president pitched his rhetoric on an ambitious high modernist plane, but he directed the actions of his administration with late modernist timidity, constrained, to be sure, by pressure from a restless public. The profound disconnect between talk and action gives the game away. The *aims* of democratic government have shifted, even if the language of politics has yet to catch up. High modernist government was an austere prophet, demanding the destruction of the muddled present to make room for the perfect future. Late modernist government is more like a kindly uncle, passing out chocolate chip cookies to his favorite nieces and nephews. He doesn't wish to transform them. He just wants them to be happy—most particularly, with him.

If high modernism in power was an engine of perfection, late modernism has become a happiness machine. It feels bound to intervene anywhere it has identified groups that were somehow victimized, disabled, troubled, below average, offended, uncomfortable—actually or potentially unhappy. Its actions are the political equivalent of handing out a chocolate chip cookie: government today desperately wishes to be seen doing something, anything, to help, and be recognized for its good intentions. There are no boundaries to intervention, but no epic outcomes either. Elected officials know perfectly well that the public is on the move, and are terrified of the consequences. Their chief ambition is to persuade us that they feel our pain, are on our side, have given a little money to our favorite cause, if only we, the public, allow them to last out their terms in peace.

Interventionism has substituted a thousand tactics for a single bold strategy. Programs seem scarcely intelligible in terms of their stated purposes, and, like the stimulus, need to be legislated at exhausting length. President Obama's signature program, the Patient Protection and Affordable Care Act, sprawled over 900 pages of contradictory minutiae: the word "waiver" appeared 214 times. The Dodd-Frank bill, which tightened regulation of the U.S. financial system in 2010, covered 848 pages. For comparison, it took 31 pages in 1913 to establish the Federal Reserve, 37 to wrap up the Social Security Act of 1935.

The itch for microcosmic social adjustments is not an American invention. The democracies of Europe surrendered to it first, and with far more conviction. The European Union's proposed constitution of 2004, for example, contained 400 articles (the U.S. Constitution has seven) and 855 pages, in which every conceivable strand of right-thinking opinion was awarded a chocolate chip cookie.

For Britain, Paul Ormerod compiled a list of the Early Day Motions of Parliament—a procedural device that allows any MP to seek the government's support for a pet project.

> *On a single day chosen at random in 2004, the British government was urged . . . to hold a full inquiry into political opinion polls; give air quality a higher priority; take firm action against "disablism"; give a posthumous VC to Lieutenant-Colonel Paddy Mayne; introduce Northern Ireland-wide standards for care and access to arthritis treatments; press for the introduction of regulations to improve safety standards in European holiday resorts; increase the amount of funding to hospices; not bring back the poll tax; ensure that members of the British Diplomatic Corps can work safely in Bangladesh; deal firmly with attacks on NHS staff; propose the suspension of the E.U.-Israel Association Agreement; set up an independent public inquiry into Gulf War Syndrome; support the Pay Up For Pensions march; invest in the East Coast mainline railway; ban smoking in public; make clear the cost to Oxfordshire County*

Council of an asylum centre; support small business in legal action against large foreign multinationals; apologize for claiming Iraq had WMDs; amend the finance bill to allow people to invest in films; and, finally, abolish the need to reballot to maintain trade union political funds.[170]

Ormerod's assessment: "The urge to intervene, to be seen to be doing something, has reached epidemic proportions."[171]

The effect of this secular trend has been to engage the legitimacy of elected governments across the entire surface of society, but to do so thinly and ineffectively, like oil on water. From obesity to climate change, nothing is so personal or so cosmic that it can't be reckoned a failure of government. If political power has become the guarantor of happiness, then politicians must take the blame for the tragic dimension of human life. Democracy, as a system, must be held accountable for every imperfection and anxiety afflicting the electorate. Political intervention, though a gesture of appeasement to the public, has compounded the distrust it aimed to nullify. The stimulus and health-care bills energized the revolt of the Tea Party, and the E.U. constitution, for all its genuflections before accepted opinion, went down in defeat.

Failure, I repeat, is a function of government claims and public expectations. High modernist governments claimed that they could do anything to achieve perfection. Rhetorically, their present-day heirs have taken on this burden too, to which they have added the claim that they can intervene anywhere to promote happiness. The history of these claims in action can best be described as a humbling collision with reality. Failure has been the rule, and the impact of failure has been to bleed legitimacy away from the democratic process.

The public, for its part, has tended to accept government claims at face value. The ambitious rhetoric of the last 100 years has evolved into the natural language of democracy, and the public now takes it for granted that government could solve any problem, change any undesirable condition, if only it tried. The late modernist urge to intervene, with its aimless meandering, has been interpreted by the public as either tyranny or corruption—never, somehow, as the ineffectual pose of a kindly uncle. Yet government interventions have chased public grievances. Ormerod's endless list of parliamentary claims of competence can find a mirror image in the equally endless expectations of government culled by Manuel Castells from Occupier statements:

> ... *controlling financial speculation, particularly high frequency trading; auditing the Federal Reserve; addressing the housing crisis; regulating overdraft fees; controlling currency manipulation; opposing the outsourcing of jobs; defending collective bargaining and union rights; reducing income inequality; reforming tax law; reforming political campaign finance; reversing the Supreme Court's decision allowing unlimited campaign contributions from corporations; banning bailouts of companies; controlling the military-industrial complex; improving the care of veterans; limiting terms for elected politicians; defending freedom on the Internet* ...[172]

The public has judged government on government's own terms, but added bad intentions. My analysis of this complex set of relations arrives at a different place: high modernist claims exceeded government's capacity for effective action. Late modernist dithering can be explained more economically by political necessity than by elaborate conspiracy theories. In both cases, failure ensued with apparent inevitability. The obvious question to pose is whether it was, in fact, inevitable—and to that question I now turn.

PAUL ORMEROD AND WHY MOST THINGS FAIL

Brasilia was built. I have been there: it's a creepy place. The failure of Brasilia consisted in the growth of the unplanned city, which swallowed the original, and in the disappointing economic returns. Kubitschek had intoned the magical words, modernization and progress. None of that happened with Brasilia.

Modern governments have many achievements to their credit. They have built superhighways and helped to eradicate smallpox and polio. But they have promised many more things—nothing less than the good life—and they have asked for increasing control over wealth and power to get there. Failure has been a function of extravagant promises and great expectations.

At some point around the turn of the new millennium, elites lost control of information, and power arrangements began to flip. Assured of the public's wrath, elected governments have acted, or failed to act, motivated by a terror of consequences. Legitimacy was equated with the deflection of blame, and the aim of governing became to exhibit a lack of culpability.

"Instead of seeking to achieve political *objectives*, people seek certain physical and moral *qualities*," writes Pierre Rosanvallon. "Transparency, rather than truth or the general interest, has become the paramount virtue in an uncertain world."[173] Punished whether they moved forward or back, governments have agonized in an endless loop of failure, real and perceived, at many levels, everywhere.

In Greece, birthplace of democracy, what passes for a government was made answerable to a "troika" of international institutions, following the catastrophic economic failure of 2008. The political system teetered on the edge: the elections of May 2012 benefited radical leftist, communist, and ultra-nationalist parties, left the country deadlocked, and necessitated new elections in June. Trust in government, by one measure, sank to 14 percent in 2013.[174]

In Spain, three years after the *indignados* had condemned the failure of the country's "obsolete and anti-natural economic model," unemployment stood at 25 percent, and youth unemployment surpassed 50 percent.[175] Seventy-five percent of the public disapproved of President Mariano Rajoy's handling of the economy—but 85 percent disapproved of the chief opposition leader.[176] Trust in government fell to 18 percent.

In Italy, the most powerful political figure of the last decade, Silvio Berlusconi, was convicted of tax fraud, although there seemed to be little likelihood that he would ever spend a single day in prison. The government was a fragile coalition of cats and dogs mashed together after two months of political gridlock. The rising new party, the Five Star Movement, was led by a former comedian turned blogger who called himself Beppe Grillo—Jiminy Cricket. Trust in government had declined to 15 percent.

The emergence of antiestablishment parties like Five Star throughout much of Europe signaled the exasperation of the public with democratic politics as usual. These parties originated in the bipolar fringes of the political spectrum, or else came from nowhere, yet all shared a radically different set of claims from those of the mainstream right and left: their promises were all about blame and punishment. The enemy they wished to eliminate were capitalists, bankers, immigrants and foreigners, the E.U. Some insurgent parties, like France's National Front and Greece's

Coalition of the Radical Left, actually hovered on the threshold of power. Others, like Britain's UK Independence Party, were substantial enough to horrify the elites. In every case, the utopian projects of high modernism and the timid intervention of late modernism were rejected in favor of a politics of pure negation.

In the U.S., government failure at times resembled a preemptive strike on the public. Leaked classified documents revealed that the National Security Agency had placed billions of mobile phone and web communications, including those of American citizens, under surveillance. In May 2013, the IRS admitted that it had targeted President Obama's political opponents for audits in the run-up to the 2012 elections, and had consistently denied tax-exempt status to groups associated with the Tea Party. At airports and federal buildings, typical interactions placed members of the public in the role of suspects and supplicants before the armed power of the state. Nervousness on the part of government could be gauged by the urge to militarize: the Department of Education, NASA, and the Fish and Wildlife Service each funded their own SWAT teams. The belief that Big Government posed the greatest threat to Americans was by no means a Tea Party eccentricity: in one December 2013 poll, 72 percent of respondents were of this opinion.[177]

Failure pervaded the most basic functions of government. In October 2013, the American public watched while their elected officials in the executive and legislative branches failed to agree on a budget. For 16 days, until a budget was finally cobbled together, the federal government staggered about in a zombie-like state of semi-existence. In the following month, after three years of preparation, the technical and procedural elements of the president's health-care law crashed and burned at the moment of takeoff. Public support for the program nose-dived in parallel—to 36 percent in one January 2014 poll.[178] Other traditional government activities, like border control and the Postal Service, seemed to have embraced failure as their mission.

Our political system—let's call it by the proper name: representative democracy—was buckling under the stress of constant failure. At the same time that politicians were blamed for displaying unprecedented levels of partisanship, voters were said to be abandoning the Democratic and Republican Parties "in droves," and 60 percent of Americans, according to one survey, believed that a third major party was needed.[179] There was no contradiction in these reports. Together, they accurately depicted the rupture between the public and the people it kept electing to office. Public trust in government during JFK's time fluctuated between 70 and 80 percent. By 2013, at the start of President Obama's second term, trust had reached a level worthy of Silvio Berlusconi: 19 percent.[180]

As I review this depressing litany of failure, the key question is whether it could have been otherwise. Even if government claims have been excessively ambitious, it may be that government capabilities can achieve *some* level of success on *some* of the great issues that have troubled democratic politics for a century, and so satisfy, to *some* degree, the heightened expectations of the public. If the answer is yes, then we must ask more pointed questions about the competence and good faith of democratic governments. If the answer is no, however, we face an even more disturbing possibility: that democratic politics are fought over issues that democratic governments have no power to resolve.

Finding the boundaries to government action has been considered the business of ideology. I intend to come at the question from a different direction. My guide will be Paul Ormerod, a British economist with a gift for statistical analysis.[181] In *Why Most Things Fail,* Ormerod's abiding interest was to understand human action in the framework of complex systems. An action can be an individual decision or a government program. A complex system can be a company or a nation. For analytical purposes, it's all the same. The heart of the matter, for Ormerod, was how closely an actor's *intention* matched up with the *results* of his action.

His title gives the answer away. Ormerod found no obvious connection between the results of actions in a complex environment and their stated intentions. That holds true for you and me, for corporations like Apple and Google, and for the federal government. Most things fail, because our species tends to think in terms of narrowly defined problems, and usually pays little attention to the most important feature of these problems: the wider *context* in which they are embedded. When we think we are solving the problem, we are in fact disrupting the context. Most consequences will then be unintended.

Ormerod's findings are by no means definitive, but I consider them extremely persuasive. He has moved the argument about the boundary conditions for government from the realm of ideology—that is, of morality and politics—to that of possibility, of a more realistic understanding of how humanity interacts with the world. Morality and politics should be-gin where Ormerod concluded: with the possible.

This isn't remotely the case today. Political life in democratic coun-tries revolves around ambitious intentions and claims of competence that will fail, necessarily, on first contact with reality.

The same can be said for business, with one crucial difference. Ormerod compared the failure rates of companies with the extinction rates for species: "The precise mathematical relationship which describes the link between the frequency and size of the extinction of companies," he wrote, "is virtually identical to that which describes the extinction of biological species in the fossil record. Only the timescales differ."[182] Consider the implications. Companies *intend* to survive, indeed to thrive, and act on those intentions. They research the market environment, draft strategic plans, seek to maximize their advantages and minimize their weaknesses. Yet, ultimately, their failure rate is "virtually identical" to the random pattern of animal extinction.

The difference is that failing companies go out of business and are replaced by new companies, while government accumulates failure, mak-ing it, systemically, much more fragile.

Ormerod examined the performance of democratic governments on those issues that perennially engaged their ambitions: what I have called their claims to competence. Take unemployment as an obvious example. Every contemporary government has claimed the ability to reduce unem-ployment. The architects of the stimulus bill passed in 2009 claimed that it would save or create 3.5 million jobs and significantly lower the unem-ployment rate. It would do so by spending a lot of money. Of necessity, that has been the chosen economic tool of government. Since World War II, Ormerod noted, governments have absorbed a much larger chunk of the national output in pursuit of worthy goals such as full employment. In Britain, where excellent statistics have been kept from the Victorian era onward, the size of the public sector as a proportion of the economy has doubled since 1946, compared to the period 1870–1938. Yet the difference in the average unemployment rate before and after the expansion of gov-ernment was statistically negligible.

A similar historical trajectory describes every wealthy democratic country, including the U.S. The public sector grew enormously, while long-term unemployment rates remained unaffected. The stimulus cost nearly $800 billion, but its effect on unemployment, if any, was still a subject of debate. "Whatever benefits may have arisen from this massive increase in the role of the state, reducing unemployment, the primary cause of poverty, has not been one of them," Ormerod concluded.[183]

Another clear-cut issue was crime. Enforcing the law and preserving the security of persons and property has been a basic function of government since the Bronze Age. You would expect that as governments grew in wealth and reach, the crime rate would decline, but in fact the opposite occurred. Between 1960 and 1980, the U.S. crime rate tripled. Today, after strict enforcement of "three strikes and out" laws and the accumulation of an all-time high prison population, the crime rate remains double what it was in the years following World War II. Britain and the major countries of continental Europe, involving a variety of economic models and attitudes toward lawbreaking, have also seen sharp spikes in their crime rates. An analyst from Mars, unblinkered by ideology, might conclude that the efforts of democratic governments to prevent or reduce or punish crime appeared largely disconnected from actual crime rates.[184]

A parallel disconnect exists with regard to poverty, income inequality, and geographical segregation along class, ethnic, or religious lines. Democratic governments for decades have labored mightily, and spent immense amounts of money, to raise citizens out of poverty, redistribute income more fairly, and integrate neighborhoods to promote cohesive communities. Despite these persistent exertions, little has changed. At best, poverty, inequality, and segregation have endured unchanged. In most cases, conditions have worsened. Results have failed to match intentions.

For Ormerod, government failure was an inescapable consequence of the human condition. Even *Homo informaticus,* with his smart devices and connectivity, was a very limited organism when it came to processing information. Actors within a complex system—even expert actors, armed with doctorates and reams of scientific research, and wielding the awesome power of the state—were blind to the perturbations caused by their actions. The component parts of such systems interacted in mysterious and fundamentally unpredictable ways. A mild racial preference at the individual level, for example, could result in marked racial segregation at the system level.[185] Singling out a section of the system as a "problem" to be solved by government action propelled a chain of unintended, and usually undesired, consequences. No matter what strategy or technology was applied, the future continued to hide behind a veil of uncertainty. Prophecy and control were illusions.

> *Humans, whether acting as individuals or making collective deci-sions in companies or governments, behave with purpose. They take decisions with the aim of achieving specific, desired outcomes. Yet our view of the world which is emerging is one in which it is either very difficult or even impossible to predict the consequences of deci-sions in any meaningful sense. We may intend to achieve a particu-lar outcome, but the complexity of the world, even in apparently simple situations, appears to be so great that it is not within our power to ordain the future.* [186]

This description of reality makes a hash of many modern assump-tions—that science and technology can penetrate the future, for instance. Or that given enough information, any problem can be solved. Or that so-cial relations can be rationalized according to some visionary principle. If Ormerod is right, most democratic contests today are fought over phan-tom issues, and democratic politicians, to get elected, must promise to de-liver impossibilities. If, in truth, they have displayed excessive partisan-ship, it may be because team play between political organizations—the tally of wins and losses—retains a reality to which they desperately cling, as a drowning man will clutch a bit of floating debris.

If it isn't within our power to ordain the future, an irresistible tempta-tion will be felt by political actors to confuse progress with the negation and condemnation of the present. That has already transpired with the sectarian public. From Tahrir Square to Zuccotti Park, the public has re-jected the legitimacy of the status quo while refusing to get involved in spelling out an alternative.

A preference for negation as a political style has begun to spread among the very people who are responsible for the preservation of the po-litical status quo. For this paradoxical development, much of the responsi-bility, I believe, falls to President Obama, whose sectarianism from the heights brings him back to my story.

BARACK OBAMA AND THE JOYS OF NEGATION

The hypothesis of the revolt of the public, if true, must have profound consequences for the conduct of government. Hierarchy, slow to respond

and easy to surprise, has lost the argument in the information sphere before it began. Trust and legitimacy have bled away from those whose task
it is to summon the collective will to action. Rulers everywhere are pale,
trembling prisoners of their own rhetoric. Democratic rulers, for purely
historical reasons, are condemned to propose ambitious projects and assert extravagant claims of competence: that's the way the game is played.
But the game of democracy is now at war with reality. The result has been
persistent failure.

There is a democrat's dilemma that is no less perilous than the dictator's. Politicians must promise the impossible to get elected. Elected officials must avoid meaningful action at all costs.

In JFK's time, the public and the elites averted their gaze from the
emperor's nakedness. In contrast, we paraded the failures of President
Bush in Iraq and President Obama with the stimulus in the manner of
defeated chieftains at a Roman triumph. Democratic life, as I write these
lines, has been reduced to the exhibition and contemplation of the emperor's naughty bits. A way out of the utopian ambitions of modern democracy was needed, in order for democratic government to subsist.

All this by way of explanation for the rise and resurrection of Barack
Obama.

The president has been mocked by opponents for having "community organizer" on his resume, but that work aligned him, from the first,
with the rhetoric and self-image of a rebellious public. The community organizer is expected to expose, denounce, whip up indignation. He dwells
constantly on the many injustices of the established order, and he demands change on a heroic scale. The change itself is pushed off to some
other responsible party—usually, a government agency. The organizer
deals in negation, not action. The president's vision of democratic government can be described in similar terms.[187]

Barack Obama campaigned for the presidency in 2008 as an insurgent from the Border, but it was clear that, initially, he wished to govern
from the Center by implementing big programs in the tradition of FDR
and LBJ. This was a tricky pivot, and, as I have shown, the president never
managed to pull it off. The programs he espoused became a drag on his
popularity. Those that were implemented into law, like the stimulus,
sparked the Tea Party uprising that dismantled his ruling coalition in the
2010 midterm elections.

At this critical juncture, the president took the measure of the changed landscape and adjusted his ambitions accordingly. Whether by plan, or, as I think more likely, by temperament, he resumed the posture of a righteous outsider calling out a corrupt establishment. He distanced himself rhetorically from the power of his office, from the Center, and abandoned the claims of competence and heroic projects that had led his administration to failure and defeat.

Few observers, then or now, have grasped how deeply against the grain of history this approach was. American presidents are supposed to be doers and achievers—masters of legislation, policy, and politics. President Obama seemed uninterested in fitting into that mold. He had risen on a tidal wave of hostility against authority, and he had been smashed down when he, in turn, was perceived to be the authority. The public was angry and disgusted with government. Henceforth he would be the voice of that anger and disgust. The veteran community organizer would embrace and reinforce the public's distrust of the established order.

The president became chief accuser to the nation. Liberated by the partisan divisions in Congress from the need to pursue a positive legislative program, he wrapped himself in the warm blanket of combative rhetoric, and turned his back on the strenuous give-and-take of democratic politics.

Between 2010 and the presidential elections in 2012, a large number of issues and episodes earned President Obama's condemnation. All fit a politically divisive "wedge" profile: racism in the shooting of Treyvon Martin, economic injustice and the inequities of the market system, putative violations of the rights of women, immigrants, gays. In a remarkable political maneuver, the president's reelection campaign ignored his achievements in office and portrayed him, once again, as an insurgent battling the status quo. His opponent, Mitt Romney, found that his career as a successful businessman assigned him to the millionaires' cabal that really ran the country. The president, as accuser, could shrug off the burdens of incumbency. Two years after the disaster of the Tea Party revolt, Barack Obama won reelection with relative ease.

The broad features of the Obama style can be identified in an address to Planned Parenthood delivered on April 26, 2013: that is, six months after he had been reelected and was as free as any American political figure ever can be to speak his mind. The president first selected a divisive issue—in this case, abortion and birth control. He then framed the subject in terms of vague but powerful forces that wished to trample on the rights of ordinary citizens.

> *So the fact is, after decades of progress, there's still those who want to turn back the clock to policies more suited to the 1950s than the 21st century. And they've been involved in an orchestrated and historic effort to roll back basic rights when it comes to women's rights.*
>
> *Forty-two states have introduced laws that would ban or severely limit access to a woman's right to choose....*
>
> *In North Dakota, they just passed a law that outlaws your right to choose, starting as early as six weeks, even if the woman is raped. A woman may not even know that she's pregnant at six weeks....*
>
> *That's absurd. It's wrong. It's an assault on women's rights.*[188]

You would expect the president to argue at some length against each of these egregious injustices, name the culprits, and announce a White House strategy to defeat those who wish to turn the clock back to the 1950s. But this is precisely where President Obama differs from his predecessors. Despite the apparent severity of the assault on women's rights, few specifics and no plans for action were mentioned. The health-care law got a nod, together with a plea to the audience, community organizer-style, that they "spread the news" about the program, but no connection was made to the effort to roll back basic rights. The president offered his accusations in a manner that was curiously detached, more descriptive than argumentative.

He concluded with these words: "I want you to know that you've also got a president who's going to be right there with you fighting every step of the way." The battle and even the battleground appeared to be rhetorical, but the implication seemed to be that, without his accusatory voice, the anti-women forces would conspire in the shadows and triumph.

An even more striking example of President Obama's embrace of negation was found in remarks he delivered before another friendly audience at the Center for American Progress, on December 4, 2013. Again the subject chosen was a wedge issue: this time, economic inequality. The president began with an admission of the vast chasm separating the public from their government.

> *Between a reckless shutdown by congressional Republicans in an effort to repeal the Affordable Care Act, and admittedly poor execution on my administration's part in implementing the latest stage of the new law, nobody has acquitted themselves too well these past few months. So it's not surprising that the American people's frustrations with Washington are at an all-time high.*[189]

The president, however, believed that the public's frustrations were not merely the result of transient political events. They had deep structural causes. Economic inequality and lack of mobility drove the public's anger and despair. America, the president noted, had once been a land of economic opportunity, in large part because of the vast programs of his high modernist predecessors, from Lincoln to LBJ, on which he heaped much nostalgic praise. "But starting in the late 1970s," he continued, "this social compact began to unravel."

> *As values of community broke down, and competitive pressure increased, businesses lobbied Washington to weaken unions and the value of the minimum wage. As a trickle-down economy became more prominent, taxes were slashed for the wealthiest, while investments in things that make us all richer, like schools and infrastructure, were allowed to wither.*
>
> *... And the result is an economy that's become profoundly unequal, and families that are more insecure.*

As in the Planned Parenthood address, President Obama's villains in the story of inequality remained shadowy and nameless. It was unclear from the president's words whether the businesses that lobbied Washington did so from malice or necessity, and no explanation was offered for the decline of community values and the rise of trickle-down ideas. But the forces of selfishness, though nebulous and undefined, were powerful enough to transform the tenor of American life from opportunity to degradation. Once his rhetoric moved into accusatory mode, the president turned specific:

So the basic bargain at the heart of our economy has frayed. . . . This increased inequality is most pronounced in our country, and it challenges the very essence of who we are as a people. . . . The problem is that alongside increased inequality, we've seen diminished levels of upward mobility in recent years. A child born in the top 20 percent has a 2-in-3 chance of staying at or near the top. A child born in the bottom 20 percent has a 1 in 20 chance of making it to the top. . . . Statistics show not only that our levels of inequality rank near countries like Jamaica and Argentina, but that it is harder today for a child born here in America to improve her station in life than it is for children in most of our wealthy allies— countries like Canada or Germany or France. They have greater mobility than we do, not less. . . . The decades-long shifts in the economy have hurt all groups: poor and middle class; inner city and rural folks; men and women; and Americans of all races. . . . A new study shows that disparities in education, mental health, obesity, absent fathers, isolation from church, isolation from community groups—these gaps are now as much about growing up rich or poor as they are about anything else.

I find it difficult to imagine another president, in any historical period, drawing such an unrelentingly dark portrait of the United States. "The combined trends of increased inequality and decreasing mobility pose a fundamental threat to the American Dream, our way of life, and what we stand for around the globe." Clearly, Barack Obama found the country over which he presided to be in the grip of moral and material disintegration. And while this wasn't the first time he had made similar accusations, the difference in *purpose* indicated a changed approach to government.

When, in 2008 and 2009, President Obama had charged his immediate predecessors with "profound irresponsibility," he assumed a posture typical of modern presidents. He spoke as the country's political prime mover, defining a problem to make the case for his proposed solution: the stimulus. In 2013, there was no solution in sight. The president invoked his "growth agenda" and his "trade agenda," but these were slogans rather than a plan. A number of existing government programs were praised—including, inevitably, the health-care law—but nothing new was proposed.

The president was now a denouncer rather than a fixer of problems. He had described a destructive trend, but refused to make any claims of competence over it. The purpose of the exercise seemed to be to align him with the public's anger on this issue, as he perceived it.

* * *

The administration's response to controversy or scandal demonstrated its peculiar relationship to power. In each case, President Obama and his immediate advisors made a show of underlining the vast distance between the president's chosen identity—Border prophet chastising a sinful society—and the dull machinery of government. A virtuous passivity was imposed over the conventional portrait of the American president as always in command of the situation.

To cite just one example: President Obama was said to have learned on television news about the IRS inspector general's investigation of that agency for targeting Tea Party groups. His senior staff supposedly had been informed earlier, but had concluded that the matter wasn't worthy of his attention. A former senior aide blamed the scandal on "some folks down on the bureaucracy," adding, "Part of being president is there's so much underneath you because the government is so vast."[190] The president himself asserted that he "certainly didn't know anything" about the IRS inspector general's report until it was "leaked to the press."[191]

In another politician, that would sound like an artful dodge. With President Obama, if there was a dodge it was altogether on a grander scale. Although the highest political authority in the land, he had won two presidential elections by his rhetorical separation from all authority. He was a man of negation: a prophet in the wilderness. For the president and his inner circle, the federal government existed an immense moral distance "underneath" them, and was staffed by grubby bureaucrats who fully deserved the distrust of the public.

We need only recall John F. Kennedy's "I'm the responsible officer of the Government" to obtain a sense of how forlorn the exercise of political authority has become, under the pressure of a rebellious public.

Barack Obama's detachment from the levers of power caused consternation among elites generally friendly to his administration, who had mistaken his accusatory rhetoric for the voice of traditional activism. Dana Milbank of the *Washington Post* chided "Obama, the uninterested president," complaining that "he wants no control over the actions of his administration."[192] A satire in the liberal *New Yorker* hammered at the same point: "President Obama used his radio address on Saturday to reassure the American people that he has 'played no role whatsoever' in the U.S. government over the past four years," it deadpanned.[193]

The implication seemed to be that the president was trying and failing at industrial-age, high modernist politics. If my analysis has come anywhere near the truth, that did not remotely describe the situation. Barack Obama, I believe, represented a new and disconcerting development in democratic politics: the conquest of the Center by the Border, and the rise of the sectarian temper to the highest positions of power.

It's important to revisit these terms. According to Douglas and Wildavsky, the Border identified itself as the negation of the Center. The sectarian temperament was formed in alienation from the inequality and corruption of hierarchy. By this logic, the rule of the sectarian Border must mean the self-negation of government: the alienation of power from itself. To govern at the heart of this contradiction was the essence of the Obama style. Failure was condemned preemptively, from the rooftops: failure of the previous political leadership, of outmoded economic theories, of the protection of basic rights, of "community values" and society as a whole. Condemnation served to prove the president's good faith, and to rally the public—not, indeed, behind the institutions of the federal government or the democratic process, but behind his administration and his person. Legitimacy adhered to qualities intrinsic to Barack Obama, sectarian prophet, the president who was going to be fighting side by side with the public every step of the way.

As for democracy, its value was made contingent on specific outcomes. A process that allowed women's rights to be trampled and businessmen to promote inequality could not in good conscience be tolerated. Thus the election of Barack Obama made democracy legitimate, rather than the other way around. His defeat could only have been the result of conspiracy by secretive forces, and would have justified the public's flooding the streets in *indignado*-style protests. Something like this speculative scenario had come to pass in Egypt. Against the authoritarian Hosni Mubarak, democracy, for the public, had meant elections. Against the legitimately elected Mohamed Morsi, democracy meant purging the government of the Muslim Brotherhood and its religious mandates.

But representative democracy, as it actually exists, is a procedural business. Either it tolerates pluralistic outcomes or it will degenerate into chaos or coronations. More to the point, the president demanded outcomes that—to paraphrase Ormerod—were not within the power of government to ordain. Economic inequality, for example, has grown everywhere despite the best intentions of democratic governments. In the U.S., it increased under the Bush administration but worsened under President Obama's. The president has managed to detach his own claims of competence from the "problem" of inequality, and thus escaped the democrat's dilemma, but he did nothing to bridge the gulf between democratic politics and reality.

The accusatory style of government must be understood as a pathological development, a deformation, brought about by the underground struggle between the public and authority. Like all politicians, Barack Obama needed a viable political space from which to maneuver. In his particular case, he was squeezed between the ambitious failures of modern democracy and the predations of a networked public. After the defeat of 2010, the president decided on a strategy that placed the public's chosen weapon against authority—negation—at the center of government. He divorced his political personality from his official position, a paradox best explained as a desperate response to severe external pressures. His personal success made it likely that he will have imitators.

Yet the public remained as before: unsubdued, unquiet, unhappy. It could erupt at any moment, as it did in 2010. President Obama was able to mimic the public's voice, but he was not its chosen instrument; he's riding a tiger, and must constantly sharpen his rhetorical attacks to avoid having it turn against him. This can only intensify the public's corrosive distrust of the political system. When that distrust is validated by the highest elected officials, outright rejection of democracy becomes a defensible position, to be invoked at the next, inevitable, failure of government.

NIHILISM AND DEMOCRACY

The grand hierarchies of the industrial age feel themselves to be in decline, and I'm disposed to agree. They evolved to operate on a more docile social structure—one in which far less information circulated far more slowly among far fewer persons. Today a networked public runs wild among the old institutions, and bleeds them of the power to command attention and define the intellectual and political agenda.

Every expert is surrounded by a horde of amateurs eager to pounce on every mistake and mock every unsuccessful prediction or policy. Every CRU has its hacker, every Mubarak his Wael Ghonim, every Barack Obama his Tea Party. Nothing is secret and nothing is sacred, so the hierarchies some time ago lost their heroic ambitions and now they have lost their nerve. They doubt their own authority, and they have good reason to do so.

This great strategic reversal has produced few alternatives to the ideas and ideologies that dominated the industrial age. The public rides on new technologies and platforms, but as users rather than makers: it is uninterested in leveraging technical innovation to formulate its own ideology, programs, or plans. The public opposes, but does not propose. So in the second decade of the new millennium, political arguments resemble a distorted echo of the French Revolution or Victorian England: we still quarrel in terms of *left* and *right, conservative* and *liberal,* even while the old landscape has been swept clean and the relevance of these venerable labels has become uncertain.

The lack of new alternatives, of a way out, has trapped democratic politics in a perpetual feedback loop of failure and negation. And negation, invoked from every corner and without relief, has driven the democratic process to the edge of nihilism—the belief that the status quo is so abhorrent that destruction will be a form of progress.

I have touched on the question of nihilism before: the time has come to confront it squarely. A dose of social and political nihilism—a suicide wish—becomes inevitable, if you grant the hypotheses I have sought to establish in previous chapters. *If* the industrial-age hierarchies of contemporary democracy are suffering a crisis of authority, *if* the public is on the

Figure 26: Nihilist's night at the movies.[194]
Photo of the Grand Lake Theater, Oakland, CA © 2011 David Gans

move and expecting impossibilities, *then,* all things equal, the system will continue to bleed away legitimacy—*and* there will be those who argue it should be put out of its misery.

One concern is to discover the point at which such a chain of reasoning turns fatal. This is a tough question to parse analytically. "Legitimacy" is a kind of authorizing magic: so far as I know, it's impossible to quantify. Words may be said that have never been said before. A president, for example, may condemn the political system over which he presides. But the impact is unclear. Opinion polls, which gyrate around dramatic events, can offer measurements of distrust, but only through a glass, darkly.

My intention in this chapter is to tell a story in which nihilism is possible—and possibly about to go viral. A growing chorus of voices now affirms, with passionate conviction, a preference for nothingness—*nihil*—over the present state of affairs. All you need is ears to hear its negations and condemnations from many corners of the information sphere. Under certain circumstances, let me suggest, this chorus could swell into the public's mainstream opinion.

Virtually none of those who rail against the established order belong to the economically downtrodden or the politically oppressed; rather, they are middle class, well educated, mostly affluent. So part of my story must be an attempt to understand how such persons can arrive at political views that, if taken seriously, would entail their own destruction.

I want to analyze that creature of the shadows, the nihilist, in the environment that made his evolution possible.

FROM DECADENCE TO NOTHINGNESS, STOPPING AT STRANGE PLACES IN BETWEEN

In this late, tired age of democracy, large numbers of people believed that life was getting worse. The climate was changing for the worse—we had the Intergovernmental Panel on Climate Change to tell us that every year. "Warming of the weather system is unequivocal," the IPCC warned in 2013, "and, since 1950, many of the observed changes are unprecedented over decades to millennia."[195] The fault lay with us—more particularly, with our economic system: global warming was "anthropogenic," human-made. Our punishment took the form of extreme weather events like the killer hurricane Sandy, which devastated New York City in 2012. An environmentalist group claimed to have gathered 280,000 signatures of Sandy "survivors" petitioning the White House for "climate action now."[196] President Obama agreed to the extent of turning to accusatory mode on the subject. Rising ocean levels had "contributed to the destruction" in New York, he charged, and the cost of extreme weather events could be "measured in lost lives and lost livelihoods, lost homes, lost businesses, hundreds of billions of dollars in emergency services and disaster relief."[197]

The economy was getting worse. For liberals, this belief justified continued intervention by the government. For conservatives, it justified attacking the president and his ambitious high modernist rhetoric. For the American public, according to one poll, the decline of the economy was an apparently "intractable judgment," with only 25 percent dissenting.[198]

Political life was getting worse. I listed multiple failures of democratic governments in the last chapter. These took place in the open, in full view of the public, and they were difficult to blame on a single person, party, or ideology. Failure seemed to be systemic. Political elites were at once dogmatically partisan and weak. The public, unlike in President Kennedy's day, was unforgiving. Compared to the "greatest generation," the present generation had failed its way into a politics of decadence and despair.

It shouldn't come as a surprise that Barack Obama, with his keen sectarian taste for condemnation, took it for granted that American life was getting worse in many ways. Whether the question at hand was extreme weather or economic inequality, the president in his statements described a society in moral and material decline. It hadn't always been thus. Like every thinker—right and left, public and elites—who abominated the present order of things, President Obama looked nostalgically to the righteous past.

> *During the post-World War II years, the economic ground felt stable and secure for most Americans, and the future looked brighter than the past. And for some, that meant following in your old man's footsteps at the local plant, and you knew that a blue-collar job would let you buy a home, and a car, maybe a vacation once in a while, health care, a reliable pension. For others, it meant going to college—in some cases, maybe the first in your family going to college. And it meant graduating without taking on loads of debt, and being able to count on advancement through a vibrant job market.*[199]

But the golden age of high modernism was over. In the 1970s, the president explained, "this social contract" had unraveled, and we entered on our own fallen times.

American politics, and I think democratic politics globally, fretted under the shadow of the heroic past. Great projects had been attempted once, and the result had been stability, security, advancement. Today, conditions were deteriorating along many fronts, but the system appeared unable to generate fixes. The economy, for example, was universally believed to be getting worse, but the conversation among the elites and the public alike fixated on the symptoms of decline, on persistent unemployment, on inequality, lack of mobility, the outrageous salaries of CEOs, rather than on policy changes that might turn the situation around. President Obama had consigned his predecessor's tax cuts to the dustbin of outmoded theories. His effort to engage in large-scale economic policy, the stimulus, had failed on its own terms. Now there was no debate about a new tax cut or a new stimulus. The political process appeared sterile and exhausted, and the politicians were afraid.

Here was the overarching feeling of our age: that we were the decadent children of a great generation, and that no way back could be found, no exit from the quicksand into which we were sinking, because that quicksand was us. The natural urge to find responsible parties and assign blame was baffled by the immense number of targets. In the U.S., but also in Britain, France, Spain, and Italy, right and left governments had alternated, with results that could scarcely be teased apart. Ideologies, political parties, elections—the formal choices of democracy all ended, it appeared, in the same failed place.

Under the circumstances, the system bearing the weight of so many imperfections—representative democracy—began to lose its authorizing magic. This could be seen from the top of the pyramid and from below.

From the top: democratic politics had become the guarantor of individual happiness, yet the voters felt viscerally unhappy about their lives, unhappy, too, with politics and politicians in this hour of decay—any number of opinion surveys, in country after country, attested to this fact.[200] With growing desperation, democratic governments intervened in individual lives to achieve what they claimed were benevolent ends, yet the electorate saw in these efforts little more than usurpation and corruption. The Tea Party and the Occupiers, polar opposites, both had reacted against a government that intruded on everyone and failed everywhere. The contract that bestowed legitimacy on elected officials was being shredded. The politicians understood this, but labored under the conviction, probably correct, that the voters would punish rhetoric that failed to promise heroic improvements. They could, like President Obama, divorce themselves from their positions, but this would only aggravate the hemorrhage of legitimacy.

From below: a public on the march perceived the institutions of democracy to be indistinguishable from every other hierarchy of the industrial age. Presidents and prime ministers, congresses and parliaments, appeared remote, self-serving, hopelessly bureaucratic at best, debauched by money at worst. The public did not feel represented by their elected representatives, and spoke of them as a class apart. The *indignados*, who had a way with words, conveyed in their slogans a clear sense of separation from the political class: "You don't represent us." "The markets rule and I never elected them." "We are not anti-system, the system is anti-us." The negation, even the destruction, of democratic politics was now detached in the public's mind from the *ideal* of democracy.

That ideal still retained some authorizing power. The main *indigna-do* faction called itself Real Democracy Now. The Occupiers claimed to stand for the 99 percent, the Tea Partiers for the people against the government. To the public in revolt, however, the ideal of democracy could not be reconciled with the top-down control that characterized the standing institutions of representative democracy.

Some groups, like the Tea Party in the U.S. and the Five Star in Italy, participated in elections, but did so in a spirit of sectarian rejection of the Center. Barack Obama had done the same in 2008. Others, like most *indignados,* assumed a "neither-nor" attitude, and abstained from voting. In either case, the public, comprised of amateurs, took a simple view of democracy: it was *direct.* When Wael Ghonim wished to settle a controversial point on his Facebook page, he polled his readers. The Tea Party Patriots' website followed an identical procedure. The anarchist assemblies of the Occupiers allowed everyone to speak and required general agreement before arriving at a decision.

These were not alternatives to representative democracy. A nation of millions couldn't be governed by online surveys or anarchist assemblies. The elites, of course, had little interest in reforming the system: they wished to cling to the top of the existing pyramid. The sectarian public, always suspicious of hierarchy, had never believed that new structures would deliver happier results. The established order had failed, persistently, but there was no talk of alternatives, no pressure for reform, no faith—as I'll have occasion to note—in revolution.

The crisis of authority was a crisis of democracy. The public's assault on the institutions was often an assault on the democratic process.

Elected officials were routinely described as tyrannical by insurgents from the right. A favorite political conceit used by the Tea Party was the American Revolution, with Barack Obama playing the part of King George. Nobody seriously advocated a violent overthrow, but the metaphor was telling. Like the president, Tea Partiers believed that it hadn't always been so, but their time horizon for "our nation's decline" was much longer—"it has taken us a hundred years or so to reach our present state of crisis."[201] According to Mark Meckler and Jenny Beth Martin of the Tea Party Patriots, the gist of this crisis was the trampling on the rights of Americans by a government voracious for power.

*We felt threatened because a government that once existed to pro-
tect our rights to life, liberty, and the pursuit of happiness had become the primary obstacle to the exercise of those rights. Our government had broken through its constitutional restraints, seized
power over everything from our financial markets to our home
loans, and aimed to go even farther, seeking control over things as
large as our health-care system, and as small as the menus in school
cafeterias.*[202]

The sense of betrayal evident in these words strangely echoed President Obama's statements about a "misguided philosophy that has dominated Washington," and his belief that powerful forces were engaged in
an "orchestrated and historic effort to roll back basic rights." The sectarian temper found different targets from the perspectives of the right and
the left, but all agreed on the malevolence of the Center, even when that
Center had been endorsed by the voters.

To insurgents from the left, elected government was plainly a tool of
the corporations. "The will and goal of the system is the accumulation of
money," explained an *indignado* manifesto.[203] The "Declaration of the
Occupation of New York City" was even more explicit: "We come to you at
a time when corporations, which place profit over people, self-interest over
justice, and oppression over equality, run our governments."[204] A participant at the Puerta del Sol demonstrations in Madrid struggled to convey the
enormity of the movement's negations: "It's a peaceful extra-parliamentary
political explosion aimed against all the system in its totality, national and
international, against the bankers, the businessmen, the labor unions, the
political parties, the institutions, the communications media."[205]

These were words only—but that such words represented a repudiation of democracy by an alienated public I take to be beyond question.
The rhetoric connected to reality. Across the world, support for democracy was ebbing; the scholars who measure such things had little doubt on
that score.[206] Democracy was disintegrating in Egypt and wobbled on a
knife's edge in Venezuela, Turkey, Greece, and many more countries.
Matters stood differently in Western Europe and the U.S., yet even there
legitimacy and loyalty to the system often appeared contingent on achieving desired outcomes, rather than the will of the voters.

Elites in the old democracies manifested a certain irritation with their decadent politics, coupled with open admiration for authoritarian methods that "worked." China was the favorite example. Tom Friedman, columnist in the *New York Times*, wrote in 2009, "There is only one thing worse than one-party autocracy, and that is one-party democracy, which is what we have in America today." He went on to explain that one-party autocracy had "drawbacks," but if it "is led by a reasonably enlightened group of people, as China is today, it can also have great advantages. That one party can just impose the politically difficult but critically important policies needed to move a society forward in the 21st century."[207]

Legitimacy, in other words, depended on outcomes, and in democratic America outcomes were a muddle compared to those in authoritarian China. The CEO of General Electric, in a televised interview, seemed to agree with this judgment. Speaking specifically of China, he said, "The one thing that actually works, state-run communism . . . may not be your cup of tea, but their government works."[208] The interviewer, Charlie Rose, observed, "They get things done."

Condemning the "stale political arguments" in Washington, President Obama, in his State of the Union address on January 28, 2014, offered to work with a divided Congress, but pointedly added, "But America does not stand still—and neither will I. So wherever and whenever I can take steps without legislation to expand opportunity for more American families, that's what I'm going to do."[209] A sectarian president seemed to be suggesting that the democratic Center could not get things done.

While elites longed for a political system that worked, the public, for its part, perceived a politics submissive to hierarchy, corrupted by the will to power. The public had no love for Chinese-style autocracy, and, given its mutinous temper, scarcely distinguished between authoritarian and representative institutions. Democracy, from this perspective, appeared like another structure of control.

* * *

Pierre Rosanvallon has told a persuasive tale to explain how voters fell out of love with a political system that raised them, in theory at least, to the status of sovereign.

Historically, the preferred strategy of democracy has been more democracy, Rosanvallon observed. Progress meant the expansion of the franchise. Marginalized groups—workers, women, racial and religious minorities—could conceive of no greater political conquest than full voting rights. The democratic ideology turned, primordially, on inclusiveness. Implicit in the long struggle for universal suffrage was the promise that, once all the people were inside the system, something magical would happen: the good society. "It would put an end to corruption," explained Rosanvallon. "It would ensure the triumph of the general interest."[210]

In fact, inclusion and alienation have progressed in lockstep. Rosanvallon contended this was no paradox—it was cause and effect. Look around: every adult citizen can vote, yet nothing remotely magical has happened. Nothing has changed. Instead, we, the voters, were abandoned to our own imperfect selves, muddling through the necessarily procedural and uninspiring machinery of representative government.

Here was one source of public "disenchantment" with democracy: the pivot, it may be, away from an ideology of inclusiveness toward a society of distrust. But there was a deeper source of discontent, derived from what can only be described as a world-historical trauma.

A generation ago, faith in revolution still provided a standard of progress—a promised land for those who considered themselves radicals. I have touched on this before, from a different perspective. Once upon a time, high modernist governments presumed they could cure the human condition. They could make the world anew. All they needed was a transcendent project, like the collectivization of agriculture or the building of Brasilia. The debate, back then, was whether revolution should be achieved suddenly and violently, in "one great night" that transformed social relations, or gradually and democratically, by means of incremental reforms.

That faith has died. I won't dwell on the cause of death, but will only state an incontrovertible fact: there are no serious political actors today who believe in the reality, much less the desirability, of revolution. In consequence, radical and democratic politics, which shared the same utopian end point, have lost their directional coherence. The word "progress" itself has become impolite, an embarrassment. Nobody has a clue which way that lies.

Government's loss of faith in radical sociopolitical fixes marked the boundary between high modernism and our later, wearier version—experienced, I repeat, as a fall from grace rather than an increase in understanding. The "resolute singularity" of high modernist action was replaced by an irresolute multiplicity of tactical zigzags. The scowl of the prophet gave way to the twitches of the kindly uncle. Such changes were not flattering to the elites on whom they were imposed.

To advocates of radical change—and this came to include the public in revolt—the death of revolution resembled a blow to the head. They, too, lost their strategic vision, became disoriented, blind to the big picture. Absent the goal line of revolution, radicals found themselves able to mobilize only on a "case-by-case" basis, against some immediately felt injustice.[211] Rather than defeat or overthrow the government, they sought to control its actions toward the specific case that engaged their energies. And they did so by pure force of negation.

Radicalism, which once aimed to transform society, now more modestly (but, it may be, more successfully) labored to browbeat democratic governments into acknowledging an endless string of failures in need of correction. "To be radical," Rosanvallon affirms, "is to point the finger of blame every day; it is to twist a knife in each of society's wounds. It is not to aim a cannon at the citadel of power in preparation for a final assault."[212] Thus the itch for condemnation, and disdain of positive programs, that has shaped the behavior of the sectarian public.

Revolution, whatever its cost in human life, was an ideal grounded in utopian optimism. Hopelessness, however realistic, drives prophets to the wilderness, to feed on locusts and wild honey and dream of a messiah. Here is Henry Farrell, blogger, academic, social democrat, a sensible thinker, brooding on the sterility of what he calls our "post-democratic" age:

> The problem that the center-left now faces is not that it wants to make difficult or unpopular choices. It is that no real choices remain. It is lost in the maze, able neither to reach out to its traditional base (which are largely dying or alienated from it anyway) nor to propose grand new initiatives, the state no longer having the tools to implement them. When the important decisions are all made outside democratic politics, the center-left can only keep going through the ritualistic motions of democracy, all the while praying for an intercession.[213]

A system that began by promising perfection had at last delivered nothingness. Governments were powerless, politics were lost in the labyrinth, democracy was a hollow ritual, a falsehood. Nothingness was the only reality, and it presided over nations. To strike at nothingness seemed at least like *something:* a step forward, an intercession to be prayed for. So we were back to the cinematic nihilism of *V for Vendetta:* "With enough people, blowing up a building can change the world." We were back to the real-world nihilism of the London rioters in August 2011: "Bare SHOPS are gonna get smashed up so come get some (free stuff!!!) fuck the feds we will send them back with OUR riot!"

I want to be extremely clear about what I'm suggesting. A vast structural collision—preeminently, the revolt of the public against authority—has left democratic governments burdened with failure, democratic politics far removed from reality, and democratic programs drained of creative energy, and thus of hope. At this point, the nihilist makes his appearance. He is not a philosopher with an elaborated ideology, or a political figure leading an organization. Membership in the Nihilist Party cannot be had for love or money. Rather, the nihilist is merely reacting, as all human beings must, to the pressures applied by his environment: which means, in this case, that he is acting to destroy that environment.

If I'm correct with this line of analysis, the nihilist, while essentially at war with himself, will happily bring down the entire edifice of democracy as part of his suicide pact. He has taken radicalism to its logical extreme. He doesn't mean to conquer power or replace it with some new deal, only to obliterate the institutions that stand in his way: "Fuck the feds." And if this is truly the case, I think it's worth spending a few moments examining this political mutant, on whom so much of the future seems to hinge.

PORTRAIT OF THE NIHILIST AS THE SUM OF OUR NEGATIONS

What is this uncanny beast, born of the Fifth Wave and now stalking into the uncertain future? After all the talk of public and authority, of network and hierarchy, where—you ask—does he fit in?

Above all, he is seized and animated by a very particular feeling. I will characterize this feeling more explicitly later. Here, let me begin by saying that it partakes of alienation. The world of the nihilist does not belong to the nihilist. It belongs to the forces of selfishness and to repulsive people.

He considers his elected government to be a thing apart, and beneath contempt. That is the view from below. George W. Bush told him that the invasion of Iraq was about weapons of mass destruction, but none were

Figure 27: A political slogan in the age of negation.[214]
No Justice, No Peace, Fuck the Police March, © 2012 Glenn Halog is licensed under CC BY-NC 2.0.

found there. Barack Obama explained to him that the stimulus would cap unemployment, but millions more lost their jobs. José Luis Zapatero refused even to mention the word "crisis" to him, while economic disaster ravaged Spain. I called these episodes failures of government, but that is not how the nihilist sees them. He thinks his rulers are liars and cheats, and he fills the web with angry rants on the subject.

He can do that because he's extremely well connected, in the current sense of that word. He's *Homo informaticus* run amok. At the high end of his communications skills, he might be a hacker in Anonymous, vandalizing Sony's corporate database. At the low end, he could be a young rioter coordinating a looting expedition on his messaging service. The nihilist comes to life through his digital devices. Without them he would sink to a condition identical to nothingness: he would be silent. Instead, he is fantastically well informed about those few odd topics that obsess him, and he produces a torrent of hard-core negations posted about the world around him.

Being connected, the nihilist is networked. He can link to others just as destructive as himself, and bring them together in a flash of real-time mayhem. And there are always others: the nihilist isn't one but many. He belongs with the public when he's interested in an affair, as sometimes he is, but his predilections are sectarian to an absolute extreme. He is morbidly, monstrously, *against*. He imagines he would be happy if the society in which he lives were wiped out tomorrow.

In politics, this impulse pushes him way beyond rejection or revolt. The nihilist is a political black hole, allowing no light or mass to escape his violent embrace. Yet he's not a professional agitator, as he surely would have been in the last century. He's a private person, an amateur in politics moving among other amateurs. Nihilism, in him, isn't a full-time job—it's a latent condition. It erupts on a case-by-case basis. The fuse might be lit by some news on his Twitter stream about the war in Afghanistan or the flood of immigrants into his country. Or he might just reach a tipping point in that all-consuming feeling that partakes so much of alienation. Then he becomes what he is: an agent of annihilation.

In the assembly of protesters, his is the loud, irreconcilable voice. In the peaceful demonstration, his is the hand heaving a Molotov cocktail through the shop window. In confrontation with police, he is eager to shed blood. In online forums, he is fertile with ideas to hack, expose, paralyze the institutions that run the world. He is the bomber, the random shooter: a terrorist without a cause.

I could go on. He is possessed by a fuzzy but apocalyptic sense of doom, for example. The world, he holds, is going to rack and ruin. To push it along is the best thing. The government could fix everything and solve our problems if it tried—for all his alienation, the nihilist is convinced of that, and the most persuasive evidence he has of government corruption is that life keeps getting worse.

But enough—I want to get to the heart of the matter. I am arguing here that the nihilist haunts democratic politics like a specter portending disaster, but I don't believe the most significant factor pertains to what he is, or what he thinks, or even what he has done. The disquieting truth about his emergence is where he comes from. The threat to the future, if there is such, originates in his past.

The nihilist benefits prodigiously from the system he would like to smash. He's *not* marginalized—*not* a street person, *not* a forsaken soul, *not* a persecuted minority. He stands in a very different relation to the established order than did, say, an industrial worker in Victorian England or a Catholic in communist Poland. He's not a sufferer in any sense, whether relative to historical standards or to the world today. On meeting him, you would not recognize him as someone alien to you. Talking to him, I would not necessarily think that he's a different type of person from me. In the way such things get reckoned today—statistically, in the gross—he *is* you and me.

The mortal riddle posed by the nihilist is that he's a child of privilege. He's healthy, fit, long-lived, university-educated, articulate, fashionably attired, widely traveled, well informed. He lives in his own place or at worst in his parents' home, never in a cave. He probably has a good job and he certainly has money in his pocket. In sum, he's the pampered poster-boy of a system that labors desperately to make him happy, yet his feelings about his life, his country, democracy—the system—seethe with a virulent unhappiness.

Feelings of this sort compelled Daphni Leef to pitch her tent on Rothschild Boulevard to demand the destruction of "swinish capitalism." She came from an affluent family. She was a film school graduate and held a job as a video editor. Compared to most people anywhere or anytime, hers was a privileged life. Yet she seethed with a sense of injustice because she couldn't afford her old apartment. She felt the system was fundamentally rapacious, and she would bring it down to shorten her commute. "We all deserve more" was her one commandment. In the clouded mind of the nihilist, that "more" stretched infinitely toward utopia.

Similar feelings drove the "neither-nor" *indignados* to turn their backs on representative democracy. Historically, Spain had recently emerged from poverty and military dictatorship, and the current generation, even after the crash of 2008, was the wealthiest, best educated, and socially and politically freest the country had known. Yet those who raised the banner of "neither-nor" seethed with an irreconcilable feeling of grievance: like Leef, they felt they deserved infinitely more, and were willing to tear down a system that had failed to give it to them.

> *"Our parents are grateful because they're voting," said Marta Solanas, 27, referring to older Spaniards' decades spent under the Franco dictatorship. "We're the first generation to say that voting is worthless."* [215]

So here we have a privileged class in revolt against itself. Here we have the beneficiaries of democracy loathing democracy and clamoring for its demise, even without an alternative in sight. Like the character in the cartoon, the nihilist hates the knotty branch on which he sits, and conceives the idea that it should be sawed off. Does he know he will plunge to earth and break his neck? Maybe he does know—nihilism is a suicide pact. Or, possibly, does he think he will levitate in the air, defying the laws of gravity? Maybe he does think this way—nihilism is a call for the obliteration of history, and, at its most obdurate, a declaration of war on cause and effect.

I ask you to ponder the words of the young *indignada* I just cited. She said her parents were grateful for electoral democracy. Her generation was the first to make a virtue of ingratitude. José Ortega y Gasset, a fellow Spaniard, once discerned a "radical ingratitude" in the type of modern person he called "mass man" and portrayed as the spoiled child of history. Mass man is heir to a long and brilliant past. The good things in life in the world he was born into—security, freedom, wealth, vacations to warm places—are in fact the outcome of a specific historical process, but mass man doesn't see it that way. Newly risen to education and prosperity, he imagines himself liberated from the past, and has grown hostile to it as to any limiting factor. The good things in life have always been there. They seem detached from human effort, including his own, so he takes them as given, part of the natural order, like the air he breathes. Gratitude would be nonsensical. Mass man accepts the gifts of the system as his due, but will tear up that system root and branch, present and past, if the least of his desires is left unfulfilled.[216]

The nihilist is by no means identical to Ortega's mass man, but both share certain family traits. More accurately than alienation, a radical ingratitude describes the feeling that makes the nihilist tick. His political and economic expectations are commensurate with his personal fantasies and desires, and the latter are boundless. He expects perfection. He insists on utopia. He has, in Ortega's words, "no experience of his own limits," at least not as something he should accept in good grace. Every encounter with the human condition, every social imperfection and government failure, triggers the urge to demolish. Fortified by the conviction that he deserves more, he feels unconquerably righteous in his ingratitude—a feeling sometimes validated by late modernist governments bent on the promotion of universal happiness.

All this matters only diagnostically: as a symptom of a sickness of the system. The way I have characterized him, the nihilist looks to be a blurry figure, a part-timer lacking a program or an organization. He might be networked but he is also nameless. The riddle he poses is whether, in any sense, under any combination of events, he could gain enough momentum to damage or wreck the democratic process.

The answer shouldn't be difficult to arrive at. Follow the thread of this book to one *possible* conclusion, and you will be there.

The nihilist, it seems to me, isn't necessarily an alienated individual, a clever V figure behind a Guy Fawkes mask, bent on blowing up the status quo. A lone-wolf attacker like Anders Breivik, who killed 77 random persons in Norway because he hated immigrants, is only a glimpse, a warning, of more horrific possibilities. From the evidence of the preceding chapters, it should be clear that the bundle of destructive impulses I have called the nihilist represents a latent tendency in the public in revolt. Potentially, he is a multitude. Under certain conditions, *he* could be *you*.

Every public in the story I have told mobilized from a privileged position. That was true materially, politically, morally. None were paupers. None were pariahs. The public was constituted in this condition: it did nothing to achieve it other than appear on the scene. The protesters in Tahrir Square were the sons and daughters of the well-off Egyptian middle class. They were born to privilege. The *indignados,* offspring of the first generation in Spain to rise out of poverty and tyranny, cherished the ambitious expectations of a privileged class. Tea Partiers, Occupiers, protesters in Turkey, Iran, Venezuela, Ukraine—all wielded negation as a birthright. Command of the information sphere, distinguishing feature of our moment, was bestowed on the public by companies like Google, Facebook, and Twitter.

Born to privilege, the public must maintain *some* relationship to the institutions and individuals that raised it out of necessity and bondage. If the past is acknowledged, that relationship must be one of indebtedness. The Romans littered their homes with carved images of illustrious ancestors. But when, as is the case today, the public rejects history and longs to start again from zero, its relationship to the institutions that sustain it will be one of radical ingratitude. Once privilege is felt to be natural, a matter of birth rather than previous effort, the phantom that is the nihilist becomes flesh in the rebellious public—and any failure, any fall from perfection, will ignite a firestorm of discontent.

I called this a latent condition. Latency has been sometimes actualized—this book can be read as a series of variations on that theme. From above, governments have failed habitually, and are doomed to fail while they continue to promise the impossible. The public, from below, has seized on each failure to batter the ruling institutions, on occasion with a nihilistic contempt for the consequences. In between, attempting to mediate the conflict, stand the clumsy mechanisms of representative democracy. The answer to the riddle of the nihilist, I said, wasn't particularly difficult to arrive at. Those who worry about the future of democracy—and I count myself in that number—have good reason to do so.

ZOMBIE DEMOCRACY, A MASS EXTINCTION HORROR SHOW

The old industrial world is passing away. This mode of organizing humanity, so brilliantly successful for a century and a half, has been overwhelmed by too much information, too much contradiction. The elites who manage the system no longer believe in a way forward. Stuck in the muck, they strive simply to endure: *après moi le deluge.*

The nihilist—the public as destroyer of worlds—twists his knife into institutions that often resemble a body without a soul. You can pick examples at random: the daily newspaper, the political party, even modern government. Such institutions retain outwardly imposing structures, but they seem to lack vital signs, and can only stagger, zombie-like, from crisis to crisis.

My concern from the start has been with representative democracy. I worry that it, too, may be passing away. I wonder whether Farrell was right to assume that democratic politics, as practiced today, are also a body without a soul.

By that literary turn of phrase I mean something very specific. I mean an institution that clings to life and still wields power, but has been bled dry of legitimacy. It has no true authority or prestige in the eyes of the public, and it survives by a precarious combination of inertia and the public's unwillingness to produce an alternative. It exists by default. That, for example, is the condition of mainstream political parties in the old democracies—Republican and Democrat, Tory and Labour, Socialist and Gaullist, Christian Democrat and Social Democrat. Even their names have been bled dry of meaning. They exist by default.

Legitimacy is about *information*. Compared to the effects on the mind of a police raid or an exploding drone, it's soft. Once again we confront the idea of power as a game of rock-paper-scissors, except we now possess an interesting data point, manifested, as always, in the guise of a riddle. We know that paper sometimes beats scissors. Wael Ghonim began the overthrow of Hosni Mubarak on a Facebook page. But we don't yet have an inkling about the process that made this revaluation possible.

So let me tell a story about the stories we tell ourselves—how they explain and justify, how they live and how they perish.

Every great institution is justified by a story. That story connects the institution to higher political ideals and ultimately to the moral order of the world. It persuades ordinary people—you and me—that, if we wish to do the right thing, we should act as the institution requires of us. The story bestows the authorizing magic I have called legitimacy.

High modernist government, for example, told a story about perfecting social relations by the application of power and science. On this basis, it razed entire neighborhoods, without much protest, to make room for housing projects like Cabrini-Green. The Federal Reserve, in Alan Greenspan's time, told a story about mastery over the economy by means of esoteric knowledge. It allowed the institution to argue, persuasively, that a casino atmosphere was the most prudent approach to the money supply.

Such stories aren't surface gloss. They influence our behavior directly. This is why paper sometimes beats scissors: soft words ignite powerful historical memories, and the public takes to the streets. Political actors, consequently, tend to dispute with one another the ownership of the grand narratives. In his first inaugural address, President Obama made a case for expanded opportunity by appealing repeatedly to the Founding Fathers and the Constitution.[217] Yet the Tea Party, we know, made the Constitution central to its argument that the president had trampled on the country's founding principles. America's political future looked to be decided by whoever controlled the story of its past—not a particularly unusual or paradoxical situation.

A great catastrophe has overwhelmed many long-standing stories of legitimacy. They are dying out in droves.

Since each story purports to explain a shifting human reality, it must rely on institutional gatekeepers who interpret messy events according to tidy plotlines. That has been the business of Christian bishops and White House press secretaries: to impose the justifying story on the chaos of events. But we have seen that the evolution of technology hasn't been kind to mediators. The public's conquest of the information sphere has meant the overthrow of the gatekeepers—often accompanied by the collapse of the stories that imbued their institutions with authority and prestige.

Consider the case of Abu Ghraib. Perverse digital images from that Baghdad prison made a hash of a carefully articulated U.S. story justifying the invasion of Iraq. Almost immediately, these images spread beyond the reach of any authority, including the U.S. government. In a bizarre juxtaposition of two informational eras, the photos of Abu Ghraib were going viral on the web and garnering obsessive international attention, while the secretary of defense pondered whether to make them *officially* public.

The Middle East today resembles a graveyard of narratives. In Tunisia and Egypt, aging rulers—like our own secretary of defense—simply didn't grasp how preposterous their messages sounded in the context of available information. Collapse of the official story in both countries *preceded* the collapse of the regime: when towering figures stood exposed as clueless pygmies, the end was close at hand.

The region's *counter*-narratives have also been swept away by events. The rejection of Israel failed to ensure tranquility or legitimacy for Syria's Bashar Assad. Al Qaeda's doctrine that local dictators would never be toppled unless the "far enemy"—the United States—was first terrorized into retreat has been utterly discredited. Pro-Western or anti-Western, pro-regime or pro-violence, most established ideologies in Arabic-speaking nations are being consumed in a prodigious bonfire of the narratives.

Closer to home, the justifying stories of democracy are coming unraveled. Faith in the magic of universal suffrage has gone up in smoke. Trust that elected officials truly represent the people stands at an all-time low. The myths of revolution, high modernism, and the ability of government to remake the human condition now appear like childish fairy tales. Not even an advocate of Big Government like Barack Obama could persuade himself of their reality. Late modernist claims that happiness can be calibrated by kindly-uncle interventions have never won the acceptance of a distrustful public. That pillar of top-down democracy, Lippmann's hero, the expert-bureaucrat, melted down like the Wicked Witch in 2008.

The authority of institutions that surround and support modern democratic government—journalism, academia, science—has been systematically challenged, with disastrous consequences for mediated domains like the news business and the politics of climate change. The conflagration has already engulfed government itself, with its ambitious promises and habitual failures, and it may reach all the way up to the narrative of the all-embracing nation-state, stripping political life to a cold nakedness, as writer Anthony Olcott, citing Marx and the *Manifesto,* suggests:

> *All fixed, fast-frozen relations, with their train of ancient and venerable prejudices and opinions, are swept away, all new-formed ones become antiquated before they can ossify. All that is solid melts into air, all that is holy is profaned....*[218]

It is at this point, and to do this work, that the nihilist arrives on the scene.

* * *

To the extent that the institutions of democracy remain lashed to the industrial mode of organization, they risk becoming part of an immense cultural extinction event.

I am compelled to add that the timeline and even the inevitability of this calamity are uncertain. Deep beneath the mass extinction of justifying stories, beneath the failure of government and the living death of democracy, the slow-motion collision of the public against authority, at once cause and consequence of those surface dramas, grinds on. Elites can't preserve a status quo that the public is unwilling to transform. Turbulence sweeps the landscape but never arrives at the next stage, as if the world-historical clock, the Big Ben of human events, has stopped dead at midnight. That is where we are today. We may be here a long time yet.

So I am also compelled to ask about the degree of yield, of contingency, in this lost hour between our exhausted era and the unformed future. If, as Marxists and Calvinists insist, we are like bugs stuck in the solid amber of history, then the writing of this book has been a pleasant but ultimately pointless exercise. I have no evidence that we are so fated, however, and I have no faith in inevitabilities. Even if I accept that social and political structures constitute a kind of destiny, *they* are precisely what is at play today.

Otherwise, I may as well shrug my shoulders and say, like John Searle's determinist at the restaurant, "I think I'll just sit here and wait to see what I order."

Grant me, for the sake of argument, that history hasn't frozen solid—not entirely. What, then, of the conflict between the public and authority? It must erupt out of the depths and become personal. By this I mean that, in a world of contingent outcomes, each of us will be faced with choices, and that our choices will come wrapped in a fatal question.

The choices are the obvious ones of picking sides, of involvement and noninvolvement. The question will relate to the vastness of the system within which the conflict is taking place, and the smallness of each person. If modern government, for all its wealth and power, can't ordain the future of complex systems, what difference can it possibly make whether we, in our smallness, embrace one side or the other, choose *this* rather than *that?*

All the wounded vanity of our decadent age will be rolled up in that one question.

I acknowledge that I have now slipped out of analysis and plunged into the realm of speculation, but here we are. This is how I perceive the situation. The analysis of the preceding chapters has been an attempt to *map,* however crudely, a new sociopolitical environment that is as unprecedented as it has been unnoticed. But a map is just an instrument. There's still the matter of getting to the right places—of navigating to the "X" on the map that marks the right relation to this environment for someone, like me, who remains an unreconstructed supporter of representative democracy.

That will be the theme of the next chapter.

CHOICES
AND
SYSTEMS

This chapter is more speculative and less analytical than the preceding ones. You stand warned. The reason for the change should be apparent. At some point, I needed to cash in my analysis. If the world is as I have described, *something* follows. Something must be done or changed or cut loose from our previous understanding. Otherwise, I have merely added my camel's straw to the vast weight of negation crushing democratic politics today.

I began my story with an information tsunami and ended with that rough beast, the nihilist, and with democracy, as actually practiced, staggering into a maze of failure and self-doubt. Now I wish to parse the *choices* available to the players—the public, the government, you and me—in this turbulent landscape. Ultimately, the question in my mind is whether any combination of choices can chart a path out of the labyrinth, into the open sunlight.

I originally titled the chapter "What Is to Be Done," which conveyed my intention all too blatantly. Having portrayed a system deformed by relentless but poorly understood forces, I felt obliged to offer a fix. I learned, however, that I'm not comfortable posing as a prophet or even as an advocate. I can think of no reason why you should act on anything I have to say—unless, of course, you were driven by motives and ideals similar to mine in the first place.

I won't pretend to have discovered an escape hatch from our enervated age, and I won't indulge in idle negation. So I settled on identifying choices. They *are* to be found in the new landscape. You, reader, must decide on yours. Mine, I will make known.

Some choices lead to chaos, some choices lead to China, but the truly perplexing analytic question is how to tell one from the other in a complex environment. I am persuaded by Paul Ormerod's argument: even the colossal machinery of modern government has been unable to ordain the future. The crisis of democracy arose from the denial of that fact. We want to build Brasilia over and again, to leap ahead 50 years into a future that is always more rational than the present. At a minimum, we demand that our politicians talk as if they can use the power of government to perfect the human condition, when we have known, since 1991, that they have no notion how to do so.

In the reality interpreted by Ormerod, most things must fail, including ambitious government projects, because the world is too unpredictable and nonlinear. But if that is the case, what difference can a personal choice make? The intelligent reader will at once understand this to be another question entirely: In what social and political environment could *personal* choices make a difference? The search for an answer is a major thread in this chapter.

The habits of high modernism have led to certain default assumptions: that only the top of the pyramid can impose meaningful social, political, and economic change, for example. Only the highest reaches of government, therefore, have the capacity to choose the path ahead. The rest of us belong to the inert masses. These assumptions were always undemocratic in spirit, but, more importantly, they have been falsified by the experience of the last 50 years. Heroic top-down initiatives have failed, habitually and in their own terms. The masses have awakened to political life in the unruly public, and the tremendous energies released by the Fifth Wave have surged entirely from below. Ideologies justifying hierarchical control over society have faltered, fallen, and begun to go extinct.

The central theme of this book has been the war of the two worlds, high and low, but that has entailed a radical reversal of roles, with amateurs, people from nowhere, swarming up the slopes of the pyramid to trample on the preserves of the chosen few. The simple world of the public, now networked and online, has thoroughly perturbed the complex system administered, for better or worse, by the elites. The question I have is whether the two spheres can be brought into better alignment from the perspective of representative democracy.

Consider this chapter a reflection on how choices, personal and political, can influence the functioning of democracy.

IF STRUCTURE IS DESTINY, THEN THE PERSONAL WILL TRUMP THE POLITICAL

Drill down into the networks that have enabled the public to confound authority, and you soon arrive at what I would call the *personal sphere.* This is the circle of everyday life, experienced directly, in all its local specificity.

Here the choices meaningful to an individual get generated: spouse, children, friends, career, faith. Government and high politics fill in the background. To imagine they can ordain or legislate happiness at this level is a modern illusion.

Because the personal sphere is tightly clustered, information seldom strays more than one or two causal links away from action. A friend mentions a job opening in his company, you apply for the position. This is the equivalent of seeing that truck bearing down on you, and using the information to step out of the way. It's immediately and demonstrably effective. A few longer links to more distant acquaintances, or friends of friends, make possible personal participation in large-scale clusters: the network.

The evolution of *Homo informaticus*, who, when interested in an affair, deploys digital devices to interact personally with a network of millions, triggered the great phase change in the public's relationship to political authority.

If the revolt of the public at times has resembled the struggle of the personal against the official and categorical, it is equally true that the industrial age often seemed intent on bulldozing every personal, local, or historical feature out of the landscape. Government in the 20th century looked into the personal sphere, found it illegible to its purposes, and sought to impose on it symmetry and uniformity.

The modern state, through its officials, attempts with varying success to create a terrain and a population with precisely those standardized characteristics that will be easiest to monitor, count, assess, and manage. The utopian, immanent, and continually frustrated goal of the modern state is to reduce the chaotic, disorderly, constantly changing social reality beneath it to something more closely resembling the administrative grid of its observations.[219]

In democracies, the impulse to standardize usually led to some version of Brasilia—the geometric city without sidewalks or neighborhoods, built in the wilderness to escape the irrational clutter of the past. Government, in high modernist mode, imposed a bargain on the silent masses: surrender your personal sphere in exchange for social perfection. That adventure has been part of my story. It ended badly, as we know, but the price paid for the failure of government went beyond the big issues I have touched on—inequality, unemployment, and so forth. Choices were sucked out of the personal sphere, where causal links are short and effective. They flew all the way to the top of a very high pyramid, to be absorbed by elites who must contend, at each step, with the nonlinearities and unintended consequences of causation within a complex system.

Vandalism and gang violence at Cabrini-Green offered a glimpse into what transpires when personal choices stand blocked by a standardizing logic.

* * *

Only a generation ago, structural necessity dictated that hierarchy must grow steeper, more controlling, more efficient. There were two political parties, two automakers, three TV networks, one newspaper for every city, all functioning with little energy and no input from below. The Taylorist spirit ruled. The top could command the bottom in minute detail. The bottom was a formless, inert mass, activated solely by commands from the top. That was the structural destiny of the industrial age. Nothing else was really possible. The public was offered a narrow band of choices—Republican or Democrat, Chevy or Ford—unless it wished to opt out of the system and all its benefits.

Today the polarities have been reversed. The public has options—that is the single defining feature of the Fifth Wave. The public has options, and everywhere has cashed them in to pull the elites down and lower the height of the political pyramid. Ordinary people have turned the tables on the standardizing bureaucracies, and now insist that their tastes and interests be imposed on the larger system. They demand personalized service. They crave latte without milk—not just from Starbucks, but from their government.

Rulers and ruled find the distance between them tightened until neither can stir without elbowing the other. Daphni Leef, with her commuter's insurgency, and Barack Obama, with his detachment from institutional power, exemplify a new crowding of the personal into the political. The old, stately pyramid is sagging. Its walls look brittle. The nihilist awaits his hour. This would appear to reflect the structural destiny of our own times.

But destiny comes in the guise of a historic choice. We have options—not just the nihilists among us, but everyone, including those, like me, who have never given up on representative democracy. The options in this case involve an analytical assessment. By an accident of history, our democracy became industrialized and Taylorized. That is its present form, how it appears in the public's mind. But the tide of history is now moving in the opposite direction. Government as pure hierarchy and authority has lost much of its legitimacy, and is under assault along many fronts.

The analytic question is whether democracy must remain industrialized to endure. Or to put it somewhat differently: whether democracy will suffer or thrive if the steep pyramid of power gets collapsed into a tighter structure. Or to put it personally: whether people like me, uncomplicated defenders of our system of government, are condemned forever to defend the system in its present form, against the predations of history.

Cyber-utopians and cyber-pessimists have debated the importance of new media to democratic activism. Research on the subject remains inconclusive, but I am posing a different kind of question in any case. My question concerns the intrinsic necessity of industrial modes of organization to democratic government, and the intrinsic destructiveness of a public organized in digital networks, riding the tsunami of information.

I don't see this as an especially tough puzzle. If I set aside, for the moment, the negations and contradictions of the public, the answer emerges from the body of evidence presented in this book. The failure of government isn't a failure of democracy but a consequence of the heroic claims of modern government, and of the constantly frustrated expectations these claims have aroused. Industrial organization, with its cult of the expert and top-down interventionism, stands far removed from the democratic spirit, and has proven disastrous to the actual practice of representative democracy. It has failed in its own terms, and has been seen to fail, and it has infected democratic governments with a paralyzing fear of the public and with the despair of decadence.

The nihilist is dangerous in part because he's right. Zapatero was egregiously mistaken when he imagined that the Spain of 2008 was not in the grip of an economic crisis. President Bush was equally mistaken about Iraq, President Obama about the stimulus. These were very unlike political personalities, espousing very different ideologies, but they were similar in one crucial respect: they believed they could ordain the future. They embodied a system that had lost touch with reality. If democracy is to be judged on their performance, it would be hard not to lapse into negation.

So it comes down to alternatives. The most effective alternative to the steep pyramid of industrialized democracy isn't direct democracy on the Athenian model or cyber-democracy in the style of Wael Ghonim's Facebook page. It's the personal sphere: the place where information and decisions move along the shortest causal links. To the extent that choices are returned to the personal from the political, they can be disposed directly, in the light of local knowledge, as part of an observable series of trial and error. Personal success can be emulated and replicated. Personal failure will not implicate the entire system.

I note that the present trajectory is heading mostly in the opposite direction. The public wishes to impose the personal on the political, in the same manner that it has imposed a personalized mode of doing business on capitalism. Here's a contradiction: for all its disdain of politicians, the public has often behaved as if happiness were indeed a gift bestowed by presidents. The apocalyptic anger of the Occupiers and the *indignados* was the dark side of a muddled utopian vision that demanded the impossible from authority. Even the Tea Partiers, for all their libertarianism, assumed that the legitimate role of political power was to "protect" the pursuit of happiness.

The public, I mean to say, has been fully complicit in the failure of government. And the question of alternatives must extend beyond the formal organization of democracy to our expectations of what democratic government can deliver.

TELESCOPIC PHILANTHROPY, OR THE POLITICS OF THE IMPOSSIBLE

As I wrote these lines, opinion polls showed that a majority of Americans disapproved of President Obama's handling of the economy. The president, who prided himself on his political instincts, was well aware of the numbers, and countered with a condemnation of a system that fosters economic inequality. These are the great issues of American politics, and have been so since the rise, late in the 19th century, of high modernist ideals.

I won't pretend to certainty in understanding what the public has in mind when it evaluates a president's "handling" of the economy. But I imagine it expects epic outcomes in the economic field, such as high growth and dramatically lowered unemployment, imposed by a ruler who enjoys command and control of the system. President Obama, in some way, has disappointed these expectations. The failure of the stimulus probably weighed heavily on public opinion—but this is a piece of circular logic. President Obama proposed the stimulus because he believed, correctly, that epic economic outcomes were expected of him as president.

Yet the claims of modern government with regard to the economy have been falsified many times over. President Obama, from the top of the power pyramid, resembled a bystander to economic developments far more than a heroic figure with command and control. His post-2010 sectarian rhetoric recognized this implicitly. He would rather have condemned inequality than proposed big economic initiatives, because, politically, it appeared more rational.

The federal government and the U.S. economy are two aspects of the same monstrously complex social system. Their interactions are uncertain, nonlinear, and prolific with unforeseen consequences. To judge a president's "handling" of the economy as if he were managing the mortgage and checking account of his own personal sphere is a gross inversion of reality—but I suspect that is precisely what the public has done for a generation and more. If, during this time, politicians have made claims for government that are untethered from reality, and have consequently failed to deliver the impossible, we should not be surprised. Success with the public on election day has entailed failure the day after.

The alternative I wish to consider comes in two parts. The first has to do with *honesty* in our expectations. Presidents can't handle the economy. They have no clue how to do it. The experts who advise them rarely have what N.N. Taleb has called "skin in the game": they pay no penalty when they are wrong, as they were, catastrophically, in 2008, and immediately again, with the stimulus, in 2009.

When it comes to economic questions, politicians should be rewarded for the modesty of their claims rather than the heroic ambition of their rhetoric. Sitting presidents should be applauded for discarding the pose of papal infallibility, and speaking about uncertainty, risk, and trade-offs. The more people we elect to office who grasp the concept of trial and error, which means nothing more than learning from mistakes, the happier we should be.

Whether this alternative is practicable I leave for you, wise reader, to decide. But it *is* a choice. You and me, and every member of the public, can

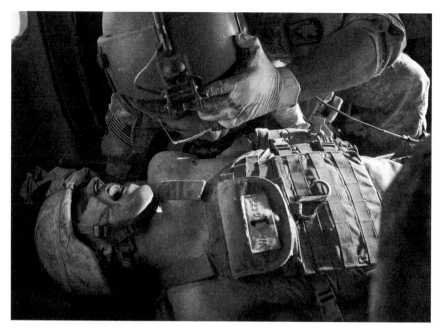

Figure 28: The meaning of round numbers. *"In Toll of 2,000, New Portrait of Afghan War," from the New York Times, August 21, 2012* © *2012 The New York Times. All rights reserved. Used by permission and protected by the Copyright Laws of the United States. The printing, copying, redistribution, or retransmission of this Content without express written permission is prohibited.*

bend our political demands to reality, as we *must* do with our private needs, when managing our affairs in the personal sphere. The ideal of government as master of the economy is an artifact of the industrial age. Today we know perfectly well that the whirlwind of aggregated activity we call "the economy" isn't like a factory floor, to be orchestrated by some maestro according to Taylorist principles.

So the choice we face is pretty stark: align our demands with the knowledge of our historical moment, or stay under the shadow of the failed ambitions of the past.

Aligning the public's expectations with historical reality should have a ripple effect on ideology. The old categories will themselves be re-aligned. The immanent faith in political power and pseudo-experts, the latter-day feeling of decadence and impotence—all of that, ultimately, will be swept away, replaced by political quarrels and emotions that actually connect to the possibilities of the moment.

I hasten to add, however, that seizing the choice before us doesn't require some sort of Pauline conversion. You *may* keep your old political faith and still break new ground—but you may *not* treat reality like an enemy, and you may not compound failure with dishonesty.

There is a second part to this choice. The standards used to evaluate government projects are also inventions of the industrial age. We, the public, are invited to take sides, to applaud or condemn presidents, based on some statistical abstraction, some *number*—the gross domestic product, for example, or the unemployment and poverty rates. We saw the unemployment rate used like a baseball score in the controversy surrounding the stimulus. The number shows the public who's winning the political game.

Numbers like the GDP fulfill a rhetorical function. They partake of the prestige of science, appearing superior to the confused jumble of reality as actually experienced. They sustain the high modernist claim that we can know at a glance the truth about vast systems.

But we know that we *don't* know. The number is an illusion. If I lose my job, I understand what this signifies in all the intimate details, because I have direct access to my personal sphere. If I am told that the unemployment rate went up from 5.1 to 5.6 percent over the last month, I have no idea what this signifies. I lack access to the reality behind the number. The rise could reflect the machinations of greedy corporations or a corrupt government, or the effects of a natural disaster, or plain misfortune, or any combination of these and many other possibilities.

Even if the unemployment rate measured the actual number of unemployed Americans—it doesn't[220]—and even if I set aside the vexing question of whether the government should be responsible for employment, playing politics by the number is a frivolous game of make-believe. Politics is nothing like baseball. In the end, the most persuasive story wins, not the highest score. That is true whenever government tries to impose a specific outcome on a complex system. In the Iraq and Afghanistan wars, for example, the tally of dead American military personnel has been used as a surrogate measure, but the success or failure of war policies have depended entirely on who wins the argument about the rightness of the cause. Abraham Lincoln, who oversaw the most horrific slaughter of U.S. troops in history, is today considered our greatest president.

Much of the negation poisoning the democratic process has stemmed from a confusion of the personal and the statistical. I may hold down an excellent job, but the failure of the stimulus to meet its targets infuriates me. I may live in peaceful Vienna, Virginia, safe from harm—but a report that several Americans have died violently in Kabul appears like a fatal failure of authority. By dwelling on the plane of gross statistics, I become vulnerable to grandiose *personal* illusions: that if I compel the government to move in this direction or that, I can save the Constitution, say, or the Earth, or stop the war, or end poverty now.

Though my personal sphere overflows with potentiality, I join the mutinous public and demand the abolition of the established order.

This type of moral and political displacement is nothing new. The best character in the best novel by Dickens, to my taste, is Mrs. Jellyby of *Bleak House,* who spent long days working to improve "the natives of Borrioboola-Gha, on the left bank of the Niger," while, in her London home, her small children ran wild and neglected. Dickens termed this "telescopic philanthropy"—the trampling of the personal sphere for the sake of a heroic illusion.

> *Mrs. Jellyby, sitting in quite a nest of waste paper, drank coffee all the evening and dictated at intervals to her eldest daughter. She also held a discussion with Mr. Quale, the subject of which seemed to be—if I understood it—the brotherhood of humanity, and gave utterance to some beautiful sentiments. I was not so attentive an auditor as I might have wished to be, however, for Peepy and the other children came flocking about Ada and me in a corner of the drawing-room to ask for another story; so we sat down among them and told them in whispers "Puss in Boots" and I don't know what else until Mrs. Jellyby, accidentally remembering them, sent them to bed.*[221]

The revolt of the public has had a telescopic and Jellybyan aspect to it. Though they never descended to details, insurgents assumed that, by symbolic gestures and sheer force of desire, they could refashion the complex systems of democracy and capitalism into a personalized utopia. Instead, unknowingly, they crossed into N. N. Taleb's wild "Extremistan," where "we are subjected to the tyranny of the singular, the accidental, the unseen, and the unpredicted." In that unstable country, "you should always be suspicious of the knowledge you derive from data."[222]

I can't command a complex social system like the United States, but I can control my political expectations of it: I can choose to align them with reality. To seize this alternative, I must redirect the demands I make on the world from the telescopic to the personal, because actionable reality resides in the personal sphere. I can do something about losing my job, for example, but I have no clue what could or should be done about the unemployment rate. I know directly whether a law affects my business for better or worse, but I have no idea of its effect on the gross domestic product. I can assist a friend in need, but I have little influence over the natives of Borrioboola-Gha, on the left bank of the Niger.

Control, however tenuous, and satisfaction, however fleeting, can *only* be found in the personal sphere, not in telescopic numbers reported by government.

A telescopic philanthropist, from the moral heights, would call this selfishness or escapism. Yet selfishness, it seems to me, would entail the demand that the government meet all my needs. Escapism would mean burying my personal responsibilities under a concern for the brotherhood of man. Mrs. Jellyby, as depicted by Dickens, was a selfish escapist. That is not *necessarily* the case with those who choose to anchor their expectations to the realities of the personal sphere.

From within the short causal links of that intimate space, I *can* engage the tangled web of politics and government, form opinions, and act, if I wish, on those opinions. I can join vital communities of interest, and participate in philanthropic activity, including protests on behalf of radical change. I can exult when my ideals triumph on the great stage of the world, and feel despondent when they are defeated. That is allowed.

What I *cannot* do is demand certainty of complexity, or expect that statistical formulas and numbers, accessible only to a chosen few, will have the power to ordain the future. What I *should* not do is pour a corrosive stream of rejection and negation on a democratic system that has struggled, and mostly failed, to meet my impossible demands and expectations.

ADVICE TO THE PRINCE, OR THE ART OF GOVERNMENT IN SOCIETIES OF DISTRUST

The most consequential choices available under the conditions that prevail at the moment concern the public—you, me—and its political expectations. Such choices are grounded in true contingency: I *can* align my expectations with reality or with utopian illusions. Nothing is settled. The power to decide is mine (yours, ours).

Government also faces epochal choices. Hierarchy and bureaucracy, the expert and the trained professional, are losing favor with the public. The pyramid is shrinking: the distance between top and bottom has grown uncomfortably tight. Wael Ghonim, anonymous administrator of a Facebook page, was sought out by powerful members of the Mubarak regime as a negotiator during the 2011 protests. He had just walked out of a secret prison, where state security had kept him for 11 days.

Power and persuasion have headed in different directions. Legitimacy currently belongs to actions and persons as much as to institutions. Democratic government is everywhere surrounded by a rebellious networked public. Institutional changes, even radical ones, are possible, but they will not arrive as the result of necessity or the laws of history. They must be chosen.

I will tread lightly in my discussion of government, for an obvious reason. For me, there's no contingency in the question. I can choose my expectations of government, but I have no way to *impose* these expectations on the human beings and structures that embody the government. Since I don't wish to dabble in utopian fantasies, or sound like King Lear railing at the storm, my options in dealing with this subject are limited.

But I can't avoid consideration of the choices of government without leaving a large, inexplicable hole in the center of my story.

Let me begin with the ideal, if only to dismiss it. In the best of all possible circumstances, government will assume the shape that dominates the imagination of a historical period. Modern government, creature of the industrial age, would give way to *networked* government, able to exploit "small world" links to reduce, formally, the distance between power and the public.[223] Political issues—proposed legislation, for example—would be debated and resolved on a much vaster virtual stage, on which ordinary people, no less than elected or bureaucratic elites, have their say. The output of government would be crowdsourced and thus sanity-checked.

This won't happen. Hierarchy is too stubborn a structure. The self-interest of the top and the *dis*interest in wielding power of the sectarian bottom make it almost certain that the current structures will endure. The pyramid is losing height, but it almost certainly won't flatten altogether. Barring some unforeseen and unprecedented breakthrough, the organization of government, like that of corporations, will remain top-down.

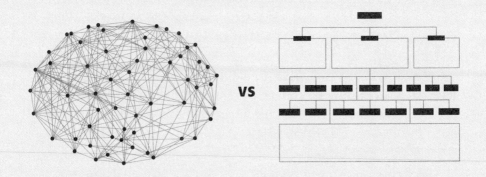

Figure 29: Structural destiny: network against hierarchy.[224]

In a non-perfect world, which happens to be the one we actually live in, hierarchical government, democratic government, must find ways to regain legitimacy without yielding on every point to the negations of a networked public. The decisive choices, I believe, concern the handling of that perturbing agent, information.

Hierarchy, as a structure, has proven transcendentally inept in dealing with digital platforms. Despite a lot of brave modernizing talk, social media and the new communication technologies remain a profound mystery to government, while those at the top of the pyramid continue to detest the intrusion of amateurs and the rude informality of the web. Hence their serial amazement each time the public rides digital tools to materialize, as from thin air, on the streets.

Government's awkward attempts to embrace digital technology provide the most revealing examples of its incapacity. According to a December 2011 study, some 56 federal agencies owned 1,489 .gov domains—but 400 of these domains redirected the user to another government site, 265 didn't work, and 20 were "under development." There seemed to be no guiding principle for hosting federal websites: the number per agency varied from 160 to two. A total of 150 different web publishing systems and 250 different web hosting providers were used to run the government's 11,000 sites. Main users of this crazy quilt of technology and information were "federal workers, followed by researchers and the press."[225]

This was information from the old elites of the industrial age to their brethren, filtered, almost symbolically, through digital systems instead of paper reports. The public need not apply, and was not interested in any case. The USA.gov site, to take just one example, described itself as "The U.S. Government's official web portal." That sounded important and ambitious. Between 2010 and 2011, however, the site garnered around 0.02 percent in "daily reach," or total traffic of the web—less than half the daily reach of Icanhascheezburger.com, a website featuring humorous photos of cats. Currently, the U.S. government's official web portal ranks 1,751 in popularity among U.S. websites, and 6,303 globally.[226]

When government has tried to reach the wider public through digital media, it has failed in spectacular fashion. The online insurance marketplace that was part of the new health-care system cost the federal government $400 million and took three years to develop. According to the *New York Times,* the website was supposed to be a "one-stop, click-and-go hub for citizens seeking health insurance." Instead, it crashed and burned on delivery. Merely to log on was impossible for many users. An insurance executive was quoted by the *Times* as saying, "The extent of the problem is pretty enormous. At the end of our calls, people say, 'It's awful, just awful.'"[227] But this should surprise nobody. The government has no idea of how to interact with the public other than from the top down. That is how federal agencies structured their 11,000 websites.

Like the CIA after 9/11, those responsible for developing the health insurance website insisted that they had failed because of insufficient funding. "The staff was heroic and dedicated, but we did not have enough money, and we all knew that," one administrator claimed.[228] In reality, we have seen, the failure of government has been systemic. It has followed the pattern of Greek tragedy, in which excessive pride, or hubris, brings the hero to ruin. Modern government believed it could conquer uncertainty and ordain the future. It couldn't—and when it tried, it failed. In the present case, government believed it could create a vast "marketplace" on command, and simplify it to a few clicks per transaction. It couldn't do that, either.

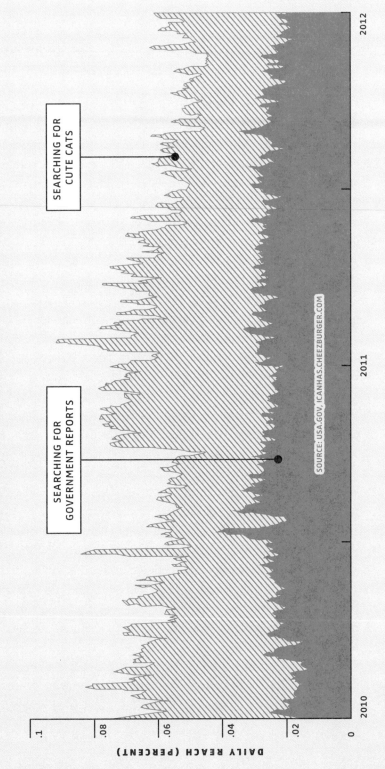

Figure 30: The public is more interested in cute cats than government reports.[229]

The tragic flaw wasn't incompetence with regard to technology. It was the illusion of control—preeminently, the inherent urge of hierarchy to control information.

On this matter, government has arrived at a fundamental choice. It can continue to squeeze a top-down framework on a networked culture, as if the social and technological reordering of the new millennium could be wished back to 1989. The terms of government's increasing proximity to the public will then be dictated by forces external to government, and, it may be, indifferent or hostile to democracy.

Alternatively, government can opt to participate in its historical re-alignment with the public, and retain a measure of control by moving information online in ways that are legible to the bottom of the pyramid. Even if interactivity—the back-and-forth of a truly networked system—is restricted, the production process of government can be made manifest at every step. Networked government, I said, is today a utopian ideal: open government, in my judgment, remains a possibility.

For government to communicate with the public online to any extent, official language must be radically altered in style and length. That is also a choice, and by no means a trivial or superficial one. Consider the making of laws by the two houses of Congress. Each proposed bill can be posted, each version, alteration, or amendment noted in real time, but that is not enough. When, like the stimulus, a law is 1,000 pages long, it becomes indigestible by the public. In fact, it is almost certainly indigestible to most of the elected representatives who vote on it—an instance of top-down ambition trumping the democratic process.

When government goes online, it will no longer be speaking just to itself. If the government chooses to feed information directly to the public at every level of operation, it must learn the language of the public, even if it limits the public's ability to talk back. Laws will be shorter, for example. How much shorter? I have no idea, but I imagine a lot less than 1,000 pages. The public, not the government, will set that boundary, indirectly, through the information sphere.

Brevity from government isn't a crazy dream. If our grandparents could deliver Social Security in 37 pages, we can produce much less consequential tax or budgetary decisions on a similar scale. It's the government's call.

That is only one speculative illustration of what might happen if government chose to work its drafts out in the open, online. The legal and pseudo-technical jargon clogging most official communications would also be reduced to a minimum. The current incentives for opaqueness would be replaced by a need for persuasiveness. Bureaucracy would behold itself through the cold eyes of the public. That alone might be transformative. The interventions and interpretations of regulators would be compared, transparently, to the original intent of a law. Instead of 11,000 agency websites, there would a single matrixed .gov web, extending as deep into the global information sphere as our elected officials can tolerate.

This can be tried step-by-step. It can be embraced sequentially by portions of the federal government in a rare shot at trial and error. But something along these lines will either be done *by* the government or likely will be done *to* it. The public is on the move. The age, recall, is stuck at midnight. I don't do prophecy, so call it speculation. But I feel certain that, to the extent government stands aloof from the global information sphere, to that exact degree the information sphere, in the form of Tea Party-like revolts and Wikileaks-style revelations, will burst back, uninvited and destructive, into the precincts of power.

* * *

The reason to push information out to the public isn't primarily so it can participate in making law or policy. The public's engagement with laws or policies has always been determined by its interest in an affair, and that, in turn, has been limited by the fractured nature of the public. For any given political issue, a vital community, obsessed with the subject, may jump on the case. Most of the population will yawn and turn away. Only in the rarest of instances will shared points of reference arouse a politically significant multitude—and even then, it may or may not represent the will of the majority. The public, we must always remember, is not, and can never be, identical to the people.

The point isn't to pull the public up to the top of the pyramid in some sort of king-for-a-day "e-government" exercise, but to push the output of the elites to the personal sphere, where the public lives and makes decisions.

The revolt of the public against authority can be framed as a contest between two disparate ways of looking at the world: the institutional and the practical. Institutions can perceive only generic abstractions, like the unemployment rate or the GDP. They are blind to the accumulation of detail that is everyday life. Practical knowledge fills that gap: it consists of local idiosyncrasies that are impossible to generalize. This can be as simple as knowing which car dealerships in the neighborhood cheat on repairs and which medical practitioners go by the book rather than the patient.

The choice of openness depends on the direction in which information *should* flow to guide effective action.

A supporter of democracy would argue, purely on principle, that information should flow from government out to the public, where it can be plugged into the matrix of everyday decisions. But I believe the same answer obtains from the perspective of efficacy in achieving outcomes. The failure of government has proceeded in parallel with the devaluation of practical knowledge.

Intoxicated with the possibility of perfection, high modernist rulers endeavored to reduce local reality to the administrative grid of their observations. They wanted society at ground level to look like Brasilia or Cabrini-Green. The public, too, came to imagine that *personal* fulfillment depended on *institutional* action, and adjusted its expectations of democracy accordingly. We stand late in that cycle of top-down ambition and failure, with the public in revolt, the elites horrified by their own weakness and decadence, and the collision between the two worlds crushing practical *and* institutional knowledge into nothingness.

Government can choose otherwise. By pushing its business online, it will demolish the mystique of institutional knowledge. You and I, as members of the public, will observe the messy birthing process of official statistics, and connect any pertinent information directly to our everyday experience. I (you, us) will have the opportunity to make personal decisions with a reasonable understanding of how complexity, bearing the aspect of government, will factor into the decision. If I run a business, for example, I will receive early warning of possible regulations that may affect my profit margins.

I (and you) can then take appropriate action. I can plunge into the complexity of the political world, if I wish, and participate in a lobbying campaign. More importantly, I can move within my personal sphere, where meaningful choices reside, to position myself and my business in whatever I believe to be the right relation to government. I can still make bad decisions. In fact, I probably will—I can't ordain the future any more than Alan Greenspan or President Obama could. But my failure will redound on me, not on the government—and I will be able to apply practical knowledge immediately to repair my circumstances, rather than wait for action from remote and formulaic institutions. I will conduct my life with humility, according to trial and error, rather than double down on error and expect power to deliver success.

By placing before the public the early drafts of government business, elected officials and their expert-bureaucrats will bring themselves down to earth. They will allow the public to catch them in the act of making assumptions, trade-offs, best guesses. Government will be demystified, as nature was after the scientific revolution. This will temper the public's expectations of the outcome. If the minutes of the risk commission's meeting in L'Aquila had been immediately posted online, the criminal prosecutions that ensued probably would have been avoided: scientific failure would have been understood to be a consequence of the limits of human knowledge.

To any who care to look, it will be apparent, in real time, that the veil of uncertainty clouds the vision of presidents and Fed chairs, no less than that of ordinary men and women. Once that fact is admitted, the loss of magical powers might well be compensated by a gain in legitimacy. I don't consider this a paradox, only the difference between observing actions based on illusion or reality.

Tremendous energies have been released by people from nowhere, networked, self-assembled, from below. That is the structural destiny of the Fifth Wave—the central theme of my story. Democratic government in societies of distrust can choose to ride the tsunami or be swamped by it. The latter choice will leave government mired in failure and drained of legitimacy. It will leave democracy, I fear, at the mercy of the first persuasive political alternative.

FINALE
FOR
SKEPTICS

My thesis, again, is a simple one. The information technologies of the 21st century have enabled the public, composed of amateurs, people from nowhere, to break the power of the political hierarchies of the industrial age. The result hasn't been a completed revolution in the manner of 1789 and 1917, or utter collapse as in 1991, but more like the prolonged period of instability that preceded the settlement of Westphalia in 1648. Neither side can wipe out the other. A resolution, when it comes, may well defy the terms of the struggle. None is remotely visible as I write these lines.

If my thesis is true, we have entered a historical period of revolutionary change that cannot achieve consummation. Institutions are drained of trust and legitimacy, but survive in a zombie-like state. Governments get toppled or voted out, but are replaced by their mirror images. Hierarchies are brought low, but refuse to yield the illusion of top-down control. Hence the worship of the heroic past, the psychology of decadence—the sense, so remarkable in a time of radical impermanence, that there's nothing new under the sun.

Very little about my thesis can be considered original. I said this at the outset, and reiterate it now. The events that make up the bulk of my story have received massive amounts of attention from high and low. But attention has riveted on the singular and the tactical: beyond generalizing turbulence in the Middle East into an "Arab spring," many connections have been missed.

I have aimed at the strategic, at the big picture, folding Napster and blogging and Climategate into the same insurgency that swept Barack Obama to office and knocked Hosni Mubarak off his pharaoh's throne. I have portrayed a public in revolt against authority in every domain. So maybe that has been my contribution.

It should be apparent by now that I'm less interested in originality than in democracy, which has been caught in the crossfire between the public and authority—sometimes, as in Egypt, literally so. The revolutionary impulse of the age has been fueled by strangely personal utopian expectations. The failure of democratic governments to deliver on equality, social justice, full employment, economic growth, cheap apartments, happiness, and a meaningful life, has driven the public to the edge of rejection of representative democracy as it is actually practiced. Some have gone over the edge. Failure has bred frustration, frustration has justified negation, and negation has paved the way for the nihilist, who acts, quite sincerely, on the principle that destruction of the system is a step forward, regardless of alternatives.

Anders Breivik, Norwegian, affluent and well educated by global standards, posted a 1,518-page manifesto online abominating the system that had pampered him, then detonated a bomb near the prime minister's office in Oslo and personally shot dozens of young kids to death. Consider him a premonition. The longer the collision between public and authority grinds on unresolved, the more likely we are to endure a multiplication of Breiviks.

And we already know what that looks like. Al Qaeda, the nihilist wing of political Islam, has shown the way.

A number of contingencies flow from my thesis, choices open to government and to the public. I have touched on them with what might have been appalling brevity. I can choose to orient my demands on life toward the personal instead of the political. This will shift meaningful decisions to the relative freedom of the personal sphere, away from remote institutions lost in the wonderland of complexity. Government can choose to push out the drafts of its business into the open, online, where they can be scrutinized by any who care to do so. This will provide early warning of official interventions at the personal level, and explode the myth of command and control—thus aligning the public's expectations with reality.

I honestly don't know whether these choices, if taken, would restore the legitimacy of the democratic system in the eyes of the public. But it would counter much of the distrust, and that would be a step in the right direction.

One large question remains. The skeptical reader has been asking it since the first chapter. How (he wonders) can he be sure that my thesis, with all that follows, is *right?* The answer is: he can't be sure. That's not how analysis works. In fact, that's not how human knowledge works. We can never know with certainty that any proposition is right. We can only try to show that, so far, it hasn't been proven wrong. Analysts thrive on counterfactuals and falsification—or at least they should.

As an analyst, I must take the skeptic's question seriously. I must be an extreme skeptic myself. Since my thesis can never be shown to be completely right, I must take care to understand *where* and *how* it can be wrong.

IF MY STORY HAS BEEN FICTION, THE NULL HYPOTHESIS MUST BE TRUE

Every thesis is simply a description of the world. From this description *something* must follow, some demonstrable effect or change—otherwise, there's no point to raising the subject. Effects can be immediate or more distant and higher-level. Because a thesis must rely on abstractions like "the public" and "authority"—or, for that matter, "gravity" and "relativity"—it is to the effects that we must look for both support and falsification. Eddington's findings in Brazil and Principe, for example, were in line with the predictable effects of Einstein's general theory of relativity.

Identifying effects in human affairs is beyond tricky, because the instances are so few and the causes interact rather bafflingly with each other. The analyst must live with a higher degree of uncertainty and imprecision than a physical scientist would tolerate. I wish I could offer you a number, like Einstein's curvature of light, to prove or disprove my story. But I can't. If I tried, it would be a symptom that I had succumbed to the industrial delirium for numerology.

Honest analysis *does* require that the thesis be stated clearly, and that effects be identified with as much precision as possible.

My thesis describes a world in which, as a result of changes in information technology, two structural forces are found in permanent collision: the public, organized in networks, and government (authority), organized hierarchically.

The overall effect has been constant political turbulence. Everywhere the status quo is attacked and under stress—yet nowhere has the revolt of the public crystallized into a completed revolution. Since, for structural and historical reasons, such a tidy end point is unlikely to come soon, I would expect a proliferation of Egypt-style protests that threaten or overturn regimes, but fail to reorganize into a new order.

A first-level effect can be seen in the character of the public. Opposition to governments and policies has been self-organized rather than controlled, conducted by amateurs rather than professionals, and outcome-oriented, usually *against,* rather than ideological. These traits appear to be intrinsic to sectarian networks. I would therefore expect more people from nowhere, in the *indignado* and Tea Party mold, to erupt on the political scene—true for democracies and authoritarian regimes alike. I'd also expect representative democracy, as a system, to come under increasing challenge when desired outcomes fail to materialize.

The behavior of late modern government, too, counts as a first-level effect. Government today is slow to respond, afraid to advance, unwilling to yield. In democratic countries, it is habitually drawn into promising outcomes that it has no clue how to deliver. The public's conquest of the information sphere has left rulers dazed and confused. They know that heroic actions are expected of them, but also that every initiative will be contested and every failure amplified. The contradiction is structural and invariable, if the thesis holds.

Under such conditions, I would expect democratic governments to intervene ever more thinly and erratically over the surface of society, to give the appearance of doing something, of being in charge. More broadly, I'd expect politicians and governments in democratic countries to promise *more* while risking *less*. Laws and policies, for example, will continue to inflate in length, allowing the authors to generate *some* words that appear, however vaguely, to have ordained the future.

I turn to higher-level effects with trepidation: these are difficult to trace in the maze of complexity, but happen to carry enormous significance for the particular story I have told. So what I'm going to place before you, reader, is an interpretation, a story derived from another story, about the indirect effects of my thesis that seem most powerful to me.

By far the most consequential higher-level effect has been the near-fatal hemorrhage of legitimacy from established institutions. I say "near-fatal" because in democracies the institutions have survived in the mode of the living dead. They exist but can only stumble clumsily around the political landscape. In authoritarian countries, matters stand somewhat differently. The regime and ruling party of Mubarak in Egypt are dead and buried, but similar institutions, run by much the same people, have replaced the old regime. In Libya, Tunisia, and elsewhere, an institutional chaos prevails.

In all cases, I believe, the feeble pulse of the institutions can be traced to the unforgiving trauma inflicted by the public. I would expect such assaults to persist, bringing about continuing declines in public trust of government, increased levels of negation and condemnation of the system in public discussion, more leaked documents believed to be damning to rulers, and a proliferation of street protests. I would look for entities external to government, such as corporations and NGOs, to absorb many of the functions traditionally assigned to the brain-dead institutions. Government could begin to unbundle.

Additional higher-level effects include a progressive loss of inhibition by the public in its attacks on authority, the rise of antiestablishment political groups, and the possibility, lurking in the shadows, of the nihilist and his fever dream of annihilation. I would therefore expect ever more frequent calls for the overthrow of government and the abolition of the system. Pariah parties, like the National Front in France and the Five Star in Italy, will enjoy electoral success. Violence could explode at any moment, though the precise circumstances needed to light the fuse are unknown to me and probably unknowable.

Finally: in the political environment described by my thesis, government must make it a priority to defend itself against the public. I would expect the Chinese regime, for example, to be far more concerned with surveillance and control of the Chinese public than with foreign adventures—and to court risk overseas primarily to manipulate domestic opinion. The same would apply to our own federal government. It will treat the American public like the enemy and deal with foreign enemies mostly to impress the public.

In democracies, elected officials will be tempted to gain favor by distancing themselves from the democratic process. I would expect a number of would-be Barack Obama imitators, who seek to rule by disdain of power and to head systems they profess to abhor. I'm not sure whether this is possible for political players who lack the president's gift of contradiction, but many, I expect, will try.

Let me stop here. I have laid out, in as much detail as I can, the conditions under which my analysis can be falsified, but my job isn't quite over yet: one more step is required. To respond to the question posed by that pesky skeptical reader, I need to flip my thesis upside down, like a pancake. I must present a "null hypothesis."

First, I must explain what that bit of jargon means.

* * *

Suppose the evidence I have submitted in this book turned out to be a series of random accidents and coincidences—sound and fury, signifying nothing. I believe, for example, that the events of 2011 folded into a meaningful whole, a phase change in the revolt of the public and the crisis of authority—but suppose I am radically mistaken. Suppose these events were unrelated to each other in any way. If what I took to be signal turned out to be noise, so that nothing new—no effects, direct or indirect—would follow logically from my description of the world, *that* would be the null hypothesis. It's the theory of the persistence of the status quo.

The null hypothesis to my story would describe some version of the world in which cyber-skeptics like Malcolm Gladwell live. (But note that it could not match Gladwell's contentions exactly: these, I insist, have been falsified by events.) In this world, hierarchical institutions still rule unchallenged. Properly interpreted, 2011 turns out to be a series of local events, largely manufactured or at least co-opted by powerful elites utilizing copy-cat tactics. The public and its weak-bond networks can irritate but never seriously threaten the authority of modern government.

The overall effect of the null hypothesis is a political environment safely entrenched within the processes of the industrial age. Government actions and policies are sheathed with authority and persuasiveness, while government failures implicate specific politicians or parties but never the system as a whole. You should expect, under such conditions, for political life to be characterized by continuity rather than disruption. Protests occur, but they target specific rather than systemic issues. Public opinion will be more forgiving—even, on occasion, as gentle as it was with JFK over the Bay of Pigs.

A first-level effect is the nature of the opposition: it's loyal rather than radical, shares many basic assumptions with those in power, and sits comfortably inside the political system. If this is true, Republicans and Democrats, Tories and Labour, will take turns running the government, and the public will accept the monotony in the manner of a dull but tolerably successful marriage. Counter-hierarchies of professional agitators might be found in the world of the null hypothesis, but eccentric political organizations, inspired by bloggers or comedians or Facebook pages, will never encroach on the power pyramid.

A crucial first-level effect of the null hypothesis concerns information: it belongs to the institutions and remains effectively under their influence. Persuasion is practiced mostly by the elites, whose voices and phrases are echoed by the public over the information sphere. Discussion focuses on "problems" and "solutions" rather than the failure of the established order. You should expect public opinion to align with elite opinion, and the information sphere to serve as a pillar of the system rather than as the means for its subversion.

Higher-level effects will reflect the tenacity of the industrial mode of organization. Institutions retain the full measure of legitimacy: they rule uncontested. Government embarks on ambitious interventionist projects at home and abroad. The public and its purported eruptions are really the manipulations of interested parties, insiders playing at populism. The public lacks reality: it is a phantom, without the will to stand apart or against.

In this environment, you should expect a substantial measure of trust in government, few leaks of damning official documents, mutual deference and limited negation in political disputes. When, as at present, the trend in every instance appears to run in the opposite direction, you should suspect a conflict among the institutions rather than posit the revolt of a fictitious public.

Even in democracies, the preferred government style will be command and control—coupled, however, with reduced interest in policing the public. The Chinese and U.S. governments will take for granted the loyalty, or at least the forbearance, of the population, and will concentrate their energies on projections of power in pursuit of social improvement and the national interest. Established political parties will absorb new political factions and tendencies. They will wield great influence over affairs, but will be checked on occasion by visionary leaders who, from the top of a very steep pyramid, implement ambitious schemes.

So there they are: my thesis and the null hypothesis. If events resemble my description of the world, I am not necessarily right in any final sense. But if they appear more accurately described by the null hypothesis, then my thesis is false. It is up to you, skeptical reader, to decide.

Before you do so, I have one more bit of evidence I wish for you to consider. Much has happened in the months since I began to write this book.

THE FUTURE'S UNCERTAIN, BUT THE PRESENT IS ALWAYS HERE

At college, I took a class in Latin American social revolutions, taught by a professor who had just published a book on Chile. The professor had a mantra about the Chilean revolution. "The Marxist Allende government might not last," he said more than once, "but its reforms are irreversible." In his book, he had banished contingency from human events. He had fallen in love with the word *irreversible*. It was fall semester. That September, a week or so after the class began, Augusto Pinochet and the Chilean military overthrew Allende and the Marxists, and reversed all their reforms in as complete and permanent a fashion as history, which never stops, allows us to judge.

My poor professor's book suffered the academic equivalent of crib death.

I learned a lesson—one that had nothing to do with Latin American social revolutions. I learned about the blindness of experts and the folly of prophecy. Years later, Philip Tetlock was to put scholarly integrity around this insight, in *Expert Political Judgment*. On reading Tetlock's data, I found myself fascinated but not in the least surprised.

I am, at present, keenly aware of another lesson from that class. Books that interpret events will sooner or later be falsified by events—you just hope it's later. Over the last few months, I have scrutinized my information stream with intense curiosity and something less than philosophic detachment.

Let me make the events flowing over that information stream a first cursory test of my thesis and the null hypothesis. Of necessity, I will be brief—superficial. I am coming to the end of my story, and I have no wish to linger unreasonably.

But I won't be coy. A description of the world of yesterday, today, this very instant, will have little in common, so it seems to me, with the null hypothesis. That might change tomorrow, but I can only deal with what I can see from where I stand.

* * *

On November 21, 2013, Viktor Yanukovych, elected president of Ukraine, backed away from an association treaty with the European Union. The move infuriated a large segment of the Ukrainian public, which had come to see the E.U. as a guarantor against government abuses and corruption. That same day, Mustafa Nayyem, an online journalist just a few months older than Wael Ghonim, summoned the Ukrainian public to the streets with a post on Facebook: "Let's meet at 10:30 p.m. near the monument to independence in the middle of the Maidan," the central square in Kiev.[230] About 50 protesters were already there when Nayyem arrived, but the crowd swelled to 100,000 within days. Eventually hundreds of thousands, quite possibly millions, participated throughout the country.

It became known as the Euromaidan revolt: three months of protests, government repression, and political violence, culminating on February 22, 2014, when Yanukovych gave up the fight and fled to Russia. He was, I noted, the elected president, but his removal was considered by the insurgents to be a victory for democracy. For them it was the outcome, not the process, that counted.

Events in Ukraine have repeated the patterns of the revolt of the public under the conditions of the Fifth Wave. My interest in the matter starts and ends with that.

The protesters of Maidan resembled in important ways those in Tahrir Square and Puerta del Sol. They were young and tech-savvy, and they belonged to a cluster of contradictory ideologies and mutually hostile ethnic groups. Some of the leading figures were Russian speakers, for example. Nayyem was a Muslim born in Afghanistan. Yet the anti-foreigner hard right also brought a considerable presence to the protests: Yanukovych characterized the uprising as a "nationalist coup."[231]

The rebels were united in opposition to Yanukovych. The uprising gained force on a platform of negation: like their precursors of 2011, the Ukrainian insurgents wished to be rid of the political status quo without having much of an idea about what to put in its place. When they triumphed and the government collapsed, the political situation in Ukraine remained as it had always been: fractured. To one observer, the idealism of Euromaidan constituted "a classic popular revolution."[232] To another, the aftermath was a mere "change of political elites."[233]

Like so many other nations, Ukraine seemed frozen in a world-historical midnight between the old order and radical change.

Information technology didn't cause the Ukrainian revolution, but the revolution would have been difficult to organize, and might have reached a different outcome, without recourse to cell phones and digital platforms like Facebook and YouTube. The street battles in the dead of winter captured the imagination of the global public. Every instance of government-instigated bloodshed entered the information sphere, with predictable effects on opinion. While the government lived in a past nostalgic for Soviet-style repression, the young protesters understood the speed of information and the power of demonstration effects.

> *This generation watches little TV, gets its news and information on-line.... The organizers of the recent protests took advantage of this. Amateur broadcasting on Ustream and YouTube quickly spread the news of the events. Independent, crowd-funded radio and television networks used the same low-budget streaming technology to deliver live content from an attic in Kiev. Every movement of the unpopular Berkut (the Ukrainian special forces) was closely followed on Facebook and Twitter; supporters were mobilized to defend tents erected by protesters.*[234]

Ukraine is an invertebrate country: it lacks strong institutions, a true Center. The Yanukovych government functioned in the manner of a mafia family. Yet even that was too slow-moving, too much hierarchy, in the hands of persons of a certain age, to respond effectively to a networked public in revolt. Nayyem called the government leadership "too old." "If you asked Yanukovych or some others about Facebook," he wrote, "they wouldn't understand what it can do."[235]

The rebels' desire to eradicate the established order placed them in an ambivalent relationship to democracy. They wanted what they wanted: elimination of the government, and the democracy and rule of law exemplified by E.U. countries. They succeeded only in their negation. Euromaidan wasn't a coup, as Yanukovych alleged. It was a sectarian revolt. Participants aspired to purity in democratic ideals, but were unwilling to invest their energies on the messy details of democratic government. They left Ukraine as they found it, at the mercy of events.

The new prime minister, a leading voice at Maidan, submitted to E.U.-mandated economic reforms with a despair bordering on nihilism. "We are a team of people with a suicide wish—welcome to hell," he said.[236] His words were remarkable for their honesty. His political circumstances precluded even the pretense of command and control.

* * *

In Venezuela, sporadic protests assumed the character of a self-conscious street uprising on February 12, 2014. University students began the trouble, but were soon joined by the opposition parties and a considerable segment of the educated class. Specific complaints about crime, inflation, and a bad economy added up to the usual demand for radical change. The protesters wanted the government of President Nicolás Maduro to be gone.

Like Hugo Chavez, his predecessor and mentor, Maduro was a creature of the age of mass movements and top-down control. From his perch at the top of the pyramid, the street protests could only be the work of "fascist groups" agitating for a coup.[237] That Viktor Yanukovych had offered an identical interpretation of events in Ukraine demonstrated the power of hierarchy to mold perspective.

Intransigence followed logically from that perspective. Confronted with the public's demand for change, Maduro, like Yanukovych, opted instead for a show of force. Some 40 persons were said to have died in the street battles that ensued.

As I write this, Maduro remains in office, and it would not be an improbable outcome if he served out his term. But the protests also continue. The violence and disruption continue. Events in Venezuela bear no resemblance to the null hypothesis. The government has focused largely on survival. The country is stuck between today and tomorrow.

Persuasion belonged to the networked public. Chavez long ago bullied mass media into silence, but Venezuelans were deep into social media, and 14 million out of a population of 30 million owned cell phones. Protesters coordinated their movements using the smartphone walkie-talkie application Zello.[238] Other digital platforms allowed them to flood the information sphere with images of large opposition crowds and government violence. The demonstration effects were powerful and effective. One opinion poll showed that nearly 54 percent of Venezuelans believed that they were living under a dictatorship.[239] In another survey, 55 percent said they did not consider their government a democracy.[240] Maduro retained the support of many groups, but the heart of the conflict lay in the failure of his government, the inability of the Venezuelan ruling elites to match their own ambitious rhetoric.

The demographic profile of the rebels should be familiar by now. They were young, many of them university students, nearly all from the well-educated and globally connected middle class. "I've got a rock in my hand and I'm the distributor for Adidas eyewear in Venezuela," one protester told the *New York Times*. Other insurgents, according to the *Times*, included "a manicurist, a medical supplies saleswoman, a businessman, and a hardware store worker."[241] The anti-Maduro uprising belonged to the same affluent networked public we have encountered in multiple settings—and was propelled, here as elsewhere, by a sectarian rejection of the established order.

Venezuela could be Tunisia or Egypt or Ukraine. The public was on the move. A semi-authoritarian government struggled to keep control of the streets. The outcome will no doubt differ from country to country, but the structure followed by events has been shaped, I believe, by the same tectonic forces.

* * *

Recent upheavals in Thailand followed a recognizable pattern. In January 2014, large crowds of protesters successfully "occupied" government buildings. Crowds also disrupted polling stations during the February general elections. Violence associated with the protests led to two dozen deaths. The conflict continued into the spring, and appeared to have brought the Thai political system to the brink of paralysis.

I am interested in only one aspect of this episode. The insurgents in Thailand, once again, were not the poor but the urban elites and the educated middle class. Their cause wasn't social revolution but the abolition of the political status quo. Candidates representing this group had regularly failed to win a majority in national elections. The response has been a rejection of the electoral process.

Protesters pressed for a "people's council" to take charge of the government, untainted by the vote. Composition of the "council" was left undefined, but its purpose was clear enough. It was expected to deliver what democracy could not: the liquidation of the ruling party and negation of the established order. A leader of the opposition insisted that the street protests would continue until the "regime is wiped out."[242] He was speaking about an elected government.

Prizing desired political outcomes over mere democratic procedures follows naturally from the public's disdain of established institutions.

In Turkey, the government of our old friend Recep Tayyip Erdogan stood in the same relation to the public as that of Thailand. It kept winning elections and losing legitimacy, in this case because of a destructive relationship with the information sphere. Erdogan was outraged by what he called the "curse" of social media. He had tamed Turkish mass media, and it plainly seemed to him unnatural, a trampling of the sanctities, that the public should continue to communicate without his permission. But the public did communicate, on Twitter and YouTube and elsewhere, and Erdogan, for all his illusions of control, became its target.

On February 25, 2014, a recorded telephone call was leaked to YouTube, purporting to show Erdogan instructing one of his sons to "take out" money from a safe in Erdogan's home and "dissolve it" ahead of a corruption investigation.[243] Additional calls were posted—less incriminating but still unflattering to the prime minister. Erdogan's reaction was what you would expect from an official ensconced at the top of the hierarchy. He labeled the call to his son a "fabrication," brushed off the rest, and concentrated his energy on punishing the offending media, primarily YouTube and Twitter. The scandal, for him, wasn't what he had said in the apparent recordings, but the insult to his dignity and the collusion of social media in that act.

Erdogan became entangled in a legal and political war against social media. He swore to "eradicate" Twitter, and blocked the platform, as well as YouTube, in Turkey. Users easily circumvented the censorship, with the help of instructions from Twitter that the company had previously posted for Venezuelans during a ban imposed by the Maduro government. To the West, the Turkish government, once a model of freedom in the Muslim world, now appeared to be "one of the world's most determined internet censors." Within Turkey itself, Erdogan and his party continued to win elections handily, but street protests were gathering momentum: more than 100,000 turned out in Istanbul on March 12, summoned, inevitably, on Twitter.[244] May 1 street confrontations led *The Economist* to wonder whether Turkey was headed for "another summer of unrest."[245]

The answer was unknowable before the fact. However, if the world described by my thesis has any connection to reality, I would expect Erdogan's actions to be guided primarily by the need to survive politically. Under the perilous conditions of the Fifth Wave, governments cling more than they rule.

In Egypt, Defense Minister al-Sisi and the military, having overthrown an elected government in the name of the people, mostly gave up the pretense of legality in the following months. They concentrated instead on the repression of political opponents. Hundreds of Muslim Brothers have been sentenced to death, leading al-Sisi to boast that the

Brotherhood was "finished." [246] Like Erdogan's threat to eradicate Twitter, this bit of rhetoric, with its high modernist bravado, said more about the military regime's delusions than about its capabilities.

The people of the web who had organized the anti-Mubarak protests found themselves under severe pressure from the new regime. Blogger Alaa Abd El Fatah was slapped around in his home, then arrested by "20 men—some of whom were masked and carrying heavy arms." [247] Ahmed Maher, Wael Ghonim's 2011 partner and the guiding spirit behind the "April 6 Movement" Facebook group, was also detained. Ghonim himself had left the country, stating that "Egypt no longer welcomes those who are like me." [248]

To all appearances, matters stood exactly where they had been before January 25, 2011. Under the surface, everything was different. *Homo informaticus* had broken the mystique of authority in Egypt. There was no going back—no return to the passive obedience of the illiterate, parochial villager. The public knew it, and the regime knew it as well. It was the rationale behind the persecution of online activists.

Al-Sisi aspired to the presidency, and his fate will provide a powerful signal with regard to the claims I have made in this book. If he can repress his way into a stable and long-lasting dynasty in the mode of Nasser and Mubarak, my analysis will be falsified. This isn't an impossible outcome. The future—just ask my old professor—is unknown.

But as I observe, from afar, recent events in Egypt—and in Ukraine, Venezuela, Thailand, Turkey—I confess to many misgivings about the future of democracy, but far fewer doubts about the restlessness of the public or the crisis of authority.

THE OLD DEMOCRACIES AND THE NEW STRUCTURE OF INFORMATION

I wish to conclude with the old democracies: Europe and the United States. After the end of World War II, the material success of these countries lifted the prestige of their system of government to the heights. Capitalism and the industrial revolution were invented here, and scientific management too—the *apparent* ability to become rich beyond the dreams of previous generations because of brilliant top-down planning. The digital world was born here: the tsunami of information could be said to originate in that unstable seismic region south and east of San Francisco Bay.

The ideals of equality, of the people as sovereign, of the public as more than a rabble, were also strongest here, part of the domestic political DNA.

The 20th century saw the rise of mass movements dedicated to the destruction of liberal democracy. Each, in turn, was defeated to the point of extinction. With the fall of communism and implosion of the Soviet Union in 1991, no alternative system was left to oppose the democracies. They had triumphed with a completeness rarely seen in history. As early as 1989, political scientist Francis Fukuyama, in his famous essay "The End of History?," could speculate about a world wholly dominated by the democratic ideology:

> *What we may be witnessing is not just the end of the Cold War, of the passing of a particular period of post-war history, but the end of history as such: that is, the endpoint of mankind's ideological evolution and the universalization of Western liberal democracy as the final form of human government. This is not to say that there will no longer be events to fill the pages of Foreign Affairs' yearly summaries of international relations, for the victory of liberalism has occurred primarily in the realm of ideas or consciousness and is as yet incomplete in the real or material world. But there are powerful reasons for believing that it is the ideal that will govern the material world in the long run.*[249]

Following the horrors of 9/11, Fukuyama and his ideas were derided as triumphalist nonsense. But he was only half wrong. Fukuyama, a Hegelian, argued that Western democracy had run out of "contradictions": that is, of ideological alternatives. That was true in 1989 and remains true today. Fukuyama's mistake was to infer that the absence of contradictions meant the end of history. There was another possibility he failed to consider.

History could well be driven by *negation* rather than contradiction. It could ride on the nihilistic rejection of the established order, regardless of alternatives or consequences. That would not be without precedent. The Roman Empire wasn't overthrown by something called "feudalism"—it collapsed of its own dead weight, to the astonishment of friend and foe alike. The centuries after the calamity lacked ideological form. Similarly, a history built on negation would be formless and nameless: a shadowy moment, however long, between one true age and another.

The end of the Cold War, in which Fukuyama discerned the millennial triumph of democracy, appears in hindsight to have been the high-water mark for the prestige and legitimacy of this system. Once the external pressure applied by communism was removed, democratic countries lost their internal cohesion, and began the slow descent into negation. The failures of high modernism became painfully evident, when detached from the epic canvas of a life-and-death struggle. The industrial mode of organization, with its militaristic respect for rank, had placed democratic government at a great distance from the governed. Lacking a shared enemy and the urgency of a war footing, public and authority discovered they stood on the opposite sides of many questions.

Then the Fifth Wave swept over the political landscape, giving voice and image and persuasive power to the insistent negations of the public. The result, if my analysis has any validity, has been the bleeding out of legitimacy and the living death of many democratic institutions.

Recent events in Europe fit into this pattern. In France, for example, three successive presidential elections reversed the previous mandate, but the difference was imperceptible, and the common denominator was failure. Less than a year after the election to the presidency of socialist François Hollande, protests had erupted over his economic and tax policies, while Hollande himself reached record lows in popularity.[250] In March 2014, the socialists suffered a disastrous defeat in local elections. Hollande dismissed his prime minister. Another mandate appeared headed for reversal.

The impotence of the established parties turned a sectarian public toward political groups less inhibited in their condemnation of the system. From the left, insurgent parties like Syriza in Greece and the Five Star Movement in Italy increased their share of the vote by attacking capitalism and politics as usual. Insurgent parties of the right, dubbed by *The Economist* "Europe's Tea Parties," were also making dramatic progress at the polls.[251] Their negations ranged from the anti-immigrant and anti-E.U. disposition of France's National Front and Britain's Independence Party to the openly neo-Nazi rhetoric of the Golden Dawn faction in Greece.

The sickness of European democracy was demonstrable and generally acknowledged by the Europeans themselves. The virulence of the malady seemed less clear. Part of the difficulty is that complex systems often look indestructible just before they collapse. That was true of the Soviet Union and the Mubarak regime, for example. European democracy, by comparison, does *not* look indestructible: it has the feel of an established religion, to which everyone belongs by force of habit, but which few, in their hearts, believe in any longer. Idle to speculate what it would take to sweep it aside. It is always useful to remember history, however: not so long ago, Europe was the world's leading exporter of anti-democratic ideologies and movements.

* * *

The theme of recent American politics was once again failure, specifically, the inauspicious rollout of the new health-care program and President Obama's efforts to recover from the consequences.

I have already noted the botched delivery of the health insurance website. Here is Clay Shirky's take on the planning process followed by the government to develop the $400 million site:

> *The management question, when trying anything new, is "When does reality trump planning?" For the officials overseeing Healthcare.gov, the answer was "Never." Every time there was a chance to create some sort of public experimentation, or even just some clarity about its methods and goals, the imperative was to deny the opposition anything to criticize.*
>
> *At the time, this probably seemed like a way of avoiding early failures. But the project's managers weren't avoiding those failures. They were saving them up.*[252]

President Obama responded to critics with his uniquely dialectical style of rhetoric. On the one hand, he seemed to accept responsibility, and to offer an apology of sorts. "We fumbled the rollout on this health-care law," he said. "I completely get how upsetting this can be for a lot of Americans." That was Barack Obama, the president, speaking.

But Obama the sectarian prophet, with his detachment from government and disdain of its works, was also to be heard from: "I was not informed directly that the website would not be working . . . . I don't think I'm stupid enough to be going around saying this is going to be like shopping on Amazon or Travelocity, a week before the website opens, if I thought that it wasn't going to work." "The federal government does a lot of things well. One of the things it does not do well," the president noted, "is information technology procurement."[253]

Barack Obama's political gift lay in the condemnation of wrongs. As he wrestled with malfunctioning features of the health-care law, the president grew visibly uncomfortable with having to advocate a positive program. "What most people I hope also recognize," he complained, "is that when you try to do something big like make our health-care system better that there're going to be problems along the way, even if ultimately what you're doing is going to make a lot of people better off."[254]

Once enrollment in the new program climbed to eight million, the president asserted, "The repeal debate is and should be over."[255] This was a remarkable statement, in equal parts sectarian certitude and Center blindness. Like Hosni Mubarak with the internet and the British authorities after the London riots, President Obama appeared to be searching for the off switch that would silence a quarrelsome public.

He was unlikely to find it. The health-care program remained unpopular. Not surprisingly, the Republican Party was expected to exploit the issue for the midterm elections. The burden of positive government would not soon be removed from the president's shoulders.

President Obama's recent difficulties continued a pattern of bipolar reversals of fortune that characterized democratic politics in the age of the Fifth Wave. Since 2008, in the U.S., elections every two years have repudiated the previous choice. We saw much the same in France. Britain, Spain, and Italy have each flipped from left to right or back the other way within the last few years. With the possible exception of Italy, whose young prime minister has been called the country's "last chance," the electorates in these countries felt a corrosive distrust of the current crowd in power.[256]

Let me submit, as my parting word, a warning to the skeptic: the democratic process is in peril of self-negation. The public's mood swings are driven by failures of government, not hope for change. Each failure bleeds legitimacy from the system, erodes faith in the machinery of democracy, and paves the way for the opposite extreme. Democracy lacks true rivals today as an ideal and an ideology. Fukuyama was indeed half right. But there is a decadence in certain historical moments, an entropy of systems, propelled by an internal dynamic, that makes no demands for alternative ideals or structures before the onset of disintegration. At some point, failure becomes final.

The failure of democracy plays no part in the null hypothesis, but it becomes a possibility in the framework of my thesis. A rebellious public, sectarian in temper and utopian in expectations, collides everywhere with institutions that rule by default and that blunder, it seems, by habit. Industrial hierarchies are no longer able to govern successfully in a world swept to the horizon by a tsunami of information. An egalitarian public is unwilling to assume responsibility under any terms. The muddled half-steps and compromises necessary to democracy may become untenable under the pressure applied by these irreconcilable forces.

Democracy isn't doomed. As an analyst, I have rejected prophecy and destiny as tools of the trade. I see the future with no greater clarity than you, reader. But processes at play *today,* right now, if continued, could well lead to the crumbling of what has always been a fragile system of government.

Strange to say, this possibility never gets discussed explicitly—only in indirections about China or about shutting down some policy debate. I wrote this book, in part, to invite the discussion. I did so in the manner of a man who notices a fire blazing in a corner of a locked room: I don't want to start a panic, only some sane talk among the occupants about how best to put the thing out.

TRUMP, BREXIT, AND FAREWELL TO ALL THAT

RECONSIDERATIONS

The Revolt of the Public was first published in June 2014. I intended the book to be the description of a conflict that was sweeping the world yet remained invisible to most observers. The development of new information technologies, I believed, had shattered the categories we inherited from the industrial age. Powerful political forces were unleashed, strange and uncouth players gained ascendancy, and much mayhem resulted—but our minds were turned in the wrong direction, and all the chaos somehow transpired beneath the horizon of public awareness. Hence I used the words *subterranean* and *tectonic* to characterize the struggle.

Events since publication changed all that. The election to the presidency of Donald Trump, in particular, had the effect of a volcanic eruption that thrust into the open, for everyone to see, the fractured and mangled pieces of the old status quo. The June 2016 Brexit referendum, which determined Britain's breakaway from the European Union, was only slightly less of a jolt. The keepers of established wisdom now know they got reality terribly wrong, even if they are too dazed and disoriented to work out just how. Beyond the howls of pain and rage, many elements of the struggle I identified in 2014 have entered the general conversation.

A mobilized public, elites bleeding out authority, the failure of government, and the catastrophic collapse of democracy: Are there themes, post-Trump, that absorb more obsessive levels of attention?

In the clear light of hindsight, I'm amused by the unease I felt about utilizing dramatic language to tell my story. I thought long and hard about *nihilist* and *nihilism,* for example. The terms fit the evidence before me. Individuals and groups had been spawned by the conflict that combined the total negation of the established order with a predilection for random violence. They considered the mass murder of strangers to be a form of progress. In parallel, a rhetorical style elaborated on the web relied entirely on rage and repudiation, making every online political dispute likely to self-destruct in a "shitstorm" of personal abuse and death threats.

That was the reality of the case. But analysts have scruples, and I was concerned about sensationalizing a subject that held plenty of drama on its own account.

Today, everyone's a nihilist. President Trump is a nihilist, many times over: Political commentator Andrew Sullivan, who writes of "Trump's mindless nihilism," describes the president as "careening ever more manically into a force of irrational fury."[257] For his part, Eugene Robinson warns in the pages of the *Washington Post,* "We will all pay a price for Trump's nihilism."[258] The president's former strategist, Steve Bannon, was accused of fostering "the uncontrolled release of rage. . . . It is nihilism, a desire to burn it all down and damn the consequences." But Trump's predecessor in the White House, Barack Obama, turns out to be a nihilist too—and at least one bewildered commentator has proclaimed (again in the *Washington Post*), "We're all political nihilists now."[259]

I also wondered whether I had exaggerated the weakness of liberal democracy, and, by harping on the voices of negation, had myself contributed to a loss of confidence in our system. I need not have worried. Since electoral calamity overtook the elites in 2016, shouting your loss of faith in democracy from the rooftops has become fashionable. "Our democratic republic is in far more danger than it was even a few weeks ago," journalist E.J. Dionne exclaimed in a bad week of December 2017.[260] Political scientist Yascha Mounk accused President Trump of being "on the verge of staging a coup against independent institutions and the rule of law."[261] Mounk had previously warned of a "rebellion against multiethnic democracy in the United States," then had expanded the disaster zone: "This is not just the problem of particular societies, but one that affects virtually every liberal democracy around the world."[262] Other observers perceived a "worldwide crisis" driven by "illiberalism" and "populism."[263]

Parallels were drawn between the U.S. today and the Weimar Republic, which spawned Adolf Hitler. Barack Obama, for one, took up the theme. Comparing the present moment to Hitler's "Vienna of the late 1920s," the former president added ominously, "And then 60 million people died."[264] In keeping with the temper of the times, the *Washington Post* devised a new, appropriately apocalyptic motto: "Democracy Dies in Darkness." For many in politics and the news media, the darkness was already here.

On democracy, as it happened, mine had been a small, uncertain voice in the crowd's deafening roar.

The aim of this chapter is to extend my analysis to the events that caused such an uproar. Beyond the existential shock that Trump and Brexit represented, I must, at some level at least, come to grips with a world of troubles: the collapse of mainstream political parties in France and Germany, the failure of popular young leaders in Italy and Greece, the slow-motion crack-up of the European Union, the rise and fall of a blood-drenched "Caliphate" in the heart of the Levant, the viral diffusion of terror and random slaughter. Then there's the vexing question of populism—a term that implies much more than it explains.

Though the word "Reconsiderations" appears on the title, I don't believe—with one important exception—that there's much to reconsider. On the whole, the thesis I put forward in 2014 has held up pretty robustly. The public, if anything, is more alienated and angry at authority than I supposed. The elites, forever astonished by events, oscillate between panic and moral outrage. The institutions that hold up the status quo are falling to pieces around them. Rough, ungainly characters, devoid of institutional loyalties, tramp impatiently in the wings. In the U.S., Hungary, and the Philippines, they have gained power and strut on center stage.

Elected officials in democratic nations seek to curry favor with the public by distancing themselves from the democratic process. Donald Trump achieves this with his tweets. France's Emmanuel Macron has dreamed out loud of an Olympian presidency. Less stable democracies have lurched, in plain daylight, toward authoritarianism. Venezuela and Turkey, while retaining the forms of liberalism, have become virtual dictatorships.

The great unraveling of the institutions has proceeded faster, further, and deeper than I imagined possible in 2014. Here is the exception I mentioned above: my reconsidered analysis. I think I identified, roughly, the forces driving the tempest forward—but I failed to reckon the speed with which it was advancing. It was a significant omission. In a few short years, the political landscape has been transformed into a bedlam of irreconcilable factions. Violent and profane language that would have been unthinkable in 2014 is routinely used. Vital communities of interest constituted and empowered by the web have degenerated into online mobs and war-bands that exist purely to attack. The nihilist, killer of innocents, has materialized among us over and over again.

Should we then yield to the doom and despair of the moment, and come to terms, somehow, with the passing away of democracy? That question will haunt, specter-like, every thought and theme in this chapter. The fate of democracy, I believe, is inextricably bound to the fate of the elites in democratic nations. The current elite class, having lost its monopoly over information, has been stripped, probably forever, of the authorizing magic of legitimacy. The industrial model of democracy is dysfunctional and discredited. That is the current predicament. Every step forward must start there.

We need to understand more clearly the conditions of legitimacy under democratic rule. The revolt of the public is out in the open. The focus of analysis must move to a crisis of authority that has infected our sources of information—think "fake news" and "post-truth"—and rattled our political class into postures of panic and paralysis. The question agitating every defender of democracy is: How can this be reversed? A more precise phrasing would be: How are *legitimate* elites selected in a democratic society? The answer, let me suggest, will go a long way to resolve, for good or evil, that haunting question about the death of democracy.

ETERNAL SURPRISE OF THE ELITES, OR THE WORLD TURNED UPSIDE DOWN

On Tuesday, November 8, 2016, 135 million Americans took part in one of the great democratic rituals in the world: the election of a new president. The outcome had been foretold with rare certainty. Hillary Clinton was a former senator and secretary of state, and was a chieftain and leading fundraiser of the Democratic Party. Donald Trump shared none of these attributes. He had gained fame as a rich real estate developer and reality TV personality, but his experience in government at any level added up to absolute zero. Clinton had money, endorsements, an organization in every state. Trump lacked all of these advantages. He fought with and fired his staff, divided Republican loyalties, and went out of his way to alienate the articulate elites—notably, the news media. The *New York Times* gave Trump a 15 percent chance of winning. Others offered worse odds.[265]

Nearly unanimously, the country's political and media elites expected Hillary Clinton to be the next president. The voters decided otherwise.

The shock dealt by the election of Donald Trump to the structures these elites controlled was therefore extreme. More than a year on, balance has yet to be restored. Trump's victory was, in reality, a highly improbable event; but to many, then and now, it felt like a pure impossibility, a violent attack on settled truth. While announcing "the most stunning upset in American history," talking heads on television stammered and wept.[266] Suddenly, every aspect of social and political life seemed up for grabs.

The sense of impossibility was compounded by the strangeness of the man. Trump was a billionaire who rode a golden elevator to his Fifth Avenue penthouse, yet he claimed to speak for "the forgotten men and women of our country." For all his celebrity, he had been a minor player on the national stage. He lacked political alliances, an ideological following, institutional connections. He said and did things that should have blown up his campaign many times over. He was a favorite of the evangelicals, even though he'd been married three times, and, in an unguarded moment, had boasted of grabbing women "by the pussy." His signature issue was a hard line on immigration, yet his mother and two of his wives were immigrants.

Even after eight years of Barack Obama's condemnations, Trump's was an impossibly dark vision of U.S. society. In his inaugural address, the new president cast his eye over the "American carnage" he had inherited:

> Mothers and children trapped in poverty in our inner cities; rusted-out factories scattered like tombstones across the landscape of our nation; an education system . . . which leaves our young and beautiful students deprived of knowledge; and the crime and gangs and drugs that have stolen too many lives and robbed our country of so much unrealized potential.[267]

The nation as a graveyard: remarkable imagery from an occupant of the White House.

Among those viscerally hostile to Trump—above all the elites and the institutions, but also Democrats and the left generally, and some conservative intellectuals—his election was received as a moral and political impossibility, a malevolent absurdity that could only be explained in terms of lies and conspiracies, whose legitimacy must be rejected and "resisted," without compromise, at all costs. Some called for members of the Electoral College pledged to Trump to vote for Clinton instead.[268] Almost immediately there was talk of impeachment on various grounds and of removal for incapacity.

The guiding principle of the opposition seemed to be that a sufficient volume of rage would wash away the election results and restore reality to the status quo before Trump. Following the election, thousands took to the streets in angry "Not my president" protests. Participants shouted "Donald Trump has got to go," even though, strictly speaking, he hadn't yet arrived. On the day after the inauguration, millions across the country joined in a Women's March against Trump's perceived misogyny. Many demonstrators wore cat-themed hats inspired by Trump's "pussy" comments—early indication of the president's uncanny ability to drive his antagonists into behavior even stranger than his own. Additional protests followed in April and May. Every week found fresh cause for outrage and scandal. Every day was doomsday for democracy. No one felt the slightest need to come to terms with this impossible man.

The fracturing of reality had a discernible cause. I will dwell on it before I'm done. Here, though, I want to pose the compulsory cosmic question: What in the world had happened? Or if you prefer: How is President Trump, disturber of the odds, object of so much fear and loathing, to be explained?

I don't believe in single answers to complex puzzles—and an election with 135 million voters swirls along a massively complex causal stream. Two elements, however, are in my opinion necessary to any answer. The first is simple and generally acknowledged. The second made the first possible, but is a bit more obscure.

I said that Trump is free of any taint of government or political experience. He's also ideologically formless—a member of his campaign staff described him, generously, as "post-ideological."[269] He has been for and against abortion in his time, for example. His supposed nationalism, on close inspection, dissolves into certain rhetorical preferences and the vague demand that the U.S. get better economic deals from the world.

The *why* of Trump's election is simple enough. A candidate that innocent of qualifications and political direction can be elected only as a gesture of supreme repudiation, by the electorate, of the governing class. From start to finish, the 2016 presidential race can best be understood as the political assertion of an unhappy and highly mobilized public. In the end, Trump was chosen precisely because of, not despite, his apparent shortcomings. He is the visible effect, not the cause, of the public's surly and mutinous mood. Trump has been for this public what the *objet trouvé* was for the modern artist: a found instrument, a club near to hand with which to smash at the established order. To compare him to Ronald Reagan, as some of his admirers have done, or to the great dictators, as his opponents constantly do, would be to warp reality as in a funhouse mirror.

The right level of analysis on Trump isn't Trump at all, but the public that endowed him with a radical direction and temper, and the decadent institutions that proved too weak to stand in his way.

The U.S. public, like the public everywhere, is engaged in a long migration away from the structures of representative democracy toward more sectarian arrangements. The public craves meaning and identity. From its perspective, late modern society, including government, exists to frustrate this desire. Caught in the collision between extraordinary personal expectations and feeble but intrusive political institutions, the nation-state, here and elsewhere, is splintering into sociopolitical shards that grow less intelligible to one another by the moment. To a Hillary Clinton, peering down from the heights of a very steep pyramid, the distant mass of Trump supporters could only look like "a basket of deplorables." Otherwise they were impossible to explain.

The political professionals who once managed the system and protected against such eruptions from below are gone with the wind. Trump's candidacy was conventionally viewed as a grassroots revolt against the Republican establishment.[270] But that turned out to be a nostalgic fiction. The 2016 primary season revealed a Republican Party bled dry of coherence and authority as an institution. The party "establishment," under any description, had cracked to pieces long before Trump arrived, and only the word remained like an incantation. Jeb Bush's risible impersonation of an establishment champion only proved the point. Bush lacked a following, barely had a pulse at the polls, and could claim nothing like an insider's clout. He had been out of office for nine years, "a longer downtime," one perceptive analyst wrote, "than any president elected since 1852 (and any candidate since 1924)."[271] The Republican worthies who endorsed him had been out of office for an average of 11 years. If this once had been the party's establishment, it was now a claque of political corpses.

For the Republican Party, in brief, the Bush campaign was a dance of the dead, and Trump's triumph became a moment of revelation and acceptance: more of a burial than a revolt.

The Democratic Party has endured an equally fatal loss of authority. Barack Obama in 2008 crushed a true establishment—fronted, as it happened, by Hillary Clinton. For eight years, Obama and his immediate circle felt no debt and little allegiance to the party organization.[272] In the 2016 Democratic primaries, more than 40 percent of the vote, and all the militant passion, went to Bernie Sanders—an old, white, dull, socialist Independent. Many of his supporters saw Clinton and other mainstream Democrats as cogs in a system they despised.

In somewhat slower motion than the Republicans, the Democratic Party is unbundling into dozens of political war-bands, each driven by the hunger for meaning and identity, all focused with monomaniacal intensity on a particular cause: feminism, the environment, anti-capitalism, pro-immigration, or racial or sexual grievance. The schism has been veiled by the generalized loathing of all things Trump, but I find it hard to envision a national party thriving on tribalism and wars of identity.

So that is the why of Donald Trump. He was the chosen instrument of an insurgent public, and no established centers of power stood in his way. The somewhat different question of how this transpired now needs to be posed. In 1980, 1990, even 2000, Trump's bizarre trajectory would have been not just impossible but politically suicidal. What has changed?

The information balance of power has changed, of course. A generation ago, the public could exist only as a passive audience. Information was dispensed on the industrial model: top-down and one to many. That was the great age of the daily newspaper and famous anchormen, on the model of Walter Cronkite. The advent of digital platforms, in a sense, created the public. People from nowhere, free of institutional entanglements, pushed the elites out of the strategic heights of the information sphere. Almost immediately, great institutions in every domain of human activity began to bleed authority—a process that, as we have seen, is now approaching the terminal stage for many of them.

That is my thesis for the revolt of the public. My claim here is that it applies in spades to every phase of the 2016 presidential contest, and helps explain how the outlandish Trump could trample so easily over once-authoritative institutions on his way to victory. He was lucky in his moment. When, like the phantom at the feast, he materialized at the head of the Republican pack, he was met by an institutional vacuum and an informational chaos.

There can be no question that Trump's online campaign "overwhelmingly outperformed" Clinton's. "Clinton's coverage was focused on scandals, while Trump's coverage focused on his core issues," concludes a study by Harvard's Berkman Klein Center for Internet and Society.[273] Evidence from the same source demonstrates convincingly the increased ability of new conservative digital media, led by Breitbart, to influence the tone of the conversation on Facebook and Twitter. Trump's own fixation with Twitter, both as candidate and president, is unusual and significant enough to merit an extended look. In another context, I intend to provide that.

Here, however, I wish to focus on that labyrinth of contradictions, which is Trump's relationship with the mainstream news media.

The facts are uncontroversial. Trump spent far less money on advertising than Clinton or his Republican opponents, yet he received a vastly greater volume of media coverage.[274] The news business seemed strangely obsessed with this strange man, and lavished on him what may have been unprecedented levels of attention. The question is why.

The answer will be apparent to anyone with eyes to see. Donald Trump is a peacock among the dull buzzards of American politics. The one discernible theme of his life has been the will to stand out: to attract all eyes in the room by being the loudest, most colorful, most aggressively intrusive person there. He has clearly succeeded to an astonishing degree. The data on media attention speaks to a world-class talent for self-promotion.[275] Again, there can be no question that this allowed Trump to separate himself from his competitors in the Republican primaries. He appeared to be a very important person. Everyone on TV was talking about him.[276] Who could say the same about Ted Cruz?

Media people pumped the helium that elevated Donald Trump's balloon, and they did so from naked self-interest. He represented high ratings and improved subscription numbers. Until the turn of the new millennium, the news media had controlled the information agenda. They could decide, on the basis of some elite standard, how much attention you deserved. In a fractured information environment, swept by massive waves of signal and noise, amid newspaper bankruptcies and many more

TV news channels, every news provider approaches a story from the perspective of existential desperation. Trump understood the hunger, and knew how to feed the beast.[277]

Paradoxically, the traditional news media felt uniformly hostile toward Trump, to the extent of abandoning its vaunted claim to objectivity. "If you view a Trump presidency as something that's potentially dangerous, your reporting is going to reflect that," stated a front-page article in the *New York Times*.[278] CNN also felt comfortable using the word "dangerous" to characterize Trump statements.[279]

Examples of journalists lining up in opposition to Trump during the elections can be multiplied at will—and it wasn't just a question of open criticism. Well-known personalities in both print and broadcast media colluded with the Clinton campaign to maximize the chances of Trump's defeat, as was revealed in a hack of her campaign manager's emails.[280] Indeed, the most damaging revelations against Trump weren't dug up by Democratic Party operatives, but leaked by NBC News to the *Washington Post*.[281]

Yet the greater paradox is that Trump almost certainly benefited from these attacks. He was able, with some justice, to portray journalists as members in good standing in the club of entitled and out-of-touch elites. The public's trust in the news stood at an all-time low—by the fall of 2016, it had fallen to 19 percent.[282] Trump had the luxury of campaigning against an unloved institution that was providing him with prodigious levels of free (if negative) publicity. When he hurled insults at Megyn Kelly of Fox News, his crowds roared with approval.

In the nineties, political scientist Thomas Patterson observed that the power to select presidential candidates had passed, effectively, from the parties to the mass media.[283] That time is over. The year 2016 showed many venerable institutions to be bare ruins of what they once were. The news business featured prominently in the wreckage. The information agenda could no longer be controlled by a handful of news organizations in chummy interaction with a few Washington grandees. Like so much else, the agenda was now a crazy quilt—a battleground. Donald Trump, novice at politics, abominated by the elites, could win a presidential election in part because he read and navigated this fractured information landscape far more intelligently than the competition.

* * *

In that improbable year of 2016, Filipino voters raised to the presidency a populist that by comparison made Donald Trump sound like an etiquette book. Rodrigo Duterte bragged to the media that, as mayor of Manila, he had roamed the streets at night and personally shot drug dealers to death. So the new president of the Philippines was either a confessed murderer or, as now seems likely, a pathological liar.

I bring up this weird story to jog our memories: the conflict that gave us Trump isn't uniquely American. The forces at play are global and secular.

In Europe, a series of electoral shocks have battered the European Union and many individual states. This predicament has been labeled a "crisis of democracy"—defined by one commentator as "a gap between elites and voters."[284] For many right-thinking Europeans, however, democracy seemed to be negating itself. Since this subject is central to my concerns, I want to reflect for a moment on the troubles of European democracy.

The place to start is with election results and their consequences.

In the January 2015 Greek general elections, a motley coalition of communists and anti-globalists came to power, grouped in a party called Syriza and headed by Alexis Tsipras, who at 40 was the country's youngest prime minister in the modern era. Syriza had existed only since 2004, but in 2015 it won, and won big, chiefly on a platform of negation and repudiation. The party stood firmly *against* the European Union, the euro, austere budgets, debt payments, capitalism, the Germans, the banks, "the rich, the markets, the super-rich, the top 10 percent."[285]

Syriza had promised what Greek voters wanted: the impossible. Reality intervened. By September 2015, the cranks and unrepentant radicals had been weeded out of the government. Greece remained in the E.U., kept the euro, put up with austerity, and bowed respectfully to capitalists, the Germans, and the banks. The promise of radical change had devolved into stasis. Under the youthful communist Tsipras, conditions for the Greek public were similar to what they had been under his middle-aged conservative predecessor. Not surprisingly, support for the populist experiment Syriza represented has collapsed, while Tsipras's ratings have "nose-dived."[286]

In February 2014, after a parliamentary maneuver, Matteo Renzi, 39, became prime minister of Italy—the youngest man ever to hold that position. He belonged to the mainstream center-left Democratic Party, but came to national politics as an outsider, having been mayor of Florence. His mandate was to tear down Italy's immobile political system from within. Because of his character and mission, the young redeemer became known as *il rottamatore*—demolition man. Renzi was free of any taint of corruption, and took the title seriously. "I'm cleaning up the swamp," he proclaimed in June 2015, curiously anticipating Trump.[287]

Renzi, like Tsipras, meant to be the negation of the status quo. A tangle of institutional interests hampered his movements: in Italy, the rules of the game aren't designed to foster reform. Renzi, the demolition man, staked his political life on changing the rules. He insisted that the central government needed greater authority, and called a constitutional referendum for December 2016 as a first step in this direction. The elite class swung in a body behind the young prime minister. Constitutional reform received the universal support of the traditional parties and of print and broadcast media, and enjoyed far more money spent on advertisement.

But antiestablishment groups like Beppe Grillo's Five Star Movement and Matteo Salvini's Northern League—the forces of populism—dominated social media.[288] An alienated public distrusted the motives behind centralization. The vote against reform surpassed 60 percent, and a few days later Renzi was gone. It was, wrote one dismayed observer, "the fall of Rome....The status quo has won."[289]

In reality the status quo had suffered a pivotal defeat. In March 2018, Renzi's Social Democrats were crushed at the polls, while populist parties received a clear majority of the vote. Italian democracy, which had proved incapable of reforming Italy's political corruption and paralysis, now faced the task of piecing together a government out of splinters of enraged opinion. Success would leave "the eurozone's third largest economy in the hands of economic populists with critical views of the E.U."[290]

For Spain, the general elections of December 2015 marked the transition from a two-party system to a fragmented and chaotic political environment. The ruling conservatives, though still the largest party, lost 64 seats and their majority in the Cortes. The reasons for the setback were many, but together added up to a mood of stark rejection by the electorate. The socialists suffered their worst showing ever. Podemos, a party that embraced the anarchist ideals of the 2011 *indignado* street revolt, and that hadn't existed in the previous election, came in third. No party could summon a majority to form a government. After ten months of paralysis, new elections were called in January 2016. This time the conservatives performed somewhat better, but the weak minority government that emerged has been stuck in a holding pattern.

All the while, in the autonomous region of Catalonia, a series of local votes favored groups that sought to break away from Spain. Catalonia was never a nation, but the Catalans, having caught the bug of identity and negation, were in revolt against history, and wished to smash through its consequences in the present order of things. In October 2017, a referendum again went the separatists' way. Local authorities declared independence. The Spanish government was compelled to send in the police, take over Catalonia's affairs, and throw the rebel leaders in prison. All of the latter had been elected democratically. Democracy, in Spain, had become an accomplice to the disintegration of national politics and of the nation-state.

And then there was Brexit.

The British vote to leave the European Union was a textbook example of democracy delivering a perplexing outcome—and of the public on a rampage. The referendum had been called by David Cameron, Conservative prime minister, to fulfill a campaign promise. Cameron himself, however, strongly opposed the exit initiative, as did the Labour and Social Democratic opposition, the respectable news media, the Archbishop of Canterbury, and a long line of foreign heads of state, starting with Barack Obama.[291] Given the thunderous pro-Europe chorus of establishment voices, the vote against—like the Trump vote in the U.S.—became a matter of *because* rather than *despite*. Caught in the grip of a glacial political order, ruled by elites who offered few alternatives, the British public opted to break some crockery. That was in May of the difficult year 2016. To this day, great uncertainty hangs over what happens next.

Britain—the "United Kingdom"—is an interesting country. As the sharp old class differences have abated, all other differences have been magnified. The official ideology of British institutions is multiculturalism, the glorification of diversity. How much this has contributed to the fragmentation of national identity would be a worthwhile topic of research. Ethnic and religious minorities remain unreconciled. The Muslim population in particular has produced perpetrators of domestic terror and Islamic State atrocities—recall the grim video images of "Jihadi John," beheader to the caliphate, with his thick London accent.[292] The Brexit vote in a sense was aimed at Jihadi John and his kind. Whether this was driven by love of country and its civic traditions or by racism and xenophobia very much depends on where you stand.

Although opinion polls had shown a tight contest, elites in Britain and Europe were utterly shocked by the outcome of the referendum. "In 1,000 years, I would never have believed that the British people would vote for this," exclaimed a baffled Labour MP.[293] Such radical disconnection from the public, even more than immigration or terror, helped explain the revolt from below implicit in the Brexit vote. Afterward, the mass media portrayed pro-Brexit voters regretting their foolish impulse, or asking, in confusion, what the E.U. actually was.[294] But it was the elites who clung to a virginal ignorance about their alienation from the public—next time, they were certain to be surprised again.

The England of the pub and the football field had struck a blow at the Britain of the institutions. On Twitter, Facebook, and Instagram, "Leave" activists had outnumbered, out-posted, and out-energized their opponents.[295] The almost willful blindness to this strategy of revolt cost David Cameron his job. His successor, Theresa May, had been against Brexit until she was for it. May proved as inept as Cameron at reading the public's mood. Under the slogan of "Strong and Stable," she called for early elections in June 2017. The voters delivered a hung Parliament, and May began her second term at the head of a weak, unstable minority government.

In parallel, the Border used the triumph of Brexit to resume its conflict against the Center. Scotland is governed by a party committed to leaving Britain, much as Britain is now committed to leaving Europe. The Scottish prime minister insists that her region will remain in the E.U., and has promised a new referendum on exiting the U.K.

The fate of Europe, like that of Britain, is slipping from the grasp of a purblind political class. The higher meaning of Brexit may be as an indicator of a great secular reversal. Globally, institutions have entered a moment of decadence and disintegration—and the E.U. has been singularly afflicted. Like the old Holy Roman Empire, it lacks a true center and a shared reason for being. Nationalists and separatists, anarchists and populists, all tear at bonds held together mostly by inertia. The question "On what *principle* must we stay?" receives at best a muddled answer.

Democracy now favors the public, and the public, at every level of social and political life, seems to want out.

* * *

In the 2017 electoral victories of Angela Merkel and Emmanuel Macron, many perceived a decisive reversal of this trend toward secession. The Center was said to have conquered, and preserved the order, in the two largest E.U. nations. After Trump's election, desperate elites had crowned Merkel the new "leader of the free world."[296] Macron inspired the same exaggerated enthusiasm—a cover of *The Economist* showed him literally walking on water.[297] The two champions, having won at the game of democracy, were expected to rescue the house of Europe from destruction.

I think this is a misreading of the facts of the case.

Stated bluntly, the September 2017 German elections were a disaster for the political status quo. The two "major" parties together barely notched 50 percent of the vote. Merkel's coalition sank to 33 percent, losing 65 seats. The opposition SPD was dealt the worst defeat in its long, proud history. The rest of the Bundestag was divided among irreconcilable cats and dogs. Four months after the elections, a majority for a new government had yet to be found. If Germany hasn't quite reached Spanish levels of political fragmentation, it's headed there. Merkel, dowager empress, looks on the ruin of her dreams and works. She can still stitch a government together, but she has lost control, and is at the mercy of events.

The situation with Emmanuel Macron is more ambivalent. If Merkel represents the tired old regime, and Trump the upsurge of chaotic new forces, Macron seeks to straddle the gulf between. His rise to the presidency was as wild and improbable, in a French context, as Trump's. His party, En Marche, was invented scarcely a year before Election Day. His voters and activists were ordinary people swept into politics for the first time. There hovers in Macron's language a vision of a society that was once glorious and can be so again: he favors words like "confidence" and "rediscover." In this, too, he comes closer in spirit than has been acknowledged to Trump's call to "make America great again."

Two great questions confront him. The first is whether it is possible to combine the tremendous political energies released by the public with the purpose and permanence of the institutions. The answer is unknown. No one has tried the experiment. The second question is whether Macron has

Figure 31: A redeemer on troubled waters.[298]
© *The Economist Newspaper Limited, London 6/17/2017.*

the skill and experience to pull the trick off, if we grant that it is possible. The answer is again uncertain, but the recent track record of political prodigies in Europe isn't encouraging. As youngest president of the Fifth Republic, Macron stands in the same unfortunate line of descent with Tsipras and Renzi.

His instincts, too, run counter to the temper of the times. He's a centralizer in a centrifugal age, for example. He has said that he aspires to a "Jupiterian" presidency—actually to *increase* the distance between power and the public.[299] He chose Versailles Palace, rococo backdrop to the Sun King, for his first important speech. While the Olympian style may have served Charles de Gaulle well, it is unlikely to be taken seriously on Twitter or Facebook. Macron is clearly tempted by the crown of the decaying empire: that is, by the ambition to become the next Angela Merkel. That way, it seems to me, lies perdition.

The odds, in sum, are stacked high against the newly delivered French president growing up to be the savior of the French established order and European democracy. But who can tell? Napoleon is reputed to have said that "impossible is not French"—and one lesson of the foregoing analysis is that it isn't *now*, either.

THE RUSSIANS ARE COMING, THE NAZIS ARE HERE, AND EVERY-WHERE YOU LOOK THERE'S DONALD TRUMP

As the outcomes of democracy turned increasingly against the elites, the elites with equal intensity worried about the failure of democracy. The tipping point, as we saw, was 2016. To many thoughtful persons, the sight of Donald Trump in the Oval Office signaled the downfall of our political system. The success of right-wing populists in Eastern and Central Europe confirmed the worst fears. Barbarians were not only inside the walls, but in charge of the government.

We have entered a time of extraordinary pessimism concerning the competence, even the legitimacy, of representative democracy. Lamentations of the most extreme kind pour out on a daily basis—here, to offer a random sample, is cultural critic Henry Giroux's take on the "failures of American democracy" under Trump:

> *A dystopian ideology, a kind of nostalgic yearning for older authoritarian relations of power, now shapes and legitimates a mode of governance that generates obscene levels of inequality, expands the ranks of corrupt legislators, places white supremacists and zealous ideologues in positions of power, threatens to jail its opponents, and sanctions an expanding network of state violence both at home and abroad.*[300]

This is how the global elite class and many others interpret what I have called the revolt of the public: as the death of democracy and a descent into authoritarian darkness. The connection between political turmoil and the new information landscape is now broadly understood, but the issue is often framed in terms of social media opening the gates to destructive or undesirable opinions. "It's the (democracy-poisoning) golden age of free speech," states an article on social media by sociologist Zeynep Tufekci.[301]

The corollary to democratic despair has been an almost mystical faith in the effectiveness of foreign dictators. Russia's Vladimir Putin, of all people, has become the hero of conspiracy theories and the *deus ex machina* of illiberalism. The belief that Russia "hacked" the presidential elections to favor Trump has become entrenched in the media and public opinion: according to one poll, over 50 percent of Americans believe Trump's dealings with Putin have been either "illegal" or "unethical."[302] The elites have seized on this putative Russian meddling as a weapon in the institutional reaction to the new president. Based on revelations, official and leaked, from the federal bureaucracy, a special counsel was appointed in May 2017 to investigate possible crimes committed by candidate Trump or his circle in collusion with Putin.

I'd like to take this dismal vision of the present state of democracy and turn it into an analytical question: *Is it, in fact, the case that the struggle between a digitally empowered public and the institutions of the industrial age has promoted the ruin of democracy and "legitimized" the authoritarian impulse, at home and abroad?* In looking for answers, my approach is going to be broad-brush and empirical. A government must do *something* to be considered authoritarian: trample on institutional checks, break the law, abuse established rights. I'm searching for instances of Giroux's "state violence." Similarly, dictatorial regimes navigating the current information environment must be shown to be more confident or aggressive in pursuit of their interests or their ideological goals.

My question is *apparently* about democracy—really about authority— yet I find it clarifying to turn first to the dictatorships. Consider: If taming social media is the fix to the present predicament, shouldn't North Korea or Cuba be our models for the future? I ask that rhetorically—and with a smile. The Kim and Castro regimes resemble nothing so much as Lenin in his mausoleum, moldering in a mummified version of the 20th century.

So let me begin, instead, with the most successful and applauded of the dictatorships: China.

China is the poster child of authoritarianism, but we know less than we think about conditions in the country. The material boom that raised millions out of poverty has brought more modern, less tangible anxieties in train. Society is persistently said to be in the grip of a "moral crisis," in which "hatred prevails over compassion" and money is made "at the cost of other people's lives"—but, of course, there's no way to quantify this.[303] It is almost certain that the population is Christianizing at a rapid rate— but actual numbers aren't available.[304] We do know that the Communist Party, led by Xi Jinping, is engaged in a ruthless "anti-corruption" campaign that has implicated high-level officials. Here the moral crisis intersects with the political system: when it comes to making money at the cost of human life, the rot starts at the top.

China's overseers call their form of government a "people's democratic dictatorship": opposites are thus reconciled in a phrase. The dictatorship side of the equation has seduced certain Western intellectuals who despair of democracy: they dream of an enlightened despot with the power to end the current political and informational chaos.[305] And, to be sure, the Chinese state has erected a massive apparatus of censorship and repression, including an "internet police" said to number in the millions. Controls over politics and media have grown harsher under Xi. Bloggers now receive long prison sentences for criticizing government policies, for example.[306] Journalists have been jailed for leaking official documents.[307] High-flying party members have been snared and broken in the purge against corruption.

The question is whether such tactics reflect strength or weakness in the regime. Given the lack of transparency, it's hard to say. My guess is that the ruling class in China, having long ago abandoned Marx, is straining after *some* ideal or principle on which to anchor its legitimacy. Xi, for his part, is pretty obviously maneuvering to increase his power at the party's expense. Hardened repression may just be a factor of the gangster-like nature of the system. Much the same could be said of China's passive-aggressive geopolitical posture. These moves may reflect internal divisions and doubts.

In any case, the concept of an enlightened dictator, with just-so repression, is a fantasy of the intellectuals. Reality is about bad choices. The regime in China survives on economic prosperity, which demands the free flow of information. But sooner or later, the economy will begin to wobble—should that information be allowed to flow? Xi has already hectored the Chinese media about "properly guiding public opinion," especially with regard to the economy.[308] He sounds, to me, like a politician on the defensive, in spin mode. Every year the Chinese government admits to thousands of "mass incidents" and labor strikes; unlike the rest of us, Xi knows their actual number. Around 700 million of his countrymen are online, and 90 percent access the web through that most subversive of devices, the smartphone.[309] China's elites are riding a tiger and know it. Whatever the future brings to this antiquated power structure, it is no more likely than North Korea or Cuba to provide the escape route from liberal democracy in the 21st century.

What, then, of Russia's Putin, the man who is said to have "a plan for destroying the West," and who in a prodigious (if conjectural) display of power and cunning has manipulated everything from the U.S. presidential elections to the price of oil?[310]

In analyzing Putin's progress, I confess that I'm at a loss on how to proceed. My perception of the reality behind both the man and his country differs radically from the accepted wisdom and much scholarly thinking. The shadow, it seems to me, is wholly out of proportion to the object. The Russian economy is roughly equivalent to Spain's. GDP per capita has declined in parallel with the oil market, and in 2016 was ranked right below the Caribbean island of Grenada. The Russian population peaked around 1990 and has lost five million since, the result of low birth rates, high abortion rates, and zero immigration. Life expectancy for males compares unfavorably with Rwanda. In a "Putin exodus," many of Russia's most talented people have left the country.

Putin commands a large military establishment that includes a nuclear arsenal. He can dispose of the wealth generated by Russian oil. He is, beyond question, a cunning and manipulative man, and he does not wish the US, Europe, or liberal democracy well. But I ask you, good reader, to maintain a sense of scale on the subject. In that spirit, I will press on as follows. The election-hacking story—heart of the Putin puzzle—I will put off to a fuller discussion of "fake news" and "post-truth." Here I intend to stick to my question: whether the Putin authoritarian style, under current conditions of information—what I have called the Fifth Wave—has grown more powerful, threatening, or seductive, relative to the old democracies.

The Putin style, let it be said, resembles that of a mafia godfather. Putin isn't Stalin, but the list of people who have died violently after crossing him—billionaires, journalists, political opponents—is impressively long.[311] It's all business, not personal (or ideological), and the sums involved are phenomenal. The hack of an offshore law firm in April 2016 revealed that an old friend of Putin's, a cellist of modest means, had fronted secret transactions totaling $2 billion.[312]

Putin portrays himself in a very different light. He belongs to a class that I would call *dictatorships of repudiation:* al-Sisi in Egypt,

Erdogan in Turkey, and the late Hugo Chávez in Venezuela are members of the club. The common thread is a rhetoric of defiance and renewal. The dictator is transformed from a murderous predator into a solitary hero struggling against overwhelming odds. The villain confronting him is some hodgepodge of globalized malevolence, with the U.S. typically pulling the strings.

For Putin, the enemy is the alliance of the United States and the European democracies. This cabal aims at nothing less than the "disintegration and dismemberment" of Russia.[313] "Our opponents want to see us disunited," he stated in 2007. "Some want to take away and divide everything, and others to plunder. . . . Those who want to confront us need a weak and ill state."[314] Putin began his career as a small cog in the enormous machine that was the Soviet state. He feels the need to explain why Russia was once a superpower, and is one no longer. The specter of decadence and disintegration, of lost glory and greatness, has come to haunt politics in nations far less troubled than Russia: in different contexts, it helped propel Trump and Macron to office. Putin's account begins with the U.S.-led destruction of the Soviet Union, and ends with the defiant rebirth of Russia.

Between the mafia boss and the restorer of Russian greatness, there's no intrinsic contradiction. Both lead to the glorification of Putin and the worship of power. Russia's foreign adventures of the last few years can be parsed either way. Tough-guy Putin moved into Crimea, Ukraine, and Syria to exploit local weakness and show up the singularly passive Barack Obama. Imperial Putin reasserted historic Russian claims in the Black Sea and eastern Mediterranean. The objective was always to frighten and impress the global elites—to force them to acknowledge the Russian dictator as a world-historical actor. In the dazed aftermath of the U.S. presidential election, this wish was granted with a vengeance.

Despite his self-righteous brutality, Putin retains levels of popularity and support that would be the envy of any American politician. The same is true of al-Sisi and Erdogan, and was true of Chávez to the end. Many factors play into this strange circumstance, including control over the story told by national media. The Russian media, for example, loves to portray the scrawny Putin in the guise of an action hero.[315] Egypt's journalists can write without blushing of al-Sisi's "flawless appearance" and "Herculean strength."[316] Yet much tighter controls over information have done nothing to enhance the image of Xi Jinping and his Chinese Communist Party.

The difference, I think, lies in the relationship to our equivocal moment in history. Putin, al-Sisi, and their kind believe, probably sincerely, that they are engaged in a war to the death against an established order dominated by foreign elites. They aim to slay the dragon of national decadence and bring to an end this unhappy age. To some extent, therefore, they can tap into the explosive political energies released by the revolt of the public, by the rage and despair over the way things stand felt by ordinary people in Russia, Egypt, and elsewhere. Their struggle is the public's, at least in this sense: the repudiation of the status quo and the desire to abolish it by fair means or foul.

Though aligned with the public's mood, the dictatorship of repudiation is best understood as a series of national episodes, lacking the ideological coherence to transform itself into a serious rival to liberal democracy. Putin's justifying crisis in Russia is nothing like that of al-Sisi in Egypt, for example, and neither is available for export. The thrust of repudiation, too, has a retrograde quality. The dictator takes up the burden of hierarchy in modern government. He will be expected to solve social and economic "problems" that he has no clue how to address, and to bring happiness to a hyper-informed and contentious public. Failure can be blamed on the enemy for only so long.

And I insist, once again, on the importance of proportion. The economies of Russia and Egypt often teeter on the verge of a nervous breakdown. Putin, the action hero, is at the mercy of the world commodities market. Al-Sisi, for all his Herculean strength, must go begging for handouts from the Gulf oil kingdoms. A possible future for one or the other might resemble the colossal wreck that is Hugo Chávez's legacy in Venezuela. Even if the way ahead is less dire, the structural reality of the dictatorship remains unaltered. Authoritarianism exaggerates precisely those elite behaviors that the public is rebelling against—and it can't repudiate itself. Putin and al-Sisi are doomed to struggle in the coils of a nihilistic age. They are not the masters or exploiters of it. Both men long for a return of the glory days of the Cold War. Their future is in the past.

So, I don't see authoritarian rulers prospering under current conditions. The 2010s bear little resemblance to the 1930s. That is the explicit answer to the "abroad" part of my question. Xi Jinping may flex China's

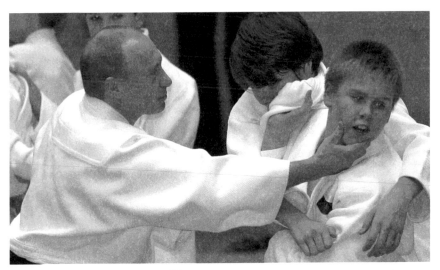

Figure 32: The dictator as action hero.[317] *Russian President Vladimir Putin attends a master class at a judo school in St.Petersburg, on Saturday, Dec. 24, 2005. Putin, a judo black belt, showed off his skills in the sport Saturday in nationwide television footage, giving a master class to students of a judo school in his home city. (AP Photo/Dmitry Lovetsky.)* © *2005 The Associated Press.*

muscle in Asia, but he knows that war will unleash domestic passions that could blow apart his precariously balanced regime. Vladimir Putin may play great power games on the edges of his rickety empire, but he's no more likely than Spain to invade Europe. China and Russia don't pretend to be rival models to democracy; they are, in fact, old-fashioned industrial-age hierarchies intent on looting their own people. Neither has been "legitimized." The restless public, riding a digital storm, is hostile to every large aggregation of power, regardless of ideology. First to be toppled in this conflict were long-entrenched dictators in the Middle East.

Authoritarianism *appears* to be advancing because so many elite voices in democratic nations say so. Democracy looks to be dying in darkness for the same reason. The source of despondency is that elite disaster, the election of Trump—and the focus of analysis must now shift to American politics, to answer the "at home" part of my question.

* * *

On August 11, 2017, white nationalists gathered in Charlottesville, Virginia, for a "Unite the Right" march against the planned removal of Confederate monuments. Among the unsavory ultras involved were neo-Nazis associated with the Daily Stormer website, the neo-Confederate League of the

South, and elements of the KKK. In the spirit of Nuremberg, a torchlight parade was expected—but it was a bring-your-own-torch party. "Each person should bring their own torches which can be bought from a local Wal-Mart, Lowes, Home Depot, etc.," were the helpful instructions of the organizers. "Tikki [*sic*] Torches are fine."[318]

Crowd sizes are difficult to reconstruct, but the protesters probably numbered in the hundreds. A somewhat larger crowd of counter-protesters included anti-racist church and progressive groups, but also hardened street fighters of the Workers World Party, Black Lives Matter, and Redneck Revolt. On the night of August 11, an impromptu tiki-torch parade took place without serious incident. On the next day, however, clashes involving the white nationalists and their opponents began early and continued into the afternoon. Police from half a dozen jurisdictions likely outnumbered both groups, but were kept out of harm's way. At 1:41 p.m., a neo-fascist sympathizer, all of 20 years of age, drove his Dodge Challenger into a crowd of counter-protesters, killing a young woman and injuring many more. As always in this visual age, the entire horror was caught on video and propagated on the web.

On the same day, President Trump offered a rambling assessment of the incident that included the following:

> We condemn in the strongest possible terms this egregious display of hatred, bigotry, and violence on many sides, many sides. It's been going on for a long time in our country. . . . Above all else, we must remember this truth: no matter our color, creed, religion, or political party, we are all Americans first.[319]

The almost universal interpretation of the president's confused statement was that he had placed the victims of Charlottesville on the same footing with the murderer, and given "a wink and a nod to white supremacists."[320] Trump poured gasoline on the fire by insisting, a few days later, that not all protesters had been "neo-Nazis and white nationalists," and included "some very fine people on both sides."[321]

It was a decisive moment for those who believed American democracy had died on Election Day. Donald Trump, president of the United States, was now openly the creature of white supremacists and Nazis. Wrote author Ta-Nehisi Coates: "His ideology is white supremacy, in all its truculent and sanctimonious power."[322] Wrote activist Bob Burnett:

"Trump now owns white supremacy."[323] Tweeted sports journalist Jemele Hill: "Trump is a white supremacist who has largely surrounded himself w/other white supremacists."[324] The "tens of millions" of Trump supporters were "white supremacists by default"—or, alternatively, were being "recruited" by neo-Nazi propaganda.[325]

For a time, elite news media became enamored of that rare and vanishing species: the American Nazi. The *New York Times* told the story of "The Voice of Hate in America's Heartland," about a young man soon to be married who happens to be "the Nazi sympathizer next door, polite and low-key at a time the old boundaries of accepted political activity can seem alarmingly in flux." Naturally, Donald Trump "helped open a space for people like him."[326] Almost simultaneously, *The Atlantic* published "The Making of an American Nazi," focused on one of the more revolting contributors to the Daily Stormer. Trump's name features 39 times, as in, illustratively: "His writing taps into some of the same anxieties and resentments that helped carry Trump to the presidency—chiefly a perceived loss of status among white men."[327]

If Russia and Putin were the hidden hand that delivered the impossible Trump to power, the Nazis, in the fevered mind of the elites, represented the monstrous outcome of this manipulation.

Books lamenting the decline and fall of our political system, authored by scholars, pundits, and pure disaster-mongers, saturated the market: *How Democracy Dies; Broken: Can the Senate Save Itself and the Country?; Can It Happen Here? Authoritarianism in America; The People vs. Democracy: Why Our Freedom Is Endangered; Russian Roulette: The Inside Story of Russia's War on America and the Election of Donald Trump; The Road to Unfreedom*; and, of course, *Trumpocracy: The Corruption of the American Republic*. These books were all published in 2018. A vast number of earlier titles could be cited.

What is one to make of such a fantastic outpouring of pessimism? I would note, first of all, that it's largely elite-driven. Millions share the sentiment—but the elites own the institutional microphones, and make the loud noise. If Trump poses an existential threat to elite authority—if he is *perceived* as posing such a threat—it isn't hard to imagine those who have managed and personified our ruling institutions for so long as projecting the threat onto the system. Democracy from that perspective means rule by the best. Authoritarianism looks like a barbarian invasion.

A second observation is that we had heard all this before. Trump was Hitler before he was inaugurated. From the first, the call was for a resistance on the model of Nazi-occupied France. Charlottesville and similar incidents, for the elites, were a confirmation, not a revelation: Trump, barbarian in the White House, has merely lived up to expectations.

This seems like an appropriate time to return to my analytical question, extracted from the cries of anguish about American democracy. Briefly: Is the U.S. now an authoritarian dictatorship? If not, is it slouching toward that goal? Is Donald Trump a tweeting version of Hitler, Mussolini, or the Grand Wizard of the KKK? Can we cite empirical evidence of Giroux's accusations—that the new administration has sought to "jail its opponents" and engaged in "state violence?"

In what follows, I'm not endorsing or resisting Donald Trump. I'm performing analysis. I'm going to compare the president's actions and policies to the accusations and condemnations of his opponents. Note that I'm also not endorsing or resisting the other side of the equation. What I'm after is a thesis that explains Trump's part, if any, in cranking up the decibels of a gigantic chorus of gloom.

We now have more than 12 months of incumbency behind us. The special counsel's investigation of collusion with Russia grinds on as I write this. I won't pre-judge the matter, other than to note that, as a path to dictatorship, "Vladimir Putin put me here" makes for a very strange choice. Beyond that, there's really nothing. Hillary Clinton wasn't prosecuted. As Michael Barone writes, "We have no political prisons full of reporters."[328] The president's travel ban remains bogged down in the courts—in that case, his instincts have been less autocratic than those of Andrew Jackson, never mind Mussolini. The wall he promised to build on the Mexican border is still unfunded by Congress, part of a thoroughly conventional tussle over immigration in which the Democrats are winning serious concessions. The attempt to "repeal and replace" Barack Obama's Affordable Care Act foundered on the structural reality of the Republican Party, a beast with too many heads and too many contradictory voices.

I don't see how, on the evidence, a case can be made that the United States is stumbling toward authoritarian rule. But I want to expand on that point. As I look over the world's democratic nations, I find little support for the thesis that their governments are becoming more violent or authoritarian. Among the old democracies, at least, the opposite is closer to the truth. Democratic governments are terrified of the public's unhappiness. They understand the crushing existential burden placed by the public on mere politics, and the likelihood of failure, and the certainty that failure will be digitally magnified. Their behavior is the opposite of authoritarian. It's a drift to dysfunction: to paralysis.

Weakness, not a will to power, accounts for the fall of Tsipras in Greece and Renzi in Italy. Paralysis seems like the right term for the government of Spain. Dysfunction describes the muddle in post-Brexit Britain, the decline of Merkel in Germany, the collapse of the political parties, the slow-motion disintegration of the E.U. and of the nation-state. A mass movement like fascism would be difficult to sustain in the age of social media. A garden-variety authoritarian dictatorship would require the unlikely cooptation of military or security forces—something visible only to the large and growing body of conspiracy theorists.

The peril to democracy under present conditions of information isn't any of these things: it's the spread of nihilism in the public and the demoralization of an elite class that has lost any claim to authority.

The August 2017 events in Charlottesville fit this pattern. Nazis and white supremacists were there in insignificant numbers when compared to, say, the huge anti-Trump protests that followed the elections. They and their "anti-fascist" antagonists exemplify the public's escape to exotic islands of identity; they are evidence, therefore, of the fracturing of American politics, not its takeover by violent mass movements. Yet these groups *did* take over the streets in Charlottesville. The cause was the abdication of the authorities. Elected officials in the city hesitated between their wish to oppose the racist protesters and their duty to preserve the peace. The police, which could have overwhelmed any disturbance, felt that its presence would actually incite violence. A single school crossing guard was posted at the intersection where the car attack occurred. She was soon removed out of fear for her safety. An independent review of the events, commissioned by the city, stated baldly:

> *The City of Charlottesville protected neither free expression nor public safety on August 12. The City was unable to protect the right of free expression and facilitate the permit holder's offensive speech. This represents a failure of one of government's core functions—the protection of fundamental rights. Law enforcement also*

failed to maintain order and protect citizens from harm, injury, and death.[329]

Here was the crisis of authority, writ small. The space abandoned by the democratic elites was immediately occupied by sectarian war-bands. None of these, by definition, were organized along old-fashioned fascist lines. That is the structural reality of our moment. So far as we know, the 20-year-old who plowed his car into the crowd at Charlottesville wasn't acting on orders from his *führer* or from anyone else. He acted on an impulse: the urge to kill and destroy. Rather than chase after Nazis or other phantoms of history, those concerned with the future of democracy should fix their attention on that young man: on the nihilist who believes, with passionate intensity, that destruction and slaughter are by themselves a form of progress.

* * *

The nihilist *impulse*—the wish to smash down whatever stands—was to a considerable extent responsible for Donald Trump. As a candidate, Trump said and did outrageous things. He trampled on every taboo sanctifying the presidential election process. This worked to his advantage. He was perceived as a worthy club in the hands of millions of "deplorables" who wanted to strike a blow at Hillary Clinton, political correctness, and the ruling elites.

The question is whether President Trump, in office, has continued to be an agent of negation and a vector for the nihilist impulse. The president, we know, is an idol-smasher and establishment-basher. But for the case to be proved, he must be shown to have wielded the massive power of the state, in a sense, against itself: to have battered, with casual abandon and without regard for the consequences, the institutions over which he presides.

The answer will depend entirely on whether you are observing the administration's behavior or parsing the president's rhetoric.

A year in, it's fairly clear that the actions and policies of the Trump administration are little different from, say, what a Ted Cruz or even a Jeb Bush administration would have implemented. From a Republican and conservative perspective, such actions and policies appear to be perfectly within the mainstream. On immigration and tax reform, in his judicial appointments and anti-regulation zeal, the president has followed prescriptions habitually endorsed by Republicans and conservatives before him.

Much the same can be said of foreign policy. Except for a strong tilt to protectionism, the Trump way on NATO and the UN, say, or China and Afghanistan, adheres pretty closely to regular Republican practice. He has been less interventionist than George W. Bush, but more aggressive—with ISIS, Iran, and North Korea, for example—than Barack Obama. And for all the talk of manipulation, he may well be tougher on Russia than his predecessor at this point in his tenure.[330]

The reasons why the antiestablishment Trump has pursued traditional Republican conservative policies need not detain us here. I simply want to establish the fact. To do so, I could cite effusive praise from pro-Trump conservatives—Newt Gingrich and Victor Davis Hanson come to mind—but I find it much more persuasive to turn to another source. Never Trump is a movement of conservative intellectuals forged during the elections. These thinkers share, in spades, the loathing of the elite class for the president's character. Many Never Trump conservatives supported Hillary Clinton. Most remain unreconciled.

Their grudging testimony on the administration's policies is therefore valuable.

Political commentator Noah Rothman, who has written of the "damage done by Trump's big mouth," nonetheless accepts that the president is governing "not as a populist firebrand but a conventional Republican."[331] Ross Douthat, a Never Trump voice in the *New York Times*, has observed with some surprise that the administration's Middle East policy is "close to what I would have hoped from a normal Republican president."[332] Yet another member of the Never Trump tribe, Rich Lowry, has conceded, "It's hard to see how a conventional Republican president would have done much better."[333]

Two observations follow from these assessments. The first is that the Trump administration's policies are not an instance of the state destroying itself. It isn't nihilism at work. For better or worse, it's Republican conservatism in power.

The second observation concerns the words "normal" and "conventional" used by these anti-Trump intellectuals. The words are striking because they have never been used to characterize Donald Trump the man—not by anyone, of any persuasion. For this, there is good reason: Trump has said and done outrageous things. He demands, and receives, impossible levels of attention—and he cashes it in with rhetoric that is *not* normal, *not* conventional, *not* mainstream, and in fact beyond anything previously experienced from a chief executive.

Trump has mastered the nihilist style of the web. That, to me, is the most significant factor separating him from the pack. His opponents speak in jargon and clichés. He speaks in rant. He attacks, insults, condemns, doubles down on misstatements, never takes a step back, never apologizes. Everyone he dislikes is a liar (see "Lyin' Ted Cruz"), a thief (see "Crooked Hillary"), a "bimbo," "bought and paid for," the equivalent of a child molester. This is American politics portrayed as the last circle of hell: treachery by the people, from the people, against the people. Taken literally, it would mean that not a single pillar of our institutions deserves to be left standing. Coming from a president, it has the feel of the state devouring itself.

Such rhetorical onslaughts would have destroyed political careers just a short time ago. They can succeed today only in the context of the great struggle that is my theme. The public, recall, has mobilized in a spirit of negation and repudiation of the status quo. It isn't interested in a positive program of reform. Because the impetus for revolt was born in the digital universe, it has inherited the style peculiar to the web—a place where every political dispute ends in obscenities, and, not infrequently, death threats. The public has absorbed this language of outrage. It too speaks in rant.

Trump's rhetorical excesses appear remarkably in tune with this environment. But there is also a political gambit being played on his part.

Politicians swept into office by the antiestablishment flood face an immediate dilemma. Once in government, they can continue to smash away at the institutions—but this will damage the economy and consequently their popularity. Alternatively, they can move to the mainstream and compromise with the elites—but this will demolish their credibility and alienate their base of support. Few have found a way out of the labyrinth. Alexis Tsipras tried each approach in turn, and failed at both.

The bizarre schizoid style of the Trump administration becomes intelligible as an attempt to escape this dilemma. Elected as an agent of negation, President Trump must now promote positive policies and programs. Any direction he takes will alienate *some* of his supporters, who are bound together largely on the strength of their repudiations. A predilection for the mainstream will alienate *most* of them.

Against this background, the loud and vulgar sound of the president's voice becomes the signal for a mustering of the political war-bands. The subject at issue is often elite behavior unrelated to policy: "fake news" in the media, for example, or an NFL star kneeling during the national anthem. Those who oppose Trump can't resist the lure of outrage. Their responses tend to be no less loud or vulgar, and are sometimes more violent, than the offending message.[334] Groups on the other side of the spectrum, now stoked to full-throated rant mode, rally reflexively to the president's defense.

I have described this process elsewhere.[335] It's a zero-sum struggle for attention that rewards the most immoderate voices—and, without question, Donald Trump is a master of the game. His unbridled language mobilizes his anti-elite followers, even as his policies appeal to more "conventional" Republicans and conservatives.

Politically, it's a high-wire act without a net. Trump was never a popular candidate. He's not a popular president. To retain his base, he must provoke his opposition into a frenzy of loathing. Ordinary Americans, inevitably, have come to regard the president as the sum of all his rants. For our confused and demoralized elites, who have no clue about the game being played, Donald Trump looks something like the Beast of the Apocalypse, a sign of chaotic end-times. Writes the normally reflective cultural critic Ian Buruma: "the act of undermining democratic institutions by abusing them in front of braying mobs is not modern at all. It is what aspiring dictators have always done."[336]

But dictators don't deal in tweets. Trump is in the style of our moment: a man from nowhere, with no stake in the system, ignorant of history, incurious about our political habits and traditions, but happy to bash and to break old and precious things in exchange for a little attention.

So I come back, one last time, to my question—only now the answer lends support to the alarmists. The predicament confronting liberal democracy, however, isn't a resurrected Hitlerism or a manipulative Putinism. It isn't even Trumpism, except as a sort of thermometer reading. The trouble is in *us*: in our readiness to generalize from the web levels of hostility and aggression inconsistent with the legitimacy of any political system. By embracing Trump in significant numbers, I mean to say, the public has signaled that it is willing to impose the untrammeled relations of social media on the fragile forms of American democracy.

FAKE NEWS, POST-TRUTH, AND MAKING THE WAY STRAIGHT FOR THE NIHILIST

The election of Donald Trump can be said to have demolished the intellectual foundations of the news business. The pretense of objectivity had been abandoned for a higher cause. The claim to furnish "all the news that's fit to print" was now refuted by the failure to grasp the shape and outcome of the contest. No one who followed the news understood the forces at play. None guessed what was coming. Continued consumption of news seemed to lack any justification, other than amusement or habit.

Dazed and demoralized, people in the media sought haphazardly to explain the disaster. They were not good at the game: a profession that is literally in broadcast mode shouldn't be expected to excel at self-scrutiny. Some wished to reclaim the mantle of authority by launching expeditions to that dark continent, Trumpland. "As The Times begins a period of self-reflection, I hope its editors will think hard about the half of America it seldom covers," wrote the *New York Times*'s public editor on the morning after.[337] Others remained unreconciled. "I blame my profession for failing to inform the public it serves," tweeted Jeff Jarvis, journalism professor and by no means the only author to assume that "information" was the antidote to "Trump."[338]

The self-critical mood didn't last. Eight days after the elections, Buzzfeed posted a long, sloppy analysis piece that made the following assertion:

> *In the final three months of the US presidential election, the top-performing fake news stories on Facebook generated more engagement than the top stories from major news outlets such as the New York Times, Washington Post, Huffington Post, NBC News, and others.* [339]

Of the top 20 fake news stories, "all but three were overtly pro-Donald Trump or anti-Hillary Clinton." The piece said nothing about the effect of fake news on public opinion, but did sound an ominous note: "This new data illustrates the power of fake election news on Facebook."

Four days later, the *New York Times* picked up on the subject: "How Fake News Goes Viral: A Case Study."[340] The case involved a false story on Twitter that sought to discredit anti-Trump protests in Austin, Texas. There followed an extraordinary flowering of media exposés about fake news, most of them implying, without quite ever affirming, that fakery had helped Trump win the election. This was capped by a *Washington Post* article purporting to have uncovered the hand of that master manipulator, Vladimir Putin, in the diffusion of fake news favoring Trump.

> *The flood of "fake news" this election season got support from a so-phisticated Russian propaganda campaign that created and spread misleading articles online with the goal of punishing Democrat Hillary Clinton, helping Republican Donald Trump, and under-mining faith in American democracy, say independent researchers who tracked the operation.*[341]

An anonymous expert was quoted as saying, "It was like Russia was running a super PAC for Trump's campaign...it worked."

If fake news deluded the masses into electing Donald Trump, and so-phisticated Russians who hated democracy were responsible for the fake news, then an explanation for 2016 had been found that absolved the news media. The question was never asked *why* people would believe fake news over the real stuff. Trust in news as an institution had imploded. News as a business had been the first casualty of the public's assault on the hierarchies of the industrial age. Information on the web existed in a state of nature, and on social media was structured by murky algorithmic priorities. All of this emptied "news" of meaning as a category of information, but none of it merited much consideration.

The prevalence of falsehood and the importance of Russian conspir-acies in the election became canonical. The news industry felt justified in taking the last logical step: in effect, a leap out of mediation over the edge to advocacy.

In a private session with the network anchors, Trump was asked what surprised him most about becoming president. "The fact that you never changed your coverage," he replied, ever attentive to media attention. "The fact that it never got better."[342] He was right. Negative coverage of the president has hovered consistently around 90 percent. According to one study, the top issue covered by mainstream news sources in 2017 was collusion between the administration and Putin's Russia.[343] The tone of coverage was even more one-sided. It was the media, of course, that gave us the caricatures of Trump as Hitler, Mussolini, and a white supremacist. It was the media that made every day into the last day of democracy in America. The rage that was once the monopoly of online politics—and poisons so much of the president's own rhetoric—now poured out of the inky pages of old-fashioned newsprint.

A side had been chosen: the other "half of America" was to be discarded. At least in the short term, it's proved to be a sound business decision. President Trump delights in tweeting about the "failing *New York Times*"—but since his election, subscriptions for the paper have increased tenfold over the previous year.[344] Viewership of cable news networks, some of which had struggled to find an audience, exploded in 2016 and continued to surge in 2017. That was true across the board: Fox, CNN, and MSNBC.[345] Half of America is a big customer base—and Donald Trump, that political peacock, always seems to sell. There was even an uptick in trust in the news, from less than 20 percent to around 27 percent, as Democrats and other opponents of Trump perceived a reliable ally in the media.[346]

But the news as an institution in a very real sense has ceased to exist. The media elites, like elites everywhere, are driven by a fever dream of undoing the outcome of the 2016 election. They desperately want the status quo before Trump back, and they are willing to bash away, Trump-like, at their own standards and even the democratic process in pursuit of that aim. I don't see how it's possible, from a posture of radical reaction, to reclaim the ideal of the news media as an honest broker of information. I don't see how journalists can be taken seriously by independent minds when they criticize President Trump's truly destructive rhetorical outbursts. All they can do is oppose one kind of tribal aggression with another, nihilism against nihilism.

Journalist Howard Kurtz sums up the conflict: "Donald Trump is staking his presidency, as he did his election, on nothing less than destroying the credibility of the news media; and the media are determined to do the same for him." But credibility, in this case, isn't necessarily a question of either-or: both the president and the institutions, including the media, have stripped themselves of authority down to a fig leaf of rage and negation. "This is, at bottom, a battle over the truth," Kurtz concludes.[347] But it's really a battle for dominance, fought on a darkling plain where truth, when encountered, is used strictly as a weapon. The media became obsessed with Russia and fake news to undermine the president's legitimacy. The president, more adept at this sort of thing, stole the phrase and now applies it liberally to those news outlets—the *New York Times*, CNN—that seem to him indistinguishable from his political enemies.

I don't wish to elide past the empirical question whether sophisticated Russians actually tried to manipulate the election with fake news. I take it for granted that they did, and that the consequences were close to nil. The kind of "sophistication" the *Washington Post* article insisted on— the word shows up three times—is entirely specialized and technical. It can get a lot of clicks for a story about Hillary Clinton's terminal illness, for example. It has nothing to do with persuasion—with changing minds. For all the sound and fury about fake news, not a shred of evidence exists that they influenced the election outcome. An analysis of online media election coverage by Harvard's Berkman Klein Center suggests the opposite: "Although fake news—fabricated and verifiable false reporting—was a phenomenon during the election, it had a minor effect on the media ecosystem of the presidential election according to our findings."[348]

The relationship between information and human behavior is exceedingly complex, but we seldom change our core beliefs because of a story we read online. That's so whether the story is true or false. On the question of influence, too, the distinction between fake and real news tends to disappear. Mark Zuckerberg, responding to questions about Facebook's role in the election, had the weight of evidence on his side when he stated, "Voters make decisions based on lived experience."[349] Predictably, Zuckerberg was harshly criticized for this comment, and has been compelled to walk it back.

* * *

The panic over fake news that followed the election soon hardened into a theory of universal self-deception. Public opinion, the account went, had become untethered from reality, and democracy was now staggering into a "post-truth" era. This phrase first gained currency after Brexit and always retained a strong British flavor—*Oxford Dictionary* made "post-truth" its word of the year for 2016. But it was the U.S. presidential election, and the scandalous rhetoric of Donald Trump, that clinched the deal.

Oxford Dictionary defined post-truth as "circumstances in which objective facts are less influential in shaping public opinion than appeals to emotion and personal belief." More literal definitions could be found. "Post-truth refers to blatant lies being routine across society,"[350] one academic explained, "and it means that politicians can lie without condemnation." In its take on the subject, *The Economist* named the politician in question:

> *Post-truth politics is more than just an invention of whingeing elites who have been outflanked. The term picks out the heart of what is new: the truth is not falsified, or contested, but of secondary importance. Once, the purpose of political lying was to create a false view of the world. The lies of men like Mr. Trump do not work like that. They are not intended to convince the elites, whom their target voters neither trust nor like, but to reinforce prejudice.*[351]

It is depressing to observe how quickly the term found a home in our dismal political landscape. For elite opinion, fronting for liberal and progressive groups, post-truth became the final solution to the mystery of Donald Trump's somersault to the presidency. At some point, these people believe, fake news metastasized into false consciousness: hence Trump. "The practice of post-truth—untrue assertion piled on untrue assertion—helped get Donald Trump to the White House," declared Ruth Marcus in the *Washington Post*. "The more untruths he told, the more his supporters rewarded him for, as they saw it, telling it like it is."[352] The sincere despair in this statement masks, I think, a kind of relief. The elite disasters of 2016 were now neatly disconnected from empirical reality.

For conservatives and libertarians, post-truth aptly described an information environment dominated by liberalism and political correctness in the news media, the entertainment industry, and the university. These people recall a famous *New York Times* headline—"fake but accurate"—about a story critical of a Republican president. The main difference between "pre-truth" and the present, they insist, is that the other side is now bringing up the subject.[353]

So the meaning of post-truth is itself up for grabs.

A fair question is whether this skirmish has any place in my story. I'm going to suggest that it does have a place: that post-truth is a clumsy label for a social trajectory that leads, over broken terrain, to the nihilist and his nightmare, and beyond that to the contested grounds where the fate of the current elite class will be decided. We live in disconcerting times. Much of our mediated reality—and that entails all of our politics—has fractured along multiple lines. Digital reality, I said above, has been swallowed by the rant—and everyday life, increasingly, is digital. This is the day of the *truther,* the *denier,* the *birther.* I'm struck by how we constantly put forward, like a battered shield, the word "literally"—as in "Trump is literally Hitler." We are not inclined to tease apart our will from the world.

A profound moral and political disorientation has driven us, stumbling, to this place. The question is whether elite complaints over post-truth make sense as an explanation. We have the evidence of Brexit and Trump: can we say, in consequence, that democracy has degenerated into an empire of lies? Two elite claims are of particular interest here, and deserve deeper reflection: that the internet is "the definitive vector of post-truth," and that certain populist politicians, with President Trump in the vanguard, now use deceit to communicate a "brutal empathy" with the public's prejudices. [354]

Let's consider each in turn.

From the first, elites have treated the web as an existential threat. Teachers forbade students any taste of that forbidden fruit. The Pentagon, taking no chances, blocked access to social media in the building. The news media, which purports to interpose layers of editors and fact-checkers between the journalist and the public, routinely portrays the web as the mother of all lies. Anyone can say anything and publish it. No penalties are incurred for peddling falsehoods, even intentional ones.

In the actual evolution of the web, true or false have come to matter less than like or dislike, friend or unfriend, follow or unfollow. The great platforms of social media labor relentlessly to "harvest your attention"—Zeynep Tufekci's phrase—by nudging you toward the like-minded, telling you what you already know, giving you what you have always wanted. [355] The effect—in journalist Matthew d'Ancona's phrase—has been "online huddling." [356] The public, which as a whole has risen in revolt against the established order, in its parts appears determined to defend a *partial* status quo—some source of identity or self-recognition that is placed beyond the reach of doubt or change. Online stories that reinforce the source of identity are consumed as nourishment for the soul, regardless of accuracy. They confirm, externally, a subjective order. Only in this way does Trump get to be literally Hitler.

This development is troubling on many levels, but it can't be used to explain radical political change—a move away from democracy to authoritarian populism, for instance. The web's force of gravity draws me to myself. Social media solidifies my private status quo. I'm encouraged to feel smug and certain in my views: whatever lies I consume I already believe. Change would require dissatisfaction with my previous views, a move *away* from what I have been. That simply never happens on the web. The rage and rant of digital content *presupposes* a loss of trust in institutional authority that elite ideas about post-truth seem to rationalize away.

On the broader subject of lies on the web, a very different sense of the matter has been advanced by Andrey Miroshnichenko in his brilliant little book, *Human as Media*. Miroshnichenko discerns a "viral editor" eternally at work online: a "distributed being of the internet, a sort of Artificial Intelligence" composed of every user, which performs many of the same functions of fact-checking and review claimed by the media. The digital universe, Miroshnichenko holds, is not indifferent between truth and falsehood:

> *If a lie is significant, it will circulate until it reaches witnesses and experts who will denounce it, because they know the truth. If a lie is insignificant, no one will denounce it; but it won't circulate.*
>
> *Every example of a lie on the internet, actually, is an example of the disclosure of this lie.*[357]

That is the strong version of a thesis I believe to be generally valid. If fake news had become a salient part of the 2016 campaign, for example, it would have been exposed and exploded. If it wasn't exposed, it was because it never crossed the public's awareness threshold. Politically, it did not matter. Post-truth in relation to the web describes a vast and elaborate body of lies, but very little deception and practically no impact.

What of Donald Trump and his fabricated empathy? The president stands at the swirling center of post-truth—and not without justice. He will say (or tweet) whatever it takes to shock the opposition into outrage. When it comes to voter fraud, the size of his crowds, the unemployment and murder rates, and many, many other topics, Trump can't resist the urge to bend reality to his theme. The *New York Times*, *Washington Post*, and CNN have kept a running tally of presidential falsehoods—in January 2018, the *Post* reported with a certain excitement that the president had broken the threshold of 2,000 "false or misleading claims." The article went on, "The longer the president has been on the job, the more frequently he touts an assortment of exaggerated, dubious or false claims."[358]

In the elite imagination, however, post-truth involves the power of lies to "shape public opinion" by pandering to prejudice. I'm not sure Trump's fabrications fit this scheme. They deceive very few, and the effect, beyond commanding attention, is never flattering. Before and after the election, most Americans held a negative view of the man. In one May 2016 survey, 6 percent of Trump *supporters* said they liked him personally, and only 43 percent agreed with his political positions. These voters were driven largely by hostility to Hillary Clinton.[359] A review of those who cast their ballots for Trump in November discovered an unstable coalition of perspectives, with highly fractured views on issues such as immigration and combating terrorism. How the lies of candidate Trump played across such diverse groups would be tough to determine.[360]

In fact, it's difficult to measure the impact of deceit on an election. By the same token, if you are going to argue that the impact was large for the 2016 presidential race, you need to muster convincing evidence. Merely to say, "But he lied—and he won," though accurate enough as a description, says nothing about causation.

The elite vision of a post-truth era ultimately rests on a fallacy. It assumes that there was once a time when voters acted on some sort of rational calculus based on "objective facts," and were immune to "appeals to emotion and personal belief." Consider Matthew d'Ancona's condemnation of the tactics used by Brexit advocates: "This was Post-Truth politics at its purest—the triumph of the visceral over the rational, the deceptively simple over the honestly complex."[361] But that has always been the way. All the cunning dictators, like Hitler and Mussolini, persuaded by appealing to raw emotions—but so did the great democrats, from Pericles to Lincoln and Martin Luther King Jr. It's how human persuasion works.

Jonathan Haidt, one of the truly original minds in contemporary American psychology, uses a metaphor of the "elephant" for our powerful passions and instincts, and of a helpless "rider" for the rationalizing intellect. He then summarizes the latest research on persuasion:

> When does the elephant listen to reason? The main way that we change our minds on moral issues is by interacting with other people. We are terrible at seeking evidence that challenges our own beliefs, but other people do us this favor, just as we are good at finding errors in other people's beliefs. When discussions are hostile, the odds of change are slight. The elephant leans away from the opponent, and the rider works frantically to rebut the opponent's charges.

> But if there is affection, admiration, or a desire to please the other person, then the elephant leans toward that person, and the rider tries to find the truth in the other person's arguments.[362]

Donald Trump, disliked even by his supporters, stood little chance of changing the minds of voters in the 2016 campaign, whether he spoke truth or lies. But that is not the point I want to make by bringing in Haidt as my witness. My point concerns the elite class. Nobody feels affection or admiration for the elites. The public has no desire to please them: it strives, rather, to knock the elites off their high perches into the dust. For the class that rules and speaks on behalf of national institutions to be stripped of authority—to lose the power to persuade—has been a traumatic and terrifying event. As Haidt would expect, the elites have chosen not to question their own worldview: they blame the lies of populists like Trump instead. That is their notion of post-truth.

Yet there may be more to this term, I am convinced, than is found in dictionary definitions or the self-serving denials of the elites. To tease out the content, though, I must first ask you, reader, to follow me into fairly tricky cognitive territory.

* * *

"What is truth?" Pontius Pilate asked—but that way lies madness. The notion that facts descend on us from a pure Platonic sphere, untainted by interpretive frames, has a powerful hold on the modern imagination. The

CIA insists that it delivers *intelligence,* never policy, for example. Dealing in virginal data sounds more scientific. But what does data look like, devoid of structure? Nietzsche thought the whole thing was a rationalist prejudice. Marxists maintain that truth is a class construct—postmodernists, that it is a justification for power. And the father of Platonic truth was himself a proponent of the "noble lie."

Thankfully, I am not interested here in the nature of truth. That is a mystery for the ages. My concern is with those shared interpretations of reality that provide the reasons and explanations necessary to political life. I'm going to argue that a crisis of authority can't help but trigger a crisis of uncertainty. An overabundance of digital information in the hands of the public has buried alive many of the grand narratives that were once our shared source of meaning. With the fatal decline of the elites, the truth, like so much else, has begun to unbundle.

I want to make my terms very clear. I don't believe reality is malleable, variable, or constructed. Reality is as unyielding as a policeman's club. Unlike that club, however, the *shared* reality of 320 million persons can't be experienced directly: it's mediated. For the last century and a half, the elites, and even more the institutions they manage, have been the arbiters of mediated certainty and truth. The government addressed social "problems" and placed difficult national episodes in perspective. The news media selected for the public's attention a handful of topics and events. Scientific institutions gave out trusted advice on health and other specialized matters.

Each of these institutions possessed a semi-monopoly over the information in its own domain. They were keepers of the stories that explained us to ourselves. They uttered, from above, the authoritative truth.

What happens when the mediators lose their legitimacy—when the shared stories that hold us together are depleted of their binding force? That's easy to answer. Look around: we happen. The mirror in which we used to find ourselves faithfully reflected in the world has shattered. The great narratives are fracturing into shards. What passes for authority is devolving to the political war-band and the online mob—that is, to the shock troops of populism, left and right. Deprived of a legitimate authority to interpret events and settle factual disputes, we fly apart from each other—or rather, we flee into our own heads, into a subjectivized existence. We assume ornate and exotic identities, and bear them in the manner of those enormous wigs once worn at Versailles.

Here, I believe, is the source of that feeling of unreality or post-truth so prevalent today. Having lost faith in authority, the public has migrated to the broken pieces of the old narratives and explanations: shards of reality that deny the truth of all the others and often find them incomprehensible.

Let's examine Donald Trump in this context. The president tells falsehoods. As might be expected, his opponents have condemned him as a deliberate liar—and this might well be the case. But many of Trump's lies seem politically pointless. Why would he complain about voter fraud in an election he won? What impact can the size of an inaugural crowd possibly have? Another thesis, no less problematic, can account for such odd behavior. The president may just be a creature of our fractured age: he speaks, subjectively and symbolically, from inside a shard of Trumpian truth. In that shallow place, where the world and his will are one, he can invent, at will, an endless supply of reasons for righteous rants.

At least the president is held accountable for his 2,000 falsehoods. The elites dwell in their own fragment of truth yet seem blissfully unaware. They tell us Trump is Hitler. They explain that their defeat is a conspiracy of lies. They insist that the world can be returned to what it was before November 2016. Most damaging, they are as willing as Trump to demolish the historical reality of their own institutions. An acting attorney general can refuse to implement a presidential executive order, for example. The head of a consumer agency can deny the chief executive's authority to appoint her successor. A minor foreign service official can resign with a very public letter directing the secretary of state to "stop the bleeding" or "follow me out the door."[363]

No behavior is too fantastic if it raises the black flag of reaction against Trump. At the televised Grammy music awards, Hillary Clinton was invited to read from a book that claimed President Trump is, in essence, deranged. A female comic had a photo taken of herself holding up, in the style of Islamist executioners, something that looked like the president's severed head.

Truth, for the elites, has come to mean that democracy will die in darkness unless the elected president is somehow overthrown.

Extremist kooks and cranks have always enjoyed wild conspiracy-mongering more than dull reality. With the collapse of the mediator class, this toxic mindset is seeping into the mainstream. When the neo-Nazis of the Stormer look on America, they see a "race war" against whites, and "filthy Jew terrorists" in charge of the government. That is crazed bigotry posing as truth. But when the elites look on the neo-Nazis, they don't see a tiny band of attention-starved bigots: they discern instead the awful consequences of Donald Trump in power. Nazis become a symbolic judgment on Trump—much as, for Trump, electoral fraud is a symbolic judgment on his enemies. Even if objectively false, both propositions embody truth as it *should* be. Once that door is open, strange things start to happen. The very liberal news media has glamorized neo-Nazis and racialists by lavishing attention on them wholly disproportionate to their numbers, making creepy marginal characters seem like important actors in U.S. politics.

It isn't irrelevant to point out that, in 2016, the media did the same with Donald Trump.

Truth at the university, social psychologist Jonathan Haidt notes, is increasingly subservient to social justice.[364] The reality of the world for the "antifas"—young members of self-styled anti-fascist groups—consists of a *V for Vendetta*-like melodrama of oppression and revenge. The antifas have always believed that Hitler's Germany and contemporary American life are fundamentally the same. That is their sliver of truth. Within the circle of the web and the war-band, it probably appears irrefutable.

Unlike the elites, antifas have taken the resistance to Trump's election to its logical conclusion: violence, they proclaim, must be met with violence.

NO! In the Name of Humanity—We REFUSE to Accept a Fascist America!

We recognize that the Trump/Pence Regime is illegitimate because it is fascist, that fascism must be stopped before it is too late, and that this means that the masses of people in their millions must be led to rise up and drive it from power.[365]

This fantasy of revolution hasn't yet occurred—but there has been real violence. Masked, black-clad antifa types have attacked pro-Trump and right-wing gatherings. Conservative speakers in universities have

Figure 33: Antifa take to the streets at Berkeley.[366]

been bullied into silence. The February 2017 antifa riot in Berkeley to muzzle one such speaker ended with at least six persons injured and $100,000 in property damage.

The unbundling of truth makes the business of democracy ever more difficult to conduct. As we fly ever farther apart, we can only hear each other when we scream. The result (I repeat) has been paralysis for democratic government. In nearly every instance of provocation and violence, officials at every level, elected and appointed, have chosen to play the part of silent observers. No arrests were made in the Berkeley riots. Few persons were arrested in Charlottesville after a day of street fighting—and most were "drunk people."[367] This, I am persuaded, is where the fuzzy notion of post-truth acquires a club-like reality. The bearers of democratic legitimacy and agents of democratic law have become uncertain of their actual power. The keepers of the grand narratives, of our cosmic truths, appear unable to find a path to right action. The elites in their institutions are petrified by self-doubt.

Among the political left, there has been a robust debate whether to applaud or condemn antifa violence. The authorities that make life-and-death decisions are more concerned with not ending up on the wrong side of history. In the era of post-truth, with reality up for grabs, nobody wants to be perceived as *anti*-anti-fascist.

* * *

On an evening in June 2015, at the Emmanuel African Methodist Episcopal Church in Charleston, South Carolina, a young man stood up from a Bible studies meeting, pulled out a pistol, and began shooting. Nine of the 13 persons present were murdered, including the pastor, an 87-year-old choir member, and a state senator. All of the dead were black. The killer, 21, was white and called himself a "white nationalist," but was unknown to his victims. While bringing down death on people at prayer he is reported to have said, "I have to do it . . . and you have to go."[368]

In the early hours of a morning in June 2016, a young man entered the Pulse, a gay nightclub in Orlando, Florida, and began firing a semi-automatic weapon methodically into the patrons crowded there. Within a few minutes 49 persons had been murdered and 58 injured, some very seriously. The killer, 29, was an American of Afghan descent, unknown to his victims. In a call to a police dispatcher he "swore his allegiance" to ISIS, the Islamist sect that had recently conquered a large swath of territory in Iraq and Syria. He had been "triggered" into mass slaughter, the shooter said, by U.S. bombing raids against ISIS.[369]

On a night in October 2016, during the last act of the Route 91 Harvest music festival in Las Vegas, Nevada, shots rang out from the 32nd floor of the Mandalay Hotel overlooking the festivities. Ten minutes later, 58 concertgoers had been murdered and hundreds lay wounded. The killer was 64, retired, well-off, and utterly disconnected from the people on whom he inflicted such suffering before committing suicide. He gave no reason for the atrocity, and none has been identified to this day.

I believe there's a relationship between our fractured reality and the rise of the nihilist—persons and groups that consider destruction and mass murder to be a form of progress. The nihilist lurks in a broken sliver of truth that is impossible to debate or refute. There, he experiences absolute grievance and the absolute negation of the system, the repudiation of everything that stands and of everyone he encounters. Not just politics but all of humanity, he holds, must be purified and made new. As the last righteous person, the nihilist aims to bring this about in the blood of random strangers. He acts out the violence that so many others perpetrate verbally and virtually on the web; he is, in that sense, the avenging angel of post-truth, and the rant made flesh.

Even as democratically elected officials watch their authority dissipate in a fog of uncertainty, the nihilist commits his crimes with absolute conviction. The assurance of being compelled—"triggered"—protects him from any sense of responsibility. In the midst of death and carnage, he feels innocent as a lamb. Guilt for his crimes must fall on the social order: he is merely an instrument of justice. "I have to do it . . . and you have to go." Osama bin Laden, a precursor of the type, chortled and giggled in an infamous video as he related the story of the death of thousands on 9/11.

The true nihilist today is more earnest. He disgorges manifestos and judgments by the ton. "Unfortunately . . . I am in a great hurry," wrote the Charleston shooter, "and some of my best thoughts, actually most of them have to be left out and lost forever."[370] He survived to spew out another manifesto in prison. These documents are mawkish and abstract, a rhetoric disconnected in tone, logic, and sense of proportion from the violence, yet bearing an uncanny resemblance to the reflexive negations of the public. In the nihilist's bloodstained vision of the world we discern a familiar landscape. His clamors *de profundis* recall our everyday repudiations. Somehow, large numbers of citizens have come to believe, like him, that the system has failed, and the social order must be smashed. A case can be made that the president of the United States is among them. The nihilist, that righteous monster, appears to be a reasonably faithful likeness of us, in a more advanced state of moral decomposition.

The blind impulse to destroy became a nation-state with the advent of the Islamic State of Iraq and Syria in 2014. A vast chunk of land, with a population of millions, was partitioned out of the region, to be ruled by a sect that exalted death. "I swear we are a people who love drinking blood," boasted a Palestinian adherent of ISIS on video. "We came to slaughter you."[371] That promise was over-fulfilled. The abominations perpetrated by ISIS matched the worst horrors of the 20th century. Victims were beheaded, crucified, burned alive in cages. Slavery was revived. Captive women were made into sex slaves and drowned if they refused the part. Untold hundreds of thousands were indeed slaughtered. Millions were uprooted, loosening a red-rimmed tide of desperate migrations and terror, not just regionally but on the democratic world.

Yet the perpetrators—mostly young, male, and media-savvy—perceived themselves as the restorers of virginity in human relations. They craved pure, authentic lives, and looked forward to an age of innocence once the stain of the past had been washed clean in blood. More than the Syrian and Iraqi military, or the West, their enemy was history. Here is Abu Bakr al-Baghdadi, caliph of the caliphate, on the subject:

> *Indeed the Muslims were defeated after the fall of their caliphate. Then their state ceased to exist, so the disbelievers were able to weaken and humiliate the Muslims, dominate them in every region, plunder their wealth and resources, and rob them of their rights. They accomplished this by attacking and occupying their lands, placing their treacherous agents in power to rule the Muslims with an iron fist, and spreading dazzling and deceptive slogans such as: civilization, peace, co-existence, freedom, democracy, secularism, baathism, nationalism, and patriotism.*[372]

In February 2015, minions of the Islamic caliphate entered Mosul Museum and smashed the statuary there. The act seemed to horrify Western elites far more than any massacre. French president François Hollande called it "barbaric"—an attack on "people, history, memories, culture."[373] That was precisely the strategic objective. As it does with its beheadings, ISIS made a show of the destruction. In a five-minute video, posted online, burly bearded men huff and puff and pull the ancient idols down, taking sledgehammers and jackhammers to the fallen figures. The frenzy is at times shown in slow motion, to romantic effect. This is vandalism as political theater, performed for the edification of the world. The lesson was simple. Since the seventh century, the human race has been entangled in lawlessness and moral chaos. The implicit solution was equally simple. ISIS didn't mean to change history but to end it.

Viewers of the video, in brief, were being invited to jackhammer their way to utopia.

Although followers of ISIS speak in an opaque theological jargon, there's nothing peculiarly Muslim or religious about yearning to escape the coils of history. We have stumbled across this theme before. Catalans imagine that the past has robbed them of nationhood. Vladimir Putin dreams of rescuing Russia out of the dead carcass of the Soviet Union. Donald Trump has condemned our "American carnage." The right-wing populist government of Poland has made it illegal to bring up the subject of Polish collaboration with Nazi war crimes. The left-leaning city fathers of

Figure 34: ISIS declares war on history.[374] *A video posted on internet on February 26, 2015 shows ISIS or Daech (Daech) or "Islamic State" group militants destroying statues inside the Nineveh museum, northern Iraq. Some of the statues date from 8th century BC. Photo by Balkis Press/Sipa USA (Sipa via AP Images.) © 2015 The Associated Press.*

Seattle, Washington, have transmuted Columbus Day into "Indigenous Peoples' Day."

The repudiation of history—in effect, of our present reality and hence of ourselves—is among the most powerful motives propelling the revolt of the public. It's the shortest route to nihilism and the logical justification for the death cult. In the turgid manifesto of one prolific lone killer, the word "history" recurs 510 times, like a ritual curse.[375]

The ISIS message resonated with thousands from Western countries who flocked to join the caliphate. Many knew just a few words of Arabic. A significant minority was of non-Muslim origin.[376] They chose barbarism over boredom, becoming actors in the apocalyptic drama instead of software programmers back home.

Brutal sectarians could carve out a nation-state because the U.S. and its allies had abandoned the region. Demoralized by failure in Iraq, the Western elites came to believe that intervention in the Middle East only made a bad situation worse. They embraced paralysis as the best policy. The result was Charlottesville on a continental scale. As the powers representing order and democracy withdrew to safety, the forces of chaos and violence moved in. The last U.S. troops departed the area in December 2011. They left behind, President Obama maintained, a "sovereign, stable, and self-reliant Iraq."[377] But in June 2014 ISIS fighters routed the Iraqi army at Mosul and swept onward. The caliphate was proclaimed a short time later.

Given the terrible consequences, there is much blame to apportion—but that is not my purpose here. The point of this particular story is that paralysis isn't irreversible. Faced with the grim reality of a terrorist nation-state, the U.S. and many European democracies were stirred to action. The elites awoke to the *truth* of the situation, and behaved appropriately. President Obama, for all his distrust of interventionism, returned U.S. forces to Iraq in November 2014 as part of a coordinated effort aimed at ISIS. President Trump, who has also scoffed at foreign adventures, accelerated this process. In July 2017, ISIS was pushed out of Mosul. In October, it was defeated in Raqqa, a place of symbolic religious importance to the sect. The Islamic caliphate, once the size of Great Britain, is now broken and on the run. The caliph, al-Baghdadi, has gone so deep underground that no one is sure whether he's alive or dead.

This is a success story. The ruling elites shouldered rather than evaded their responsibility. The real-life outcome was more or less what was intended. The democracies acted vigorously and triumphed. The carriers of nihilism were crushed. Good news may be hard to decipher in a post-truth era, but here is food for thought.

Much speculation and hand-wringing have been poured out on the public for its mutiny against the established order. But the public, all along, has insisted that the revolt is about the elites. That, at least, is my judgment. It was elite failure in the context of the Fifth Wave of information that set the wheel of change to turning, and it's with elite choices, including the possibility of reforming industrial-style democracy, that I would like to conclude my story.

THE FATE OF THE INDUSTRIAL ELITES AND THE UNCERTAIN FUTURE OF LIBERAL DEMOCRACY

In a 2009 interview with the *Los Angeles Times*, Harvey Weinstein, powerful film producer, made the following claim about his institution: "Hollywood has the best moral compass, because it has compassion. We were the people who did the fundraising telethon for the victims of 9/11. We were there for the victims of Katrina and any world catastrophe."[378] Weinstein, whose personal worth was in the hundreds of millions, could best be described as an elite of the elites: friend of Barack Obama and

Hillary Clinton, generous contributor to the Democratic Party and progressive causes, maker and breaker of movie stars. The day after Donald Trump's inauguration, Weinstein joined a women's march held in Sundance, Utah, to protest the new president's sexist views.

But in October 2017, the *New York Times* and *The New Yorker* reported that Weinstein had sexually assaulted or harassed dozens of women, including famous actresses, over a span of decades. Some of the incidents were violent physical attacks. Others betrayed bizarre and perverse behavior. All were committed with impunity, as the victims were afraid to speak out against such a ruthless and well-connected potentate, and Weinstein's institution, the film industry, turned its moral compass in some other direction. The media revelations broke the silence. As a growing number of women went public with grotesque stories of impropriety, Weinstein's place in the Hollywood hierarchy tottered. He was fired from his own company on October 8.

The well-deserved fall of Harvey Weinstein sparked one of the most remarkable episodes in the annals of any elite class. Suddenly, women began to speak out on the past predations of powerful men. Many of the accused were household names, highflyers in politics, the news media, and, of course, the entertainment industry. Most were tainted beyond repair or forced out of public life. A Republican candidate for the Senate in Alabama, though heavily favored, was defeated after reports surfaced of sexual misconduct. He was a flag-bearer for the religious right, but he stood accused of soliciting sex from an underage girl. Sexual scandal drove a Democratic senator from Minnesota to resign. He was said to be a "committed feminist," but he had been photographed groping a woman's breasts, so he had little choice but to go. Several members of the House announced their departure after reports were published of their misbehavior. A well-known morning news show host for NBC News was removed from his job for sexual misconduct. The White House correspondent for the *New York Times* was "suspended" while allegations of harassment were looked into.

As was the case with Weinstein, most of the men involved had been protected by their institutions. They were examples of structural corruption. The fall, when it came, implicated much more than flawed individuals.

I bring up this sordid tale for a reason.

The recovery of truth requires the restoration of trusted authority. At the moment, that is nowhere in sight. The question before us is whether the current elite class can ever resume that function. The crisis of authority, currently at the stage of paralysis, will otherwise continue to warp and fracture the top-down model of liberal democracy long managed by this class.

Can the industrial elites find redemption? The defeat of ISIS demonstrates that when elites act with confidence in a cause that is shared across partisan and social lines, they can easily scatter the barbarian warbands. Modern government still holds unparalleled power and wealth at its disposal. Liberal democracy remains unchallenged as a system. Elite authority today is threatened not by any specific movement or group but by the relentless intensity of the public's negations: a stance that is reflexively *anti*-government, *anti*-system, and sometimes *anti*-democracy. The mood is driven by a near-universal perception of failure at the top. ISIS, after all, needed to be confronted in large part because of a long string of policy disasters and evasions of the truth touching Iraq, the Arab Spring, and the Syrian civil war.

To have any hope of reversing this trend, the elites must counter negation with a positive vision—a shared adventure—that includes and persuades the public. Politicians must tell a story about the world that stirs the imagination of voters. The people at the top must raise the public's understanding to a higher plane. In the attempt, however, they will collide head-on with the social imperatives of the system they represent. The industrial model of liberal democracy isn't particularly democratic in structure. It's a steep hierarchy that operates in broadcast mode only. The *distance* between top and bottom is very great. The chasm of distrust will be difficult to bridge. And as elite fear and loathing of the public has increased, so has the craving for distance and isolation.

Elites today have no idea how to speak to the public or what to say to it. They have shown little interest in trying. The hyper-educated individuals who ran the Clinton campaign were utterly indifferent to public opinion: they believed in big data. An algorithm nicknamed "Ada" delivered "simulations" of opinion to the campaign staff.[379] Ada was the public as elites wish it would be: safe, clean, and speaking only when spoken to. The voter in the flesh was clearly perceived by this group as an alien and frightening brute. His very existence was deplorable. The shock of Election Day followed naturally from such distortions of distance.

The men flushed out by the sexual scandals of the past year measured their success in terms of distance. They leveraged their exceptional talents to transcend the rules by which ordinary people are judged. Great institutions protected and indulged them. Physical contact with the public was ritualized to advantage. Other elites flattered them constantly. You became, in your own eyes, a superb humanitarian. You were a role model to those beneath you. You could be a rapist but also a moral compass to the nation.

Because of the heights to which they had risen, these men felt invulnerable—and they weren't far off the mark.

The elites that govern democratic nations have shown zero interest in leaping over the chasm to reach the public. In fact, they seem headed in the opposite direction. The crisis of democracy, viewed from the top, implicates a digital information landscape that brings the public with its destructive urges into terrifying proximity. The response has been a kind of political claustrophobia—regularly triggered, for example, by Donald Trump's blatherings on Twitter.[380] The frenzy over fake news is part of this pathology. It has pushed Facebook and Google to design opaque filtering algorithms—a small step, it may be, toward converting the information sphere into Ada, the mechanical doll that tells only happy news.[381]

The industrial elites, I mean to say, have lashed their fate to that of the battered model in which they have thrived. Their political projects seek to restore distance rather than authority. Their hope is to silence the public, not persuade it. Hillary Clinton ran for president on a promise to keep the deplorables in their place. Angela Merkel clings to office to suppress the secret Nazi inside every German voter. Europe's hate-speech laws ban conversations that are offensive to the elites. Our own federal government spends millions in extreme security and policing measures to keep the public a safe distance away.

I can't predict whether top-down democracy will endure, but the momentum of events over the past decade and more is pushing the democratic world in a specific direction. First, the great hierarchical institutions of the industrial age are toppling—the political parties, as we have seen, are in a state of dissolution, and even chunks of the nation-state are splintering off. The times favor fragmentation, if not disintegration. Second, the present elite class has disqualified itself from reforming the system. It has no interest in taking on the job, and would have no clue how to proceed if it tried. The elites, like Icarus, appear content to glide above the masses until it's too late to avoid a crash.

Lastly, the question of political distance has become decisive in the many-sided brawl over the established order. The democratic principle of access to the people in power is at war with the industrial-age ideal of rule by remote, disinterested experts—and our representative system is too broken to mediate a settlement. Secular trends at present promote the reduction of distance. Secret depravity, in consequence, has become open scandal. The walls are closing in on the tainted keepers of the status quo—and the possible consequences, I think, are significant enough to bear a bit of speculation.

* * *

The conquest of political distance must deal with hard structural reality. Rage, populism, and tweeting at odd hours amount to little more than a stylistic posture. In the end, the pyramid must be flattened. Donald Trump, archetype populist, chose a cabinet of relative "outsiders" instead of the usual establishment types.[382] This will change nothing in the perception of distance. The outsiders have now climbed to their high perches and interact with the public mostly through multiple layers of insiders below them. The distance stays the same. Every failure of government, therefore, will continue to be compounded by an alienated and unforgiving public.

With regard to President Trump, I doubt that flattening federal institutions was ever a thought in his head. This is a man who strives for bigness in politics, and loves to name towers after himself.

The 2016 elections may prove a pivotal moment on this front, nonetheless. The fractured nature of our political life became impossible to ignore. Shocked elites began to speak of the "Divided States of America."[383] In that spirit, Democratic state and city governments proclaimed their defiance of the electoral outcome. "We've got the scientists, we've got the lawyers, and we're ready to fight," announced California's Jerry Brown.[384] Before the election, Brown had joked that he would "build a wall around California" if Trump won.[385] By October 2017, he seemed to a progressive admirer to have erected a "parallel universe to Donald Trump's America" in his state.[386] On immigration, taxes, the environment, and many other issues, Brown staked out positions that were diametrically opposed to the federal government. He even conducted a breakaway foreign policy, choosing a visit to the Vatican to dismiss the president's importance to global climate policy-making: "The Trump factor," he said, "is small, very small indeed."[387]

Trump's mandates from on high must collide with Brown's wall in California, a state Hillary Clinton won by three million votes. The immediate result has been conflict—a mirror-image version of the guerrilla war waged by Republican governors against the Obama administration. To cite just one example: Brown has signed a bill that exempts state law enforcement from assisting federal immigration agencies. The Trump administration, with much pomp and noise, has taken the state of California to court over the matter.[388] The clash is another instance of the crack-up of authority into mutually hostile fragments—ultimately, into paralysis.

Yet mapped to the larger quarrel of the public with the elites, this partisan tussle looks to be pregnant with practical and ideological possibilities.

In an age of partial truths and enraged political war-bands, big national "solutions" imposed from above by the federal government are likely to ignite fierce repudiation, if not revolt. That was the case with Barack Obama's stimulus and health-care legislation. Opposition gave rise to the Tea Party, which demolished the Obama coalition in the 2010 midterms. That has also been the case with Donald Trump's "big, beautiful" policies, many of which have been checked or overturned by the likes of Jerry Brown. Distance, that toxic cloud over contemporary politics, is perceived by the public to emanate from a specific address on Pennsylvania Avenue in Washington, D.C. Large majorities of Americans, before and after the 2016 election, have identified "Big Government" as the top threat to the nation.[389]

If the federal government is now an agent of division and polarization, state and local government, as well as certain private entities, can become rallying points of community. The negation of the nation-state must mean either anarchy or devolution to the city-state.

Already urban and media elites, old apostles of centralization, have rediscovered the virtues of federalism and states' rights. Andrew Cuomo, governor of New York, declared shortly after the election that New Yorkers held moral and political principles that were "fundamentally different" from Trump's vision of America: "We respect all people in the state of New York." Cuomo went on:

It's the very core of what we believe and who we are. But it's not just what we say, we passed laws that reflect it, and we will continue to do so, no matter what happens nationally. We won't allow a federal government that attacks immigrants to do so in our state.[390]

The case has been made that people of the left and the right can preserve their peculiar values—Cuomo's "what we believe and who we are"—by embracing something called "localism." Since we dwell in separate valleys of culture and politics, runs the argument, we should empower these to the fullest extent consistent with national unity.[391] In one possible future, all democratic countries will be Switzerland.

The pieces of the unbundling nation-state will have flatter hierarchies and a greatly reduced distance between the public and power. That's a simple matter of numbers. The public will push harder against local magistrates who are closer at hand, and local interests will loom larger in national decisions. We can get a sense of how this works by looking to Italy, where in 2016 the newly elected mayor of Rome, a member of the Five Star Movement, killed the city's bid to host the 2024 Olympics. The enraged mandarin at the head of the National Olympic Committee called the decision "demagogic and populist."[392] He lives in a city of palaces and hierarchies—the mayor, in the Rome of trash removal and sewage disposal.

The rise of local power would make it feasible to digitize government on the model of Estonia, something that, for many reasons, lies beyond the reach of gargantuan-sized national bureaucracies. Estonia's population is just over a million. Its model applies to U.S. cities and counties, and maybe the smaller states. Still, the redesign of modern life being attempted in this small Baltic nation has the potential to scale globally:

E-Estonia is the most ambitious project in technological statecraft today, for it includes all members of the government, and it alters citizens' daily lives. The normal services that government is involved in—legislation, voting, education, justice, healthcare, banking, taxes, policing, and so on—have been digitally linked across one platform, wiring up the nation.[393]

If the experiment succeeds, government activity and information will be flattened to the level of the web—that is, of everyday life. Our personal and official identities would then begin a process of synchronization to a degree scarcely conceivable since "the masses" entered history near the end of the 19th century.

From these speculative heights, we can glimpse more sweeping changes. Once government goes digital, it becomes possible to alter its structure, even to redirect its purpose. As imagined by the Pirate Party of Iceland, government can evolve into more of a transactional platform—part Facebook page, part Amazon marketplace—and less of an all-knowing solver of problems. Political expectations would be drastically adjusted. So would the relationship of information and power, reversing, at last, the pathological imbalances of the Fifth Wave. Direct democracy, in the form of referendums, would be invoked regularly, to good ends and bad.

To ask why these changes aren't happening is to circle back to the beginning of the conversation. The people at the top are unable and unwilling to reform or adapt. The distance to the bottom has protected the elites from their own inertia and decadence. If, as the evidence suggests, that distance is rapidly decreasing, then an entire ruling class, and a familiar mode of dealing with and talking about politics and the uses of power, face the possibility of extinction.

Let's consider how this may come to pass.

* * *

The revolt of the public will *not* necessarily usher in an authoritarian age. It does *not* necessarily foster populism. It is *not* necessarily destructive of liberal democracy. The revolt of the public, as I envision the thing, is a technology-driven churning of new people and classes, a proliferation and confusion of message and noise, utopian hopes and nihilistic rage, globalization and disintegration, taking place in the unbearable personal proximity of the web and at a fatal distance from political power. Every structure of order is threatened—yes. Nihilism at the level of whole societies, in the style of ISIS, is a possible outcome. But no particular system is favored or disadvantaged—and nothing is ordained.

Many aspects of human welfare have flourished in tandem with the revolt of the public. Over the last generation, in Asia, hundreds of millions have made the extraordinary leap out of ancestral poverty to the digital lifestyle. Except for a few retrograde nations like Russia, standards of living have risen everywhere. Between 2000 and 2015, global life expectancy went up by five years. In Africa, the increase was 9.4 years.[394]

The same technology that has disrupted social and political relations also connects, informs, and entertains billions of individuals and families. Twenty-eight years after the initial release of the World Wide Web, the online population was estimated at between three and four billion. The number of mobile phone users approached five billion. Half the world's population was literally on the move: in 2017, four billion passengers took an airplane flight to some far destination.

The economy, often portrayed as faltering and unequal, and thus a main determinant of political instability, has in fact performed tolerably well. While the crisis of 2008 dealt an incalculable blow to the system, it was followed by years of slow but steady growth, then a strong surge forward. For the democratic nations of North America and Europe, 2017 turned out to be a boom year. The E.U. experienced its strongest growth in a decade. Unemployment was high but rapidly declining and closing in on pre-2008 levels.[395] Germany, for all its struggles to form a government, remained a powerhouse, with an unemployment rate under 4 percent. The Spanish economy, whose collapse in 2008 shattered the country's political consensus, by 2017 had rebounded to pre-crisis levels of prosperity.[396] Even Italy, which had seen its economy flatline for two decades, was on the move again. For the bulk of the E.U. population, life in material terms was sweet.

By most measures, the U.S. has done better than Europe. Growth has been sustained for seven years. Unemployment has reached a 17-year low. Even laggard sectors like manufacturing are prospering and hiring. Despite the incessant talk about inequality, the benefits of the boom have spread deep and wide. The biggest decline in unemployment has been among those with the least education, for example. Adult men and women had identical unemployment rates in 2017: 3.7 percent.[397] Black and Hispanic unemployment have fallen to historic lows. Old-fashioned American ingenuity has reinvented the oil and natural gas extraction industry, moderating energy costs for all.

Attempts to explain the revolt of the public in terms of economic distress would seem to contradict this large body of data. Such explanations have proliferated anyhow. The dominant story holds that "globalism's losers"—shorthand for socioeconomically backward people, most of them white and male—have declared war on progress while demanding a return to some imagined past. This is Hillary Clinton's theory of the 2016

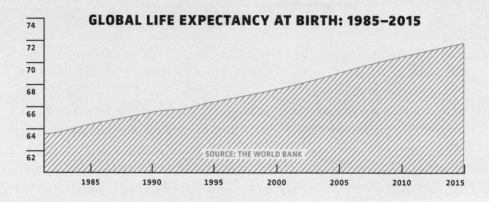

GLOBAL LIFE EXPECTANCY AT BIRTH: 1985–2015

SOURCE: THE WORLD BANK

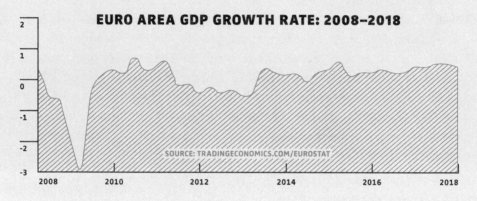

EURO AREA GDP GROWTH RATE: 2008–2018

SOURCE: TRADINGECONOMICS.COM/EUROSTAT

Figure 35: Not the worst of times.[398]

election. In March 2018, Clinton observed that her voters had come from places that were "optimistic, diverse, dynamic, moving forward," whereas Trump had appealed to those who "didn't like blacks getting their rights . . . don't like women getting jobs . . . don't want to see that Indian-American succeeding more than you are."[399] Here was the hidden meaning of "making America great again." In a different context, this accounted for little England's divorce from Europe. The deplorables, to everyone's surprise, kept outvoting their betters.

I find evidence in support of the economic explanation to be rather thin on the ground. There is, among the public, a complete lack of trust in the ability of government and the political class to manage the economy. The perception of elite failure clearly extends to the economic domain. But this, I believe, is part of a much more pervasive crisis of authority— and a far wider horizon of failure. White working-class voters put Donald Trump over the top in a few key states—but he won booming Texas and

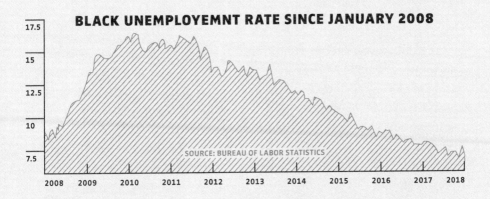

BLACK UNEMPLOYEMNT RATE SINCE JANUARY 2008

SOURCE: BUREAU OF LABOR STATISTICS

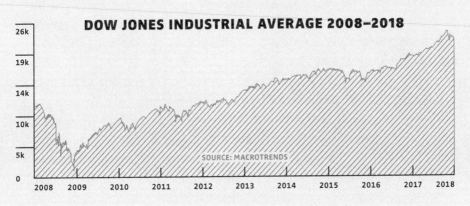

DOW JONES INDUSTRIAL AVERAGE 2008–2018

SOURCE: MACROTRENDS

Florida by larger margins than Rust Belt Pennsylvania. One in-depth analysis of Trump voters found them more likely to be "fiscal conservatives" or "free marketeers" than the regressive types suggested by Clinton.[400] Another detailed analysis showed that "affluent Republicans" provided Trump's core support in the primaries, while "about two-thirds" of his voters in the presidential election "came from the better-off half of the economy."[401]

Brexit voters defied predictions of economic disaster, and, on one account, were not disproportionately male, working class, or poor.[402] In Italy's 2018 general elections, the rich North backed one populist party, the poor South another. Filipinos who elected the outrageous Rodrigo Duterte were concerned with crime and corruption rather than economic issues.[403] It's difficult to discover a correlation here, much less a cause.

So I come to the abiding paradox that defines our predicament. An affluent, well-educated, hyper-connected public is in revolt against the system that has bestowed all of this bounty upon it. The great motive power of the revolt isn't economic resentment but outrage over distance and failure. Everyday life is increasingly digital and networked. From dating to hailing a cab, most social and commercial transactions occur at the speed of light. This mode of life incessantly collides with the lumbering hierarchies we have inherited from the industrial age. Modern government, above all, is institutionally unable to grasp that it has lost its monopoly over political reality. It behaves as if imposture and depravity will never be found out—but under the digital dispensation, everything is found out. The public is accustomed to proximity but finds the exercise of power removed an impossible distance away: reasons are never given, questions are never answered, and in this way begins the long, foul rant that is our moment in history.

The immediate target of revolt is an elite class that has failed persistently, on its own terms. The elites once were wrapped in the mantle of authority and delivered grandiose national projects, but now the public knows them too well, and they can only mutter and stammer, demoralized. They loathe the public for their humiliation. Politicians have lost faith in the idea of service, or the common interest, or the promotion of some universal cause or ideology: they exist, in office, merely to survive, or more accurately to be seen surviving, to suck up the attention of mass and social media. It has come to pass that presidents are chosen from the casts of reality TV shows. Political actors more and more resemble the real actors in Hollywood, whose company they keep and whose perverse predilections they seem to share.

Under the watchword of resistance, the elites are leading a massive reaction of the institutions against electoral results dictated by the public: populism. The counter-attack has been relentless and along multiple fronts. If the elites win their bet, then democracy, at last, will be truly up for grabs, even in the full light of day. If the elites are defeated, however, the inevitable question is what, exactly, this will mean.

Liberal democracy predates the industrial world and is now struggling to survive it. It must shake off many of the forms and the rhetoric of the past 150 years in the manner of a snake shaking off its skin, and for the same reason: in order to grow. The digital universe has brought into being an overactive public whose numbers are unprecedented in human experience. Political room must be found for it somehow. The current elite class is probably unable and certainly unwilling to entertain this transformation. So far as the public is concerned, the elites have forsaken their function and thereby lost any claim to legitimacy.

Yet democracy in a complex society can't dispense with elites. That is the hard reality of the situation. Much more is involved than a need for specialized or esoteric knowledge. Today's tastes may run to egalitarianism, but across history and cultures the only way to organize humanity, and get things done, has been through some level of command and control within a formal hierarchy. We are probably hardwired to respond to this pattern. The pyramid can be made flatter or steeper, and a matrix of informal networks is invariably overlaid on it, but the structural necessity holds. Only a tiny minority can be bishops of the church. This may seem apparent when it comes to running a government or managing a corporation, but it applies with equal strength to the dispensation of certainty and truth.

If my analysis is anywhere close to the mark, the re-formation of liberal democracy, and the recovery of truth, must wait on the emergence of a *legitimate* elite class.

* * *

How does one group replace another at the top of the pyramid? The study of social change is burdened with many preconceptions regarding the primacy of economic factors, the exploitation and liberation of minority groups, the rise and fall of the bourgeoisie or the proletariat, and so forth. By a stroke of luck, I lack the erudition to take a stand on any of these weighty subjects. Instead, I'll revert to an old analytic trick and pose a simpler question.

How is a legitimate hierarchy formed?

In *Invertebrate Spain* (1921), the great Spanish thinker José Ortega y Gasset argued that such hierarchies occur quite naturally and spontaneously. In every group and occasion of life, Ortega observed, there are individuals who appear admirable to the rest. By the rightness of their feelings, actions, and expressions, these individuals become "exemplars"—they are "selected" by the majority as models of humanity. Psychologists today speak of "social mimicry" or "mirroring": the body language of the dominant person in a room tends to be unconsciously assumed by everyone else. Ortega insisted that the dynamic transcended mere imitation. This wasn't a question of hairstyles or clothing fashions. In all that counted, he claimed, it was a reorientation in the depths. The highest conceptions of public and private life were manifested in living persons, not abstract principles. The many who hoped to lift up their lives aspired to be, in some fashion, like these superior few.[404]

On this account, hierarchy arises out of a natural impulse to self-improvement, and is legitimate when, in an almost Darwinian manner, it is "selected."

Ortega held the process to be the driving force of history. The "reciprocal action between the masses and select minorities," he wrote, "is the fundamental fact of every society and the agent of its evolution for good or evil." Ortega's masses we now call the public. By "select minorities" he meant the admirable few: elites who, at their best, lavish their creative energies on the effort to sustain and enrich the fabric of contemporary life. These are the truly superior artists and technologists, preachers and politicians.

In the right relation between elites and the public, the former act as exemplars to the latter. They embody and live out the master narratives. We can think of George Washington returning to his farm after the Revolution as a striking example. Abe Lincoln in his childhood log cabin and Tom Edison chasing the perfect filament also fit the type. It almost didn't matter what these historic figures were like in person: whether they were lovable or jerks. The outline of their lives had displayed magnificently admirable traits, and previous generations of Americans agreed with Ortega on the power of exemplarity to raise human life to a higher plane.

The quality that sets the true elites apart—that bestows authority on their actions and expressions—isn't power, or wealth, or education, or even persuasiveness. It's *integrity* in life and work. A healthy society is one in which such exemplary types draw the public toward them purely by the force of their example. Without compulsion, ordinary persons aspire to resemble the extraordinary, not superficially but fundamentally, because they wish to partake of superior models of being or doing. The good society, Ortega concluded, was an "engine of perfection."

In a sickly society, the force of exemplarity is reversed. Elites seek to flatter and imitate the public. They make a display of popular tastes and attitudes, even as they retreat behind barricades of bodyguards and metal-detecting machines. This, of course, is what I meant by distance: a moral alienation felt even more keenly than the structural divide.

Relations between top and bottom, Ortega asserted, were "reciprocal." Elites are in some sense selected by the public. If we were to ask how that selection works, Ortega would reply: by aspiration. When elites fail the test of exemplarity—when, as is the case today, they repel rather than attract—they are *un*selected. They are stripped of legitimacy and authority. A vacuum is created that strange new archetypes will seek to fill. As Donald Trump's teleportation from his Trump Tower elevator to the White House shows, the change can occur with astonishing rapidity.

President Trump, however, is a prisoner of the public's repudiations, of the attempt to impose a narrow symbolic framework on sprawling reality. The president, I stated above, perceives the world from a fractured place. That's another way of saying that his life has shown the opposite of integrity. He is not the one we have been waiting for. Legitimacy depends on a shared interpretation of events: and to be shared, to be perceived equally by contradictory perspectives, a story must go light on raging at symbolic phantoms in favor of the demonstrable and the concrete.

To the extent that Ortega has accurately mapped the path to elite legitimacy, we are afforded a glimpse of the way forward.

The present need is for a re-formation of the system and the restoration of authority. The practice of democracy must accommodate the existence of an enormous and super-opinionated public. Political action must approach the speed and proximity expected by an electorate that lives, works, and shops on digital media. The change can occur in many different ways, but a few hard truths are apparent from where I stand. The top-down political style, a relic of the last century, today appears false and fraudulent even when it is sincere. The extension of social distance as a reward for political success is perceived, rightly, as contrary to the democratic spirit. The elites now directing our great institutions are unalterably wedded to top-down control and increased distance from the rabble. Their resistance will make the necessary changes very difficult to achieve.

As members of the public, we—by which I mean you, reader, and I—are not helpless. We are not inert. We retain the power to select and unselect, and we wield that power constantly—not only in our political participation, our votes and donations, but in the books we read, the television we watch, the performances we attend, the products we purchase. If, as I believe, Ortega's framework of legitimacy was broadly correct, we can replace a failed elite class with another that is worthier of our aspirations.

Fundamental change is possible, and can come peacefully and quickly. That's the good news.

The big question is where to find a "select minority" that embodies the set of virtues required to lead democracy into the digital age, and can draw the public, by force of example, toward those virtues. Here political turbulence may lend a hand. Trump and Macron, for example, brought in tow a host of new faces, ordinary citizens previously disengaged from political activity. The two presidents love bigness and Olympian distance, but from the ranks of the new crowd may arise exemplars who can teach the public how to do democracy without negation or nihilism. Others may emerge out of the tremendous churning of new people and new modalities agitating our social life. Innovation's lightning may strike new domains: religion, so far, has remained singularly untouched. The selection of elites seems semi-Darwinian in nature. Many are called, but few will be chosen.

It may be more useful to specify exactly *what* virtues will be required under a new dispensation of liberal democracy. That, needless to say, will take us out of the realm of speculation into pure opinion. Since I am coming to the end of my story, I will, in all diffidence, offer mine.

Modern government's original sin is pride. It was erected on a boast—that it can solve any "problem," even to fixing the human condition—and it endures on a sickly diet of utopian expectations. We now know better. Since the fall of the Soviet Union, we have understood that even the most brutal application of power cannot redeem the human lot. For exactly that time, electorates in democratic nations have, in effect, lived a lie—of which the post-truth era, for all its weird pathologies, is only a second-level effect.

The qualities I would look for among elites to get politics off this treadmill are *honesty* and *humility:* old-school virtues, long accepted to be the living spirit behind the machinery of the democratic republic, though now almost lost from sight. The reformers of democracy must learn to say, out loud for all to hear, "This is a process of trial and error," and, "We are uncertain of the consequences," and even, "I was wrong." Elected officials must approximate the ability of scientists and businessmen—and, for that matter, ordinary households—to identify failure and move on. Honesty means that the relationship to truth, as truth is perceived, matters more than ambition or partisan advantage. Humility means that the top of the pyramid looks to the public as a home it will return to rather than a carnivorous species from which to hide. Truth must be spoken even when it hurts the speaker or the audience. Distance must be reduced to a minimum, even at the risk of physical danger.

So I would borrow one more virtue, from *The Wizard of Oz:* courage.

Is this scenario realistic? Who knows? Stranger things have happened. Infections stimulate their own specific antibodies. The era of post-truth and the rant may induce a powerful demand for simple honesty and humility. I'm not forecasting the rule of saints any time soon. That isn't necessary. Nor am I expecting a revolutionary transformation, in which, say, the president of the United States governs in his pajamas while sitting at his laptop. History doesn't work like that. The forms and ideals of Enlightenment democracy are still alive in the industrial model. Many aspects of this model will survive and evolve in any future iteration of democracy. The crucial move if we are to surmount our predicament isn't transformation but *reorientation,* a turn in direction away from top-down control, bureaucratic power, and the high valuation of distance as a reward for political success. Such a reorientation strikes me as perfectly possible.

In the end, everything will hinge on the public: on us. If Ortega was correct, then we have lost the right to rant about our rulers. Instead, we must go about the job of selecting their successors. We can lavish our attention and our energies strictly on politicians who seem unwilling to lie or simplify or distort to advantage. We can identify and raise up those who refuse to climb above us. That's one fork in the path ahead: another leads to nihilism. Either way, the choice is ours.

CHAPTER 1

1 Peter Lyman and Hal R. Varian, "How Much Information 2003?" (School of Information Management and Systems, University of California at Berkeley, 2003), http://www2.sims.berkeley.edu/research/projects/how-much-info-2003.

2 Study data courtesy of Hal R. Varian.

3 See Yochai Benkler, *The Wealth of Networks* (2006); Clay Shirky, *Here Comes Everybody* (2008) and *Cognitive Surplus* (2010); Glenn Reynolds, *An Army of Davids* (2006). I would also recommend Anthony Olcott's *Open Source Intelligence in a Networked Age* (2011), Jeff Jarvis's *Public Parts* (2011), and John Battelle's *The Search* (2005).

4 Walter Lippmann, *The Phantom Public, 9th ed.* (Transaction Publishers, 2009), 67.

CHAPTER 2

5 Image courtesy of Morningside Analytics.

6 On Suleiman, see "Egypt Blogger Jailed for 'Insult,'" BBC, February 22, 2007, http://news.bbc.co.uk/2/hi/middle_east/6385849.stm; on Douma, see "Egypt Activist Ahmed Douma Convicted for Morsi Insult," BBC, June 3, 2013, http://www.bbc.co.uk/news/world-middle-east-22758415.

7 On Sánchez, see Andrew Hamilton, "Yoani Sánchez, Cuba's Popular Blogger, Has Been Beaten Up for Describing Life," *Telegraph*, November 28, 2009, http://www.telegraph.co.uk/news/worldnews/centralamericaandthecaribbe-an/cuba/6678937/Yoani-Sanchez-Cubas-popular-blogger-has-been-beaten-up-for-describing-life.html; on Nguyen Hoang Vi, see Emily Alpert, "Dozens Detained, Jailed in Crackdown on Vietnam Bloggers," *Los Angeles Times*, February 12, 2013, http://articles.latimes.com/2013/feb/12/world la-fg-wn-report-vietnam-bloggers-jailed-20130212.

8 Joe Parkinson, "Amid Turkey Unrest, Social Media Becomes a Battleground," *Wall Street Journal*, June 3, 2013, http://blogs.wsj.com/middleeast/2013/06/03/amid-turkey-unrest-social-media-becomes-a-battleground/?mod=e2tw.

9 Nicholas Kristof, "The Daily Me," *New York Times*, March 18, 2009, https://www.nytimes.com/2009/03/19/opinion/19kristof.html.

10   "Music Industry Files Motion For Preliminary Injunction Against Napster," *RIAA Gold & Platinum News*, no date, http://riaa.com/newsitem.php?news_year_filter=&resultpage=106&id=FBD85765-00D7-2B2D-1D29-74FDD0F0826B; James Nicolai, "Creative Groups Slam Napster in Court Brief," *PC World*, September 11, 2000, http://www.pcworld.idg.com.au/article/80045/creative_groups_slam_ napster_court_brief/.

11   No known source site, usually identified as "web photo."

12   Wael Ghonim, *Revolution 2.0: The Power of the People Is Greater Than the People in Power, A Memoir* (Houghton Mifflin Harcourt, 2012), 90.

13   See Roland Schatz, "How To Define Awareness Thresholds," Media Tenor, 6th International Agenda-Setting Conference, Lugano, October 27, 2005, at http://www.agendasetting.com/2005/speakers_ppt/Schatz.pdf. Schatz is founder and president of Media Tenor International; I am a member of Media Tenor's Board of Advisors. On adoption of innovations, see Everett M. Rogers, *Diffusion of Innovations*, 5th ed. (Free Press, 2003).

14   My chart.

15   Screen capture from Dream TV broadcast posted on YouTube, https://www.youtube.com/watch?v=V690GO7YzgA.

16   Data courtesy of Arbor Networks.

CHAPTER 3

17   Mary Douglas and Aaron Wildavsky, *Risk and Culture: An Essay on the Selection of Technological and Environmental Dangers* (University of California Press, 1985).

18   Ibid., Kindle location 1172.

19   Ibid., Kindle location 1591.

20   Walter Lippmann, *Public Opinion* (Transaction Publishers, 1993. Originally published by Macmillan, 1922).

21   The two-step flow of influence theory was introduced by Paul Lazarsfeld and others, based on a study of the 1944 presidential elections. For its application to Twitter, see Shaomei Wu, Winter A. Mason, Jake M. Hofman, and Duncan J. Watts, "Who Says What to Whom on Twitter," presented at the World Wide Web Conference, 2011, http://www.wwwconference.org/proceedings/www2011/proceedings/p705.pdf.

22   Roland Schatz, "Rebuilding Reputation Won't Work Without the Full Picture," slides presented at the 11th International Agenda-Setting Conference, 2010, http://issuu.com/mediatenor_international/docs/rebuilding_reputation.

23   Malcolm Gladwell, "Small Change: Why the Revolution Won't Be Tweeted," *The New Yorker*, September 27, 2010, https://www.newyorker.com/magazine/2010/10/04/small-change-malcolm-gladwell.

24   Clay Shirky, *Here Comes Everybody: The Power of Organizing Without Organizations* (Penguin Books, 2008).

25   Clay Shirky, "The Political Power of Social Media: Technology, the Public Sphere, and Political Change," *Foreign Affairs*, 90, no. 1 (January–February 2011).

26   All the *Homo informaticus* charts are mine.

27   Wael Ghonim, *Revolution 2.0: The Power of the People Is Greater Than the People in Power, A Memoir* (Houghton Mifflin Harcourt, 2012), 137.

CHAPTER 4

28   Nassim Nicholas Taleb, *Antifragile: Things That Gain From Disorder* (Random House, 2012).

29   Al Jazeera, "Transcript: Egypt's Army Statement. Statement of Abdul Fatah Khalil al-Sisi, Head of Egyptian Armed Forces, Announcing the Overthrow of President Morsi," July 3, 2013, http://www.aljazeera.com/news/middleeast/2013/07/201373203740167797.html.

30   "An Interview with Mohamed ElBaradei, Who Hopes for Reconciliation in Egypt,"*Washington Post*, August 2, 2013, http://www.washingtonpost.com/opinions/an-interview-with-mohamed-elbaradei-who-hopes-for-reconciliation-in-egypt/2013/08/02/e409eac0-fab4-11e2-8752-b41d7ed1f685_story.html. Shortly after this interview was published, ElBaradei resigned to protest the Armed Forces' violent repression of the Muslim Brotherhood.

31   John Dewey, *The Public and Its Problems* (Ohio University Press, 1927).

32   Walter Lippman, *The Phantom Public*, 9th ed. (Transaction Publishers, Ninth Edition, 2009), 55.

33   José Ortega y Gasset, *La Rebelion de las Masas* (Revista de Occidente, 1930), 47.

34   Frederick Winslow Taylor, *The Principles of Scientific Management* (Public domain book, 1911), 16.

35   Maciej Lukasiewicz, "History's Turning Point," *Rzeczpospolita*, October 16, 2003, http://www.worldpress.org/Europe/1698.cfm.

36   Wael Ghonim, *Revolution 2.0: The Power of the People Is Greater Than the People in Power, A Memoir* (Houghton Mifflin Harcourt, 2012), 184.

CHAPTER 5

37   Pierre Rosanvallon, *Counter-Democracy: Politics in an Age of Distrust* (Cambridge University Press, 2008), 9.

38   Manuel Castells, *Networks of Outrage and Hope: Social Movements in the Internet Age* (Polity Press, 2012), 112.

39   Manifiesto "Democracia Real Ya," my translation, http://www.democraciarea-lya.es/manifiesto-comun/.

40   Fernando Cabal, ed. *Indignados! 15 M* (Mandala ediciones, no date), Kindle location 135.

41   Castells, *Networks of Outrage*, 128 forward.

42   Manifiesto "Democracia Real Ya."

43   Javier M. Faya, "Fabio Gándara, Portavoz de iDemocracia Real Ya!: 'Yo Votaré el Domingo,'" *Diario de Burgos*, May 19, 2011, http://www.diariodeburgos.es/noticia.cfm/Espa%C3%B1a/ 20110519/fabio/gandara/portavoz/democracia/real/ya/votare/domingo/31CA6909-036C-F947-4C5DA36DC9652FB4.

44   Photo by Juan Santiso.

45   Cabal, *Indignados! 15 M*, Kindle location 451.

46   Castells, *Networks of Outrage*, 141.

47   Unless otherwise specified, all economic data in this chapter comes from the World Bank Data Catalog website, http://datacatalog.worldbank.org/.

48   "El PSOE Solicitará al Congreso de Diputados Que Se Reconozcan los 'Derechos Humanos' de los Simios," *El Mundo*, May 24, 2006, http://www.elmundo.es/elmundo/2006/04/24/sociedad/1145890969.html.

49   "Zapatero Admite Que el Dato del Paro es 'Objetivamente Negativo,'" *Cinco Dias*, December 10, 2008, http://cincodias.com/cincodias/2008/11/04/economia/1225938222_850215.html.

50   Castells, *Networks of Outrage*, 122.

51   "Facebook Facts & Figures for 2010," *Digital Buzz*, March 22, 2010, http://www.digitalbuzzblog.com/facebook-statistics-facts-figures-for-2010/.

52   Noah Efron, "The Israeli Summer," *The Huffington Post*, July 31, 2011, http://www.huffingtonpost.com/noah-efron/the-israeli-summer_b_914389.html; Harriet Sherwood, "Israeli Protests: 430,000 Take to the Streets to Demand Social Justice," *The Guardian*, September 4, 2011, http://www.theguardian.com/world/2011/sep/04/israel-protests-social-justice; Asher Schechter, "A Short Guide to Israel's Social Protest," *Haaretz*, July 11, 2012, http://www.haaretz.com/news/national/a-short-guide-to-israel-s-social-protest-1.450369.

53   Harriet Sherwood in *The Guardian* cites a figure of 90 percent.

54   See, for example, Melanie Lidman, "Scale of Social Protests Surprises Experts," *Jerusalem Post*, August 11, 2011, http://www.jpost.com/National-News/Scale-of-social-justice-protests-surprises-experts.

55   Yoav Fromer, "Generation א: The Selfish Goals of the Tel Aviv Tent Protesters," *Tablet*, August 17, 2011, http://www.tabletmag.com/jewish-news-and-politics/75270/generation-aleph.

56   Economic data from the World Bank Data Catalog website, http://datacata-log.worldbank.org/; see also Tia Goldenberg, "Israeli Protests: Poorest Sit Out Demonstrations," *Huffington Post*, August 12, 2011, http://www.huffington-post.com/2011/08/12/israel-protests-poorest_n_925446.html.

57   Both quotes from Fromer, "Generation א."

58   Naama Cohen-Friedman, "Social Activists: The Revolution Is Here," *Ynetnews.com*, July 30, 2011, http://www.ynetnews.com/arti-cles/0,7340,L-4102107,00.html.

59   Fromer, "Generation א."

60   Herb Keinon, "Trajtenberg Oversees First Meeting of 'Rothschild Team,'" *Jerusalem Post*, August 9, 2011, http://www.jpost.com/Diplomacy-and-Politics/Trajtenberg-oversees-first-meeting-of-Rothschild-Team.

61   David Graeber, "Occupy Wall Street's Anarchist Roots," *Al Jazeera*, November 30, 2011, http://www.aljazeera.com/indepth/opinion/2011/11/201111287 2835904508.html; Nathan Schneider, "Thank You, Anarchists," *The Nation*, December 19, 2011, http://www.thenation.com/article/165240/ thank-you-anarchists#; "Translating Anarchy: Interview with Mark Bray, OWS Organizer and Author of the New Book Translating Anarchy: The Anarchism of Occupy Wall Street," OccupyWallStreet, September 12, 2013, http://occupywallst.org/ article/translating-anarchy-occupy-wall-street/.

62   Castells, *Networks of Outrage*, 199.

63   "#OCCUPYWALLSTREET: A Shift in Revolutionary Tactics," *Adbusters*, July 13, 2011, https://www.adbusters.org/blogs/adbusters-blog/occupywallstreet.html.

64   "2012 Platinum PR Awards: WOW! Awards," *PRNews*, August 15, 2012, http://www.prnewsonline. com/featured/2012/09/15/2012-platinum-pr-awards-wow-award-3/.

65   Castells, *Networks of Outrage*, 188.

66   "Declaration of the Occupation of New York City," #OccupyWallStreet, NYC General Assembly, http://www.nycga.net/resources/documents/declaration/.

67   Castells, *Networks of Outrage*, 186.

68   Andy Kroll, "VIDEO: Obama: Occupy Wall St. 'Expresses the Frustrations the American People Feel,'" *Mother Jones*, October 6, 2011, http://www.mother-jones.com/mojo/2011/10/obama-biden-occupy-wall-street.

69   Glenn Thrush, "W.H. with the '99-Percenters,'" *Politico*, October 16, 2011, http://www.politico.com/politico44/perm/1011/obama_preoccupied_ 2e1e701c-9e52-4e29-a7a3-1d074659996b.html.

70   "The BlackBerry Riots," *The Economist*, August 13, 2011, http://www.econo-mist.com/node/21525976.

71   "One in Four Riot Suspects Had 10 Previous Offences," BBC, September 15, 2011, http://www.bbc.co.uk/news/uk-14926322.

72   Josh Halliday, "London Riots: How BlackBerry Messenger Played a Key Role," *The Guardian*, August 8, 2011, http://www.theguardian.com/media/2011/aug/08/london-riots-facebook-twitter-blackberry.

73   *Four Days in August: Strategic Review Into the Disorder of 2011, Final Report*, Metropolitan Police Service, March 2012, 105, http://content.met.police.uk/cs/Satellite?blobcol= urldata &blobheadername1=Content-Type&blobheadername2=Content-Disposition&blobheadervalue1 =application%2Fpdf&blobheadervalue2=inline%3B+filename%3D%22145%2F595%2Fco553-114DaysInAugust.pdf%22&blobkey=id&blobtable=MungoBlobs&blobwhere=1283551523589&ssbinary=true.

74   "London Riots: Young Rioters Say They're Proud to Steal," *Mirror*, August 11, 2011, http://www. mirror.co.uk/news/uk-news/london-riots-young-rioters-say-146880.

75   Riots Communities and Victims Panel, *After the Riots: The Final Report of the Riot Communities and Victims Panel*, no date, 22, http://www.fredsakademiet.dk/ordbog/sord/riots.pdf.

76   Doug Gross, "British PM Proposes Social Media Ban for Rioters," CNN, August 12, 2011, http://www.cnn.com/2011/TECH/social.media/08/11/london.riots.social.media/index.html.

77   From Joe Lustri, *bogieharmond*, http://www.flickr.com/photos/68146720@N05/6356999163/in/photolist-aFKhnR-avSxur.

78   Wael Ghonim, *Revolution 2.0: The Power of the People Is Greater Than the People in Power, A Memoir* (Houghton Mifflin Harcourt, 2012), 102.

79   The Urban Dictionary offers a helpful definition of "lulz" for the uninitiated: "Lulz is the one good reason to do anything from trolling to rape. After every action taken, you must make the epilogic dubious disclaimer, 'I did it for the lulz.'" https://www.urbandictionary.com/define.php?term=lulz.

80   The best summary of Anonymous participation in OWS, which includes the YouTube videos, is Sean Captain's "The Real Role of Anonymous in Occupy Wall Street," *Fast Company*, October 11, 2011, http://www.fastcompany.com/1788397/real-role-anonymous-occupy-wall-street.

81   Castells, *Networks of Outrage*, 185.

82   Stéphane Hessel, *Time for Outrage*, (Hachette Book Group, 2010), 11.

CHAPTER 6

83   Anecdotes and quotes on the Einstein-Eddington episode taken from Walter Isaacson's *Einstein: His Life and Universe* (Simon & Schuster, 2007), 255-267.

84   Wikipedia Commons. This image is available from the United States Library of Congress's Prints and Photographs Division under the digital ID cph.3b46036.

85   From the World Bank Data Catalog website.

86   Both dictators took a personal interest in the development of science. See Richard Overy, *The Dictators: Hitler's Germany, Stalin's Russia* (W.W. Norton & Company, 2004).

87   Henry H. Bauer, "Science in the 21st Century: Knowledge Monopolies and Research Cartels," *Journal of Scientific Exploration*, 18, no. 4, (2004): 643-660, http://henryhbauer.homestead.com/21stCenturyScience.pdf.

88   "Trouble at the Lab," *The Economist*, October 18, 2013, http://www.economist.com/news/briefing /21588057-scientists-think-science-self-correcting-alarming-degree-it-not-trouble.

89   *The Climategate Emails*, ed. John Costella, (The Lavoisier Group, March 2010), http://www.lavoisier.com.au/articles/greenhouse-science/climate-change/climategate-emails.pdf.

90   Ibid., 10.

91   Ibid., 30.

92   Ibid., 34.

93   Ibid., 33.

94   Ibid., 34.

95   Ibid., 144.

96   Ibid., 89.

97   Ibid., 57.

98   Ibid., 129.

99   James Delingpole was the author. http://blogs.telegraph.co.uk/news/james-delingpole/100017393/climategate-the-final-nail-in-the-coffin-of-anthropogenic-global-warming/.

100   "Colleague defends 'ClimateGate' professor," BBC, December 4, 2009, http://news.bbc.co.uk/2/hi/8396035.stm.

101   Gordon Gauchat, "The Politicization of Science in the Public Sphere: A Study of Public Trust in the United States, 1974 to 2010," *American Sociological Review*, 77, no. 2, (2012): 157-187, https://www.asanet.org/sites/default/files/savvy/images/journals/docs/pdf/asr/Apr12ASRFeature.pdf; Eurobarometer: Science and Technology Report, European Commission, June 2010, http://ec.europa.eu/public_opinion/archives/ebs/ebs_340_en.pdf.

102   Roger A. Pielke Jr., "Lessons of the L'Aquila Lawsuit," *bridges*, vol. 31, (October 2011), http://sciencepolicy.colorado.edu/admin/publication_files/2011.36.pdf.

103   "L'Aquila's Earthquake: Scientists on the Dock," *The Economist*, September 14, 2011, http://www.economist.com/node/21529006.

104   John Dollar, "The Man Who Predicted an Earthquake," *The Guardian*, April 5, 2010, http://www.theguardian.com/world/2010/apr/05/laquila-earthquake-prediction-giampaolo-giuliani.

105   Dollar, "Man Who Predicted Earthquake," and Pielke, "Lessons of L'Aquila Lawsuit."

106   Ibid.

107   "L'Aquila Quake: Italy Scientists Guilty of Manslaughter," BBC, October 27, 2012, http://www.bbc. co.uk/news/world-europe-20025626.

108   An excellent evaluation of the state of the art in the forecasting of earthquakes is found in Nate Silver's *The Signal and the Noise: Why So Many Predictions Fail—But Some Don't* (The Penguin Press, 2012), 142–175.

109   *The Climategate Emails*, 84.

110   Bob Woodward, *Maestro: Greenspan's Fed and the American Boom* (Simon and Schuster, 2000), Kindle location 507.

111   Ibid., Kindle location 602-609, 641.

112   Ibid., Kindle location 396.

113   The *New York Times* and *Washington Post*, in particular, seemed to cover two mutually hostile Alan Greenspans. See Woodward, *Maestro*, Kindle locations 2426, 2452.

114   Woodward, *Maestro*, Kindle location 3878.

115   Data via Wikipedia Commons.

116   "After Alan," *The Economist*, October 13, 2005, http://www.economist.com/node/5025627.

117   Walter Lippman, *Public Opinion* (Transaction Publishers, 1993. Originally published by Macmillan, 1922), 233-4.

118   I have excluded agencies employed by the government to fund its own activities, such as the IRS and the Office of Management and Budget.

119   Silver, *The Signal and the Noise*, 29.

120   Andrew Ross Sorkin, *Too Big to Fail: The Inside Story of How Wall Street and Washington Fought to Save the Financial System—and Themselves* (Penguin Books, 2009), 439-440.

121   Ibid., 448-9.

122   Ibid., 368.

123   Silver, *The Signal and the Noise*, Kindle location 388-397.

124   Ibid., Kindle location 397 forward.

125   Nassim Nicholas Taleb, *Fooled by Randomness: The Hidden Role of Chance in Life and in the Markets* (Random House Trade Paperbacks, 2004), 79-91.

126   "Obama Delivers Speech on Economy," *New York Times*, June 9, 2012, http://www.nytimes.com/2008/06/09/us/politics/09transcript-obama.html?pagewanted=all.

127   Barack Obama, "Remarks on the National Economy," Government Printing Office, February 4, 2009, http://www.gpo.gov/ dsys/pkg/DCPD-200900057/pdf/DCPD-200900057.pdf.

128   Christina Romer and Jared Bernstein, "The Job Impact of the American Recovery and Reinvestment Plan," no publisher given, January 9, 2009, https://www.economy.com/mark-zandi/documents/The_Job_Impact_of_the_American_Recovery_and_Reinvestment_Plan.pdf.

129   Source: Bureau of Labor Statistics, White House. From Silver, *The Signal and the Noise*, Kindle location 742.

130   Silver, *The Signal and the Noise*, Kindle location 722-743.

131   Ibid., Kindle location 743-754.

132   "Greenspan Admits 'Mistake' That Helped Crisis," Associated Press, October 23, 2008, http://www.nbcnews.com/id/27335454/#.UpFaY8Tkv74.

133   Ibid.

134   Silver, *The Signal and the Noise*, Kindle location 344-349.

135   Paola Sapienza and Luigi Zingales, "Anti-Trust America: A Trust Deficit Is Driving Our Economy Down," *City Journal*, February 27, 2009, http://www.city-journal.org/2009/eon0227pslz.html.

136   "74% Want to Audit the Federal Reserve," Rasmussen Reports, November 8, 2013, http://www.rasmussenreports.com/public_content/business/general_business/november_2013/74_want_to_audit_the_federal_reserve; "US Investors Trust Financial Adviser Over Bernanke, Survey Finds," SmartBrief, February 7, 2012, http://www.smartbrief.com/02/07/12/us-investors-trust-financial-advisers-over-bernanke-survey-finds#.UpNjicTkv75.

137   Copyright *New York Times*, Nicolas Felton, illustrator.

138   Erik Brynjolfsson and Andrew McAfee, *Race Against the Machine: How the Digital Revolution Is Accelerating Innovation, Driving Productivity, and Irreversibly Transforming Employment and the Economy*, (Digital Frontier Press, 2011), 9, 40.

139   Toby Elwin, "The Cost of Culture, a 50% Turnover of the Fortune 500," https://tobyelwin.com/fortune-500-turnover/.

140   "Creative Destruction Whips Through Corporate America," Innosight, Winter 2012, http://www.innosight.com/innovation-resources/strategy-innovation/upload/creative-destruction-whips-through-corporate-america_final2012.pdf.

141   Data courtesy of Richard Foster.

142   My combined chart.

143   Paul Ormerod, *Why Most Things Fail: Evolution, Extinction and Economics* (Pantheon Books, 2005), Kindle location 66.

144   Duncan J. Watts, *Everything Is Obvious, Once You Know the Answer: How Common Sense Fails* (Crown Business, 2011), Kindle location 3312.

145   Taleb, *Antifragile*, 8.

146   Ibid., 126.

147   Jeanne Meister, "Job Hopping Is the 'New Normal' for Millennials: Three Ways to Prevent a Human Resource Nightmare," *Forbes*, August 14, 2012, http://www.forbes.com/sites/jeannemeister/2012/08/14/job-hopping-is-the-new-normal-for-millennials-three-ways-to-prevent-a-human-resource-nightmare/.

CHAPTER 7

148   Thomas W. Benson, *Writing JFK: Presidential Rhetoric and the Press in the Bay of Pigs Crisis* (Texas A&M University Press, 2004), 39.

149   Ibid., xv–xix.

150   Ibid., 37–38.

151   Ibid., 36.

152   Ibid., 36–42.

153   "Text of Obama Speech on the Economy," CNBC, January 8, 2009, http://www.cnbc.com/id/28559492.

154   Yuri Maltsev and Roman Skaskiw, *The Tea Party Explained: From Crisis to Crusade* (Open Court, 2013), Kindle location 1526.

155   The entire Santelli rant can be watched at http://www.youtube.com/watch?v=bEZB4taSEoA.

156   Maltsev and Skaskiw, *The Tea Party Explained*, Kindle location 1558.

157   Ibid., Kindle location 1858.

158   In *Networks of Outrage and Hope*, Manuel Castells takes this co-optation to be self-evident.

159   Maltsev and Skaskiw, *The Tea Party Explained*, Kindle location 1717.

160   See, for example, Eric Alterman, James Antle, Ayesha Kazmi, Sally Kohn, Doug Guetzloe, Frances Fox Piven, and Douglas Rushkoff, "Occupy Wall Street and the Tea Party Compared," *The Guardian*, October 7, 2011, http://www.theguardian.com/commentisfree/cifamerica/2011/oct/07/occupy-wall-street-tea-party; Peter Aldhous, "Occupy vs. Tea Party: What Their Twitter Networks Reveal," *New Scientist*, November 17, 2011, https://3quarksdaily.com/3quarksdaily/2011/11/occupy-vs-tea-party-what-their-twitter-networks-reveal.html.

161   Gary C. Jacobson, "Barack Obama, the Tea Party, and the 2010 Elections," *Extensions*, Summer 2011, http://www.ou.edu/carlalbertcenter/extensions/summer2011/Jacobson.pdf.

162   Rob Cottingham, "The Obama Online Campaign, by the Numbers: Quantifying the Impact of Social Media in 2008," Social Signal, November 22, 2008, http://www.socialsignal.com/blog/rob-cottingham/the-obama-online-campaign-by-the-numbers.

163   Jacobson, "Barack Obama, the Tea Party."

164   For the best-argued and most incisive analysis of this trend in the news media, see Thomas E. Patterson, *Out of Order*, (Vintage Books, 1993). One citation should suffice (Kindle location 179): "After the 1992 election, I asked several of the nation's top journalists why they portray the candidates as liars. 'Because they are liars,' was the most common response . . . "

165   James C. Scott, *Seeing Like a State: How Certain Schemes to Improve the Human Condition Have Failed* (Yale University Press, 1998).

166   Ibid., 347.

167   Ibid., 117–130.

168   Ibid., 128.

169   "Text of Obama Speech on the Economy," CNBC.

170   Paul Ormerod, *Why Most Things Fail: Evolution, Extinction, and Economics* (Pantheon Books, 2005), 236.

171   Ibid., 236.

172   See Chapter 4 for fuller quote and context.

173   Pierre Rosanvallon, *Counter-Democracy: Politics in an Age of Distrust* (Cambridge University Press, 2008), 257-9.

174   Anna Manchin, "Trust in Government Sinks to New Low in Southern Europe," Gallup World, October 30, 2013, http://www.gallup.com/poll/165647/trust-government-sinks-new-low-southern-europe.aspx.

175   World Bank Data Catalog website.

176   "Support for Spain's Government Grows as Graft Scandal Recedes—Poll," Reuters, October 6, 2013, https://www.reuters.com/article/idUS-BRE99503W20131006.

177   Jeffrey M. Jones, "Record High in US Say Big Government Biggest Threat," *Gallup Politics*, December 18, 2013, http://www.gallup.com/poll/166535/record-high-say-big-government-greatest-threat.aspx.

178   "Health Care Law: 74 Percent Rate Their Health Insurance Good or Excellent," Rasmussen Reports, February 10, 2014, http://www.rasmussenreports.com/public_content/politics/current_events/healthcare/health_care_law.

179   "Political Polarisation: United States of Amoeba," *The Economist*, December 7, 2013, http://www.economist.com/news/united-states/21591190-united-states-amoeba; Richard Wolf, "Voters Leaving Republican, Democratic Parties in Droves," *USA Today*, December 22, 2011, http://usatoday30.usatoday.com/news/politics/story/2011-12-22/voters-political-parties/52171688/1; Jane C. Timm, "Majority of Americans Want a Third Party," MSNBC, October 14, 2013, http://www.msnbc.com/morning-joe/majority-americans-want-third-party.

180   "Public Trust in Government: 1958–2013," Pew Research Center for the People and the Press, October 18, 2013, http://www.people-press.org/2013/10/18/trust-in-government-interactive/.

181   Ormerod belongs to a group of thinkers who in the last decade have thrown much light on the boundary conditions of what human beings can and can't know, predict, or ordain: Nassim Nicholas Taleb, Duncan Watts, James C. Scott, Philip Tetlock, Nate Silver.

182   Ormerod, *Why Most Things Fail*, Kindle location 66.

183   Ibid., 38.

184   Ibid., 236.

185   Ibid., 67–68.

186   Ibid., 99.

187   I urge the reader to browse the many job postings for "community organizer" on the web, which add up to a familiar portrait.

188   Melissa McEwan, "President Obama at Planned Parenthood," *Shakesville*, April 26, 2013, http://www.shakesville.com/2013/04/president-obama-at-planned-parenthood.html.

189   "President Obama on Inequality (Transcript)," *Politico*, December 4, 2013, http://www.politico.com/story/2013/12/obama-income-inequality-100662.html.

190   The senior aide was David Axelrod, and he can be seen making this statement at http://www.youtube.com/watch?v=mhd6XLbbtIY.

191   Wynton Hall, "President Obama on IRS Scandal: 'I Certainly Did Not Know Anything,'" *Breitbart*, May 16, 2013, http://www.breitbart.com/Big-Government/2013/05/16/Obama-On-IRS-Scandal-I-Certainly-Did-Not-Know-Anything.

192   Dana Milbank, "Obama, the Uninterested President," *Washington Post*, May 14, 2013, http://www.washingtonpost.com/opinions/dana-milbank-obama-the-uninterested-president/2013/05/14/da1c982a-bcd7-11e2-9b09-1638acc3942e_story.html.

193   Andy Borowitz, "Obama Denies Role in Government," *The New Yorker*, May 18, 2013, http://www.newyorker.com/online/blogs/borowitzreport/2013/05/obama-denies-role-in-government.html.

CHAPTER 8

194   Screen shot of video, http://hellaoccupyoakland.org/occupy-oakland-forum-police-actions/.

195   Climate Change 2013, *The Physical Science Basis: Summary for Policymakers, Intergovernmental Panel on Climate Change*, (Cambridge University Press, 2013), https://www.ipcc.ch/report/ar5/wg1/.

196   Will Wrigley, "Hurricane Sandy Survivors Demand Climate Change Action From Obama," *Huffington Post*, February 11, 2013, http://www.huffingtonpost.com/2013/02/11/hurricane-sandy-climate-change_n_2664563.html.

197   Office of the Press Secretary, "Remarks by the President on Climate Change," The White House, June 25, 2013, http://www.whitehouse.gov/the-press-office/2013/06/25/remarks-president-climate-change.

198   "Are Things Getting Better? More Americans Continue to Believe the Economy Is Getting Worse," YouGov, February 27, 2013, https://today.yougov.com/news/2013/02/27/are-things-getting-better-more-americans-continue-/.

199   "President Obama on Inequality (Transcript)," *Politico*, December 4, 2013, https://www.politico.com /story/2013/12/ obama-income-inequality-100662.html.

200   See, for example, "What's Gone Wrong with Democracy," *The Economist*, March 1, 2014, http://www.economist.com/news/essays/21596796-democracy-was-most-successful-political-idea-20th-century-why-has-it-run-trouble-and-what-can-be-do.

201   Mark Meckler and Jenny Beth Martin, *Tea Party Patriots: The Second American Revolution* (Henry Holt and Company, 2012), 6.

202   Ibid., 13.

203   Fernando Cabal, ed. *Indignados! 15 M* (Mandala ediciones, no date), Kindle location 36.

204   "Declaration of the Occupation of New York City," #OccupyWallStreet, NYC General Assembly, http://www.nycga.net/resources/documents/declaration/.

205   Cabal, ed. *Indignados!*, Kindle location 449.

206   Joshua Kurlantzick, *Democracy in Retreat: The Revolt of the Middle Class and the Worldwide Decline of Representative Government* (Yale University Press, 2013), 6–31.

207   Thomas L. Friedman, "Our One-Party Democracy," *New York Times*, September 8, 2009, http://www.nytimes.com/2009/09/09/opinion/09friedman.html?_r=3&adxnnl=1&partner=rss&emc=rss&adxnnlx=1342620027-Z4vProSA4/hgcF8nbyrltw&.

208   "Jeff Immelt: China's Communist Government 'Works,'" *RealClearPolitics* Video, December 11, 2012, http://www.realclearpolitics.com/video/2012/12/11/jeff_immelt_chinas_communist_government_works.html.

209   Office of the Press Secretary, "President Obama's State of the Union Address," The White House, January 28, 2014, http://www.whitehouse.gov/the-press-office/2014/01/28/president-barack-obamas-state-union-address.

210   Pierre Rosanvallon, *Counter-Democracy: Politics in an Age of Distrust* (Cambridge University Press, 2008), 150.

211   Ibid., 255.

212   Ibid., 255.

213   Henry Farrell, "There is No Alternative," *Aeon Magazine*, April 25, 2013, https://aeon.co/essays/the-left-is-now-too-weak-for-democracy-to-survive.

214   Screen shot from video.

215   Nicolas Kulish, "As Scorn for Vote Grows, Protests Surge Around the Globe," *New York Times*, September 27, 2011, http://www.nytimes.com/2011/09/28/world/as-scorn-for-vote-grows-protests-surge-around-globe.html?pagewanted=all&_r=0.

216   José Ortega y Gasset, *La Rebelion de las Masas* (Revista de Occidente, 1930), 86-87.

217   "President Barack Obama's Inaugural Address," *Washington Post*, January 20, 2009, http://voices.washingtonpost.com/44/2009/01/president-barack-obamas-inaugu.html.

218   Anthony Olcott, "All That Is Solid Melts Into Air," Institute for the Study of Diplomacy, May 2010, http://www.academia.edu/662725/All_That_Is_Solid_Melts_Into_Air.

CHAPTER 9

219   James C. Scott, *Seeing Like a State: How Certain Schemes to Improve the Human Condition Have Failed* (Yale University Press, 1998), 81.

220   U.S. Bureau of Labor Statistic's "How the Government Measures Unemployment," http://www.bls.gov/cps/cps_htgm.htm.

221   Charles Dickens, *Bleak House* (1852-1853), via The Literature Network, http://www.online-literature.com/dickens/bleakhouse/6/.

222   Nassim Nicholas Taleb, *The Black Swan: The Impact of the Highly Improbable* (Random House, 2007), 34–35.

223   The most lucid and readable book on networks and small worlds, in my judgment, is still Albert-László Barabási's *Linked: How Everything Is Connected to Everything Else and What It Means for Business, Science, and Everyday Life* (Perseus Books, 2002).

224   My chart.

225   Ed O'Keefe, "How Many .gov Sites Exist? Thousands.", *Washington Post*, December 20, 2011, http://www.washingtonpost.com/blogs/federal-eye/post/how-many-gov-sites-exist-thousands/2011/12/20/gIQAkGAG7O_blog.html.

226   All website data derived from alexa.com.

227   Robert Pear, Sharon LaFraniere, and Ian Austen, "From the Start, Signs of Trouble at the Health Portal," *New York Times*, October 13, 2013, http://www.nytimes.com/2013/10/13/us/politics/from-the-start-signs-of-trouble-at-health-portal.html?_r=0.

228   Ibid.

229   Chart by alexa.com.

CHAPTER 10

230   Mustafa Nayyem, "Uprising in Ukraine: How It All Began," *Open Society Foundations*, April 4, 2014, http://www.opensocietyfoundations.org/voices/uprising-ukraine-how-it-all-began.

231   Timothy Snyder, "Ukraine: The Haze of Propaganda," *The New York Review of Books*, March 1, 2014, https://www.nybooks.com/daily/2014/03/01/ukraine-haze-propaganda/.

232   Ibid.

233   Volodymyr Ishchenko, "Ukraine Has Not Experienced a Genuine Revolution, Merely a Change of Elites," *The Guardian*, February 28, 2014, http://www.theguardian.com/world/2014/feb/28/ukraine-genuine-revolution-tackle-corruption.

234   Oleh Kotsyuba, "Ukraine's Battle for Europe," *New York Times*, November 29, 2013, http://www.nytimes.com/2013/11/30/opinion/ukraines-battle-for-europe.html?_r=0.

235   Nayyem, "Uprising in Ukraine."

236   Michael Bociurkiw, "Can Ukraine's 'Political Kamikazes' Rescue the Country from Collapse?" CNN, February 27, 2014, http://www.cnn.com/2014/02/27/opinion/ukraine-new-government/.

237   "Police Clash in Venezuela with Anti-Government Protesters," BBC, March 20, 2014, http://www.bbc.com/news/world-latin-america-26676806; William Neuman, "In Venezuela, Protest Ranks Grow Broader," *New York Times*, February 24, 2014, http://www.nytimes.com/2014/02/25/world/americas/in-venezuela-middle-class-joins-protests.html?_r=0.

238   Loretta Chao, "Twitter, Other Apps Disrupted in Venezuela Amid Protests," *Wall Street Journal*, February 21, 2014, http://online.wsj.com/news/articles/SB10001424052702303775504579397430033153284.

239   "Hercon: El 53.7% de Venezolanos Considera Que Vive en Dictadura (Gobierno Raspado)," *La Patilla*, May 19, 2014, http://www.lapatilla.com/site/2014/03/30/hercon-el-53-7-de-venezolanos-considera-que-vive-en-dictadura-gobierno-raspado/.

240   "55% of Venezuelans Think Maduro's Gov't Is No Longer Democratic," *El Universal*, March 31, 2014, http://english.eluniversal.com/nacional-y-politica/140331/55-of-venezuelans-think-maduros-govt-is-no-longer-democratic.

241   Neuman, "In Venezuela, Protest Ranks Grow Broader."

242   Thomas Fuller, "Thai Protests Turn Volatile as at Least 3 Are Shot Dead," *New York Times*, December 1, 2013, http://www.nytimes.com/2013/12/02/world/asia/thailand-protests.html?_r=0.

243   "Full Transcript of Voice Recording Purportedly of Erdogan and His Son,"
       Today's Zaman, February 26, 2014, http://www.todayszaman.com/news-
       340552-full-transcript-of-voice-recording-purportedly-of-turkish-pm-
       erdogan-and-his-son.html.

244   Joe Parkinson, Sam Schechner, and Emre Peker, "Turkey's Erdogan: One of the
       World's Most Determined Internet Censors," *Wall Street Journal*, May 2, 2014,
       http://online.wsj.com/news/articles/SB10001424052702304626304579505912518706936.

245   Charlemagne, "Another Summer of Unrest for Turkey?" *The Economist*, May 3,
       2014, http://www.economist.com/blogs/charlemagne/2014/05/turkeys-
       may-day-protests.

246   "Egypt's Al-Sisi: Muslim Brotherhood Is 'Finished,'" Sky News, May 6, 2014,
       http://news.sky.com/story/1255779/egypts-al-sisi-muslim-brotherhood-is-
       finished.

247   Robert Mackey, "For Egypt's Rulers, Familiar Scapegoats," *New York Times*,
       November 29, 2014, http://thelede.blogs.nytimes.com/2013/11/29/for-
       egypts-new-rulers-familiar-scapegoats/.

248   Patrick Kingsley, "I'm No Traitor, Says Wael Ghonim as Egypt Regime Targets
       Secular Activists," *The Guardian*, January 9, 2014, http://www.theguardian.
       com/world/2014/jan/09/wael-ghonim-egypt-regime-targets-secular-
       activists.

249   Francis Fukuyama, "The End of History?" *The National Interest*, Summer 1989,
       http://www.kropfpolisci.com/exceptionalism.fukuyama.pdf.

250   Angelique Chrisafis, "François Hollande Becomes Most Unpopular French Pres-
       ident Ever," *The Guardian*, October 29, 2013, http://www.theguardian.com/
       world/2013/oct/29/francois-hollande-most-unpopular-president.

251   "Political Insurgency: Europe's Tea Parties," *The Economist*, July 4, 2014,
       http://www.economist.com/news/leaders/21592610-insurgent-parties-are-
       likely-do-better-2014-any-time-second-world.

252   Clay Shirky, "Healthcare.gov and the Gulf Between Planning and Reality," *Clay
       Shirky*, November 19, 2013, http://www.shirky.com/weblog/2013/11/
       healthcare-gov-and-the-gulf-between-planning-and-reality/.

253   "Full Transcript: President Obama's Nov. 14 news conference on the Affordable
       Care Act," *Washington Post*, November 14, 2013, https://www.washington-
       post.com/politics/transcript-president-obamas-nov-14-statement-on-health-
       care/2013/11/14/6233e352-4d48-11e3-ac54-aa84301ced81_story.html.

254   John Dickerson, "A Sorry Apology," *Slate*, November 8, 2013, http://www.
       slate.com/articles/news_and_politics/politics/2013/11/barack_obama_s_
       bad_apology_the_president_s_apology_for_the_affordable_care.html.

255   Louise Radnofsky and Colleen McCain Nelson, "Obama Says Health-Insurance
       Enrollees Reach 8 Million," *Wall Street Journal*, April 17, 2014, http://online.wsj.
       com/news/articles/SB10001424052702304810904579507922881089460.

256   Christopher Duggan, "Italy Has One Last chance with Matteo Renzi—or the Clowns Will Be Back in Charge," *Telegraph*, February 26, 2014, http://www. telegraph.co.uk/news/worldnews/europe/italy/10662452/Italy-has-one-last-chance-with-Matteo-Renzi-or-the-clowns-will-be-back-in-charge.html.

RECONSIDERATIONS

257   Andrew Sullivan, "Trump's Mindless Nihilism," *New York Magazine,* October 13, 2017, http://nymag.com/daily/intelligencer/2017/10/andrew-sullivan-trump-mindless-nihilism.html.

258   Eugene Robinson, "We Will All Pay a Price for Trump's Nihilism," *Washington Post*, November 27, 2017, https://www.washingtonpost.com/opinions/we-will-all-pay-a-price-for-trumps-nihilism/2017/11/27/2be5d924-d3b1-11e7-95bf-df7c19270879_story.html.

259   Peggy Noonan, "The Nihilist in the White House," *The Wall Street Journal,* November 21, 2014, https://www.wsj.com/articles/peggy-noonan-the-nihilist-in-the-white-house-1416533660; Aaron Blake, "We're All Political Nihilists Now," *Washington Post*, April 6, 2017, at https://www.washington-post.com/news/the-fix/wp/2017/04/06/were-all-political-nihilists-now/?utm_term=.c140b82029be.

260   E. J. Dionne, "Our Institutional Crisis Is Upon Us," *RealClearPolitics*, December 11, 2017, https://www.realclearpolitics.com/articles/2017/12/11/our_institutional_crisis_is_upon_us_135736.html.

261   Yascha Mounk, "The Real Coup Plot Is Trump's," *New York Times*, December 20, 2017, https://www.nytimes.com/2017/12/20/opinion/trump-republican-coup.html.

262   Council of Foreign Relations, "End-Times for Liberal Democracy?" Interview by Zachary Laub, Yascha Mounk, Interviewee, December 28, 2016, https://www.cfr.org/interview/end-times-liberal-democracy.

263   Sohrab Ahmari, "The Worldwide Crisis of Illiberalism," *Commentary,* June 16, 2016, https://www.commentarymagazine.com/articles/illiberalism-worldwide-crisis/; Human Rights Watch, "The Dangerous Rise of Populism: Global Attacks on Human Rights Values," *World Report 2017,* 2018, https://www.hrw.org/world-report/2017/country-chapters/dangerous-rise-of-populism.

264   CNN, "Obama Invokes Hitler Era in Warning to America," YouTube, December 9, 2017, https://www.youtube.com/watch?v=z_FWptVoBWg; Richard Cohen, "The Echoes of Weimar Germany Should Not Be Ignored," *RealClearPolitics,* December 6, 2017, https://www.realclearpolitics.com/articles/2016/12/06/the_echoes_of_weimar_germany_should_not_be_ignored_132495.html.

265   See Josh Katz, "Who Will Be President?" *New York Times,* November 8, 2016, https://www.nytimes.com/interactive/2016/upshot/presidential-polls-forecast.html; Natalie Jackson, "Huffington Post Predicts Hillary Clinton Will Win with 323 Electoral Votes," *Huffington Post,* November 7, 2016, https://www.huffingtonpost.com/entry/polls-hillary-clinton-win_us_5821074ce4b0e80b02cc2a94. The *Huffington Post* piece placed the odds of a Trump victory at 2 percent.

266   Shane Goldmacher and Ben Schreckinger, "Trump Pulls Off Biggest Upset in US History," *Politico,* November 9, 2016, https://www.politico.com/story/2016/11/election-results-2016-clinton-trump-231070.

267   "The Inaugural Address: Remarks of Donald J. Trump," The White House, January 20, 2016, https://www.whitehouse.gov/briefings-statements/the-inaugural-address/.

268   Andrew Prokop, "The Last-Ditch Push for the Electoral College to Stop Trump, Explained," *Vox,* December 19, 2016, https://www.vox.com/policy-and-politics/2016/12/16/13920444/electoral-college-trump-hamilton-electors.

269   James Hohman, "The Daily 202: Trump's Pollster Says He Ran a 'Post-Ideological' Campaign," *Washington Post,* December 5, 2016, https://www.washingtonpost.com/news/powerpost/paloma/daily-202/2016/12/05/daily-202-trump-s-pollster-says-he-ran-a-post-ideological-campaign/5844d166e9b69b7e58e45f2a/?utm_term=.c19bf393fb98.

270   See, for example, M.J. Lee, "Donald Trump vs. the Republican establishment," CNN, October 26, 2015, http://www.cnn.com/2015/10/26/politics/donald-trump-republican-establishment/index.html.

271   David Gurri, "When do the Candidates Come From? Part 2: When the Supporters Come From," *Trivial Analysis*, February 3, 2016, https://trivialanalysis.wordpress.com/2016/02/03/when-do-the-candidates-come-from-part-2-when-the-supporters-come-from/.

272   See criticism of the former president's "neglect" of the party in Donna Brazile, "Inside Hillary Clinton's Secret Takeover of the DNC," *Politico*, November 2, 2017, https://www.politico.com/magazine/story/2017/11/02/clinton-brazile-hacks-2016-215774.

273   Rob Faris, Hal Roberts, Bruce Etling, Nikki Bourassa, Ethan Zuckerman, Yochai Benkler, "Partisanship, Propaganda, and Disinformation: Online Media and the 2016 Presidential Elections," Berkman Klein Center For Internet & Society at Harvard, August 16, 2017, https://cyber.harvard.edu/ publications/2017/08/mediacloud.

274   See, for example, Nicholas Confessore and Karen Yourish, "$2 Billion of Free Media for Donald Trump," *New York Times,* March 15, 2016, https://www.nytimes.com/2016/03/16/upshot/measuring-donald-trumps-mammoth-advantage-in-free-media.html.

275   Adrienne LaFrance, "Trump's Media Saturation, Quantified," *The Atlantic,* September 1, 2016, https://www.theatlantic.com/technology/archive/2016/09/trumps-media-saturation-quantified/498389/.

276   Eric Boehlert, "All Trump, All the Time: The Donald Dominated the Airwaves in 2015," *Salon,* January 16, 2016, https://www.salon.com/2016/01/16/all_trump_all_the_time_the_donald_dominated_the_airwaves_in_2015_partner/.

277   In *The Art of the Deal*, Trump had stated, "One thing I've learned about the press is that they're always hungry for a good story, and the more sensational the better. . . . The point is that if you are a little different, or a little outrageous, or if you do things that are bold or controversial, the press is going to write about you." Donald J. Trump with Tony Schwartz, *Trump: The Art of the Deal*, (Ballantine Books, 1987), 56.

278   Jim Rutenberg, "Trump Is Testing the Norms of Objectivity in Journalism," *New York Times*, August 7, 2016, https://www.nytimes.com/2016/08/08/business/balance-fairness-and-a-proudly-provocative-presidential-candidate.html.

279   Stephen Collinson, "Why Trump's Talk of a Rigged Vote Is So Dangerous," CNN, October 19, 2016, http://www.cnn.com/2016/10/18/politics/donald-trump-rigged-election/index.html.

280   See Jack Shafer, "WikiLeaks and the Oily Washington Press," *Politico,* October 18, 2016, https://www.politico.com/magazine/story/2016/10/john-podesta-emails-wikileaks-press-214367.

281   See David A. Fahrenthold, "Trump Recorded Having an Extremely Lewd Conversation About Women in 2005," *Washington Post,* October 8, 2016, https://www.washingtonpost.com/politics/trump-recorded-having-extremely-lewd-conversation-about-women-in-2005/2016/10/07/3b9ce776-8cb4-11e6-bf8a-3d26847eeed4_story.html?utm_term=.40ee72eca553; Sharon Waxman, "How 'Access Hollywood' Found the Trump Tape – and Why NBC News Probably Leaked It (Exclusive)," *The Wrap*, October 7, 2016, https://www.thewrap.com/how-access-hollywood-found-the-trump-tape-and-why-nbc-news-probably-leaked-it-exclusive/.

282   NBC News/Wall Street Journal Survey, Study #16804, September 16–19, 2016, https://www.scribd.com/document/324821200/16804-NBCWSJ-September-Poll-9-21-Release?secret_password=gKkeD7pKqo5rYoSPNmfU&content=10079&ad_group=Online+Tracking+Link&campaign=Skimbit%2C+Ltd.&keyword=ft500noi&source=impactradius&medium=affiliate&irgw.

283   Thomas E. Patterson, *Out of Order: An Incisive and Boldly Original Critique of the News Media's Domination of America's Political Process* (Vintage Books, 1993).

284   Mike Wooldridge, "BBC Democracy Day: Europe 'Faces Political Earthquakes,'" BBC, January 20, 2015, http://www.bbc.com/news/world-europe-30864088.

285   Giorgos Christides, "Greek Radical Left Syriza Prepares for Power Under Tsipras," BBC, December 14, 2014, http://www.bbc.com/news/world-europe-30481307.

286   Helena Smith, "Alexis Tsipras: 'The Worst is Clearly Behind Us,'" *The Guardian*, July 24, 2017, https://www.theguardian.com/world/2017/jul/24/alexis-tsipras-the-worst-is-clearly-behind-us.

287   Jane Kramer, "The Demolition Man," *The New Yorker,* June 29, 2015, https://www.newyorker.com/magazine/2015/06/29/the-demolition-man.

288   See Jamie Bartlett, "How Beppe Grillo's Social Media Politics Took Italy by Storm," *The Guardian,* February 26, 2013, https://www.theguardian.com/commentisfree/2013/feb/26/beppe-grillo-politics-social-media-italy; "Most Famous Ten Politicians in Italy as of November 2016, by Number of Facebook Page Fans," Statista: The Statistical Portal, https://www.statista.com/statistics/590340/top-politicians-on-facebook-in-italy/.

289   Gianni Riotta, "The Resignation of Renzi, the Fall of Rome," *Foreign Policy,* December 5, 2016, https://foreignpolicy.com/2016/12/05/the-resignation-of-renzi-the-fall-of-rome/.

290   Stephanie Kirchgaessner, "Italy: Five Star and League Parties Likely to Form Governing Alliance," *The Guardian,* March 25, 2018, https://www.theguardian.com/world/2018/mar/25/italy-elections-five-star-movement-and-rightists-strike-deal-to-elect-speakers.

291   Anushka Asthana and Rowena Mason, "Barack Obama: Brexit Vote Would Put UK 'Back of Queue' for Trade Talks," *The Guardian,* April 22, 2016, https://www.theguardian.com/politics/2016/apr/22/barack-obama-brexit-uk-back-of-queue-for-trade-talks.

292   See, for example, "'Jihadi John' Killer from Islamic State Beheading Videos Named by Media," YouTube, https://www.youtube.com/watch?v=HEbtx-p9SsVs.

293   Steven Erlanger, "Britain Votes to Leave EU; Cameron Plans to Step Down," *New York Times,* June 23, 2016, https://mobile.nytimes.com/2016/06/25/world/europe/britain-brexit-european-union-referendum.html?_r=0&referer=http://www.powerlineblog.com/.

294   See Lizzie Dearden, "Anger Over 'Bregret' as Leave Voters Say They Thought UK Would Stay in EU," *The Independent,* June 25, 2016, http://www.independent.co.uk/news/uk/politics/brexit-anger-bregret-leave-voters-protest-vote-thought-uk-stay-in-eu-remain-win-a7102516.html; Alina Selyukh, "After Brexit Vote, Britain Asks in Google: 'What Is the EU?'" NPR, June 24, 2016, https://www.npr.org/sections/alltechconsidered/2016/06/24/480949383/britains-google-searches-for-what-is-the-eu-spike-after-brexit-vote.

295   Vyacheslav Polonski, "Impact of Social Media on the Outcome of the EU Referendum," *EU Referendum Analysis 2016,* no date, http://www.referendumanalysis.eu/eu-referendum-analysis-2016/section-7-social-media/impact-of-social-media-on-the-outcome-of-the-eu-referendum/.

296   Sunny Hundal, "Angela Merkel is Now the Leader of the Free World, Not Donald Trump," *The Independent,* February 1, 2017, http://www.independent.co.uk/voices/angela-merkel-donald-trump-democracy-freedom-of-press-a7556986.html.

297   Emile Simpson, "Macron the Conqueror," *Foreign Policy,* January 18, 2018, http://foreignpolicy.com/2018/01/18/macron-the-conquerer/, and also this: https://beholdisraelblog.files.wordpress.com /2017/06/unknown.jpg?w=219&h=236.

298   Cover is for the June 17, 2017 issue of *The Economist.*

299   See, for example, Pierre Briançon, "Macron's 'Jupiter' Model Unlikely to Stand the Test of Time," *Politico*, June 16, 2016, https://www.politico.eu/article/emmanuel-macron-jupiter-model-unlikely-to-stand-test-of-time-leadership-parliamentary-majority/.

300   Henry A. Giroux, "Gangster Capitalism and Nostalgic Authoritarianism in Trump's America," *Salon*, December 3, 2017, https://www.salon.com/2017/12/03/gangster-capitalism-and-nostalgic-authoritarianism-in-trumps-america/.

301   Zeynep Tufekci, "It's the (Democrary-Poisoning) Golden Age of Free Speech," *Wired*, January 16, 2018, https://www.wired.com/story/free-speech-issue-tech-turmoil-new-censorship/.

302   Jessica Taylor, "Majority of Americans Believe Trump Acted Either Illegally or Unethically With Russia," NPR, June 6, 2017, https://www.npr.org/2017/07/06/535626356/on-russia-republican-and-democratic-lenses-have-a-very-different-tint.

303   There's a large literature on the nature and implication of China's moral crisis, most of which I confess I have not read. My citation is from "The Moral Crisis in China," CHINASCOPE Analysis Series (December 2011), at http://chinascope.org/wp-content/uploads/2012/01/CSA20111224.pdf. For the type of incident that has sparked soul-searching on Chinese mass and social media, see Lijia Zhang, "How Can I Be Proud of My China When We Are a Nation of 1.4bn Cold Hearts?" *The Guardian*, October 22, 2011, https://www.theguardian.com/commentisfree/2011/oct/22/china-nation-cold-hearts.

304   Tom Phillips, "China on Course to Become 'World's Most Christian Nation' Within 15 Years," *Telegraph*, April 19, 2014, http://www.telegraph.co.uk/news/worldnews/asia/china/10776023/China-on-course-to-become-worlds-most-Christian-nation-within-15-years.html; Ian Johnson, "In China, Unregistered Churches Are Driving a Religious Revolution," *The Atlantic*, April 23, 2017, https://www.theatlantic.com/international/archive/2017/04/china-unregistered-churches-driving-religious-revolution/521544/.

305   See Chapter 8.

306   "China Jails Xinjiang Blogger for 19 Years Over Criticizing Government Online," Jimmy Wales Foundation, January 22, 2016, http://jimmywalesfoundation.org/china-jails-blogger-for-19-years-over-criticising-government-online/.

307   Sui-Lee Wee, "China Jails Journalist for Seven Years for 'Leaking State Secrets,'" Reuters, April 16, 2015, https://www.reuters.com/article/us-china-rights/china-jails-journalist-for-seven-years-for-leaking-state-secrets-idUSKBN0N806I20150417.

308   "State Media Should Play Due Role in Properly Guiding Public Opinion," *China Daily*, February 22, 2016, http://www.chinadaily.com.cn/opinion/2016-02/22/content_23580181.htm.

309   Marco Huang, "More Than Half of China's Population is Online – and Most Use Smartphones," *Wall Street Journal,* January 26, 2016, https://blogs.wsj.com/chinarealtime/2016/01/26/more-than-half-of-chinas-population-is-online-and-most-use-smartphones/.

310   Franklin Foer, "Putin's Puppet," *Slate,* July 4, 2016, http://www.slate.com/articles/news_and_politics/cover_story/2016/07/vladimir_putin_has_a_plan_for_destroying_the_west_and_it_looks_a_lot_like.html; Muhamed Sacirbey, "Has Putin Been Manipulating Energy Prices?" *Huffington Post,* no date, https://www.huffingtonpost.com/ambassador-muhamed-sacirbey/has-putin-been-manipulati_b_5268443.html.

311   David Filipov, "Here Are 10 Critics of Vladimir Putin Who Died Violently or in Suspicious Ways," *Washington Post,* March 23, 2017, https://www.washingtonpost.com/news/worldviews/ wp/2017/03/23/here-are-ten-critics-of-vladimir-putin-who-died-violently-or-in-suspicious-ways/?utm_term=.1bf-065caef40.

312   Jake Bernstein, Petra Blum, Oliver Zihlmann, David Thompson, Frederik Obermaier, and Bastian Obermayer, "All Putin's Men: Secret Records Reveal Money Network Tied to Russian Leader," *The International Consortium of Investigative Journalists,* April 3, 2016, https://panamapapers.icij.org/20160403-putin-russia-offshore-network.html.

313   "Vladimir the Great," *The Economist,* December 5, 2014, https://www.economist.com/news/europe/21635690-russias-president-tells-his-people-west-out-get-them-vladimir-great.

314   Anna Smolchenko, "Putin Lashes Out at West and Domestic Critics at Rally," *New York Times,* November 21, 2007, http://www.nytimes.com/2007/11/21/world/europe/21iht-russia.4.8424392.html.

315   See, for example, Alan Taylor, "Vladimir Putin, Action Man," *The Atlantic,* September 13, 2011, https://www.theatlantic.com/photo/2011/09/vladimir-putin-action-man/100147/.

316   David Kirkpatrick, "As Egyptians Grasp for Stability, Sisi Fortifies His Presidency," *New York Times,* October 7, 2014, https://www.nytimes.com/2014/10/08/world/as-egyptians-grasp-for-stability-sisi-fortifies-his-presidency.html?mtrref=undefined&gwh=28C80B42EBB13AB946FAE4C128700066&gwt=pay.

317   Screen capture of video, "Let's Learn Judo With Vladimir Putin" (2008).

318   Timothy J. Heaphy, "Final Report: Independent Review of 2017 Protest Events in Charlottesville, Virginia," Hunton & Williams LLP, 2017, https://www.huntonak.com/images/content/3/4/v4/34613/final-report-ada-compliant-ready.pdf. This review, commissioned by the city of Charlottesville, is by far the most complete and balanced source on this divisive subject.

319   Carly Sitrin, "Read: President Trump's Remarks Condemning Violence 'on Many Sides' in Charlottesville," *Vox,* August 12, 2017, https://www.vox.com/2017/8/12/16138906/president-trump-remarks-condemning-violence-on-many-sides-charlottesville-rally.

320   Erik Hananoki, "How Donald Trump Emboldened Charlottesville White Supremacists," *Media Matters,* August 12, 2017, https://www.mediamatters.org/
blog/2017/08/12/how-donald-trump-emboldened-charlottesville-white-
supremacists/217601.

321   Rosie Gray, "Trump Defends White-Nationalist Protesters: 'Some Very Fine
People on Both Sides,'" *The Atlantic,* August 15, 2017, https://www.theatlan-
tic.com/politics/archive/2017/08/trump-defends-white-nationalist-
protesters-some-very-fine-people-on-both-sides/537012/.

322   Ta-Nehisi Coates, "The First White President," *The Atlantic,* October 2017,
https://www.theatlantic.com/magazine/archive/2017/10/the-first-white-
president-ta-nehisi-coates/537909/.

323   Bob Burnett, "Trump Now Owns White Supremacy," *Huffington Post,*
October 1, 2017, https:// www.huffingtonpost.com/entry/trump-now-owns-
white-supremacy_us_59ce3ed7e4b0f3c468060dcf.

324   German Lopez, "Donald Trump's War with ESPN and Jemele Hill, Explained,"
Vox, October 10 2017, https://www.vox.com/identities/2017/9/15/16313800/
trump-jemele-hill-espn-white-supremacist.

325   See John Blake, "'White Supremacists by Default': How Ordinary People Made
Charlottesville Possible," CNN, August 24, 2017, https://www.cnn.
com/2017/08/18/us/ordinary-white-supremacists/index.html; Michael Edison
Hayden, "Neo-Nazis and White Supremacists Are Recruiting Trump Supporters Who Are Mad at Colin Kaepernick," *Newsweek,* October 12, 2017, http://
www.newsweek.com/nazis-white-nationalists-recruiting-trump-supporters-
mad-colin-kaepernick-683272.

326   Richard Fausset, "A Voice of Hate in America's Heartland," *New York Times,*
November 25, 2017, https://www.nytimes.com/2017/11/25/us/ohio-hovater-
white-nationalist.html?mtrref=www.google.com&gwh=8F7C43EBCAF07D3EC-
804B68C784B254A&gwt=pay.

327   Luke O'Brien, "The Making of an American Nazi," *The Atlantic,* December 2017,
https://www.theatlantic.com/magazine/archive/2017/12/the-making-of-an-
american-nazi/544119/.

328   Michael Barone, "Toward a Trump Republicanism," *The Washington Examiner,*
February 1, 2018, https://www.washingtonexaminer.com/michael-barone-
toward-a-trump-republicanism/article/2647767.

329   Timothy J. Heaphy, "Final Report: Independent Review," 7.

330   Michael R. Gordon, "U.S. Decision to Send Lethal Arms to Ukraine Signals Tougher
Stand on Russia," *Wall Street Journal,* October 24, 2017, https://www.wsj.com/
articles/u-s-decision-to-send-lethal-arms-to-ukraine-signals-tougher
-stance-on-russia-1514161057.

331   Noah Rothman, "Was It All Worth It?" *Commentary,* December 19, 2017,
https://www.commentarymagazine.com/politics-ideas/donald-trump-year-
in-review-unfavorable/; Rothman, "The Death Rattle of Obama's Reputation,"
Commentary, December 22, 2017, https://www.commentarymagazine.com/
foreign-policy/the-death-rattle-of-obamas-foreign-policy-record-susan-rice/.

332   Ross Douthat, "A War Trump Won," *New York Times,* December 16, 2017, https://www.nytimes.com/2017/12/16/ opinion/sunday/war-trump-islamic-state.html.

333   Rich Lowry, "Give Trump Credit Where It Is Due," *National Review,* December 20, 2017, https://www.sltrib.com/opinion/commentary/2017/12/20/rich-lowry-give-trump-credit-where-it-is-due/.

334   Carl M. Cannon, "Democrats' Year of Living Angrily," *Orange County Register,* December 30, 2017, https://www.ocregister.com/2017/12/30/democrats-year-of-living-angrily/.

335   "2016: A Hard Rain," *The Fifth Wave,* January 4, 2017, https://thefifthwave.wordpress.com/2017/01/04/2016-a-hard-rain/.

336   Ian Buruma, "Trump's Flirtation with Violence," *Project Syndicate,* July 10, 2017, https://www.project-syndicate.org/commentary/trump-flirtation-with-violence-by-ian-buruma-2017-07?barrier=accessreg.

337   Liz Spayd, "Want To Know What America's Thinking? Try Asking," *New York Times,* November 9, 2016, https://www.nytimes.com/2016/11/10/public-editor/want-to-know-what-americas-thinking-try-asking.html?rref=collection%2F-column%2FThe%20Public%20Editor&action=click&contentCollection=Public%20Editor&module=Collection&region=Marginalia&src=me&version=column&pg-type=article.

338   Jeff Jarvis, Twitter post, November 9, 2016, 12:29 A.M., https://twitter.com/jeffjarvis/status/796223123750354944?ref_src=twsrc%5Etfw.

339   Craig Silverman, "This Analysis Shows How Viral Fake Election News Stories Outperformed Real News on Facebook," *Buzzfeed,* November 16, 2016, https://www.buzzfeed.com/craigsilverman/viral-fake-election-news-outperformed-real-news-on-facebook?utm_term=.ymr3Q8YOY#.blgWQeV8V.

340   Sapna Maheshwari, "How Fake News Goes Viral: A Case Study," *New York Times,* November 20, 2016, https://www.nytimes.com/2016/11/20/business/media/how-fake-news-spreads.htmlmtrref=theweek.com&gwh=BBB362CE192362D-F24C7E91717CDBC35&gwt=pay.

341   Craig Timberg, "Russian Propaganda Effort Helped Spread 'Fake News' During Election, Experts Say," *Washington Post,* November 24, 2016, https://www.washingtonpost.com/business/economy/russian-propaganda-effort-helped-spread-fake-news-during-election-experts-say/2016/11/24/793903b6-8a40-4ca9-b712-716af66098fe_story.html?utm_term=.1a8ffb599100.

342   Howard Kurtz, *Media Madness: Donald Trump, the Press, and the War Over the Truth,* (Regnery Publishing, 2018), Kindle location 1406.

343   Craig Bannister, "Study: 90% of News Coverage of President Trump Negative in 2017," CNSNews, January 16, 2018, https://www.cnsnews.com/blog/craig-bannister/study-90-networks-trump-coverage-negative-2017.

344   Matthew J. Belvedere and Michael Newberg, "New York Times Subscription Growth Soars Tenfold, Adding 132,000, After Trump's Win," CNBC, November 29, 2016, https://www.cnbc.com/2016/11/29/new-york-times-subscriptions-soar-tenfold-after-donald-trump-wins-presidency.html.

345   Michael O'Connell, "Fox News Holds No. 1, MSNBC Thrives During Wild Year for Cable News," *The Hollywood Reporter,* December 20, 2017, https://www.hollywoodreporter.com/news/fox-news-holds-no-1-msnbc-thrives-wild-year-cable-news-1069621.

346   Art Swift, "In US, Confidence in Newspapers Still Low but Rising," Gallup News, June 28, 2017, http://news.gallup.com/poll/212852/confidence-newspapers-low-rising.aspx.

347   Kurtz, *Media Madness*, Kindle loc. 115-134.

348   Rob Faris et al., "Partisanship, Propaganda, and Disinformation."

349   Casey Newton, "Zuckerberg: The Idea That Fake News on Facebook Influenced the Election Is 'Crazy,'" *The Verge,* November 10, 2016, https://www.theverge.com/2016/11/10/13594558/mark-zuckerberg-election-fake-news-trump.

350   Kathleen Higgins, "Post-truth: A Guide for the Perplexed," *Nature*, November 28, 2016, http://www.nature.com/news/post-truth-a-guide-for-the-perplexed-1.21054.

351   "Post-Truth Politics: Art of the Lie," *The Economist,* September 10, 2016, https://www.economist.com/leaders/2016/09/10/art-of-the-lie.

352   Ruth Marcus, "Welcome to the Post-Truth Presidency," *Washington Post,* December 2, 2016, https://www.washingtonpost.com/opinions/welcome-to-the-post-truth-presidency/2016/12/02/baaf630a-b8cd-11e6-b994-f45a208f7a73_story.html?noredirect=on&utm_term=.d28be1f81d30.

353   See, for example, Steven Hayward, "Post-Truth Media Should Look in the Mirror," *Powerline,* December 6, 2016, http://www.powerlineblog.com/archives/2016/12/post-truth-media-should-look-in-the-mirror.php.

354   Matthew d'Ancona, *Post-Truth: The New War on Truth and How to Fight Back* (Ebury Press: 2017), 53, 29.

355   Tufekci, "It's the (Democracy-Poisoning) Golden Age."

356   D'Ancona, *Post-Truth*, 49.

357   Andrey Miroshnichenko, *Human as Media: The Emancipation of Authorship* (2014), 24.

358   Glenn Kessler and Meg Kelly, "President Trump Has Made More Than 2,000 False or Misleading Claims Over 355 Days," *Washington Post,* January 10, 2018, https://www.washingtonpost.com/news/fact-checker/wp/2018/01/10/president-trump-has-made-more-than-2000-false-or-misleading-claims-over-355-days/?utm_term=.fbe90eff5c34.

359   Chris Kahn, "Exclusive: Top Reason Americans Will Vote for Trump: 'To Stop Clinton'—Poll," Reuters, May 5, 2016, https://www.reuters.com/article/us-usa-election-anti-vote/exclusive-top-reason-americans-will-vote-for-trump-to-stop-clinton-poll-idUSKCN0XX06E.

360   Emily Ekins, "The Five Types of Trump Voters: Who They Are and What They Believe," Democracy Fund Voter Study Group, June 2017, https://www.voterstudygroup.org/publications/2016-elections/the-five-types-trump-voters.

361   D'Ancona, *Post-Truth*, 20.

362   Jonathan Haidt, *The Righteous Mind: Why Good People Are Divided by Politics and Religion*, (Pantheon Books, 2012), 79.

363   Dan De Luce, Robbie Gramer, "U.S. Diplomat's Resignation Signals Wider Exodus from State Department," *Foreign Policy,* December 9, 2017, https://foreignpolicy.com/2017/12/09/u-s-diplomat-resigns-warning-of-state-departments-diminished-role-diplomacy-national-security-tillerson-africa-somalia-south-sudan/.

364   Jonathan Haidt, "Why Universities Must Choose One Telos: Truth or Social Justice," Heterodox Academy, October 21, 2016, https://heterodoxacademy.org/one-telos-truth-or-social-justice/.

365   RefuseFascism.org, "What is Refuse Fascism?" https://refusefascism.org/about-contact/.

366   Mobilus in Mobilis/Wiki.

367   Joshua Eaton and Josh Israel, "Police in Charlottesville Arrested Almost as Many Drunk People as Violent White Supremacists," *ThinkProgress,* August 18, 2017, https://thinkprogress.org/charlottesville-protest-arrests-9484856f4489/.

368   Andrew Marszal and Peter Foster, "Dylann Roof: Profile of Charleston Church Shooting Suspect," *Telegraph,* June 18, 2015, http://www.telegraph.co.uk/news/worldnews/northamerica/usa/11684603/Dylan-Roof-Profile-of-Charleston-church-shooting-suspect.html.

369   A transcript of the 911 call can be found at https://info.publicintelligence.net/FL-OmarMateenTranscripts.pdf.

370   The "Last Rhodesian Manifesto" can be found at https://www.documentcloud.org/documents/2108059-lastrhodesian-manifesto.html.

371   Jack Moore, "ISIS Terrorist: 'We Are a People Who Love Death . . . Who Love Drinking Blood' of Enemies," *International Business Times,* September 17, 2014, https://midnightwatcher.wordpress.com/2014/09/17/isis-terrorist-we-are-a-people-who-love-death-who-love-drinking-blood/.

372   Abu Bakr al-Baghdadi, "A Message to the Mujahidin and the Muslim Ummah in the Month of Ramadan," 2014, https://azelin.files.wordpress.com/2014/07/abc5ab-bakr-al-e1b8a5ussaync4ab-al-qurayshc4ab-al-baghdc481dc4ab-22message-to-the-mujc481hidc4bn-and-the-islamic-ummah-in-the-month-of-ramae1b88dc481n22-en.pdf.

373   Arutz Sheva staff, "Hollande Condemns ISIS's 'Barbaric' Museum Destruction," *Arutz Sheva,* February 27, 2015, https://www.israelnationalnews.com/News/News.aspx/191923.

374   Screen capture of ISIS video.

375   Anders Breivik's Manifesto can be found at https://info.publicintelligence.net/AndersBehringBreivikManifesto.pdf.

376   Simon Cottee, "Reborn Into Terrorism: Why Are So Many ISIS Recruits Ex-Cons and Converts?" *The Atlantic,* January 25, 2016, https://www.theatlantic.com/international/archive/2016/01/isis-criminals-converts/426822/.

377   Chris McGreal, "Barack Obama Declares Iraq War a Success," *The Guardian,* December 14, 2011, https://www.theguardian.com/world/2011/dec/14/barack-obama-iraq-war-success.

378   John Horn and Tina Daunt, "In Roman Polanski Case, Is It Hollywood vs. Middle America?" *Los Angeles Times,* October 1, 2009, http://articles.latimes.com/2009/oct/01/entertainment/et-polanski1.

379   John Wagner, "Clinton's Data-Driven Campaign Relied Heavily on an Algorithm Named Ada. What Didn't She See?" *Washington Post,* November 9, 2016, https://www.washingtonpost.com/news/post-politics/wp/2016/11/09/clintons-data-driven-campaign-relied-heavily-on-an-algorithm-named-ada-what-didnt-she-see/?utm_term=.b546cac7fde2.

380   A very time-limited sampling of elite rage over Trumpian tweets: "Editorial: Trump's Twitter Tantrums Must End," *Detroit News,* November 28, 2016, https://www.detroitnews.com/story/opinion/editorials/ 2016/11/28/editorial-trumps-twitter-tantrums-must-end/94582768/; Libby Nelson, "Donald Trump Has Weaponized Twitter—with Dangerous Consequences," *Vox,* December 10, 2016, https://www.vox.com/2016/12/10/13901238/trump-twitter-harassment-criticism-jones; Justin Baragona, "Jill Abramson: 'Donald Trump and His Tweets Themselves' Are 'Fake News,'" *Mediaite,* December 11, 2016, https://www.mediaite.com/online/jill-abramson-donald-trump-and-his-tweets-themselves-are-fake-news/; Nahal Toosi, "Is Trump's Twitter Account a National Security Threat?" *Politico,* December 13, 2016, https://www.politico.com/story/2016/12/trump-twitter-national-security-232518; Dean Obeidallah, "Chilled by Trump Tweets? You Should Be," CNN, November 21 2016, https://www.cnn.com/2016/11/20/opinions/trump-tweets-on-hamilton-snl-obeidallah/.

381   Tufekci, "It's the (Democracy-Poisoning) Golden Age."

382   Michael D. Shear, "Outsiders Selected by Trump Aim to Unnerve Washington," *New York Times,* December 17, 2016, https://www.nytimes.com/2016/12/17/us/politics/donald-trump-cabinet-picks.html.

383   See, for example, "Time Calls Donald Trump 'President of the Divided States of America'" Euronews, December 7, 2016, http://www.euronews.com/2016/12/07/time-calls-donald-trump-president-of-the-divided-states-of-america.

384   John Myers, "'We're Ready to Fight.' Gov. Jerry Brown Unloads on Trump and Climate Issues," *Los Angeles Times,* December 14, 2016, http://www.latimes.com/politics/essential/la-pol-ca-essential-politics-updates-we-re-ready-to-fight-says-gov-jerry-1481739836-htmlstory.html.

385   David Siders, "Jerry Brown: We'll Need to 'Build a Wall Around California,'" *Sacramento Bee,* March 15, 2016, http://www.sacbee.com/news/politics-government/election/presidential-election/article66085062.html.

386   Tim Dickinson, "Jerry Brown's California Dream: The Rolling Stone Interview," *Rolling Stone,* October 5, 2017, https://www.rollingstone.com/politics/features/jerry-browns-california-dream-the-rolling-stone-interview-w507082.

387   Christopher Cadelago, "World Needs 'Brain Washing' on Climate Change, Jerry Brown Says at Vatican," *Sacramento Bee,* November 4, 2017, http://www.sacbee.com/news/politics-government/capitol-alert/article182789821.html.

388   Melody Gutierrez, "Gov. Brown Signs Bill Making California a Sanctuary State," *SFGate,* October 7, 2017, https://www.sfgate.com/news/article/Jerry-Brown-signs-bill-making-California-a-12255884.php; Katie Benner and Jennifer Medina, "Trump Administration Sues California Over Immigration Laws," *New York Times,* March 6, 2018, https://www.nytimes.com/2018/03/06/us/politics/justice-department-california-sanctuary-cities.html.

389   Noam Fishman and Alyssa Davis, "Americans Still See Big Government as Top Threat," Gallup News, January 5, 2017, at http://news.gallup.com/poll/201629/americans-big-government-top-threat.aspx.

390   Jelani Cobb, "Post-Election, Liberals Invoke States' Rights," *The New Yorker,* October 28, 2016, https://www.newyorker.com/magazine/2016/11/28/post-election-liberals-invoke-states-rights.

391   Joel Kotkin, "How the Left and Right Can Learn To Love Localism: The Constitutional Cure for Polarization," *Daily Beast,* December 4, 2016, https://www.thedailybeast.com/how-the-left-and-right-can-learn-to-love-localism-the-constitutional-cure-for-polarization; Bruce Katz and Jeremy Nowak, "The New Localism," *Prospect,* September 10, 2017, https://www.prospectmagazine.co.uk/politics/our-infrastructure-isnt-prepared-for-the-world-of-the-future.

392   "Rome Olympic Chief's Fury at Mayor's Bid Veto," BBC, September 22, 2016, http://www.bbc.com/news/world-europe-37436066.

393   Nathan Heller, "Estonia, the Digital Republic," *The New Yorker,* December 18 & 25, 2017, https://www.newyorker.com/magazine/2017/12/18/estonia-the-digital-republic.

394   The figures are from the World Health Organization's "Global Health Observatory (GHO)" data, at http://www.who.int/gho/mortality_burden_disease/life_tables/situation_trends_text/en/.

395   "European Union Unemployment Rates, 2000–2018," Trading Economics (chart), https://tradingeconomics.com/european-union/unemployment-rate.

396   Peter S. Goodman, "Spain's Long Economic Nightmare Is Finally Over," *New York Times,* July 30, 2017, https://www.nytimes.com/2017/07/28/business/spain-europe-economy-recovery-unemployment.html.

397   "Trump's Inclusive Jobs Boom," *Investor's Business Daily,* December 8, 2017, https://www.investors.com/politics/editorials/trumps-inclusive-jobs-boom/.

398   Data sources in clockwise order: The World Bank, tradingeconomics.com/Eurostat, Macrotrends, Bureau of Labor Statistics. My chart.

399   Allahpundit, "Hillary on 2016: I Won the Places That Aren't Looking Backwards," *Hot Air,* March 12, 2018, https://hotair.com/archives/2018/03/12/hillary-2016-won-places-arent-looking-backwards/.

400   Emily Ekins, "Five Types of Trump Voters."

401   Nicholas Carnes and Noam Lupu, "It's Time to Bust the Myth: Most Trump Voters Were Not Working Class," *Washington Post,* June 5, 2017, https://www.washingtonpost.com/news/monkey-cage/wp/2017/06/05/its-time-to-bust-the-myth-most-trump-voters-were-not-working-class/?utm_term=.d37e4f-7d3e1f.

402   "Explaining Britain's Vote to Leave the EU," *The Economist,* April 29, 2017, https://www.economist.com/news/books-and-arts/21721358-book-makes-rare-attempt-use-survey-data-find-some-answers-explaining.

403   See, for example, Nash Jenkins, "Why Did the Philippines Just Elect a Guy Who Jokes About Rape As Its President?" *Time,* May 10, 2016, http://time.com/4324073/rodrigo-duterte-philippines-president-why-elected/.

404   José Ortega y Gasset, *España Invertebrada* (Austral Espasa, 2011, original publication date 1921), 109–115.

INDEX

Notes from the Art Department

Creative Director: Tyler Thompson
Typesetting & Design: Kevin Wong
Printing: Hemlock Printers USA Inc.
Bindery: Roswell Bookbinding

Composed in Lyon Text, designed by Kai Bernau;
and Zwo, designed by Henning Krause, and Jörg Hemker.
Printed on 60lb Lynx Smooth Book White FSC Mix.
Bound with 80lb Neenah Classic Techweave Cobalt.

Inks:
- Cyan
- Magenta
- Yellow
- Black
- Pantone 807